Third SIGHAN Workshop on Chinese Language Processing 2004

Held in cooperation with ACL-2004

Barcelona, Spain
25 July 2004

ISBN: 978-1-62748-368-1

Printed from e-media with permission by:

Curran Associates, Inc.
57 Morehouse Lane
Red Hook, NY 12571

Some format issues inherent in the e-media version may also appear in this print version.

Printed by Curran Associates, Inc. (2013)

Association for Computational Linguistics
209 N. Eighth Street
Stroudsburg, Pennsylvania 18360

Phone: 1-570-476-8006
Fax: 1-570-476-0860

acl@aclweb.org

Additional copies of this publication are available from:

Curran Associates, Inc.
57 Morehouse Lane
Red Hook, NY 12571 USA
Phone: 845-758-0400
Fax: 845-758-2634
Email: curran@proceedings.com
Web: www.proceedings.com

Table of Contents

Proceedings of the

Third SIGHAN Workshop on Chinese Language Learning

Held in cooperation with ACL-2004

25 July 2004
Barcelona, Spain

ORGANIZERS:

Chair: Qin Lu & Oliver Streiter
Proceedings: Qin Lu & Oliver Streiter

PROGRAM COMMITTEE:

Andi Wu - Microsoft, USA
Changning Huang - Microsoft, China
Chu-ren Huang - Academia Sinica, Taiwan
Joyce Chai - Michigan State Univ, USA
Keh-Jian Chen - Academia Sinica, Taiwan
Li Wenjie - the Hong Kong Polytechnic University, Hong Kong
Martha Palmer - Univ. of Pennsylvania, USA
Nianwen Xue - Univ. of Pennsylvania, USA
Oliver Streiter - EURAC, Italy
Qiang Zhou - Tsinghua University, China
Qing Ma - Ryukoku University, Japan
Qin Lu - The Hong Kong Polytechnic University
Sui Zhifang - Peking University, China
Sun Maosong - Tsinghua University, China
Tom Emerson - Basis Technology Corp, U.S.A.

FURTHER INFORMATION:

Dr. Qin Lu
Department of Computing,
The Hong Kong Polytechnic University,
Hung Hom, Kowloon,
Hong Kong

Technical Program Schedule

Sunday, July 25

8:45-8:50	Welcome
8:50-9:10	*Segmentation of Chinese Long Sentences Using Commas* Meixun Jin, Mi-Young Kim, Dongil Kim and Jong-Hyeok Lee
9:15-9:35	*A Preliminary Study on Probabilistic Models for Chinese Abbreviations* Jing-Shin Chang and Yu-Tso Lai
9:40-10:00	*Document Re-ranking based on Global and Local Terms* Lingpeng Yang, DongHong Ji and Li Tang

Coffee Break

10:30-10:50	*Chinese Chunking with Another Type of Spec* Hongqiao Li, Changning Huang, Jianfeng Gao and Xiaozhong Fan
10:55-11:15	*Chinese Word Segmentation by Classification of Characters* Chooi-Ling GOH, Masayuki Asahara and Yuji Matsumoto
11:20-11:40	*Automated Alignment and Extraction of Bilingual Domain Ontology for Medical Domain Web Search* Jui-Feng Yeh, Chung-Hsiwn Wu, Ming-Jun Chen and Liang-chih Yu
11:45-12:05	*Using Synonym Relations in Chinese Collocation Extraction* Wanyin Li, Qin Lu and Ruifeng Xu

Lunch Break

13:50-14:10	*Combining Prosodic and Text Features for Segmentation of Mandarin Broadcast News* Gina-Anne Levow
14:15-14:35	*Automatic Semantic Role Assignment for a Tree Structure* Jia-Ming You and Keh-Jiann Chen
14:40-15:00	*A Large-Scale Semantic Structure for Chinese Sentences* Li Tang, Donghong Ji and Lingpeng Yang
15:05-15:25	*Aligning Bilingual Corpora Using Sentences Location Information* Weigang Li, Ting Liu, Zhen Wang and Sheng Li

Coffee Break

Poster Session

15:50-17:10 *An Integrated Method for Chinese Unknown Word Extraction*
Zhiyong Luo and Rou Song

15:50-17:10 *Adaptive Compression-based Approach for Chinese Pinyin Input*
JinHu Huang and David Powers

15:50-17:10 *Character-Sense Association and Compounding Template Similarity: Automatic Semantic Classification* Chao-Jan Chen

15:50-17:10 *Combining Neural Networks and Statistics for Chinese Word Sense Disambiguation*
Zhimao Lu, Ting Liu and Sheng Li

15:50-17:10 *A Statistical Model for Hangeul-Hanja Conversion in Terminology Domain*
Jin-Xia Huang, Sun-Mee Bae and Key-sun Choi

15:50-17:10 *Chinese Term Extraction from Web Pages Based on Compound Term Productivity*
Hiroshi Nakagawa, Hiroyuki Kojima and Akira Maeda

15:50-17:10 *The Construction of A Chinese Shallow Treebank*
Ruifeng Xu, Qin Lu, Yin Li and Wanyin Li

15:50-17:10 *Do We Need Chinese Word Segmentation for Statistical Machine Translation?*
Jia Xu, Richard Zens and Hermann Ney

15:50-17:10 *A New Chinese Natural Language Understanding Architecture Based on Multilayer Search Mechanism*
Wanxiang Che, Ting Liu and Sheng Li

15:50-17:10 *A Semi-Supervised Approach to Build Annotated Corpus for Chinese Named Entity Recognition*
Xiaoshan Fang, Jianfeng Gao and Huanye Sheng

15:50-17:10 *An Enhanced Model for Chinese Word Segmentation and Part-of-Speech Tagging*
Feng Jiang, Hui Liu, Yuquan Chen and Ruzhan Lu

SIGHAN Meeting

17:20-18:20 *Organizational Meeting*
Discussion of Future Bakeoff

Segmentation of Chinese Long Sentences Using Commas

Mei xun Jin[1], Mi-Young Kim[2], Dongil Kim[3] and Jong-Hyeok Lee[4]

Graduate School for Information Technology[1], Div. of Electrical and Computer Engineering[24], Pohang University of Science and Technology
Advanced Information Technology Research Center(Altrc)
{meixunj[1],colorful[2],jhlee[4]}@postech.ac.kr

Language Engineering Institute[3]
Div. of Computer, Electronics and Telecommunications
Yanbian University of Science and Technology
dongil@ybust.edu.cn

Abstract

The comma is the most common form of punctuation. As such, it may have the greatest effect on the syntactic analysis of a sentence. As an isolate language, Chinese sentences have fewer cues for parsing. The clues for segmentation of a long Chinese sentence are even fewer. However, the average frequency of comma usage in Chinese is higher than other languages. The comma plays an important role in long Chinese sentence segmentation. This paper proposes a method for classifying commas in Chinese sentences by their context, then segments a long sentence according to the classification results. Experimental results show that accuracy for the comma classification reaches 87.1 percent, and with our segmentation model, our parser's dependency parsing accuracy improves by 9.6 percent.

1 Introduction

Chinese is a language with less morphology and no case marker. In Chinese, a subordinate clause or coordinate clause is sometimes connected without any conjunctions in a sentence. Because of these characteristics, Chinese has a rather different set of salient ambiguities from the perspective of statistical parsing (Levy and Manning, 2003). In addition, the work for clause segmentation is also rather different compared with other languages.

However, in written Chinese, the comma is used more frequently (Lin, 2000). In English, the average use of comma per sentence is 0.869 (Jones, 1996a)[1] ~1.04(Hill, 1996), and in Chinese it is 1.79[2], which is one and a half to two more times as it is used in English. In Korean, the comma is used even less than it is in English (Lin, 2000).

Since Chinese has less morphology and no case marker, and the comma is frequently used, the comma becomes an important cue for long Chinese sentence parsing. Because more commas may appear in longer sentences, the necessity of analyzing the comma also increases.

Some handbooks about standard Chinese grammars list ten to twenty uses of the comma, according to the context. Among these uses, is occurrence at the end of a clause[3] in a sentence (Lin, 2000). About 30% of commas are used to separate the clause from its main sentence or neighbor clause(s). If the comma appears at the end of a clause, the position can naturally be set as the clause segmentation point.

This paper proposes Chinese long sentence segmentation by classifying the comma. In section 2, related work in clause segmentation and punctuation processing is presented. Comma classification criteria are then introduced, and the classification model follows. Afterwards, some experimental results show how the proposed comma classification and long sentence segmentation are effective in Chinese parsing. Finally, a conclusion will be given.

[1] The frequency of comma per sentence is calculated as = Total frequency of commas/(Total frequency of full stop + Total frequency of Question mark), based on the punctuation statistics of Jone's Phd. thesis P56,57.
[2] The calculation is based on People's Daily Corpus'98.
[3] Clause in this paper, is a predicate with its full complements, subject, object(s). According to the type of a predicate and the context, subject or object may or may not appear. Adjunct of the predicate may or may not be included in the clause.

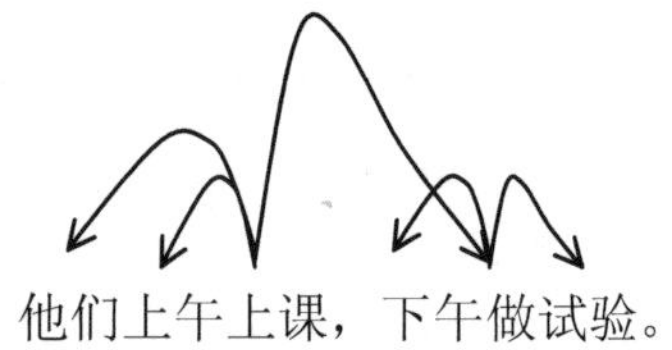

Figure1: example of a dependency relation

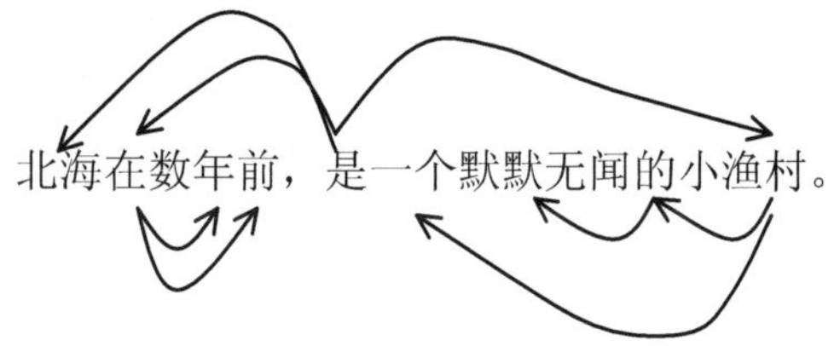

Figure2: example of a dependency relation

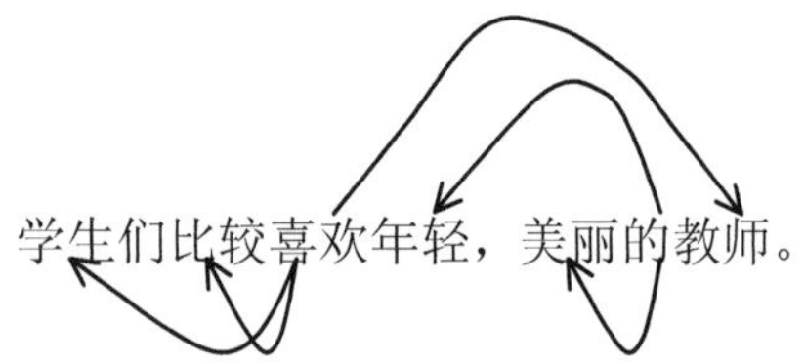

Figure 3: example of a dependency relation

Examples:

(1) 他们上午上课，下午做试验。
They have class in the morning and do experiments in the afternoon.

(2) 北海在数年前，是一个默默无闻的小渔村。
Several years ago, BeiHai City was only an unknown small fishing village.

(3) 学生们比较喜欢年轻，美丽的教师。
The students prefer young and beautiful teachers.

(4) 小明在写作业，妈妈在打毛衣。
Xiao Ming is doing homework and his mom is knitting.

(5) 尽管他很努力，但成绩不理想。
Though he studies very hard, his score is not satisfiable.

(6) 俄罗斯国内经济的发展变化，促进了两国之间的贸易往来。
The change of domestic economic development in Russia has promoted the trade exchange between two countries.

(7) 中国银行在去年十月，聘请日某公司做顾问。
Bank of China invited a Japanese company as its consoler last October.

(8) 在单位里，他是好领导，在家里，他是好爸爸。
He is a good leader in the company as well as a good daddy at home.

(9) 科研成果迅速转化为生产力，是这个开发区的特点。
The quick transfer of the scientific research achievement to industry is the characteristic of this development district.

(10) 学生们来到了操场，高高兴兴地。
The students happily come to the playground.

(11) 韩国对大连投资已连续三年增长，在大连，韩国投资企业受到各种优惠。
The investment from Korea to DaLian city has grown for three years, and all Korean investment companies in DaLian receive preferential treatment.

(12) 统计资料表明，大连对韩出口达一亿多美元。
The statistics show that the exportation from DaLian to Korea is reach to USD100,000,000.

(13) 一九九四年，通用在中国购买了四千多万美元的东西。
In 1994, TongYong Company purchased goods worthy of more than USD40,000,000.

(14) 她每天都起早，每天早上都要锻炼。
She gets up early, and does physical exercise every morning.

(15) 一号产品占据不到三成，二号产品比重达七成以上。
The occupation of the first products is less than 3/10 and the portion of the second ones is more than 7/10.

2 Related Work

2.1 Related Work for Clause Segmentation

Syntactic ambiguity problems increase drastically as the input sentence becomes longer. Long sentence segmentation is a way to avoid the problem. Many studies have been made on clause segmentation (Carreras and Marquez, 2002, Leffa, 1998, Sang and Dejean,2001). In addition, many studies also have been done on long sentences segmentation by certain patterns (Kim and Zhang, 2001, Li and Pei, 1990, Palmer and Hearst, 1997).

However, some researchers merely ignore punctuation, including the comma, and some researchers use a comma as one feature to detect the segmentation point, not fully using the information from the comma.

2.2 Related Work for Punctuation Processing

Several researchers have provided descriptive treatment of the role of punctuations: Jones (1996b) determined the syntactic function of the punctuation mark. Bayraktar and Akman (1998) classified commas by means of the syntax-patterns in which they occur. However, theoretical forays into the syntactic roles of punctuation were limited.

Many researchers have used the punctuation mark for syntactic analysis and insist that punctuation indicates useful information. Jones (1994) successfully shows that grammar with punctuation outperforms one without punctuation. Briscoe and Carroll (1995) also show the importance of punctuation in reducing syntactic ambiguity. Collins (1999), in his statistical parser, treats a comma as an important feature. Shiuan and Ann (1996) separate complex sentences with respect to the link word, including the comma. As a result, their syntactic parser performs an error reduction of 21.2% in its accuracy.

Say (1997) provides a detailed introduction to using punctuation for a variety of other natural language processing tasks.

All of these approaches prove that punctuation analyses improve various natural language processing performance, especially in complex sentence segmentation.

3 Types of Commas

The comma is the most common punctuation, and the one that might be expected to have the greatest effect on syntactic parsing. Also, it seems natural to break a sentence at the comma position in Chinese sentences. The procedure for syntactic analysis of a sentence, including the segmentation part, is as follows:

1st step: segment the sentence at a comma

2nd step: do the dependency analysis for each segment

3rd step: set the dependency relation between segment pairs

In Chinese dependency parsing, not all commas are proper as segmentation points.

First, segmentation at comma in some sentences, will cause some of the words fail to find their heads. Figure 2 shows, in example (2), there are two words, 北海 (BeiHai City) and 在 (preposition) from the left segment have dependency relation with the word 是(is) of the right segment. So, the segmentation at comma , will cause two of words 北海 (BeiHai City) and 在 (preposition) in the left segment, cannot find their head in the second step of syntactic parsing stage.

Second, segmentation at commas can cause some words to find the wrong head. Example (3) of figure 3 shows two pairs of words with dependency relations. For each pair, one word is from the left segment, and one word is from the right segment : 喜欢 (like) from the left segment and 教师(teacher) from the right, 年轻 (young) from the left and 的 (of) from the right. Segmentation at the comma will cause the word 年轻(young) to get the word 喜欢 (like) as its head, which is wrong.

Example (2) and (3) demonstrate improper sentence segmentation at commas. In figure 2 and figure 3, there are two dependency lines that cross over the commas for both sentences. We call these kinds of commas *mul_dep_lines_cross comma* (multiple lines cross comma). In figure 1, there is only one dependency line cross over the comma. We call these kinds of commas *one_dep_line_cross comma*.

Segmentation at *one_dep_line_cross comma* is helpful for reducing parsing complexity and can contribute to accurate parsing results. However, we should avoid segmenting at the position of *mul_dep_lines_cross comma.* It is necessary to check each comma according to its context.

3.1 Delimiter Comma and Separator Comma

Nunberg (1990) classified commas in English into two categories, as a *delimiter comma* and a *separator comma*, by whether the comma is used to separate the elements of the same type[4] or not. While a *delimiter comma* is used to separate different syntactic types, a *separator comma* is used to separate members of conjoined elements. The commas in Chinese can also be classified into these two categories. The commas in example (3) and (4) are separators, while those in (2) and (5), are delimiters.

However, both delimiter comma and separator commas can be *mul_dep_line_cross commas.* In example (2), the comma is a delimiter comma as well as a *mul_dep_line_cross comma*. As a separator comma, the comma in example (3), is also a *mul_dep_line_cross comma*. Nunberg's classification cannot help to identify *mul_dep_line_cross commas.*

We therefore need a different kind of classification of comma. Both delimiter comma and separator comma can occur within a clause or at the end of a clause. Commas that appear at the end of a clause are clearly *one_dep_line_cross commas.* The segmentation at these kinds of comma is valid.

[4] Same type means that it has the same syntactic role in the sentence, it can be a coordinate phrase or coordinate clause.

3.2 Inter-clause Comma and Intra-clause Comma

Commas occurring within a clause are here called intra-clause commas. Similarly, commas at the end of a clause will be called inter-clause commas. Example (2), (3) include intra-clause commas, and example (4), (5) include inter-clause commas.

3.2.1 Constituents of the Two Segments Adjoining a Comma

A segment is a group of words between two commas or a group of words from the beginning (or end) of a sentence to its nearest comma.

To identify whether a comma is an inter-clause comma or an intra-clause comma, we assign values to each comma. These values reflect the nature of the two segments next to the comma. Either the left or right segment of a comma, can be deduced as a phrase[5], or several non-overlapped phrases, or a clause.(see examples (6)~(15)). The value we assign to a comma is a two-dimensional value (*left_seg, right_seg*). The value of *left_seg* and *right_seg* can be p(hrase) or c(lause), therefore the assigned value for each comma can be (p,p), (p,c), (c,p) or (c,c).

Commas with (p,p) as the assigned value, include the case when the left and right segment of the comma can be deduced as one phrase, as shown in example (6) or several non-overlapped phrases, as described in example (7).

We can assign the value of (c,p) to commas in example (8), (9) and (10), indicating the left adjoining segment is a clause and the right one is a phrase or several non-overlapped phrases. In a similar way, commas in example (11)~(13) are case of (p,c).

If a comma has (c,c) as the assigned value, both the left segment and the right segment can be deduced as a clause. The relation between the two clauses can be coordinate (example (14)) or subordinate (example (15)).

[5] Phrase is the group of words that can be deduced as the phrase in Chinese Penn Tree Bank 2.0. A phrase may contain an embedded clause as its adjunct or complement.
(a), 在他们写完作业之后，…
(b) 他们常去的饭店，…
In example (a) ,the PP has the embedded clause as its complement. And in example (b), the embedded clause is the adjunct of the NP.

3.2.2 Syntactic Relation between Two Adjoining Segments

A word (some words) in the left segment and a word (some words) in the right segment of a comma may or may not have a dependency relation(s). For a comma, if at least one word from the left segment has a dependency relation with a word from the right segment, we say the left segment and the right segment have a syntactic relation. Otherwise the two segments adjoining the comma have no syntactic relations. **Rel()** functions are defined in table-1.

Rel()
• To check if any words of the left segment has a dependency relation with the word of the right segment. • If there is, Rel()=1 Otherwise Rel()=0.
Dir()
• To indicate how many direction(s) of the dependency relations the left and right segment have. when Rel()=1. • For one_dep_line_cross comma, Dir()=1. • For mul_dep_line_cross comma, if the directions of the dependency relations are the same, Dir()=1, else Dir()=2.
Head()
• To indicate which side of segment contains the head of any words of the other side, when Rel()=1. • When Dir()=1, if the left segment contains any word as the head of a word of the right, Head() = left; Otherwise Head()=right. • When Dir()=2, 1. According to the direction of dependency relation of these two segments, to find the word which has no head. 2. If the word is on the left, Head()=left, otherwise, Head()=right.

Table 1: functions Rel(), Dir() and Head()

For the *one_dep_line_cross comma*, the left and right segments have syntactic relation, and only one word from a segment has a dependency relation with a word from the other segment. For *mul_dep_line_cross comma,* at least two pairs of words from each segment have dependency relations. We then say that the left and right segments adjacent to the comma have multiple dependency relations. The directions of each relation may differ or not. We define a function **Dir()** as follows : if all the directions of the relations are the same, get 1 as its value, else 2 for its value. This is in table-1. We also define function **Head()** to indicate whether the left segment or the right segment contains the head word of the other when the two segments have syntactic relation. This is also shown in table 1.

In example (3) as figure 3 shows, Rel()=1, Dir()=2 and Head()=left.

3.2.3 Inter-clause Comma and Intra-clause Comma

For commas assigned values (p,p) or (c,c), the function Rel() is always 1. Commas with values (c, p) or (p,c) can be further divided into two sub-cases. Table 2 shows the sub-case of (c,p), and table 3 shows the sub-cases of (p,c).

Rel() =0	The 2nd comma of Example (8);	(c,p)-I
Rel()=1	Example (9); Head() =right = p	
	Example (10); Head() = left=c	(c,p)-II

Table 2: sub-cases of commas with value of (c,p)

Rel()=0	Example (11);	(p,c)-I
Rel()=1	Example (12); Head() =left = p	
	Example (13); Head() = right=c	(p,c)-II

Table3: sub-cases of commas with value of (p,c)

Commas with the value of (p,p), (c,p)-II and (p,c)-II are used to connect coordinate phrases or to separate two constituents of a clause. These commas are intra-clause commas.

Commas with (c,c), (c,p)-I and (p,c)-I are used as a clause boundaries. These are inter-clause commas.

An inter-clause comma joins the clauses together to form a sentence. The commas that belong to an inter-clause category are safe as segmentation points (Kim, 2001).

4 Feature Selection

To identify the inter-clause or intra-clause role of a comma, we need to estimate the right and left segment conjuncts to the comma, using information from both segments. Any information to identify a segment as a clause or a phrase or phrases is useful. Carreras and Marquez (2001) prove that using features containing relevant information about a clause leads to more efficient clause identification. Their system outperforms all other systems in CoNLL'01 clause identification shared task (Sang & Dejean, 2001). Given this consideration, we select two categories of features as follows.

(1) Direct relevant feature category: predicate and its complements.

(2) Indirect relevant feature category: auxiliary words or adverbials or prepositions or clausal conjunctions.

Directly relevant features
VC: if a copula 是 appears
VA: if an adjective appears
VE: if 有 as the main verb appears
VV: if a verb appears
CS: if a subordinate conjunction appears

Indirectly relevant features
AD: if an adverb appears
AS: if an aspect marker appears
P: if a preposition appears
DE: if 的 appears
DEV:if 地 appears
DER: if 得 appears
BA_BEI: if 把 or 被 appears
LC: if a localizer appears
FIR_PR : if the first word is a pronoun
LAS_LO: if the last word is a localizer
LAS_T : if the last word is a time
LAS_DE_N : if the last word is a noun that follows 的
No_word : if the length of a word is more than 5
no_verb: if no verb(including VA)
DEC: if there is relative clause
ONE: if the segment has only one word

Table 4: feature types for classification

To detect whether a segment is a clause or phrase, the verbs are important. However, Chinese has no morphological paradigms and a verb takes various syntactic roles besides the predicate, without any change of its surface form. This means that information about the verb is not sufficient, in itself, to determine whether segment is a clause.

When the verb takes other syntactic roles besides the predicate, it's frequently accompanied by function words. For example, a verb can be used as the complement of the auxiliary word 地 or 的(Xia, 2000), to modify the following verb or noun. In these cases, the auxiliary words are helpful for deciding the syntactic role of the verb. Other function words around the verb also help us to estimate the syntactic role of the verb. Under this consideration, we employ all the function words as features, where they are composed as the indirect relevant feature category.

Table 4 gives the entire feature set. The label of each feature type is same as the tag set of Chinese Penn Treebank 2.0 (see Xia (2000) for more detailed description). If the feature appears at the left segment, we label it as L_*feature type*, and if it is on the right, it's labeled as R_ *feature type*, where *feature type* is the feature that is shown on table 4.

The value for each feature is either 0 or 1. When extracting features of a sentence, if any feature in the table 4, appears in the sentence, we assign the value as 1 otherwise 0. The features of example (12) are extracted as table 5 describes. All of these values are composed as an input feature vector for comma classification.

L_VC =0	L_VA =0	L_VE =0
R_VC = 0	R_VA =0	R_VE =0
L_VV = 0	L_CS =0	L_AD =0
R_VV =1	R_CS =0	R_AD =0
L_AS =0	L_P =0	L_DE =0
R_AS =1	R_P =0	R_DE =1
L_DEV =0	L_DER = 0	L_BA_BEI =0
R_DEV =0	R_DER =0	R_BA_BEI=0
L_LC =0	L_DEC = 0	L_FIR_PR =0
R_LC =0	R_DEC =0	R_FIR_PR=0
L_LAS_LO =0	L_LAS_T =1	L_LAS_DE_N=0
R_LAS_LO=0	R_LAS_T=0	R_LAS_DE_N=1
L_No_word=0	L_no_verb =1	L_ONE = 0
R_No_word =1	R_no_verb =0	R_ONE =0

Table 5: the extracted features of example (12)

5 Experiments

For training and testing, we use the Chinese Penn Treebank 2.0 corpus based on 10-fold validation. First, using bracket information, we extract the type (inter-clause comma or intra-clause comma) for each comma, as we defined. The extracted information is used as the standard answer sheet for training and testing.

We extract the feature vector for each comma, and use support vector machines (SVM) to perform the classification work.

Performances are evaluated by the following four types of measures: accuracy, recall, $F_{\beta=1/2}$ for inter-clause and intra-clause comma respectively, and total accuracy. Each evaluation measure is calculated as follows.

Inter(or intra)-clause comma accuracy[6] =

$$\frac{\text{the number of correctly identified}}{\text{the number of identified}}$$

Inter(or intra)-clause comma recall =

$$\frac{\text{the number of correctly identified}}{\text{total number of the class}}$$

Inter(or intra)-clause comma $F_{\beta=1/2}$ =

$$\frac{2\times(\text{inter(or intra)} - \text{clause comma precision} \times \text{inter(or intra)} - \text{clause comma recall})}{(\text{inter(or intra)} - \text{clause comma precision} + \text{inter(or intra)} - \text{clause comma recall})}$$

Total accuracy =

$$\frac{\text{total number of correctly identified}}{\text{total number of commas}}$$

5.1 Classification Using SVM

Support vector machines (SVM) are one of the binary classifiers based on maximum margin strategy introduced by Vapnik (Vapnik, 1995). For many classification works, SVM outputs a state of the art performance.

There are two advantages in using SVM for classification:

(1) High generalization performance in high dimensional feature spaces.

(2) Learning with combination of multiple features is possible via various kernel functions.

Because of these characteristics, many researchers use SVM for natural language processing and obtain satisfactory experimental results (Yamada, 2003).

In our experiments, we use SVM^{light} (Joachims, 1999) as a classification tool.

5.2 Experimental Results

First, we set the entire left segment and right segment as an input window. Table 6 gives the performance with different kernel functions. The RBF kernel function with γ =1.5 outputs the best performance. Therefore, in the following experiments, we use this kernel function only.

Next, we perform several experiments on how the selection of word window affects performance. First, we select the adjoining 3 words of the right and left segment each, indicated as win-3 in table 7.

[6] The inter-clause comma precision is abbreviated as inter-P. Same way, Inter-R for inter-clause comma recall, ..etc.

Second, we select the first 2 words and last 3 words of the left segment and the first 3 and last 2 of the right segment, indicated as win 2-3 in table 7. Finally, we use the part of speech sequence as input.

As the experimental results show, the part of speech sequence is not a good feature. The features with clausal relevant information obtain a better output. We also find that the word window of first 2-last 3 obtains the best total precision, better than using the entire left and right segments. From this, we conclude that the words at the beginning and end of the segment reveal segment clausal information more effectively than other words in the segment.

5.3 Comparison of Parsing Accuracy with and without Segmentation Model

The next experiment tests how the segmentation model contributes to parsing performance. We use a Chinese dependency parser, which was implemented with the architecture presented by Kim (2001) presents.

After integrating the segmentation model, the parsing procedure is as follows:

- Part of speech tagging.
- Long sentence segmentation by comma.
- Parsing based on segmentation.

Table 9 gives a comparison of the results of the original parser with the integrated parser.

5.4 Comparison with Related Work

Shiuan and Ann's (1996) system obtains the clues for segmenting a complex sentence in English by disambiguating the *link words*, including the comma. The approach to find the segmentation point by analyzing the specific role of the comma in the sentence seems similar with our approach. However, our system differs from theirs as follows:

(1) Shiuan and Ann's system sieves out just two roles for the comma, while ours gives an analysis for the complete usages of the comma.

(2) Shiuan and Ann's system also analyzes the clausal conjunction or subordinating preposition as the segmentation point.

Although the language for analysis is different, and the training and testing data also differ, the motivation of the two systems is the same. In addition, both systems are evaluated by integrating the original parser. The average accuracy of comma disambiguation in Shiuan and Ann's is 93.3% that is higher than ours by 6.2%. However, for parsing accuracy, Shiuan and Ann's system improves by 4%(error reduction of 21.2%), while ours improves by 9.6 percent.

Kernel function	Inter-P	Inter-R	Intra-P	Intra-R	Inter-F	Intra-F	Total-P
linear	74.22 %	77.87 %	72.52 %	70.61 %	76.00 %	71.56 %	73.14 %
Polynomial d=2	79.84 %	81.15 %	84.51 %	83.77 %	80.49 %	84.14 %	82.86 %
Polynomial d=3	78.57 %	81.15 %	88.39 %	86.84 %	79.84 %	87.61 %	84.86 %
RBF $\gamma = 0.5$	78.46 %	83.61 %	88.64 %	85.53 %	80.95 %	87.05 %	84.86 %
RBF $\gamma = 1.5$	78.69 %	78.69 %	**89.04 %**	**89.04 %**	78.69 %	**89.04 %**	**85.43 %**
RBF $\gamma = 2.5$	**80.62 %**	85.25 %	88.24 %	85.53 %	82.87 %	86.86 %	**85.43 %**
RBF $\gamma = 3.5$	79.41 %	**88.52 %**	85.05 %	79.82 %	**83.72 %**	82.35 %	82.86 %

Table 6: experimental results with different kernel functions

Word Window	Inter-P	Inter-R	Intra-P	Intra-R	Inter-F	Intra-F	Total-P
Win3	80.45 %	87.70 %	84.33 %	80.26 %	83.92 %	82.25 %	82.86 %
Win2-3	85.60 %	87.70 %	88.00 %	86.84 %	86.64 %	87.42 %	**87.14 %**

Table 7: experimental results for word window size

	Inter-P	Inter-R	Intra-P	Intra-R	Inter-F	Intra-F	Total-P
POS sequence	75.42 %	72.95 %	80.60 %	82.02 %	74.17 %	81.30 %	78.86 %

Table 8: experimental results for using part of speech sequence

	Original parser	Integrated parser
Average dependency parsing accuracy[7]	73.8%	83.4%
Average complete sentence accuracy	23.8%	25.4%

Table 9: comparison of parsing accuracy of the original parser with the integrated parser

[7] The evaluation measures are used as it is defined in Kim (2001).

6 Conclusion

In this paper, we propose a method to segment a Chinese sentence by classification of the comma.

We define the criteria for classification, and according to the criteria, a model for classification of the comma is given. The segmentation at the comma position seems to be efficient for improving the accuracy of dependency parsing by 9.6percent. Moreover, since commas more frequently appear in Chinese language, we expect our approach including salient and refined analysis of comma usages provides feasible solutions for segmentation.

However, the accuracy for the segmentation is not yet satisfactory. Since erroneous segmentation may cause a parsing failure for the entire sentence, errors can be serious. Further research should be done to improve the performance and reduce side effects for parsing the entire sentence.

Acknowledgments

This work was supported by the KOSEF through the Advanced Information Technology Research Center (AITrc), and by the BK21 Project.

References

M. Bayparktar, B. Say and V. Akman 1998, An analysis of English punctuation: the special case of comma, *International Journal of Corpus Linguistics*, 1998

X. Carreras, L. Marquez, V. Punyakanok, and D. Roth 2002, Learning and inference for clause identification, Proceeding of 13th European Conference on Machine Learning, Finland, 2002

R.L. Hill 1996, A comma in parsing: A study into the influence of punctuation (commas) on contextually isolated "garden-path" sentences. M.Phil disseration, Dundee University, 1996

T.Joachims 1999, Making large-Scale SVM Learning Practical. Advances in Kernel Methods - Support Vector Learning, B. Schölkopf and C. Burges and A. Smola (ed.), MIT-Press, 1999

B. Jones 1994, Exploring the role of punctuation in parsing natural text, Proceedings of COLING-94, pages 421-425

B. Jones 1996a, What's the point? A (computational) theory of punctuation, PhD Thesis, Centre for Cognitive Science, University of Edinburgh, Edinburgh, UK, 1996

B. Jones 1996b, Towards testing the syntax of punctuation, Proceeding of 34th ACL, 1996

M.Y.Kim, S.J. Kang, J.H. Lee 2001, Resolving ambiguity in Inter-chunk dependency parsing, Proceedings of the sixth Natural Language Processing Pacific Rim Symposium, Tokyo, Japan, 2001

S. Kim, B.Zhang and Y. Kim 2001, Learning-based intrasentence segmentation for efficient translation of long sentences, *Machine Translation*, Vol.16, no.3, 2001

Roger Levy and Christopher Manning. 2003. Is it harder to parse Chinese, or the Chinese Treebank? In Proceeding of ACL-2003.

V.J. Leffa 1998, clause processing in complex sentences, Proceeding of 1st International Conference on Language Resources and Evaluation, Spain,1998

W.C. Li, T.Pei, B.H. Lee and Chiou, C.F. 1990, Parsing long English sentences with pattern rules, Proceeding of 13th International Conference on Computational Linguistics, Finland, 1990

Shui-fang Lin 2000. *study and application of punctuation(标点符号的学习和应用)*. People's Publisher, P.R.China. (in Chinese)

Geoffrey Nunberg 1990. *the linguistics of punctuation* .CSLI lecture notes. 18, Stanford, California.

D.D. Palmer and M.A. Hearst 1997, Adaptive multilingual sentence boundary disambiguation, *Computational Linguistics*, Vol.27, 1997

E.F.T.K. Sang and H.Dejean. 2001, Introduction to the CoNLL-2001 shared task: clause identification, Proceeding of CoNLL-2001

B. Say and V. Akman 1997, current approaches to punctuation in computational linguistics, *Computers and the Humanities, 1997*

P.L. Shiuan and C.T.H. Ann 1996, A divide-and-conquer strategy for parsing, Proceedings of the ACL/SIGPARSE 5th international workshop on parsing technologies, Santa Cruz, USA, pp57-66

Fei Xia 2000, The bracketing Guidelines for the Penn Chinese Treebank(3.0)

Vladimir N Vapnik 1995 *The nature of statistical learning theory.* New York, 1995

A Preliminary Study on Probabilistic Models for Chinese Abbreviations

Jing-Shin Chang
Department of Computer Science & Information Engineering
National Chi-Nan University
Puli, Nantou, Taiwan, ROC.
jshin@csie.ncnu.edu.tw

Yu-Tso Lai
Department of Computer Science & Information Engineering
National Chi-Nan University
Puli, Nantou, Taiwan, ROC.
s0321521@ncnu.edu.tw

Abstract

Chinese abbreviations are widely used in the modern Chinese texts. They are a special form of *unknown words*, including many *named entities*. This results in difficulty for correct Chinese processing. In this study, the Chinese abbreviation problem is regarded as an *error recovery* problem in which the suspect root words are the "errors" to be recovered from a set of candidates. Such a problem is mapped to an HMM-based generation model for both abbreviation identification and root word recovery, and is integrated as part of a unified word segmentation model when the input extends to a complete sentence.

Two major experiments are conducted to test the abbreviation models. In the first experiment, an attempt is made to guess the abbreviations of the root words. An accuracy rate of 72% is observed. In contrast, a second experiment is conducted to guess the root words from abbreviations. Some submodels could achieve as high as 51% accuracy with the simple HMM-based model. Some quantitative observations against heuristic abbreviation knowledge about Chinese are also observed.

1 Introduction

The modern Chinese language is a highly abbreviated one due to the mixed uses of ancient single character words as well as modern multi-character words and compound words. The abbreviated form and root form are used interchangeably everywhere in the current Chinese articles. Some news articles may contain about 20% of sentences that have suspect abbreviated words in them (Lai 2003). Since abbreviations cannot be enumerated in a dictionary, it forms a special class of *unknown words*, many of which originate from *named entities*. Many other open class words are also abbreviatable. This particular class thus introduces complication for Chinese language processing, including the fundamental *word segmentation* process (Chiang 1992, Lin 1993, Chang 1997) and many word-based applications. For instance, a keyword-based information retrieval system may requires the two forms, such as "立委" and "立法委員" ("legislators"), in order not to miss any relevant documents. The Chinese word segmentation process is also significantly degraded by the existence of unknown words (Chiang 1992), including unknown abbreviations.

There are many heuristics for Chinese abbreviations. Such heuristics, however, can easily break (Sproat 2002). Currently, only some quantitative approaches (Huang 1994a, 94b) are available in predicting the presentation of an abbreviation. Since such formulations regard the word segmentation process and abbreviation identification as two independent processes, they probably cannot optimize the identification process jointly with the *word segmentation* process, and thus may lose the useful contextual information. Some class-based segmentation models (Sun 2002, Gao 2003) well integrate the identification of some regular non-lexicalized units (such as named entities). However, the abbreviation process can be applied to almost all word forms (or classes of words). Therefore, this particular word formation process may have to be handled as a separate layer in the segmentation process.

To resolve the Chinese abbreviation problems and integrate its identification into the word segmentation process, this study proposes to regard the abbreviation problem in the word segmentation process as an "error recovery" problem in which the suspect root words are the "errors" to be recovered from a set of candidates according to some generation probability criteria. This idea implies that an HMM-based model for identifying Chinese abbreviations could be effective in either identifying the existence of an abbreviation or the recovery of the root words from an abbreviation. We therefore start with a unified word segmentation model so that both processes can be handled at the same time, and when the input is reduced to a single abbreviated word, the model can be equally useful for recovering its root.

As a side effect of using HMM-based formulation, we expect that a large abbreviation dictionary could be derived from a large corpus or from web documents through the training process of the unified word segmentation model automatically.

Section 2 will show our HMM models and the three abbreviation problems correspond to the three basic HMM problems. Section 3 will show the experiment setup. Section 4 will examine the experiments to guess abbreviations from root or vice versa.

2 Chinese Abbreviation Models

2.1 An Error Recovery Paradigm

To resolve the abbreviation problems, first note that the most common action one would take when encountering an abbreviation is to find its candidate roots (probably from a large abbreviation dictionary if available or from an ordinary dictionary with some educated guesses), and then identify the most probable one. This process is identical to the operation of many spelling correction models, which generate the candidate corrections according to a *reversed* word formation process, then justify the best candidate.

Such an analogy indicates that we may use an HMM model (Rabiner 1993), which is good at finding the best *unseen* state sequence, for error recovery. There will be a direct map between the two paradigms if we regard the observed input character sequence as our "observation sequence", and regard the unseen word candidates as the underlying "state sequence".

Given these mappings, we will be able to use many standard processing approaches for HMM when we have to answer some interesting questions (including root word recovery). Among all interesting questions for an HMM, we have three basic questions to ask the model (Rabiner 1993), namely the output probability of an output sequence, the best underlying state sequence and the best parameters given a training corpus.

If we can ask the HMM for abbreviation the same questions, then we will also be able to answer the question on (1) what is the likelihood that a string is an abbreviation, (2) what are the best underlying root words for an input character string that contains abbreviations, and (3) how to estimate the model parameters automatically given a corpus.

The first question is related to the problem of generating an appropriate abbreviation from a root word; the second question is linked to finding the best underlying roots from an abbreviated string, and the third question have a direct link to the construction of an abbreviation dictionary automatically from a corpus. For now we will not explore this third question, but leave it to a research that would be launched in the near future.

The most interesting question to ask is, of course, the second question in the Chinese tokenization process. Therefore, we will start with a unified word segmentation model, which has the capability to handle abbreviation problem jointly with the word segmentation process.

2.2 HMM-Q2: Unified Word Segmentation Model for Abbreviation Recovery

To integrate the abbreviation process into the word segmentation model, firstly we can regard the segmentation model as finding the best underlying words $w_1^m \equiv w_1, \cdots, w_m$ (which include only base/root forms), given the surface string of characters $c_1^n \equiv c_1, \cdots, c_n$ (which may contain abbreviated forms of compound words.) The segmentation process is then equivalent to finding the best word sequence $\vec{w}^*$ such that:

$$\begin{aligned}
\vec{w}^* &= \arg\max_{w_1^m : w_1^m \Rightarrow c_1^n} P\left(w_1^m \mid c_1^n\right) \\
&= \arg\max_{w_1^m : w_1^m \Rightarrow c_1^n} P\left(c_1^n \mid w_1^m\right) \times P\left(w_1^m\right) \\
&= \arg\max_{w_1^m : w_1^m \Rightarrow c_1^n} \prod_{\substack{i=1,m \\ w_i \Rightarrow \vec{c}_i}} P\left(\vec{c}_i \mid w_i\right) \times P\left(w_i \mid w_{i-1}\right)
\end{aligned}$$

Equation 1. Unified Word Segmentation Model for Abbreviation Recovery

where $\vec{c}_i$ refers to the surface form of w_i, which could be in an abbreviated or non-abbreviated (or any transformed) form of w_i. The last equality assumes that the generation of an abbreviation is independent of context, and the language model is a word-based bigram model. Such assumptions can be adapted to different submodels for word segmentation (Chiang 1992) as appropriate. Furthermore, in many cases, the underlying word w_i will be a *compound* word consisting of other constituent words w_{ij} (e.g., "台灣 大學"). And, the probability $P(\vec{c}_i \mid w_i)$ is not always 1 or 0, since the constituents may be abbreviated differently in different context, making the mapping of the compound ambiguous. For instance, some people may prefer to abbreviate '工業技術研究院' (Industrial Technology Research Institute; ITRI) into '工研院' (IRI) while other may prefer an abbreviation of '工技院' (ITI).

Notice that, this equation is equivalent to the formulation for an HMM (Hidden Markov Model) (Rabiner 1993) to find the best "state" sequence given the observation symbols. The parameters $P(w_i \mid w_{i-1})$ and $P(\vec{c}_i \mid w_i)$ represent the transition probability and the (word-wise) output probability of an HMM, respectively; and, the formulations for $P(w_1^m)$ and $P(c_1^n \mid w_1^m)$ are the respective "language model" of the Chinese language and the "generation model" for the abbreviated words (i.e., the "abbreviation model" in the current context). The "state" sequence in the word segmentation case is characterized by the root forms $w_1^m \equiv w_1, \cdots, w_m$, or the hidden words; and, the "observation symbols" are characterized here by $c_1^n \equiv c_1, \cdots, c_n \equiv \vec{c}_1, \cdots, \vec{c}_m$, where the surface form $\vec{c}_i \equiv c_{b(i)}^{e(i)}$ is a chunk of characters beginning at the b(i)-th character and ending at the e(i)-th character.

Such an analogy with an HMM enables us to estimate the model parameters using an unsupervised training method that is directly ported from the forward-backward or Baum-Welch re-estimation formula (Rabiner 1993) or a generic EM algorithm (Dempster 1977).

Note also that, while the above formulation is intended for finding root words in a sentence, with the help of contextual words, we can also apply the same formulation to a single abbreviated word (likely to have a compound word as its root in many cases) to find the most likely constituent words, without the help of surrounding words, but with the help of contextual constraints among its constituents.

2.2.1. Language Model

The word transition probability $P(w_i \mid w_{i-1})$ used in the language model is used to provide contextual constraints among root words. It may not be reliably estimated when the language has a large vocabulary and when the training corpus is small. To resolve this problem, we can back-off the bigram word transition probability to a unigram word probability using Katz's method (Katz 1987) for rare bigrams. We can, of course, use other smoothing methods to acquire reliable parameters. The smoothing issues, however, are not the main focus of this preliminary study.

2.2.2 Generation Model for Abbreviations

In the perfect case where all words are lexicalized, rendering all surface forms identical to their "root" forms and all words are known to the system dictionary, we will have $P(\vec{c}_i \mid w_i) = 1$, $\forall i = 1, m$, and **Equation 1** is no more than a word bigram model for word segmentation (Chiang 1992). In the presence of unknown words (e.g., abbreviations being one of such entities), however, we can no longer ignore the generation probability $P(\vec{c}_i \mid w_i)$.

For example, if $\vec{c}_i$ is '台大' then w_i could be the compound word '台灣 大學' (Taiwan University) or '台灣 大聯盟' (Taiwan Major League). In this case, the parameters in P(大學|台灣) x P(台|台灣) x P(大|大學) and P(大聯盟|台灣) x P(台|台灣) x P(大|大聯盟) will indicate how likely '台大' is an abbreviation, and which of the above two compounds is the root form of the abbreviation. Therefore, we need a method for estimating the probabilities between the abbreviations and their root forms (many of which are compound words with other constituents).

2.3 Applying Abbreviation Models

There are two problems to use the unified model which takes abbreviated words into account. First of all, since the word lattice is constructed from all possible $w_1^m \equiv w_1, \cdots, w_m$, how can we construct it without really knowing the candidate base forms of $\vec{c}_i$ in advance? We don't really want to randomly combine all possible root forms, which is not affordable in computational cost. Therefore, we have to make some smarter choices. Second, how to compute the abbreviation (output/generation) probability $P(\vec{c}_i \mid w_i)$ once the lattice is constructed with candidate root words?

2.3.1 Candidate Root Word Generation

The first problem can be resolved if we choose some highly probable constituents w that would generate each individual characters c_{ij} in $\vec{c}_i$ *independently*, and allow such Top-N candidates to form part of the complete word lattice. That is, for each individual character c_{ij}, we choose its Top-N candidates according to: $P(c_{ij} \mid w) \cdot P(w)$.

The probability $P(c_{ij} \mid w)$ here represents the character-wise generation probability of a single character from its corresponding root word. Notice that, after we apply the word segmentation model **Equation 1** to the word lattice, some of the above candidates may be preferred and others be discarded, by consulting the neighboring words and their transition probabilities. This makes the abbreviation model *jointly* optimized in the word segmentation process, instead of being optimized independent of context.

2.3.2 Abbreviation Probability

The second problem can be resolved using the following equation if w_i can be segmented into $w_i \equiv w_{i1}, \cdots, w_{iL}$, each constituent corresponding to a character in $\vec{c}_i \equiv c_{b(i)}^{e(i)}$:

$$P(\vec{c}_i \mid w_i) = P\left(c_{b(i)}^{e(i)} \mid w_{i1}^{iL}\right)$$

$$= \prod_{j=1,L} P\left(c_{b(i)+j-1} \mid w_{ij}\right) \cdot P\left(w_{ij} \mid w_{i,j-1}\right)$$

$$L = e(i) - b(i) + 1 \equiv L(i)$$

Equation 2. Abbreviation Probability.

In other words, we use the transition probability between constituent words and the character-wise generation probabilities of individual characters from a constituent word to estimate the global generation probability of the abbreviated form.

2.3.3 Simplified Abbreviation Models

It is sometimes simply not efficient to save all pairs of root compounds and their respective abbreviations in an abbreviation dictionary. Therefore, it is desirable to simplify the abbreviation probability by using some simpler features for Chinese abbreviation words. For instance, it is known that many 4-character compound words will be abbreviated as 2-character abbreviations (such as the case for the <台灣大學, 台大> pair.) It was also known heuristically that many such 4-character words are abbreviated by reserving the first and the third characters, which can be represented by a '1010' bit pattern, where a '1' means to reserve the respective character and a '0' means to delete it. Therefore, a reasonable simplification for the abbreviation model is to introduce the *length* and the *bit pattern* for abbreviation operations as additional features into the abbreviation model. If this is the case, we will have the following augmented abbreviation model.

$$P(\vec{c} \mid w) = P(c_1^m, bit, m \mid r_1^n, n)$$

$$\equiv P(c_1^m \mid r_1^n) \times P(bit \mid n) \times P(m \mid n)$$

where $\begin{cases} c_1^m : \text{surface characters.} \\ r_1^n : \text{root word characters.} \\ m\text{: length of surface characters.} \\ n\text{: length of root word characters.} \\ \text{bit: bit pattern of abbreviation} \end{cases}$

Equation 3. Abbreviation Probability using Abbreviation Pattern and Length Features.

All these three terms can be combined freely to produce as many as 7 sub-models for the abbreviation model. Note, the first term $\Pr(c_1^m \mid r_1^n)$ plays the same role as the older notation of $\Pr(\vec{c} \mid w)$, which could means a pair of <abbreviation, root> or be evaluated as the product of the per-character generation probabilities and the sub-constituent transition probabilities as outlined in **Equation 2**. This term can of course be ignored from the above augmented abbreviation model so that only very simple length and position features are used for abbreviation handling.

3 Data and Parameter Estimation

An abbreviation dictionary containing the word-abbreviation pairs is required to test the proposed models. Unfortunately, a large Chinese abbreviation dictionary is not available. Therefore, we have to collect some of the generic abbreviations, and make others manually from some named entity lists. Almost half of our collection comes from the Ministry of Education of the ROC. (http://www.edu.tw/clc/dict/). (In a future plan, a large abbreviation dictionary will be built automatically by using the proposed models.)

Eventually, we got 1547 root-abbreviation pairs. Among them, 1235 pairs are considered *simple* and 312 pairs are "*tough*" in the sense that they violate some model assumptions. For instance, we required that a root in a compound word be mapped to at least one character in its abbreviation (not to a null string), and we also assume that the word cannot be mapped to a character that is not part of the word. (For example, AB can be abbreviated as A or B but not C.) Some tough words will actually map substrings to *null* strings;

others may be *recursively* abbreviated; and yet others may change the word order (as in abbreviating "第一核能發電廠" as "核一廠" instead of "一核廠".). As a result, the tough pairs will not be handled correctly with current models.

To simplify the task, only the 1235 simple pairs are tested for evaluation. They are further divided randomly into a training set of 986 pairs (80%) and a test set of 249 pairs (20%). Since the corpus size is not large, the compound words are also manually segmented into their constituents in order to know the true alignments between each character of the abbreviation with its root form in the compound word. Admittedly, such an extremely small training set causes serious data sparseness problem during training. Therefore, the evaluated performance in this preliminary report will be highly underestimated.

The parameters are estimated in the *unsupervised* mode using a standard EM algorithm or the re-estimation method as conventional HMM models would do (Rabiner 1993). In addition, the manually segmented dictionary also allows us to estimate the model parameters in the *supervised* mode.

The unsupervised training will automatically align each character in the abbreviations to its root form in the full words. It is observed that 65.5% of the training set dictionary pairs will be aligned correctly. Other pairs are aligned partially correct.

Note that parameters $P(m|n)$ and $P(bit|n)$ can be estimated using maximum likelihood estimation by directly consulting the abbreviation dictionary since they are only related to word length and character position. It is interesting, in the first place, to check these types of parameters quantitatively to see if they reveal some abbreviation heuristics recognized by native Chinese speakers. The high frequency patterns, which are much more frequent than the ones ranked in lower places, are listed in **Table 1** and **Table 2**.

P(m|n)	Score	Examples
P(1|2)	1.00	(港|香港), (適|適用)
P(2|3)	0.67	(投縣|南投縣), (交部|交通部)
P(2|4)	0.95	(歐盟|歐洲聯盟), (暨大|暨南大學)
P(3|5)	0.73	(中研院|中央研究院), (資工系|資訊工程系)
P(3|6)	0.70	(農工系|農業工程學系), (雲科大|雲林科技大學)
P(3|7)	0.76	(廣電處|廣播電視事業處), (中科院|中山科學研究院)

Table 1. High Frequency Abbreviation Patterns [by lengths]

P(bit|n)	**Score**	**Examples**
P(10|2)	0.87	(德|德國),(美|美國)
P(101|3)	0.44	(宜縣|宜蘭縣), (限級|限制級)
P(1010|4)	0.56	(公投|公民投票), (清大|清華大學)
P(10101|5)	0.66	(環保署|環境保護署), (航警局|航空警察局)
P(101001|6)	0.51	(化工系|化學工程學系), (工工系|工業工程學系)
P(1010001|7)	0.55	(國科會|國家科學委員會), (中科院|中山科學研究院)
P(10101010|8)	0.21	(一中一台|一個中國一個台灣), (一大一小|一個大人一個小孩)

Table 2. High Frequency Abbreviation Patterns [by P(bit|n)]

Table 1 shows how word lengths will change during the abbreviation process, and **Table 2** shows which characters will be deleted from the root of a particular length. The tables quantitatively support some general heuristics for native Chinese speaker. For instance, most words will be abbreviated by deleting about half the characters in the words, as shown in **Table 1**. The data also shows that the first character in a two-character word will be retained in most cases, and the first and the third characters in a 4-character word will be retained in 56% of the cases. However, the tables also shows that around 50% of the cases cannot be uniquely determined simply by consulting the word length for its abbreviated form. This does suggest the necessity of an abbreviation model for resolving this kind of unknown words and named entities.

4 Experiments and Analysis

The unified model can be applied to a whole sentence which contains abbreviations during word segmentation. When the input is reduced to a single abbreviated word (or compound), it can also be applied to recover the underlying root constituent words (without consulting contextual words). In this paper, we will only focus on the abbreviation word recovery problems.

Two major experiments are conducted. The first experiment is to guess the most likely abbreviation form for a word using various feature combinations; the second is to guess the root word from an abbreviation. The following sections will give more details.

4.1 Guessing Abbreviations from Roots

The main task of this experiment is to guess the most probable abbreviation forms for the unabbreviated words in a word list. The abbreviation forms of a word can be enumerated by arbitrarily retaining some characters of this root word and deleting others. For example, the word "南投縣" has six possible abbreviated forms: "南", "投", "縣", "南投", "南縣" and "投縣". In general, if we have a root word of length ***L***, there could be $2^L - 2$ possible abbreviations for this root word (excluding the word itself and the null string).

The best possible abbreviation form $\vec{c}^*$ for an input word w_i can be determined as the one with the highest generation probability $P(\vec{c}_i \mid w_i)$, i.e., $\vec{c}^* = \arg\max_{\vec{c}_i} P(\vec{c}_i \mid w)$. The generation probability for a candidate $\vec{c}_i$, in turn, can be estimated by summing up all probabilities of alignments between each character c_{ij} in $\vec{c}_i$ and the suspect constituent words w_{ij} in w_i. In other words, we have

$$P(\vec{c}_i \mid w_i) = \sum_{A \in \text{all alignments}} P(\vec{c}_i, \mathrm{A} \mid w_i)$$
$$\equiv \sum_A P_A(\vec{c}_i \mid w_i)$$

where $P_A(\vec{c}_i \mid w_i)$ is the generation probability for a known alignment *A*, which can be estimated as in **Equation** 2.

For simplicity, we assume that each character in $\vec{c}_i$ will be mapped to a substring w_{ij} in w_i. In other words, we assume that the mapping between the constituents is 1-1, and no 1-0 or 0-1 mapping is possible. (In future works, such a constraint could be removed.) Also, we will assume that w_{ij} should at least contain the character that is aligned to it. (This is not always true for Chinese abbreviations. For example, "福建" can be abbreviated with its ancient location name "閩", which does not appear anywhere in its root.)

There is also a *normalization* issue in computing the probability of a particular alignment. In general, a shorter string may be preferred as the best abbreviation simply because it multiplies less probability factors when estimating the alignment probability. To reduce this effect, we intentionally scale down, by a normalization factor, the generation probabilities for those alignments that map a complete word into a single character. In fact, there are only about 10% of such alignments, and many of which are mapping a two-character word into a single character (which can be compensated by the large Pr(1|2) factor in the model. This simple normalization approach actually improves the test set performance greatly.

The following table shows the test set performance for using different features in the abbreviation probability as given in **Equation 3**. (The training set performance ranges from 94% to 98%, which suggests a good fit to the training data.)

Feature	Unsupervised				Supervised			
P(c|w)xP(wi|wi-1)	1	1	1	1	1	1	1	1
P(bit|n)	1	1	0	0	1	1	0	0
P(m|n)	1	0	1	0	1	0	1	0
Accuracy Rate(%)	68	68	61	60	72	70	61	58

Table 3. Test Set Performance for Abbreviation Generation with Combined Features.

Each column shows the test set performance for a submodel, which is identified by the features used for estimating the probability. The label '1' (or '0') indicates that the feature at the first column is used (or unused) in the submodel. For instance, the submodel of the second column ('111') uses all the features, including the word transition probability, word-to-abbreviation probability, probability for mapping n character word to a particular abbreviation bit pattern P(bit|n), and the probability for mapping n-character words into m-character abbreviations.

It is seen that supervised training acquires a little better performance than its unsupervised (EM) counterpart. Although not shown in this table, it is observed that the word transition probability and word-to-abbreviation probability in general should be used to get better performance. The table also shows that the other two features based on character positions and word lengths provide additional help. In particular, P(bit|n) seems to be more helpful than P(m|n) since it contains detailed information for retaining characters at particular positions.

The best performance is about 72% when supervised training is used and all the three types of features are used for estimating the abbreviation probability.

4.2 Guessing Roots from Abbreviations

In this experiment, we are given an abbreviation list; the goal is to guess the best root words of the abbreviations in the list. The parameters used here are acquired from human tagged alignments in a supervised manner.

To find the best root candidates of an abbreviated compound word, we need to find the candidate root words for each input character first. The candidate root words can be found from the training set whose generation probability $P(\vec{c}_i \mid w_i)$ is non-zero. The Top-N candidates can then be picked up as described earlier.

For instance, if we want to find the root words of the abbreviation "立委", and the probabilities P(立|立法) and P(委|委員) are non-zero, then we have the chance to recover the abbreviation "立委" back to the correct compound word "立法委員" , which consists of the candidate root words "立法" and "委員" for the input characters "立" and "委" respectively.

Unfortunately, the limited abbreviation dictionary we have is highly sparse. Among the 249 abbreviations in the test set, only 144 (58%) of them have their candidate root words available in the training set. The other 105 abbreviations (42%) cannot be recovered since each of them has at least one character whose candidate cannot be discovered from the training set. For this reason, we will limit ourselves to the performance of the "trainable" test set consisting of the 144 abbreviations, in order to factor out the sparseness problem pertaining to the training corpus.

Under such a restricted environment, we have tested various submodels to see how different language models and simple smoothing affect the results of this error recovery process. The results are summarized in the following table:

LM	SM?	Top-N	TR(%)	TS(%)	Best?
bigram	No	all	90.9	35	
		2	69.6	43	2
		1	46.0	45	1
unigram	No	all	44.2	44	
bigram	Yes	all	90.7	51	1
		2	69.6	51	1
		1	46.0	45	

Table 4. Abbreviation Recovery Performance.

Notations: LM: Language Model, SM?: Apply Smoothing?, Top-N: maximum number of Top-N candidate root words for each character, TR: Training Set Accuracy Rate, TS: Test Set Accuracy, Best?: Best TS Performance among all N's? (1 = yes, 2= rank 2)

The bigram language model uses $P(w_i \mid w_{i-1})$ in the unified HMM model while the unigram model uses $P(w_i)$ instead. Both of them use maximum likelihood estimation over the manually tagged abbreviation-root pairs when smoothing is not applied. When smoothing is applied, the smoothed bigram probability is acquired by linearly interpolating the unigram and bigram probabilities with an equal weight (0.5). The above table indicates that using the less complicated unigram model generally improve the test set performance significantly (from 35% to 44%). If the model parameters are smoothed, the improvement is even greater. Such results can be well expected in the current environment where the training data is very sparse.

Overall, the best test set performance is about 51% when using a smoothed bigram language model; and this can be achieved by using at most 2 Top-N candidate root words while constructing the underlying word lattice. This suggests that we don't really need to wildly enumerate all possible candidate root words for each input character with this model.

5. Concluding Remarks

Chinese abbreviations, a special form of unknown words and named entities, are widely seen in the modern Chinese texts. This results in difficulty for correct Chinese processing. In this preliminary study, the Chinese abbreviation problem is modeled as an *error recovery* problem in which the suspect root words are to be recovered from a set of candidates. An HMM-based model is thus used for Chinese in either abbreviation identification, or in the recovery of the root words from an abbreviation. By extending a simple abbreviation string into a whole text involving abbreviations, it can also be applied to the Chinese word segmentation for identifying abbreviations in a text, or for bootstrapping an abbreviation dictionary from a text corpus.

With the proposed model, the abbreviated forms can be guessed from root words at about 72% correction. The recovery of the root words from abbreviations is conducted at about 51% accuracy rate. Although further improvement is possible, the preliminary results are encouraging. In the near future, *bootstrapping* a large abbreviation dictionary from web text by applying the proposed models is planned. This should partially resolve the data sparseness problems. Such models will also be integrated into a Chinese word segmentation model to partially resolve the unknown word and named entity identification problems in the tokenization process. It is expected that more applications will rely on such models for Chinese processing.

References

Chang, Jing-Shin and Keh-Yih Su, 1997. "An Unsupervised Iterative Method for Chinese New Lexicon Extraction", *International Journal of Computational Linguistics and Chinese Language Processing (CLCLP)*, 2(2): 97-148.

Chiang, Tung-Hui, Jing-Shin Chang, Ming-Yu Lin and Keh-Yih Su, 1992. "Statistical Models for Word Segmentation and Unknown Word Resolution," *Proceedings of ROCLING-V*, pages 123-146, Taipei, Taiwan, ROC.

Dempster, A. P., N. M. Laird, and D. B. Rubin, 1977. "Maximum Likelihood from Incomplete Data via the EM Algorithm", *Journal of the Royal Statistical Society*, 39 (b): 1-38.

Gao, Jianfeng, Mu Li, Chang-Ning Huang, 2003. "Improved Source-Channel Models for Chinese Word Segmentation," *Proc. ACL 2003*, pages 272-279.

Huang, Chu-Ren, Kathleen Ahrens, and Keh-Jiann Chen, 1994a. "A data-driven approach to psychological reality of the mental lexicon: Two studies on Chinese corpus linguistics." In *Language and its Psychobiological Bases*, Taipei.

Huang, Chu-Ren, Wei-Mei Hong, and Keh-Jiann Chen, 1994b. "Suoxie: An information based lexical rule of abbreviation." In *Proceedings of the Second Pacific Asia Conference on Formal and Computational Linguistics II*, pages 49–52, Japan.

Katz, Slava M., 1987. "Estimation of Probabilities from Sparse Data for the Language Model Component of a Speech Recognizer," *IEEE Trans. ASSP-35 (3).*

Lai, Yu-Tso, 2003. *A Probabilistic Model for Chinese Abbreviations,* Master Thesis, National Chi-Nan University, ROC.

Lin, Ming-Yu, Tung-Hui Chiang and Keh-Yih Su, 1993. "A Preliminary Study on Unknown Word Problem in Chinese Word Segmentation," *Proceedings of ROCLING VI*, pages 119-142.

Rabiner, L., and B.-H., Juang, 1993. *Fundamentals of Speech Recognition*, Prentice-Hall.

Sun, Jian, Jianfeng Gao, Lei Zhang, Ming Zhou and Chang-Ning Huang, 2002. "Chinese named entity identification using class-based language model," *Proc. of COLING 2002*, Taipei, ROC.

Sproat, Richard, 2002. "Corpus-Based Methods in Chinese Morphology", *Pre-conference Tutorials*, COLING-2002, Taipei, Taiwan, ROC.

Document Re-ranking Based on Global and Local Terms

Yang Lingpeng
Institute for Infocomm Research
21 Heng Mui Keng Terrace
Singapore 119613
lpyang@i2r.a-star.edu.sg

Ji Donghong, Tang Li
Institute for Infocomm Research
21 Heng Mui Keng Terrace
Singapore 119613
{dhji, tangli}@i2r.a-star.edu.sg

Abstract

In this paper, we propose a method to improve the precision of top *N* documents by reordering the retrieved documents in the initial retrieval. To reorder the documents, we first automatically extract global key terms from document set, then use these terms and their frequency to identify local key terms in a single query or document, finally we make use of local key terms to reorder the initially retrieved documents. In our experiments based on NTCIR3 CLIR dataset, an average 10%-11% improvement can be made for top 10 documents and an average 2%-5% improvement can be made for top 100 documents.

1 Introduction

To find out what we really want from a large document set is a headache. Information retrieval (IR) is used to retrieve relevant documents from a large document set for a given query where the query is a simple description by natural language. In most practical situations, users concern much on the precision of top ranking documents than recall because users want to acquire relevant information from the top ranking documents to save their valuable time.

Traditionally, IR system uses a one-stage or a two-stage mechanism to retrieve relevant documents from document set. For one stage mechanism, IR system only does an initial retrieval. For two-stage mechanism, except the initial retrieval, IR system will make use of the initial ranking documents to automatically do query expansion to form a new query and then use the new query to retrieve again to get the final ranking documents. The effectiveness of query expansion mainly depends on the precision of top *R* (*R*<50) ranking documents in initial retrieval because almost all proposed automatic query expansion algorithms make use of the information in the top *R* documents in initial ranking documents. Figure 1 demonstrates the general processes of a two-stage IR system.

To improve the precision of top *N* ranking documents in initial retrieval, many researches have been done on the retrieval modals and indexing units.

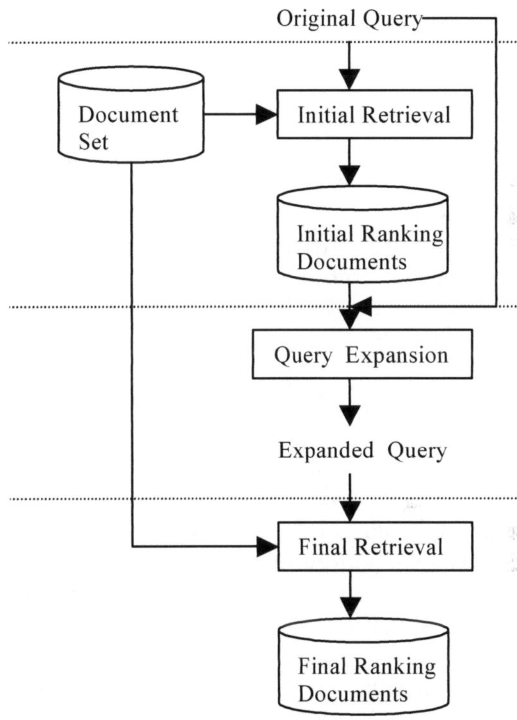

Fig. 1 Traditional Process of two-stages IR

In this paper, we propose a method to improve the precision of top *N* ranking documents in the initial retrieval by reordering the initial ranking documents in the initial retrieval. To reorder documents, we first automatically extract global key terms from document set, then use extracted global key terms and their frequencies to identify local key terms in a single document or query topic, finally we make use of local key terms in query and documents to reorder the initial ranking documents. By doing so, our method can improve the precision of top documents in initial ranking documents and help to improve the effectiveness of query expansion.

Although our method is general and can apply to any languages, in this paper we'll only focus on the research on Chinese IR system.

The rest of this paper is organized as following. In section 2, we give an overall introduction of our proposed method. In section 3, we describe what are global key terms and what are local key terms and how to acquire them. In section 4, we describe how global key terms and local key terms apply to Chinese IR system to improve the precision and quality of IR system. In section 5, we evaluate the performance of our proposed method and give some result analysis. In section 6, we present the conclusion and some future work.

2 Overview of Document Reordering in Chinese IR

For Chinese IR, many retrieval models, indexing strategies and query expansion strategies have been studied and successfully used in IR. Chinese Character, bi-gram, n-gram (n>2) and word are the most used indexing units. (Li. P., 1999) gives out many research results on the effectiveness of single Chinese Character as indexing unit and how to improve the effectiveness of single Chinese Character as indexing unit. (K.L. Kwok., 1997) compares three kinds of indexing units (single Character, bigram and short-words) and their effectiveness. It reports that single character indexing is good but not sufficiently competitive, while bi-gram indexing works surprisingly well and it's as good as short-word indexing in precision. (J.Y. Nie et al., 2000) suggests that word indexing and bi-gram indexing can achieve comparable performance but if we consider the time and space factors, then it is preferable to use words (and characters) as indexes. It also suggests that a combination of the longest-matching algorithm with single character is a good method for Chinese and if there is unknown word detection, the performance can be further improved. Many other papers in literature (Palmer, D. and Burger, J, 1997; Chien, L.F, 1995) give similar conclusions. Although there are still different voices on if bi-gram or word is the best indexing unit, bi-gram and word are both considered as the most important top two indexing units in Chinese IR and they are used in many reported Chinese IR systems and experiences.

There are mainly two kinds of retrieval models: Vector Space Model (G. Salton and M. McGill, 1983) and Probabilistic Retrieval (N. Fuhr, 1992). They are both used in a lot of experiences and applications.

For query expansion, almost all of the proposed strategies make use of the top *R* documents in initial ranking documents in the initial retrieval. Generally, query expansion strategy selects *P* indexing units (*P*<50) from the top *R* (*R*<25) documents in initial ranking documents according to some kind of measure and add these *P* indexing units to original query to form a new query. In such process of query expansion, it's supposed that the top *R* documents are related with original query, but in practice, such an assumption is not always true. The famous Okapi approach (S.E. Roberson and S.Walker, 2001) supposes that the top *R* documents are related with query and it selects *P* indexing unit from the top *R* documents to form a new query, for example, *R*=10 and *P*=25. (M. Mitra. Et al., 1998) did an experience on different query topics and it is reported the effectiveness of query expansion mainly depends on the precision of the top *R* ranking documents. If the top *R* ranking documents are highly related with the original query, then query expansion can improve the final result. But if the top *R* documents are less related with the original query, query expansion cannot improve the final result or even reduces the precision of final result. These researches conclude that whether query expansion is successful or not mainly depends on the quality of top *R* ranking documents in the initial retrieval.

The precision of top *N* documents in the initial ranking documents depends on indexing unit and retrieval models and mainly depends on indexing unit. As discussed above, bi-gram and word both are the most effective indexing units in Chinese IR.

Other effort has been done to improve the precision of top *N* documents. (Qu. Y, 2002) proposed a method to re-rank initial relevant documents by using individual thesaurus but the thesaurus must be constructed manually and depends on each query topic.

In this paper, we propose a new method to improve the precision of top *N* ranking documents in initial ranking documents by reordering the top *M* (*M* > *N* and *M*<1000) ranking documents in initial ranking documents. To reorder documents, we try to find long terms (more than 2 Chinese characters) that may represent some complete concepts in query and documents, then we make use of these long terms to re-weight the top *M* documents in initial ranking documents and reorder them by re-weighted value. We adopt a two-stage approach to acquire such kinds of long terms. Firstly, we acquire global key terms from the whole document set; secondly, we use global key terms to acquire local key terms in a query or a document. After we have acquired local key terms, we use them to re-weight the top *M* documents in initial ranking documents. Figure 2 demonstrates the processes of an IR system that integrates with our new methods. In the following sections, we'll give the details of our proposed method.

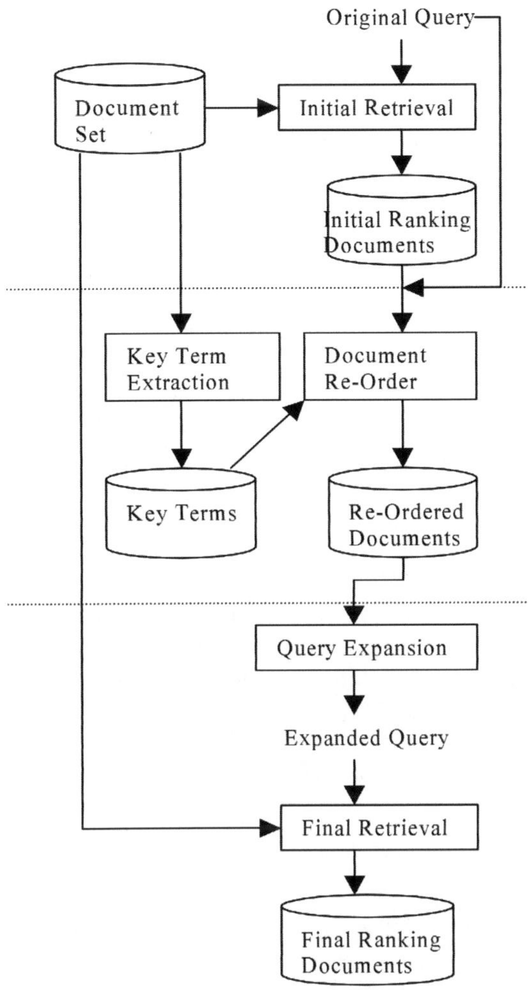

Fig. 2 Enhanced Process of IR

3 Global/Local Key Term Extraction

The global/local key term extaction concerns the problem of what is a key term. Intuitively, key terms in a documents are some conceptual terms that are prominent in document and play main role in discriminating itself from other documents. In other words, a key term in a document can represent part of the content of document. Generally, in the viewpoint of conventional linguistic studies, key terms maybe are some NPs, NP-Phrases or some kind of VPs, adjectives that can represent some specific concepts in document content representation.

We define two kinds of key terms: global key terms which are acquired from the whole document set and local key terms which are acquired from a single document or a query.

We adopt a two-stage approach to automatically acquire global key terms and local key terms. In the first stage, we acquire global key terms from document set by using a seeding-and-expansion method. In the second stage, we make use of acquired global key terms to find local key terms in a single document or a query.

3.1 Global Key Terms

Global key terms are terms which are extracted from the whole document set and they can be regarded to represent the main concepts of document set.

Although the definition of global key term is difficult, we try to give some assumptions about a global key term. Before we give these assumptions, we first give out the definition of *Seed* and key term in a document (or document cluster) *d*.

The concept *Seed* is given to reflect the prominence of a Chinese Character in a document (or document cluster) in some way.

Suppose *r* is the referrence document set (referrence document set including document set and other statistical large document collection), *d* is a document (or a document set), *w* is an individual Chinese Character in *d*, let $P_r(w)$ and $P_d(w)$ be the probability of *w* occurring in *r* and *d* respectively, we adopt 1), *relative probability* or *salience* of *w* in *d* with respect to *r* (Schutze. 1998), as the criteria for evaluation of *Seed*.

1) $P_d(w) / P_r(w)$

We call *w* a *Seed* if $P_d(w) / P_r(w) \geq \delta$ ($\delta > 1$).

Now we give out the assumptions about a key terms in document *d*.

i) a key term contains at least a *Seed*.

ii) a key term occurs at least *O* (*O*>*1*) times in *d*.

iii) the length of a key term is less than *L* (*L*<30).

iv) a *maximal character string* meeting i), ii) and iii) is a key term.

v) for a key term, a *real maximal substring* meeting i), ii) and iiI) without considering their occurrence in all those key terms containing it is also a key terms.

Here a *maximal character string* meeting i), ii) and iii) refers to a adjacent Chinese character string meeting i), ii) and iii) while no other longer Chinese character strings containing it meet i), ii) and iii). A *real maximal substring* meeting i), ii) and iii) refers to a real substring meeting i), ii), and iii) while no other longer real substrings containing it meet i), ii) and iii).

We use a kind of seeding-and-expansion-based statistical strategy to acquire key terms in document (or document cluster), in which we first identify *Seed* for a key term then *expand* from it to get the whole key term.

Fig. 3 describes the procedure to extract key terms from a document (or document cluster) *d*.

let $F_d(t)$ represents the frequency of *t* in *d*;
let *O* is a given threshold (*O*>1);

```
T = {};
collect Seeds in d into S;
for all c∈S {
    let Q = {t: t contains c and F_d(t)≥O};
    while Q ≠ NIL  {
      max-t ← the longest string in Q;
      T ← T + { max-t };
      Remove max-t from Q;
     for all other t in Q   {
         if t is a substring of max-t  {
            F_d(t)← F_d(t)- F_d(max-t);
            if F_d(t)<O  {
               removing t from Q;  }
         }
      }
    }
 }
 return T as key terms in document d;
```

Fig. 3 Key Term Extraction from document *d*

To acquire global key terms, we first roughly cluster the whole document set *r* into *K* $(K<2000)$ document clusters, then we regard each document cluster as a large document and apply our proposed key term extraction algorithm (see Fig. 3) on each document cluster and respectively get key terms in each document cluster. All these key terms from document clusters form global key terms.

There are many document clustering approach to cluster document set. K-Means and hierarchical clustering are the two often used approaches. In our algorithm, we don't need to use complicated clustering approaches because we only need to roughly cluster document set *r* into *K* document clusters. Here we use a simple K-Means approach to cluster document set. Firstly, we pick up randomly 10**K* documents from document set *r;* secondly, we use K-Means approach to cluster these 10**K* documents into *K* document clusters; finally, we insert every other document into one of the *K* document clusters. Fig. 4 describes the generel process to cluster document set *r* into *K* document clusters.

```
let K is the number of documnet clusters to get;
T←10*K documents randomly pickuped from r;
 cluster T into K clusters {K_j} by using K-Means;
for any document d in {r-T} {
   K_i← document cluster which has the maximal
similarity with d;
   insert d to document cluster K_i; }
return K document clusters {K_j|1<=j<=K};
```

Fig. 4 Cluster document set *r* into *K* clusters

Fig. 5 describes the procedure to acquire global key terms from document set *r*.

```
roughly cluster document set r to K document
clusters {K_j|1<=j<=K} (See Fig. 4);
 G = {};
 for each K_j
 {
    extract Key Terms g from K_j; (See Fig. 3)
    G ← G + g;
 }
 return G as global key terms in document set r;
```

Fig. 5 Global Key Terms Acquisition

In the processing of global key terms acquisition, the frequency of each global key term is also recorded for further use in identifying local key terms - terms in a single document or query.

3.2 Local Key Terms

Unlike global key terms, local key terms are not extracted by using key term extraction algorithm from single document or query, they are identified based on global key terms and their frequencies.

Fig.6 describes the procedure of local key terms acquisition from a single document or query *d*.

```
Given threshold X (X>10), Y (Y>100) and
document d;
L = {};
collect global key terms occurred in d and their
frequency in document set r into S = <c, tf>;
for all <c, tf>∈S {
    if tf < X  {
        remove <c, tf> from S;
    }
};
for all <c, tf>∈S {
    if c = c1c2 and <c1, tf1>∈S and <c2, tf2>∈S
    {
        if (tf1 > tf *Y and tf2>> tf*Y){
           remove <c, tf> from S;
        };
    }
};
while S ≠ NIL
{
    let Q = {<t, tf>: t is the longest string is S};
    find <max-c,max-tf> in Q where max-tf has
the maximum value;
    remove <max-t, max-tf> from S;
    if max-t occurs in d {
      L ← L + max-t;
      remove all occurrance of max_t in d;
      for all <b, tf-b>∈S where b is a substring of
max-t;
      {
         if tf-b < max-tf  {
```

```
        remove <b,tf-b> from S;
      }
    };
  }
};
return L as local key terms in document d;
```

Fig. 6 Local Key Terms Acquisition

Following are some examples of global key terms and local key terms in a query.

Example:

Query: 查询故宫博物院所举办之千禧汉代文物大展相关内容

(Find information of the exhibition "Art and Culture of the Han Dynasty" in the National Palace Museum)

Global key terms occurred in Query and their frequencies in document set:

查询 (Cha2 Xun2)– 4948
故宫 (Gu4 Gong1)– 3456
故宫博物院(Gu4 Gong1 Bo2 Wu4 Yuan4)– 727
博物院(Bo2 Wu4 Yuan4) – 772
院所(Yuan4 Suo3) – 2991
举办(Zhu3 Ban4) – 38698
千禧(Qian1 Xi3)– 11510
汉代(Han4 Dai4) – 411
汉代文物(Han4 Dai4 Wen3 Wu4) - 173
汉代文物大展(Han4 Dai4 Wen3 Wu4 Da4 Zhan3) – 133
文物(Wen3 Wu4) – 7088
文物大展(Wen3 Wu4 Da4 Zhan3) – 158
大展(Da4 Zhan3) – 2270
相关(Xiang3 Guan3) – 67990
相关内容(Xiang3 Guan3 Nei3 Rong2) – 148
内容(Nei3 Rong2) – 31165

Local key terms in Query:

汉代文物大展(Han4 Dai4 Wen3 Wu4 Da4 Zhan3)
汉代文物(Han4 Dai4 Wen3 Wu4)
文物(Wen3 Wu4)
大展(Da4 Zhan3)
故宫博物院(Gu4 Gong1 Bo2 Wu4 Yuan4)
博物院(Bo2 Wu4 Yuan4)
故宫(Gu4 Gong1)
相关(Xiang3 Guan3)
内容(Nei3 Rong2)
举办(Zhu3 Ban4)
千禧(Qian1 Xi3)
查询(Cha2 Xun2)

From the example, we can see the difference between global key terms and local key terms. For example, 院所(Yuan4 Suo3) and 文物大展(Wen3 Wu4 Da4 Zhan3) are global key terms, but they are not the local key terms of query.

4 Document Reordering

After we have acquired global key terms in document set and local key terms in every document and query, we make use of them to reorder the top *M* (*M*<=1000) documents in initial ranking documents. Suppose *q* is a query, Fig. 7 is the algorithm to reorder top *M* documents in initial ranking documents where *w(t)* is the weight assigned to local key term *t*. *w(t)* can be assigned different value by different measures. For example,

i) *w(t)* = the length of *t;*
ii) *w(t)* = the number of Chinese Characters in *t;*
iii) *w(t)* = square root of the length of *t;*
iv) *w(t)* = square root of the number of Chinese Characters in *t;* (default)

```
for each document d in top M ranking documents
{
  sim ← similary value between d and q;
  w ← 0;
  for each local key term t in query q;
  {
    if t is a local key term of d {
      w ← w + weight(t);
    };
  };
  if (w > 0) {
    sim ← sim * w;
    set sim as the new similary between d and q ;
  };
};
reorder top M documents by their new similarity values with query q;
```

Fig. 7 Process of Document Reordering

5 Experiments & Evaluation

We make use of the Chinese document set CIRB011 (132,173 documents) and CIRB20 (249,508 documents) and D-only run type query topic set (42 topics) of CLIR in NTCIR3 (see http://research.nii.ac.jp/ntcir-ws3/work-en.html for more information) to evaluate our proposed method. We use vector space model as our retrieval model and use cosine to measure the similarity between document and query. For indexing unit, we seperately use bigram as indexing and word as indexing. To measure the effctiveness of IR, we use the same two kinds of relevant measures: relax relevant and rigid relevant. A document is rigid relevant if it's high relevant or relevant with query, and a document is relax relevant if it is high relevant or relevant or partitional relevant with query. We also use PreAt10 and PreAt100 to represent the precision of top 10 ranking documents and top 100 ranking documents.

When we use our proposed method and algorithm to extract global key terms from document set *r,* we set all kinds of algorithm parameters as following:

- 10000 documents from *r* to do initial document clustering; (Fig. 4)
- 1000 document clusters; (Fig. 4)
- maximal length of key terms:30; (Fig. 3)
- minimal occurrence of key terms:2; (Fig. 3)
- minimum salience of *seed*:2; (Fig. 3)
- reorder the top 1000 documents;
- We also set X =10, Y= *100* for the algorithm to acquire local key terms. (Fig. 6)

Table 1 lists the normal results and enhanced results based on bigram indexing. The enhanced results are acquired by using our method to enhance the effectiveness. PreAt10 is the average precision of 42 queries in precision of top 10 ranking documents, PreAt100 is the average precision of 42 queries in precision of top 100 ranking documents. Column 2 (normal) displays the precision of normal retrieval, column 3 (Enhanced) displays the precision of using our proposed approach, and column 4 (ratio) displays the ratio of column 3 (enhanced) compared with column 2 (normal). Table 2 lists the normal results and our enhanced results based on word indexing.

	Normal	Enhanced	Ratio
PreAt10(Relax)	0.3642	0.4052	1.11
PreAt100(Relax)	0.1886	0.1926	1.02
PreAt10(Rigid)	0.2595	0.2871	1.11
PreAt100(Rigid)	0.1278	0.133	1.04

Table 1 Precision (bigram as indexing unit)

	Normal	Enhanced	Ratio
PreAt10(Relax)	0.3761	0.4119	1.1
PreAt100(Relax)	0.1983	0.2074	1.05
PreAt10(Rigid)	0.269	0.2952	1.1
PreAt100(Rigid)	0.1381	0.1419	1.03

Table 2 Precision (word as indexing unit)

From table 1, using bigram as indexing unit, our proposed method can improve PreAt10 by 11% from 0.3642 to 0.4052 in relax relevant measure and improve 11% from 0.2595 to 0.2871 in rigid relevant measure. Even in PreAt100 level, our method can improve 2% and 4% in relax relevant and rigid relevant measure. Fig. 8 displays the PreAt10 values of each query in relax relevant measure based on bigram indexing where the red lines represent the precision enhanced with our method while the black lines represent the normal precision. Among the 42 query topics, there are only 5 queries whose enhanced precisions are worse than normal precisions, the precisions of other 37 queries are all improved.

From table 2, using word as indexing unit (we use a dictionary which contains 80000 Chinese items to segment Chinese document and query), our method can improve PreAt10 by 10% from 0.3761 to 0.4119 in relax relevant measure and improve 10% from 0.269 to 0.2952 in rigid relevant measure. Even in PreAt100 level, our method can improve 3% and 5% in rigid and relax relevant measure.

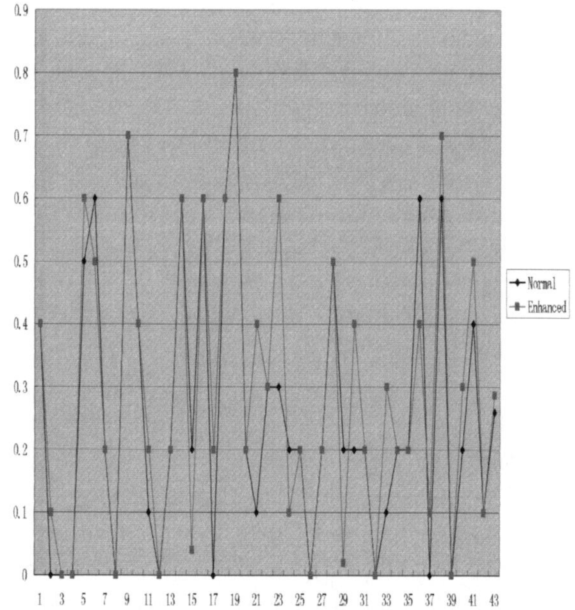

Fig. 8 PreAt10 of all queries in relax judgment

In our experiences, for the most important and effective Chinese indexing units: bigram and words, our proposed method improves the average precision of all queries in top 10 measure levels for about 10%. What lies behind our proposed method is that in most case, proper long terms may contain more information (position and Chinese Character dependence) and such information can help us to focus relevant documents. Our experience also shows improper long terms may decrease the precision of top documents. So it's very important to extract right and proper terms in documents and queries.

6 Conclusions & Future Work

In this paper, we propose a new method to improve the precision of top N retrieved documents in Chinese IR. We try to find proper and important long terms in queries and documents, then we make use of these information to reweight the similarity between queries and documents and finally reorder the top M (M>N) documents by their new similarities with query. With either bigrams or words as indexing units, the experiments show that the method can improve the performance of Chinese IR by 10%-11% at top 10 and 2%-5% at top 100 documents.

For the further work, we will try to improve the quality of global key terms and local key terms, and we will apply our method to English IR and other languages IR systems.

References

Chien, L.F. *Fast and quasi-natural language search for gigabytes of Chinese texts*. In: Proc. 18th ACM SIGIR Conf. On R&D in IR. Fox, E., Ingwersen, P. & Fidel, R. (eds.) ACM: NY, NY. Pp.112-120.

G. Salton and M. McGill. *Introduction to Modern Information Retrieval*, McGraw-Hill, 1983.

H. Schutze. 1998. *The hypertext concordance: a better back-of-the-book index*. Proceedings of First Workshop on Computational Terminology. pp: 101-104.

J.Y. Nie, J. Gao, J. Zhang and M. Zhou. 2000. *On the Use of Words and N-grams for Chinese Information Retrieval*. In Proceedings of the Fifth International Workshop on Information Retrieval with Asian Languages, IRAL-2000, pp. 141-148

K.L. Kwok. 1997. *Comparing Representation in Chinese Information Retrieval*. In Proceedings of the ACM SIGIR-97, pp. 34-41.

Li. P. 1999.*Research on Improvement of Single Chinese Character Indexing Method*, Journal of the China Society for Scientific and Technical Information, Vol. 18 No. 5.

M. Mitra., Amit. S. and Chris. B. *Improving Automatic Query Expansion*. In Proc. ACM SIGIR'98, Aug. 1998.

N. Fuhr. *Probabilistic Models in Information Retrieval*. The Computer Journal. 35(3):243-254, 1992.

Palmer, D. and Burger, J. *Chinese Word Segmentation and Information Retrieval*. AAAI Spring Symposium on Cross-Language Text and Speech Retrieval, Electronic Working Notes, 1997

Qu Y., Xu G. and Wang J. *Rerank Method based on Individual Thesaurus*. In NTCIR Workshop 2.

S.E. Robertson and S. Walker. *Microsoft Cambridge at TREC-9: Filtering track*: In NIST Special Pub. 500-264: The Eight Text Retrieval Conference (TREC-8), pages 151-161, Gaithersburg, MD, 2001.

Adaptive Compression-based Approach for Chinese Pinyin Input

Jin Hu Huang and David Powers
School of Informatics and Engineering
Flinders University of South Australia
GPO Box 2100, SA 5001
Australia
{jin.huang,powers}@infoeng.flinders.edu.au

Abstract

This article presents a compression-based adaptive algorithm for Chinese Pinyin input. There are many different input methods for Chinese character text and the phonetic Pinyin input method is the one most commonly used. Compression by Partial Match (PPM) is an adaptive statistical modelling technique that is widely used in the field of text compression. Compression-based approaches are able to build models very efficiently and incrementally. Experiments show that adaptive compression-based approach for Pinyin input outperforms modified Kneser-Ney smoothing method implemented by SRILM language tools (Stolcke, 2002).

1 Introduction

Chinese words comprise ideographic and pictographic characters. Unlike English, these characters can't be entered by keyboard directly. They have to be transliterated from keyboard input based on different input methods. There are two main approaches: phonetic-based input methods such as Pinyin input and structure-based input methods such as WBZX. Pinyin input is the easiest to learn and most widely used. WBZX is more difficult as the user has to remember all the radical parts of each character, but it is faster.

Early products using Pinyin input methods are very slow because of the large number of homonyms in the Chinese language. The user has to choose the correct character after each Pinyin has been entered. The situation in current products such as Microsoft IME for Chinese and Chinese Star has been improved with the progress in language modelling (Goodman, 2001) but users are still not satisfied.

2 Statistical Language Modelling

Statistical language modelling has been successfully applied to Chinese Pinyin input (Gao et al., 2002). The task of statistical language modelling is to determine the probability of a sequence of words.

$$P(w_1 \dots w_i) = P(w_1) * P(w_2|w_1) * \dots * P(w_i|w_1 \dots w_{i-1}) \quad (1)$$

Given the previous i-1 words, it is difficult to compute the conditional probability if i is very large. An n-gram Markov model approximates this probability by assuming that only words relevant to predict are previous n-1 words. The most commonly used is trigram.

$$P(w_i|w_1 \dots w_{i-1}) \approx P(w_i|w_{i-2}w_{i-1}) \quad (2)$$

The key difficulty with using n-gram language models is that of data sparsity. One can never have enough training data to cover all the n-grams. Therefore some mechanism for assigning non-zero probability to novel n-grams is a key issue in statistical language modelling. Smoothing is used to adjust the probabilities and make distributions more uniform. Chen and Goodman (Chen and Goodman, 1999) made a complete comparison of most smoothing techniques and found that the modified Kneser-Ney smoothing(equation 3) outperformed others.

$$p_{KN}(w_i|w_{i-n+1}^{i-1}) = \frac{c(w_{i-n+1}^{i-1}) - D(c(w_{i-n+1}^{i-1}))}{\sum_{w_i} c(w_{i-n+1}^{i-1})} + \gamma(w_{i-n+1}^{i-1}) p_{KN}(w_i|w_{i-n+2}^{i-1}) \quad (3)$$

where

$$D(c) = \begin{cases} 0 & if\ c = 0 \\ D_1 & if\ c = 1 \\ D_2 & if\ c = 2 \\ D_3+ & if\ c \geq 3 \end{cases}$$

$$\gamma(w_{i-n+1}^{i-1}) = \frac{D_1 N_1(w_{i-n+1}^{i-1}\cdot) + D_2 N_2(w_{i-n+1}^{i-1}\cdot) + D_{3+} N_{3+}(w_{i-n+1}^{i-1}\cdot)}{\sum_{w_i} c(w_{i-n+1}^{i-1})} \quad (4)$$

$$
\begin{aligned}
N_1(w_{i-n+1}^{i-1}\cdot) &= |\{w_i : c(w_{i-n+1}^{i-1}w_i) = 1\}| \quad (5)\\
Y &= \frac{n_1}{n_1 + 2n_2}\\
D_1 &= 1 - 2Y\frac{n_2}{n_1}\\
D_2 &= 1 - 3Y\frac{n_3}{n_2}\\
D_{3+} &= 1 - 4Y\frac{n_4}{n_3}
\end{aligned}
\quad (6)
$$

The process of Pinyin input can be formulated as follows.

$$W = \arg\max_W \Pr(W|A) \quad (7)$$

$$W = \arg\max_W \Pr(A|W)\Pr(W) \quad (8)$$

We assume each Chinese character has only one pronunciation in our experiments.

Thus we can use the Viterbi algorithm to find the word sequences to maximize the language model according to Pinyin input.

3 Prediction by Partial Matching

Prediction by Partial Matching (PPM)(Cleary and Witten, 1984; Bell et al., 1990) is a symbolwise compression scheme for adaptive text compression. PPM generates a prediction for each input character based on its preceding characters. The prediction is encoded in form of conditional probability, conditioned on previous context. PPM maintains predictions, computed from the training data, for larger context as well as all shorter con-texts. If PPM cannot predict the character from current context, it uses an escape probability to "escape" another context model, usually of length one shorter than the current context. For novel characters that have never seen before in any length model, the algorithm escapes down to a default "order-1" context model where all possible characters are present.

PPM escape method can be considered as an instance of Jelinek-Mercer smoothing. It is defined recursively as a linear interpolation between the nth-order maximum likelihood and the (n-1)th-order smoothed model. Various methods have been proposed for estimating the escape probability. In the following description of each method, e is the escape probability and $p(\phi)$ is the conditional probability for symbol ϕ , given a context. $c(\phi)$ is the number of times the context was followed by the symbol ϕ . n is the number of tokens that have followed. t is the number of types.

Method A works by allocating a count of one to the escape symbol.

$$e = \frac{1}{n+1} \quad (9)$$

$$p(\phi) = \frac{c(\phi)}{n+1} \quad (10)$$

Method B makes assumption that the first occurrence of a particular symbol in a particular context may be taken as evidence of a novel symbol appearing in the context, and therefore does not contribute towards the estimate of the probability of the symbol which it occurred.

$$e = \frac{t}{n} \quad (11)$$

$$p(\phi) = \frac{c(\phi) - 1}{n} \quad (12)$$

Method C (Moffat, 1990) is similar to Method B, with the distinction that the first observation of a particular symbol in a particular symbol in a particular context also contributes to the probability estimate of the symbol itself. Escape method C is called Witten-Bell smoothing in statistical language modelling. Chen and Goodman (Chen and Goodman, 1999) reported it is competitive on very large training data sets comparing with other smoothing techniques.

$$e = \frac{t}{n+t} \quad (13)$$

$$p(\phi) = \frac{c(\phi)}{n+t} \quad (14)$$

Method D (Howard, 1993) is minor modification to method B. Whenever a novel event occurs, rather than adding one to the symbol, half is added instead.

$$e = \frac{t}{2n} \quad (15)$$

$$p(\phi) = \frac{2c(\phi) - 1}{2n} \quad (16)$$

To illustrate the PPM compression modelling technique, Table 1 shows the model after string *dealornodeal* has been processed. In this illustration the maximum order is 2 and each prediction has a count c and a prediction probability p. The probability is determined from

Order 2			
Prediction		c	p
al	→ o	1	1/2
	→ Esc	1	1/2
de	→ a	2	3/4
	→ Esc	1	1/4
ea	→ l	2	3/4
	→ Esc	1	1/2
lo	→ r	1	1/2
	→ Esc	1	1/2
no	→ d	1	1/2
	→ Esc	1	1/2
od	→ e	1	1/2
	→ Esc	1	1/2
or	→ n	1	1/2
	→ Esc	1	1/2
rn	→ o	1	1/2
	→ Esc	1	1/2

Order 1			
Prediction		c	p
a	→ l	2	3/4
	→ Esc	1	1/4
d	→ e	2	3/4
	→ Esc	1	1/4
e	→ a	2	3/4
	→ Esc	1	1/4
l	→ o	1	1/2
	→ Esc	1	1/2
n	→ o	1	1/2
	→ Esc	1	1/2
o	→ d	1	1/4
	→ r	1	1/4
	→ Esc	2	1/2
r	→ n	1	1/2
	→ Esc	1	1/2

Order 0		
Prediction	c	p
→ a	2	3/24
→ d	2	3/24
→ e	2	3/24
→ l	2	3/24
→ n	1	1/24
→ o	2	3/24
→ r	1	1/24
→ Esc	7	7/24

Order −1		
Prediction	c	p
→ A	1	$1/\|A\|$

Table 1: PPM model after processing the string *dealornodeal*

counts associated with the prediction using escape method D(equation 16). $|A|$ is the size the alphabet which determines the probability for each unseen character.

Suppose the character following *dealornodeal* is *o*. Since the order-2 context is *al* and the upcoming symbol *o* has already seen in this context, the order-2 model is used to encode the symbol. The encoding probability is 1/2. If the next character were *i* instead of *o*, it has not been seen in the current order-2 context (*al*). Then an order-2 escape event is emitted with a probability of 1/2 and the context truncated to *l*. Checking the order-1 model, the upcoming character *i* has not been seen in this context, so an order-1 escape event is emitted with a probability of 1/2 and the context is truncated to the null context, corresponding to the order-0 model. As *i* has not appeared in the string *dealornodeal*, a final level of escape is emitted with a probability of 7/24 and the *i* will be predicted with a probability of 1/256 in the order-−1, assuming that the alphabet size is 256 for ASCII. Thus *i* is encoded with a total probability of $\frac{1}{2} * \frac{1}{2} * \frac{7}{24} * \frac{1}{256}$.

In reality, the alphabet size in the order- −1 model may be reduced by the number of characters in the order-0 model as these characters will never be predicted in the order- −1 context. Thus it can be reduced to 249 in this case. Similarly a character that occurs in the higher-order model will never be encoded in the lower-order models. So it is not necessary to reserve the probability space for the character in the lower-order models. This is called "exclusion", which can greatly improve compression.

Compression Method	Size	Compression Rate
Escape A(order 2)	434228	54.8%
Escape B(order 2)	332278	41.9%
Escape C(order 2)	333791	42.1%
Escape D(order 2)	332829	42.0%
Escape D(order 1)	345841	43.6%
Escape D(order 3)	332932	42.0%
gzip	434220	54.8%
compress	514045	64.8%

Table 2: Compression results for different compression methods

Table 2 shows the compression result for file People Daily (9101) with 792964 Bytes using different compression methods. PPM compression methods are significantly better than practical compression utilities like Unix *gzip* and *compress* except escape method A but they are slower during compression. The compression rates for escape method B and D are both higher than escape method C. Order-2 model (trigram) is slightly better that order-1 and order-3 models for escape method D.

In our experiment we use escape method D to calculate the escape probability as escape method D is slightly better than other escape methods in compressing text although Method B is the best here. Teahan (Teahan et al., 2000) has successfully applied escape method D to segment Chinese text.

4 Experiment and Result

We use 220MB People Daily (91-95) as the training corpus and 58M People Daily (96) and stories download from Internet (400K) as the test corpus.

We used SRILM language tools (Stolcke, 2002) to collect trigram counts and applied modified Kneser-Ney smoothing method to build the language model. Then we used *disambig* to translate Pinyin to Chinese characters.

In PPM model we used the same count data collected by SRILM tools. We chose a trie structure to store the symbol and count. Adaptive PPM model updates the counts during Pinyin input. It is similar to a cache model (Kuhn and De Mori, 1990). We tested both static and adaptive PPM models on test corpus. PPM models run twice faster than SRILM tool *disambig*. It took 20 hours to translate Pinyin (People Daily 96) to character on a Sparc with two CPUs(900Mhz) using SRILM tools. The following Table 3 shows the results in terms of character error rate. People Daily(96) is the same domain as the training corpus. Results obtained testing on People Daily are consistently much better than Stories. Static PPM is a little worse than modified Kneser-Ney smoothing method. Adaptive PPM model testing on large corpus is better than small corpus as it takes time to adapt to the new model.

	People Daily(96)	Stories
modified Kneser-Ney	5.82%	14.48%
Static PPM	6.00%	16.55%
Adaptive PPM	4.98%	14.24%

Table 3: Character Error Rates for Kneser-Ney, Static and Adaptive PPM

5 Conclusion

We have introduced a method for Pinyin input based on an adaptive PPM model. Adaptive PPM model outperforms both static PPM and modified Kneser-Ney smoothing.

References

T.C. Bell, J.G. Cleary, and I.H. Witten. 1990. *Text Compression*. Prentice Hall.

Stanly Chen and Joshua Goodman. 1999. An empirical study of smoothing techniques for language modeling. *Computer Speech and Language*, 13, 10.

J.G. Cleary and I.H. Witten. 1984. Data compression using adaptive coding and partial string matching. *IEEE transactions on Communications*, 32(4).

Jianfeng Gao, Juashua Goodman, Mingjing Li, and Kai Fu Lee. 2002. Toward a unified approach to statistical language modeling for chinese. *ACM transaction on Asian Language information processing*, 1(1), March.

Joshua Goodman. 2001. A bit of progress in language modeling. Technical Report MSR-TR-2001-72, Microsoft Research.

P.G. Howard. 1993. *The design and analysis of efficient lossless data compression systems*. Ph.D. thesis, Brown University, Providence, Rhode Island.

R. Kuhn and R. De Mori. 1990. A cache-based natural language model for speech reproduction. *IEEE Transac-tion on Pattern Analysis and Machine Intelligence*, 6.

Alistair Moffat. 1990. Implement the ppm data com-pression scheme. *IEEE Transaction on Communications*, 38(11):1917–1921.

A. Stolcke. 2002. Srilm – an extensible language modeling toolkit. In *Proc. Intl. Conf. on Spoken Lan-guage Processing*, volume 2, pages 901–904, Denver.

W.J. Teahan, Yingying Wen, and I.H. Witten R. McNab. 2000. A compression-based algorithm for chinese word segmentation. *Computational Linguistics*, 26(3):375–394, September.

An Enhanced Model for Chinese Word Segmentation and Part-of-speech Tagging

Jiang Feng
Department of
Computer Science and Engineering
Shanghai Jiao Tong University
Shanghai, China, 200030
f_jiang@sjtu.edu.cn

Liu Hui
Department of
Computer Science and Engineering
Shanghai Jiao Tong University
Shanghai, China, 200030
lh_Charles@sjtu.edu.cn

Chen Yuquan
Department of
Computer Science and Engineering
Shanghai Jiao Tong University
Shanghai, China, 200030
yqchen@mail.sjtu.edu.cn

Lu Ruzhan
Department of
Computer Science and Engineering
Shanghai Jiao Tong University
Shanghai, China, 200030
rzlu@mail.sjtu.edu.cn

Abstract

This paper will present an enhanced probabilistic model for Chinese word segmentation and part-of-speech (POS) tagging. The model introduces the information of Chinese word length as one of its features to reach a more accurate result. And in addition, the model also achieves the integration of segmentation and POS tagging. After presenting the model, this paper will give a brief discussion on how to solve the problems in statistics and how to further integrate Chinese Named Entity Recognition into the model. Finally, some figures of experiments and comparisons will be reported, which shows that the accuracy of word segmentation is 97.09%, and the accuracy of POS tagging is 98.77%.

1 Introduction

Generally, Chinese Lexical Analysis consists of two phases; one is word segmentation and the other is part-of-speech(POS) tagging. Rule-based approach and statistic-based approach are two dominant ways in natural language processing, as well as Chinese Lexical Analysis. This paper will only focus on the later one. Hence, our model is called a probabilistic model.

Scanning through the researches in this field before, we have just found two points at which the performance of a Chinese word segmentation and POS tagging system could get better. One is the on the system architecture, and the other is from the Machine Learning theory.

First, the traditional way of Chinese Lexical Analysis simply regards the word segmentation and POS tagging as two separated phases. Each one of them has its own algorithms and models. Dividing the whole process into two independent parts can lower the complexity of the design of system, but decrease the performance as well, because the two are fully integrated when a human processing a sentence. Fortunately, many researchers have already noticed it, and recent projects pay more attention on the integration of word segmentation and POS tagging, such as [Gao Shan, Zhang Yan. 2001]'s pseudo trigram integrated model, [Fu Guohong et al. 2001]'s analyzer which incorporates backward Dynamic Programming and A* algorithm, [Sun Maosong, et al. 2003]'s 'Divide and Conquer integration', [Zhang Huaping, et al. 2003]'s hierarchical hidden Markov model and so on. The experiments given by these papers also showed a great potential of the integrated models.

Besides the system architecture, another point should be noticed. A probabilistic model of word segmentation and POS tagging can be regarded as an instance of Machine Learning. In Machine Learning, the feature extraction is the most important aspect, and far more important than a learning algorithm. In the models nowadays, it seems that the features for Chinese Lexical Analysis are a little too simple. Most of them take tag sequences, or word frequencies as the distinguishing features and ignore the other useful information that are provided by Chinese itself.

In this paper, we will present an enhanced, not too complex, model for word segmentation and POS tagging, which will not only inherit the merit of an integrated model, but also take a new feature (word length) into account.

The second part of this paper will describe the model, including the input, output, and some assumptions. The third part will give some brief discussion about the model on some issues like data sparseness and Named Entity Recognition. In the final part, the results of our experiments will be reported.

2 The Model

The first step to establish the model is to make a formal description for its input and output. Here, a Chinese word segmentation and POS tagging system is viewed as with input,

$$C_1, C_2, ..., C_n$$

where C_i is the i'th Chinese character of the input sentence, and with output pairs, ($m \leq n$)

$$\begin{pmatrix} L_1 \\ T_1 \end{pmatrix}, \begin{pmatrix} L_2 \\ T_2 \end{pmatrix} ... \begin{pmatrix} L_m \\ T_m \end{pmatrix}$$

where L_i is the word length of the i'th word in the segmented word sequence, T_i is the word tag, and each (L_i, T_i) pair is corresponding to a segmented and tagged word, and $\sum_{i=1}^{m} i = n$.

It is easily seen that the distinction between this model and other models is that this one introduces word length. In fact, word length really works, and affects the performance of the system in a great deal, of which our later experiments will approve.

The motivation to introduce word length into our model is initially from the classical Chinese poems. When we read these poems, we may spontaneously obey some laws in where to have a pause. For example, in most cases, a 7-character-lined Jueju(A kind of poem format) is read as **/**/***. And the pauses in a sentence are much related to the length of words or chunks. Even in modern Chinese, word length also plays a part. Sometimes we prefer to use disyllabic words rather than single one, though both are correct in grammar. For example, in our daily lives, we always say “汽车/n 修理/v 站/n” or “汽车/n 维修/v 站/n”, but seldom hear ‘汽车/n 修/v 站/n”, where ‘修理”, “维修” and ‘修” have the same meaning. So, it is reasonable to assume that the occurrence of the word length will obey some unwritten laws when human writes or speaks. Introducing the word length into the word segmentation and POS tagging model may be in accord with the needs for processing Chinese.

Another main characteristic of the model is that it is an integrated model, because there is only one hop through the input sentence to the output word-tag sequence.

The following text will introduce how the model works. We will also inherit n-gram assumption in our model.

Our destination is to find a sequence of (L_i, T_i) pairs that maximizes the probability,

$$P(\overrightarrow{(L,T)} \mid \vec{C})$$

i.e.

$$\overrightarrow{(L,T)}_R = \arg\max_{\overrightarrow{(L,T)}} P(\overrightarrow{(L,T)} \mid \vec{C}) \quad .... 2.1$$

(For conveniece, we will use $\vec{A}$ to represent a squence of A_1, A_2, A_3...)

And,

$$P(\overrightarrow{(L,T)} \mid \vec{C}) = \frac{P(\vec{C} \mid \overrightarrow{(L,T)}) * P(\overrightarrow{L,T})}{P(\vec{C})} \quad ....2.2$$

For $P(\vec{C})$ is a constant given a $\vec{C}$, we just need to consider $P(\vec{C} \mid \overrightarrow{(L,T)})$ and $P(\overrightarrow{L,T})$.

First consider $P(\vec{C} \mid \overrightarrow{(L,T)})$. Suppose $\vec{W}$ is the vertex of words that $\overrightarrow{(L,T)}$ represents(i.e. the segmented word sequence), and the dependency assumption is like the following Bayers Network:

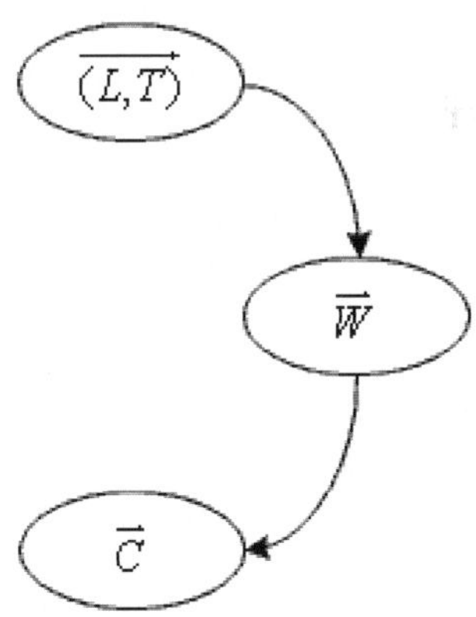

Figure 2.1: Dependency assumption among length-tag pair, word and character

So, we have,

$$P(\vec{C} \mid \overrightarrow{(L,T)}) = P(\vec{C} \mid \vec{W}) * P(\vec{W} \mid \overrightarrow{(L,T)}) \quad ..2.3$$

Because $\vec{W}$ is the segmentation of $\vec{C}$, $P(\vec{C} \mid \vec{W})$ is always 1, and by another assumption that the occurrence of every word is independent to each other, then

$$P(\vec{W} \mid \overrightarrow{(L,T)}) = \prod_{i=1}^{m} P(W_i \mid (L_i, T_i)) \quad ....2.4$$

where $P(W_i \mid (L_i, T_i))$ means the conditional probability of W_i under L_i and T_i. For example,

P("学习"|2, v) is the conditional probability of "学习" under a 2-charactered verb which may be computed as (the number of "学习" appearing as a verb) / (the number of all 2-charactered verbs). With 2.3 and 2.4, $P(\vec{C} \mid \overrightarrow{(L,T)})$ is ready.

Then consider $P(\overrightarrow{L,T})$, which is easy to retrieve when we apply n-gram assumption. Suppose n is 2, which means that (L_i, T_i) only depends on (L_{i-1}, T_{i-1}).

$$P(\overrightarrow{L,T}) = \prod_{i=1}^{m} P((L_i, T_i) \mid (L_{i-1}, T_{i-1})) \quad \text{........2.5}$$

Here $P((L_i, T_i) \mid (L_{i-1}, T_{i-1}))$ means the probability of a Tag T_i with Length L_i appearing next to Tag T_{i-1} with Length L_{i-1}, which may be computed as (the number of $(L_{i-1}, T_{i-1})(L_i, T_i)$ appearing in corpus) / (the number of (L_{i-1}, T_{i-1}) appearing in corpus). So, $P(\overrightarrow{L,T})$ is also ready.

Combining formula 2.1, 2.2, 2.3, 2.4 and 2.5, we have,

$$(\overrightarrow{L,T})_R = \underset{(L,T)}{\operatorname{argmax}} \prod_{i=1}^{m} P(W_i \mid \begin{pmatrix} L_i \\ T_i \end{pmatrix}) * P(\begin{pmatrix} L_i \\ T_i \end{pmatrix} \mid \begin{pmatrix} L_{i-1} \\ T_{i-1} \end{pmatrix}) \quad \text{..2.6}$$

Now, the enhanced model is complete with 2.6. When establishing the model, we have made several assumptions.

1. the dependency assumption between tag-length pairs, words and characters like the Bayers network of figure 2.1
2. Word and word are independent.
3. n-gram assumption on (T,L) pairs.

The validation of these assumptions is still somewhat in doubt, but the computational complexity of the model is decreased.

All the resources required to achieve this model are also listed, i.e., a word list with probability $P(W_i \mid \begin{pmatrix} L_i \\ T_i \end{pmatrix})$, and an n-gram transition network with probability $P(\begin{pmatrix} L_i \\ T_i \end{pmatrix} \mid \begin{pmatrix} L_{i-n+1} \\ T_{i-n+1} \end{pmatrix}, \ldots, \begin{pmatrix} L_{i-1} \\ T_{i-1} \end{pmatrix})$.

The algorithm to implement this model is also rather simple, and using Dynamic Programming, we could finish the algorithm in O(cn), where n is the length of input sentence, and c is a constant related to the maximum ambiguity in a position.

3 Discussion

Though the model itself is not difficult to implement as we have presented in last section, there are still some problems that we will be probably encountered with in practice. The first one is the data sparseness when we do the statistics. Another is how to further integrate Chinese Named Entity Recognition into the new, word-length-introduced model.

3.1 Data Sparseness

The Data Sparseness happens when we are calculating $P(\begin{pmatrix} L_i \\ T_i \end{pmatrix} \mid \begin{pmatrix} L_{i-n+1} \\ T_{i-n+1} \end{pmatrix}, \ldots, \begin{pmatrix} L_{i-1} \\ T_{i-1} \end{pmatrix})$. After the word length is introduced, the need for larger corpus is greatly increased. Suppose we are using a tri-gram assumption on length-tag pairs, the number of tags is 28 as that of our system, and the max word length is 6, then the number of patterns we should count is,

$$28 * 6 * 28 * 6 * 28 * 6 = 4{,}741{,}632.$$

To retrieve a reasonable statistical result, the scale of the corpus should at least be several times larger than that value. It is common that we don't have such a large corpus, and meet the problem so called Data Sparseness.

One way to deal with the problem is to find a good smoothing, and another is to make further independent assumption between word length and word tag. The word length sequence and word tag sequence can be considered independent. That means,

$$P(\begin{pmatrix} L_i \\ T_i \end{pmatrix} \mid \begin{pmatrix} L_{i-n+1} \\ T_{i-n+1} \end{pmatrix}, \ldots, \begin{pmatrix} L_{i-1} \\ T_{i-1} \end{pmatrix}) = P(L_i \mid L_{i-n+1}, \ldots, L_{i-1}) * P(T_i \mid T_{i-n+1}, \ldots, T_{i-1}) \quad \text{...3.1}$$

Now, the patterns to count are just as many as those of a traditional n-gram assumption that only assumes the dependency among tags.

3.2 Named Entity Recognition Integration

Named Entity Recognition is one of the most important parts of word segmentation and POS tagging systems, for the words in word list are limited while the language seems infinite. There are always new words appearing in human language, among which human names, place names and organization names are most common and most valuble to recognize. The performance of Named Entity Recognition will have a deep impact on the performance of a whole word segmentation and POS tagging system. The research on Named Entity Recognition has appeared for many years. No matter whether the current performance of Named Entity Recognition is ideal or not, we will not discuss it here, and instead, we will just show

how to integrate the existing Name Entity Recognition methods into the new model.

During the integration, more attention should be paid to the structural and probabilistic consistency. For structural consistency, the original system structure does not need modifying when a new method of Named Entity Recognition is applied. For probabilistic consistency, the probabilities outputted by the Named Entity Recognition should be compatible with the probabilities of the words in the original word list.

Here, we will take the Human Name Recognition as an example to show how to do the integration.

[Zheng Jiahen, et al. 2000] has presented a probabilistic method for Chinese Human Name Recognition, which is easy to understand and suitable to be borrowed as a demonstration.

That paper defined the probability for a Chinese Human Name as:

$$P(ns \mid ik) = F(i) * E(k) \quad \text{......3.2}$$

$$P(np \mid ijk) = F(i) * M(j) * E(k) \quad \text{......3.3}$$

Where each one of "*i*", "*j*", "*k*" represents a single Chinese characters, "*ik*", "*ijk*" are the strings which may be a human name, "*ns*" means a single name when "*j*" is empty, "*np*" means plural name when "*j*" is not empty, $F(i)$ is the probability of "*i*" being a family name, $M(j)$ means the probability of "*j*" being the middle character of a human name, $E(k)$ means the probability of "*k*" being the tailing character of a human name, $P(ns \mid ik)$ is the probability of "*ik*" being a single name, and $P(np \mid ijk)$ is the probability of "*ijk*" being a plural name. $F(i)$, $M(j)$, and $E(k)$ are easily retrieved from corpus, so $P(ns \mid ik)$ and $P(np \mid ijk)$ can be known.

However, $P(ns \mid ik)$ and $P(np \mid ijk)$ do not satisfy the requirements of the word length introduced model. The model needs probabilities like $P(w \mid (l,t))$, where w is a word, t is a word tag, and l is the word length. Therefore, $P(ns \mid ik)$ needs to be modified into $P(ik \mid nh, 2)$, for *ik* is always a 2-charactered word, and likewise, $P(np \mid ijk)$ needs to be modified into $P(ijk \mid nh, 3)$, where "nh" is the word tag for human name in our system.

$P(ns \mid ik)$ is equivalent to $P(nh, 2 \mid ik)$ and $P(np \mid ijk)$ is equivalent to $P(nh, 3 \mid ijk)$. $P(ns \mid ik)$ can be converted into $P(ik \mid nh, 2)$ through following way,

$$P(ik \mid nh,2) = \frac{P(nh,2 \mid ik)P(ik)}{P(nh,2)} = \frac{P(nh,2 \mid ik)P(i)P(k)}{P(nh,2)} \quad \text{......3.4}$$

where "*i*", "*k*" have the same meaning with those in 3.2 and 3.3. and *nh* is the tag for human name.

In this formula, "*i*" and "*k*" are assumed to be independent. $P(nh, 2)$, $P(i)$, $P(k)$ are easy to retrieve, which represent the probability of a 2-charactered human name, the probability of character "*i*" and the probability of character "*k*". $P(nh, 2 \mid ik)$ is computed from 3.2. Thus, the conversion of $P(nk \mid nh, 2)$ to $P(nh, 2 \mid ik)$ is done.

In the same way, $P(np \mid ijk)$ can be converted into $P(ijk \mid nh, 3)$ by:

$$P(ijk \mid nh,3) = \frac{P(nh,3 \mid ijk)P(ijk)}{P(nh,3)} = \frac{P(nh,3 \mid ik)P(i)P(j)P(k)}{P(nh,3)} \quad \text{......3.5}$$

Finally, the Human Name Recognition Module is integrated into the whole system. The input string $C_1, C_2, \ldots, C_n$ first goes through the Human Name Recognition module, and the module outputs a temporary word list, which consists of a column of words that are probably human names and a column of probabilities corresponding to the words, which can be computed by 3.4 and 3.5. The whole system then merges the temporary word list and the original word list into a new word list, and applies the new word list in segmenting and tagging $C_1, C_2, \ldots, C_n$.

4 Conclusion & Experiments

This paper has presented an enhanced probabilistic model of Chinese Lexical Analysis, which introduces word length as one of the features and achieves the integration of word segmentation, Named Entity Recognition and POS tagging.

At last, we will briefly give the results of our experiments. In the previous experiments, we have compared many simple probabilistic models for Chinese word segmentation and POS tagging, and found that the system using maximum word frequency as segmentation strategy and forward tri-gram Markov model as POS tagging model (MWF + FTMM) reaches the best performance. Our comparisons will be done between the MWF+FTMM and the enhance model with tri-gram assumption. The training corpus is 40MB annotated Chinese text from *People's Daily*. The testing data is about 1MB in size and is from *People's Daily*, too.

	MWF+FTMM	**New Model**
WSA	95.24%	**97.09%**
PTA	97.12%	**98.77%**
Total	92.50%	**95.90%**

Table 4.1: The accuracy by word, with named entity not considered

	MWF+FTMM	**New Model**
WSA	93.86%	**95.68%**
PTA	93.89%	**95.72%**
Total	88.13%	**91.59%**

Table 4.2: The accuracy by word, with named entity considered

	MWF+FTMM	**New Model**
WSA	69.46%	**82.63%**
PTA	72.58%	**80.33%**
Total	50.42%	**66.38%**

Table 4.3: The accuracy by sentence, with named entity not considered

	MWF+FTMM	**New Model**
WSA	63.86%	**74.78%**
PTA	61.40%	**67.41%**
Total	39.21%	**50.42%**

Table 4.4: The accuracy by sentence, with named entity considered

NOTES:

MWF: Maximum Word Frequency, a very simple strategy in word segmentation disambiguation, which chooses the word sequence with max probability as its result.

FTMM: Forward Tri-gram Markov Model, a popular model in POS tagging.

MWF+FTMM: A strategy, which chooses the output that makes a balance between the MWF and FTMM as its result.

WSA (by word): Word Segmentation Accuracy, measured by recall, i.e. the number of correct segments divided by the number of segments in corpus.
(In a problem like word segmentation, the result of precision measurement is commonly around that of recall measurement.)

PTA (by word): POS Tagging Accuracy based on correct segmentation, the number of words that are correctly segmented and tagged divided by the number of words that are correctly segmented.

Total (by word): total accuracy of the system, measured by recall, i.e. the number of words that are correctly segmented and tagged divided by the number of words in corpus, or simply WSA * PTA.

WSA (by sentence): the number of correctly segmented sentences divided by the number of sentences in corpus. A correctly segmented sentence is a sentence whose words are all correctly segmented.

PTA (by sentence): the number of correctly tagged sentences divided by the number of correctly segmented sentences in corpus. A correctly tagged sentence is a sentence whose words are all correctly segmented and tagged.

Total (by sentence): WSA * PTA.

Named entity considered or not: When named entity is not considered, all the unknown words in corpus are deleted before evaluation. Otherwise, nothing is done on the corpus.

According to the results above (Table 4.1, Table 4.2, Table 4.3, Table 4.4), the new enhanced model does better than the MWF + FTMM in every field. Introducing the word length into a Chinese word segmentation and POS tagging system seems effective.

This paper just focuses on the pure probabilistic model for word segmetation and POS tagging. It can be predicted that, with more disambiguation strategies, such as some rule based approaches, being implemented into the new model to achieve a multi-engine system, the performance will be further improved.

5 Acknowledgements

Thank Fang Hua and Kong Xianglong for their previous work, who have just graduated.

References

Sun Maosong, Xu Dongliang, Benjamin K Tsou. 2003. *Integrated Chinese word segmentation and part-of-speech tagging based on the divide-and-conquer strategy.* International Conference on Natural Language Processing and Knowledge Engineering Proceedings, Beijing.

Zhang Huaping, Liu Qun, et al. 2003. *Chinese lexical analysis using hierarchical hidden Markov model.* 2nd SIGHAN workshop affiliated with 41th ACL, Sapporo Japan

Fu Guohong, Wang Ping, Wang Xiaolong. 2001. *Research on the approach of integrating chinese wordd segmentation with part-of-speech tagging. Application Research of Computer.* (In Chinese)

Gao Shan, Zhang Yan. 2001. *The Research on Integrated Chinese Word Segmentation and Labeling based on trigram statistical model. Natural Language Understanding & Machine Translation (JSCL-2001)*, Taiyuan. (In Chinese)

Zheng Jiahen, Li Xin, et al. 2000. *The Research of Chinese names recognition method based on corpus. Journal of Chinese Information Processing.* (In Chinese)

Character-Sense Association and Compounding Template Similarity: Automatic Semantic Classification of Chinese Compounds

Chao-Jan Chen

LATTICE, University Paris VII, Paris, France

chen_chaojan@yahoo.com.tw

Abstract

This paper presents a character-based model of automatic sense determination for Chinese compounds. The model adopts a sense approximation approach using synonymous compounds retrieved by measuring similarity of semantic template in compounding. The similarity measure is derived from an association network among characters and senses, which is built from a formatted MRD. Adopting the taxonomy of CILIN, a system of deep semantic classification (at least to the small classes) for V-V compounds is implemented and evaluated to test the model. The experiment reports a high precision rate (about 38% in outside test and 61% in inside test) against the baseline one (about 18%).

1. Introduction

Sense tagging is an important task in NLP. It is supposed to provide semantic information useful to the application tasks like IR and MT. As generally acknowledged, sense tagging is to assign a certain sense to a word in a certain context by using a semantic lexicon (Yarowsky, 1992, Wilks and Stevenson, 1997). In addition to word sense disambiguation (WSD) for known words, sense determination for words unknown to the lexicon poses another challenge in sense tagging. This is especially the case in NLP of Chinese, a language rich in compound words. According to the data in (Chen and Lin, 2000), about 5.51% of unknown words is encountered in their sense-tagging task of Chinese corpus. Instead of proper names, the cross-linguistically most common type of unknown words, compound words constitute the majority of unknown words in Chinese text. According to Chen and Chen (2000), the three most dominant types of Chinese unknown words are: compound nouns (about 51%), compound verbs (about 34%), and proper names (about 15%). While the identification and classification of proper names is an issue already well discussed in Chinese NLP researches, the sense determination of unknown compounds remains a subject relatively less tackled.

1.1 Shallow vs. Deep Classification

While *word sense* might be conceptually vague and controversial in linguistics and difficult to define (Manning and Schütze, 1999), *sense tag* is more concrete and can be defined according to the specific need of the NLP tasks in question. For example, in a task of semantic tagging or classification, *sense tag* can be the semantic class from a thesaurus. Or otherwise, in a task of machine translation, the equivalent foreign word from a bilingual dictionary can be chosen as *sense tag*. In this paper, it is the *sense tag* so defined that is meant by the term *sense*. The notion *sense determination* then refers to the assignment of sense tag to a word without using contextual information. It is so called to be distinguished from *sense tagging*, which requires contextual information. Under such a definition, *semantic classification* can be regarded as a case of sense determination using the taxonomy of a certain thesaurus, in which a *semantic class* is a *sense tag*.

According to Wilks and Stevenson (1997), a task assigning *broad* sense tags like HUMAN, ANIMATE in WordNet is referred to as *semantic tagging*, different from *sense tagging*, which assigns more *particular* sense tags. In fact, a similar distinction can also be made for semantic classification according to the target level of the semantic classes in the taxonomy tree: a task aiming at the top-level classes can be called *shallow* semantic classification (like Lua, 1997), while a task aiming at the bottom-level classes can be called a *deep* semantic classification[1] (like Chen and Chen, 2000). Since many top-level semantic classes, like TIME, SPACE, QUALITY, ACTION, etc., are often already reflected in the syntactic information, a shallow semantic classification does not actually provide much semantic information independent of syntactic tagging. It is therefore the deep semantic classification that the paper is concerned about.

[1] Take the word 攻擊('attack') for example. According to CILIN (a thesaurus widely used in Chinese semantic classification, see 3.1), it can be classified to shallow-levels as major class H (ACTIVITY) or as medium class Hb (MILITARY ACTIVITY). It can also be classified to deep-levels as small class Hb03 (specific military operations: ATTACK, RESIST, and COUNTERATTACK) or as subclass Hb031 (ATTACK).

1.2 Previous Researches

In the previous researches of automatic semantic classification of Chinese compounds, compounds are generally presupposed to be endocentric, composed of a head and a modifier. Determining the class of the head is therefore determining the class of the target compound (Lua, 1997, Chen and Chen, 2000). This head-determination approach has two advantages: (1) it is simple and easy to implement (2) it works effectively for compound nouns, the dominant type of compounds, since most of them are head-final endocentric words.[2] However, there exist considerable exocentric compounds, for which such a simple algorithm does not work successfully. It is especially the case for compound verbs like V-Vs[3]. For example, 打死 is a V-V compound meaning 'to kill by beating'. Obviously, neither the sense of 打 ('beat') nor that of 死('die') is appropriate to be assigned to the compound 打死 as the sense of 車 ('car') can be assigned to 電車('tram', literally 'electricity-car') as a general meaning.

A second problem encountered in compound semantic classification is that there are considerable *out-of-coverage morphemes*, which are not listed in the lexicon, as remarked in (Chen and Chen, 2000). Moreover, even a morpheme is listed, the given senses are not necessarily appropriate to the task. For example, in the search of compound morphological rules in (Chen and Chen, 1998), some appropriate senses of morphemes have to be added manually to facilitate the task. Obviously this causes a great difficulty to an automatic task, especially to the example-based models which rely on the similarity measurement of the modifier morphemes to disambiguate the head senses (Chen and Chen, 1998, 2000). An alternative approach is thus needed to solve the problems of exocentric compounds and lexicon incompleteness.

Therefore in this paper I will present a non head-oriented model of Chinese compound sense determination, in which lexicon incompleteness will be overcome by exploring the association between characters and senses in a MRD. The sense of an unknown compound can be approximated by retrieved synonyms. Its sense tag can be assigned according to a certain MRD. This model facilitates an automatic system of deep semantic classification for unknown compounds. In this paper, a system for V-V compounds is implemented and evaluated. The model can however be extended to handle general Chinese compounds, like V-N and N-N, as well.

2. Compound Sense Determination

2.1 Compounding Semantic Templates

Most of the Chinese compounds are composed of two constituents, which can be bound morphemes of one character or free words of one or more characters. The two-character compound is a most representative type because its components can be bound morphemes as well as free words. The handling of two-character compounds becomes therefore the focus in this paper.

As in general Chinese compounding, a two-character compound is usually semantically compositional, with each character conveying a certain sense. The principle of semantic composition implies that under each compound lies a semantic pattern, which can be represented as the combination of the sense tags of the two component characters. The combination pattern is referred to as *compounding semantic template* (denoted by S-template) in this paper; compounds of the same S-template are then referred to as *template-similar* (denoted by T-similar). Since T-similar compounds are alike in their semantic compositions, they are supposed to possess roughly the same meaning and to be put under a considerably fine-grained semantic class. Take the compound verb 打破 for example. This compound suggests the existence of a *S-template* of HIT-BROKEN, as the senses of the two component characters 打 and 破 are respectively 'hit' and 'broken'. The S-template HIT-BROKEN refers to a complex event schema [to make something BROKEN by HITting]. This S-template can also be found in many other compounds with a similar meaning:打碎,擊碎,敲破,敲碎...etc. Obviously such T-similar words can make a good set of examples for the example-based approach to the sense determination, if an effective measure of word similarity is available for their retrieval.

2.2 Compound Similarity

As a critical technique, word similarity is generally used in the example-based models of semantic classification. The measure of word similarity can be

---

[2] Though a compound noun and its head are strictly speaking in a hyponym relation, they are usually categorized as members of the same class. For example, in CILIN,車('car', 'vehicle') and most of the compounds X-車 are put under the same class Bo21 (VEHICLES), where X can be a morpheme designating the energy source (like horse, cow, electricity) or the load content (like passenger, merchandise).

[3] An introspection on the two-character verbs in CILIN shows that about 48% of them are semantically exocentric, which means the semantic class of a compound X-Y in CILIN is equal neither to that of X nor to that of Y. As to the endocentric V_1-V_2, V_1 and V2 are about equally likely to be the head of a compound verb according to the introspection.

divided into two major approaches: taxonomy-based lexical approach (Resnik 1995, Lin 1998a, Chen and Chen 1998) and context-based syntactic approach (Lin 1998b,Chen and You 2002), which is not the concern in this context-free model. However, two problems arise here for the taxonomy-based lexical approach. First, such similarity measures risk the failure to capture the similarity among some semantically highly related words, if they happen to be put under classes distant from each other according to a specific ontology[4]. Second, as mentioned, the appropriate senses of some characters just cannot be found in the thesaurus. One major reason why dictionaries do not include certain character senses is that many of such characters are used in contemporary Chinese only as bound morphemes not as free words, when the senses in question are involved. However, such senses could be kept in the compounds in the lexicon, so they might be covert but not inextricable.

To remedy the effects of such lexicon incompleteness, I propose an approach to retrieve the *latent* senses[5] of characters and the *latent* synonymy among characters by exploring association among characters and senses. The idea is that if a character C appears in a compound W, then according to semantic composition, the sense of C must somehow contributes to S, the sense of W. Therefore the association strength between character C and sense S in a MRD is supposed to reflect the potentiality of S to be a sense of C. By transitivity, such association between characters and senses allows to capture association among characters. A new way to measure word similarity of two compounds can be thus derived based on the association strength of the corresponding component characters. This measure actually reflects the S-template similarity between two compounds and can be used to retrieve for a compound its T-similar words, which are potentially synonymous.

2.3 Synonyms and Sense Approximation

The acquisition of synonyms plays an important role in the sense determination of a word. When a native-speaker is capable of giving synonyms to a word, he is considered to understand the meaning of that word. In fact, such a way of sense capturing is also reflected in how the senses of words can be explained in many dictionaries[6]. Moreover, as some researches propose, synonyms can be used to construct the semantic space for a given word (Ploux and Victorri, 1998, Ploux and Ji, 2003). In such a semantic space, each synonym with different nuance occupies a certain area. As visually reflected in this approach, retrieving a proper set of its synonyms means the ability to well capture the senses of a word. In fact, my model of automatic sense determination for a compound is exactly built upon the retrieval of its near synonyms, the T-similar compounds as previously described.

2.4 Model Representation

With a S-template similarity measure, one can retrieve, for a given compound, its potential synonymous T-similar compounds. Then the sense tags of the retrieved compounds can be used to determine the sense tag of the target compound. The model of compound sense determination can be thus composed of two modules, as illustrated in Fig.1.

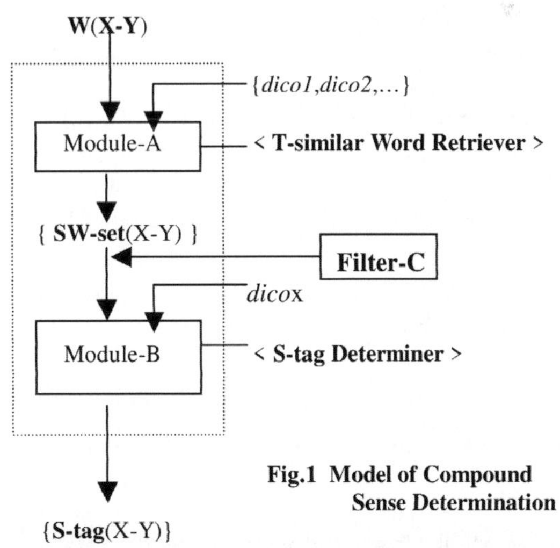

Fig.1 Model of Compound Sense Determination

Module-A (<T-similar Word Retriever>) is to find the potential synonyms ({**SW-set**(X-Y)}) of a given compound (X-Y) by using association information provided from dicos {dico1, dico2,...}. Module-B (<S-tag Determiner>) is to obtain the most likely

[4] Take an example in CILIN (a Chinese thesaurus, see 3.1). KILL(殺死), BUTCHER(屠宰), and EXCUTE(處決) are three concepts all meaning 'cause to die'. However, the words expressing these three ideas are respectively put under small classes Hn05, Hd28, and Hm10, respectively under medium class Hn: *Criminal Activities*(惡行), class Hd: *Economical Production Activities*(生產), and class Hm: *Security and Justice Activities*(公安, 司法). We wonder if any measurement based on that hierarchy can capture the similarity among the words situated in these three small classes in CILIN, for those words share only a common major class H, denoting vaguely *Activities*, which includes 296 small classes and 836 subclasses.

[5] Here the term *latent* is used only to mean 'hidden, potential, and waiting to be discovered'. It has nothing to do with the LSI techniques, though they both evoke the same meaning of *latent*.

[6] Especially in Chinese dictionaries, it is often the case that several synonymous words are given as explanation to the meaning of a word, especially when it is a compound verb.

sense tags ({**S-tag**(X-Y)}) according to dicox for the target word by using the output of Module-A. The component filter-C is optional, which passes only the T-similar words with the same syntactic category as the target compound, if it is already known. In fact, a system of semantic classification can be so created by choosing dico2 as dicox and the S-tag is then the semantic class in CILIN (as in section 4).

3 Character-Sense Association Network

Before exploring the critical measurement of association among characters and senses needed in the model, I have to briefly present the lexical sources in use and to define the idealized dictionary format adopted in this task.

3.1 Lexical Sources

The lexical sources used to implement my system include:

(1) **Sinica Corpus**: a balanced Chinese corpus with 5 million words segmented and tagged with syntactic categories. (Huang et al., 1995)

(2) **HowNet**: an on-line Chinese-English bilingual lexical resource created by Dong. It is used in this paper as a Chinese-English dictionary registering about 51,600 Chinese words, each assigned with its equivalent English words and its POS. (http://www.keenage.com/)

(3) **CILIN**: a Chinese thesaurus collecting about 53,200 words. CILIN classifies its lexicon in a four-level hierarchy according to different semantic granularities: 12 major classes (level-1), 95 medium classes (level-2), 1428 small classes (level-3), and 3924 subclasses (level-4). The words in the same small class can be regarded as semantically similar, but only the words in the same subclasses can be surely regarded as synonyms[7].(Mei et al., 1984)

3.2 Idealized Dictionary Format (*dico*)

The idealized dictionary, denoted as ***dico***, is actually a formatted MRD defined as follows:

A *dico* is a set of <*W-S*> correspondence pairs, where *W* is a word, and *S* is a sense tag. **(1)**

In the system implementation in this paper, two *dico*s are converted respectively from HowNet and CILIN for the calculation of the association measures among characters and sense tags with different types of sense tags adopted. For HowNet, the English equivalent words are used as sense tags to form dico1. For CILIN, the subclasses are used as sense tags to form dico2.

3.3 Character-Sense Association

All the semantic information provided by a *dico*, as defined in (1), can be in fact represented as a network with links between two domains: *W* domain (words) and *S* domain (sense tags). In such a viewpoint, polysemy is then a one-to-many mapping from W to S, while synonymy a one-to-many mapping from S to W. If we further link a component character C of a word W to one of the S linked to W, such a C-S link might intuitively reflect a potential sense S for the character C, probably a *latent* sense of C, as previously described in section 2.2. We can use a statistical association measure, like MI or χ^2, to extract such C-S links. The statistically extracted C-S association can then lead to the finding of latent senses for a character. The revelation of a latent character-sense association will further lead to the retrieval of new synonymy relation between characters. Symmetrically, the revelation of a latent character-sense association will also lead to the retrieval of the potential polysemy of a character. As illustrated in the Z-diagram below, supposed that *C*1 is already associated to *S*1 and *C*2 to *S*2, the retrieval of *latent sense S*1 to *C*2 will, meanwhile, lead to the finding of an association between *C*1 and *C*2 (*latent synonymy*), and an association between *S*1 and *S*2 (*latent polysemy*).

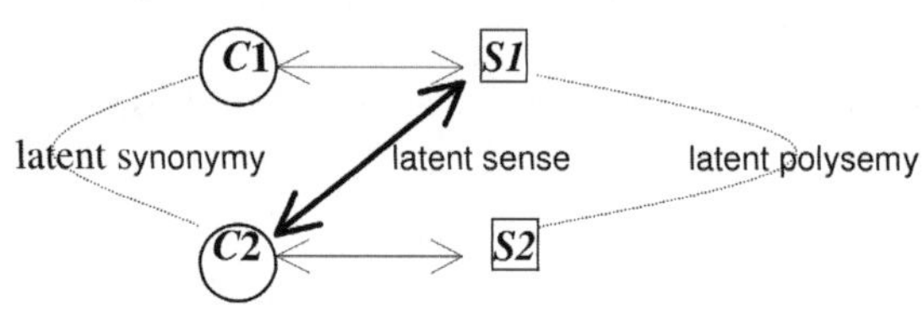

Fig. 2 Z-diagram of C-S links

The *directed* association measure from a character to a sense, denoted as CS-asso(C_i,S_j), can be defined as follows:

$$\alpha(C_i, S_j) = [\, freq(C_i,S_j)^2 / (\, freq(C_i)+freq(S_j)\,)\,]\ \hat{}\ 0.5$$

$$\text{CS-asso}\,(C_i, S_j) = \alpha\,(C_i,S_j)\,/\,\text{Max}_k\,\{\,\alpha\,(C_i,S_k)\,\} \qquad \textbf{(2)}$$

where freq(C_i,S_j) is the number of the words in the MRD that contain character C_i and is tagged with sense S_j, while freq(C_i) is the number of words

[7] Take two verbs 買('to buy') and 賣('to sell') as examples to demonstrate the taxonomy of CILIN. Both of the two verbs are grouped in the small class He03 (commercial trade), which is under the major class H (activities) and the medium class He (economic activities). However, the two antonyms are put under two different subclasses, respectively He031 (buying) and He032 (selling).

containing character C_i, and freq(S_j) the number of words tagged with sense S_j.[8] Likewise, the *directed* association measure from a sense to a character, denoted as SC-asso(S_i,C_j), can be defined as follows[9]:

$$\alpha(S_i,C_j) = [\, freq(S_i,C_j)^2 / (freq(S_i)+freq(C_j))\,]\ \hat{}\ 0.5$$
$$SC\text{-}asso(S_i,C_j) = \alpha(S_i,C_j) / Max_k \{ \alpha(S_i, C_k) \}, \quad (3)$$

Consequently, by link of a C_i-S_j-C_k chain (a latent synonymy), the directed association measure for a character C_i to another character C_k is defined as a combination of two types of directed association measures, the maximal association measure CC-asso1(C_i ,C_k) and the over-all association measure CC-asso2(C_i ,C_k), with respective weights of 1-ω and ω (the value ω is by default set at 0.5).

$$asso\text{-}chain(C_i,S_j,C_k) = (asso\,(C_i,S_j) * asso\,(S_j,C_k))\ \hat{}\ 0.5$$
$$f1\,(C_i,C_k) = Max_j \{asso\text{-}chain\,(C_i,S_j,C_k)\}$$
$$CC\text{-}asso1(C_i,C_k) = f1\,(C_i,C_k) / Max_m \{f1\,(C_i,C_m)\}$$
$$f2\,(C_i,C_k) = \Sigma_j\, asso\text{-}chain(C_i,S_j,C_k)$$
$$CC\text{-}asso2(C_i,C_k) = f2\,(C_i,C_k) / Max_m \{f2\,(C_i,C_m)\}$$
$$CC\text{-}asso = (1\text{-}\omega) * CC\text{-}asso1 + \omega * CC\text{-}asso2 \quad (4)$$

3.4 S-Template Similarity Measure

Supposed that $W_i(C_{i1}$-$C_{i2})$ and $W_j(C_{j1}$-$C_{j2})$ are both two-character compounds, a measure of word-word directed association (denoted as WW-asso) from W_i to W_j can be defined based on the CC-asso between their corresponding component characters:

$$\beta\,(W_i,W_j) = \{ CC\text{-}asso(C_{i1},C_{j1}) * CC\text{-}asso(C_{i2},C_{j2}) \}\ \hat{}\ 0.5$$
$$WW\text{-}asso(W_i,W_j) = \beta\,(W_i,W_j) / Max_k \{ \beta\,(W_i,W_k) \} \quad (5)$$

Since the corresponding characters of two T-similar compounds must share the same sense tags and thus have strong CC-asso, the measure WW-asso(W_i,W_j) indicates, in fact, how T-similar for a compound W_j to a target W_i, compared with other compounds. WW-asso(W_i,W_j) is therefore taken as the measure of S-template similarity (denoted as T-similarity).

Applying the S-template similarity measure in (5), now the T-similar Word Retriever (<TWR>) can give for a compound X-Y the list of its most T-similar compounds from the corpus and their T-similarity scores. As to the <S-tag Determiner>, it receives as input the output T-similar words from <TWR>. Among the input T-similar words, the ones known to $dico_x$, are picked out and their sense tags (S-tag) with the T-similarity scores (WW-asso) are used, as in the formula (6), to calculate the likelihood score Λ for a compound **V-V_i** to possess a certain **S-tag$_j$**. Therefore a set of ranked possible semantic classes for the compound X-Y can be given ({**S-tag**(X-Y)}).

$$\lambda(V\text{-}V_i,\ S\text{-}tag_j) = \Sigma_j\ WW\text{-}asso\,(V\text{-}V_i,\ SW_k) \quad (6)$$
,where SW_k is a known word in $dico_x$ and $S\text{-}tag_j$ is one of the S-tages to SW_k
$$\Lambda(V\text{-}Vi,S\text{-}tag_j) = \lambda(V\text{-}V_i,S\text{-}tag_j) / Max_n \{ \lambda(V\text{-}V_i,\ S\text{-}tag_n) \}$$

4. System Implementation

4.1 Classification for V-V Compounds

Based on the model proposed, a system of semantic classification can be implemented for two-character V-V compound verbs by using dico2 as the dicox in the Module-B (the S-tag now is the semantic class in CILIN). The V-V compounds are chosen as subjects in this system because the choice can best distinguish the present model from the previous head-orientated approaches. As the involvement of only V characters make training data homogeneous, it simplifies the association network and reduces largely the computational complexity. However, the partial system for V-V compounds can be easily extended to handle V-N compounds and N-N compounds as well when the character-sense association network for N characters is established.

Since only the V characters are involved, a subset of <W-S> pairs of dico1 (HowNet) and dico2 (CILIN) is extracted to calculate the association measures and then the T-similarity measure. The subset contains only the <W-S> pairs whose W are one-character or two-character verbs. In CILIN the verbs are put under the major classes from E to J, designating the concepts of attributes (E), actions (F), mental activities (G), activities (H), physical states (I), and relations (J). By choosing only the words in the above 6 major classes, the nominal senses of characters (A: human, B: concrete object, C: time and space, D: abstract object) are supposed to be excluded. Besides, the occurrence frequency of a character in a mono-character word will be double weighted, since in this case the word sense is surely contributed by that character alone.

Let us take the V-V compound 捕獲 ('to catch by hunting', literally 'hunt-catch') for example to see how the model operates. Based on the

[8] The formula α in (2) is actually a simplified approximation to the χ^2 -test measure by supposing that freq(C,S) is much smaller than freq(C) and freq(S). In fact, MI (mutual information) is another association measure frequently used in Chinese NLP. For example, it is successfully used for the character-POS association measure in the task of syntactical classification for Chinese unknown words (Chen et al., 1997). However, a heuristic evaluation on some randomly picked examples shows that it seems to be outperformed by the χ^2 measure in this task.

[9] It must be noted that the measures of directed association (2) and (3) are asymmetric in that they give different values for the association from Ci to Sj and for the one from Sj to Ci because their normalization factors are not the same. That is why the notion *directed* is added here to point out the asymmetry.

association network created from HowNet, the characters associated to 捕 and 獲 are listed in List 1 and List 2 (only the 10 top ranked are listed here), the 20 top ranked T-similar compounds of 捕獲 are listed in List 3 with their similarity scores, syntactic categories and semantic classes, if they are known in CILIN. Among the 20 T-similar compounds retrieved, 10 of them (the grayed ones) can be found in CILIN; 9 of them (the framed ones) can be considered as good synonyms of 捕獲, while other 7 (the starred ones) considered semantically really close. In this particular example, 80% (16/20) of the T-similar compounds can be considered as at least near synonymous, while 50%(8/16) of them can be actually found in CILIN to serve the automatic semantic classification.

捕 1.0000	抓 0.8832
緝 0.9634	擒 0.8673
捉 0.9165	佔 0.8629
逮 0.9073	獲 0.8558
拿 0.9022	奪 0.8306

List 1

獲 1.0000	賺 0.8694
得 0.9402	俘 0.8687
擒 0.9146	捉 0.8641
拿 0.9076	捕 0.8632
收 0.9034	繳 0.8614

List 2

捕獲 1.0000 VC H m051	緝捕* 0.8316 VC Hm051
緝獲 0.9634 VC H m051	佔得 0.8113 VC
捕得 0.9402 VJ	獲得* 0.8046 VJ Je121
逮獲 0.9073 VC	獵獲 0.8036 VC
拿獲 0.902 2 VC Hm051	捕抓* 0.7970 VC
緝拿* 0.8744 VC Hm051	擒拿 0.7872 VC Hb141
擒獲 0.8673 VC	攫獲 0.7853 VC
捕捉* 0.8641 VC	逮捕* 0.7832 VC Hm051
捕到 0.8380 VC	奪得 0.7809 VC Je121
捉拿* 0.8318 VC Hm051	扣得 0.7790 VC

List 3

Applying the formula for the likelihood score of semantic class determination in (6), we have the 4 top ranked semantic classes for 捕獲 predicted by the system as follows:

(1) Hm051 (逮捕 'arrest')
(2) Je121 (取得 'acquire')
(3) Hb121 (攻佔 'attack and occupy')
(4) Hb141 (俘虜 'capture as war prisoner')

In this case, the standard answer of class Hm051 for the compound 捕獲 is ranked as the first candidate, while the second ranked candidate class Je121 ('acquire') is also reasonable, which can be considered rather correct in a certain way by human judgment. In fact, according to the native speaker's instinct, the 4th ranked candidate class Hb141 ('capture') is also quite suitable to the meaning of the verb 捕獲, though that is not what it is classified in CILIN. However, to avoid the subjective interference of human judgment and particularly to make the evaluation task automatic, the evaluation in the following sections will be made by machine only according to the standard classification in CILIN.

4.2 Experiment Results

For evaluating the performance of the system, 500 V-V compounds are randomly picked out from CILIN to form the test set. Two modes of evaluation experiments are carried out: both modes adopt dico2 (CILIN) in Module-B (dicox=dioc2) to determine semantic classes, while the inside-test mode uses dico2 (CILIN) in Module-A and the outside-test mode uses dico1 (HowNet) in Module-A, to obtain association network and retrieve the T-similar words. To make the test compounds *unknown* to the model, the semantic classes of the test compounds have to be *invisible* to CILIN, while the *invisibility* should not undermine the training of the association network in Module-A. The effect is done by dynamically withdrawing a word from dico2 in Module-B each time when it is in test. Two ways of evaluation can be made: by verifying the answer to the level of small class (level-3) and to the level of subclasses (level-4). The accuracy is calculated by verifying if the correct answer or one of the correct answers (if V-V is polysemous) according to CILIN can be found in the first n ranked semantic classes predicted by the system. The performance of a random head-picking model is offered as the baseline. In this baseline model, one of the semantic classes of X and Y is randomly chosen as the semantic class of the compound X-Y.

	Level-3(Small Class)			Level-4(Subclass)		
n	outside	inside	Baseline	outside	inside	Baseline
1	**39.80%**	**61.60%**	**18.83%**	**36.60%**	**60.40%**	**17.34%**
2	56.80%	76.00%	31.40%	52.80%	74.40%	29.12%
3	64.40%	83.80%	40.21%	59.80%	80.80%	37.54%

Table 1. Performance for 500 V-V compounds

The results in Table 1 show that the system achieves a precision rate of 60.40% for inside test and 36.60% for outside test in level-4 classification against the baseline one of 17.34%. Not to our surprise, the performance of classification to level-3, a slightly shallower level, is slightly better: 61.60% for inside test and 39.80% for outside test. Table 1 also shows that the system can achieve a correction rate of 59.8% (outside) and 80.80% (inside) for including the correct answer in the first 3 ranked candidate classes in level-4, 64.40% (outside) and 83.80% (inside) in level-3, all much better than the baseline ones, 37.54% and 40.21%.

4.3 A Pseudo-WSD Problem

If the correct semantic class can be found in a

limited number of candidates, context information can be used to help determine which candidate is more likely to be the proper one, just as a WSD task does. Take again the example of the compound 捕獲 in section 4.1, which the system classifies most likely as: '**arrest**', '**acquire**' and '**attack-occupy**'. Obviously the verbs in the three classes should take different stereotypes of objects: respectively **person**, **thing**, and **place**. Therefore it is not difficult to determine the correct semantic class of the verb in question by using context information, in this case the type of the object. Through this example, we can see that the high inclusion rate of the correct answer in the top ranked classes has in fact a great significance: the ranking of the top candidates can be further adjusted and eventually ameliorated by context information, and thus the task of class determination can become a pseudo-WSD problem, in which domain various techniques are well available (Manning and Schutze, 1999). The performance of the present non-contextual system of automatic semantic classification is then expected to be improvable with the eventual help of a good context-sensitive WSD system, though it is out of the scope in this paper. Therefore the correct inclusion rate of top n ranked classes is also the concern of this paper.

4.4 Endocentric vs. Exocentric Compounds

Table 2 shows the performance of the system on the endocentric compounds (with heads) and on the exocentric ones (without heads) in level-3. Among the 500 V-V compounds, the endocentric V-V compounds have much higher precision rates than the exocentric ones. But even for the exocentric compounds, the precision rate of the system is 49.28% in inside test and 27.05% in outside test, while the correct inclusion rate of top 3 ranked classes achieves 74.64% in inside test and 51.69% in outside test. Such a performance is in fact rather encouraging since it shows that this model has overcome the inherent difficulty met by a head-oriented approach.

	Outside		inside	
n	+Head	-Head	+Head	-Head
1	**48.81%**	**27.05%**	**70.69%**	**49.28%**
2	68.26%	40.58%	84.83%	64.11%
3	73.38%	51.69%	90.69%	74.64%

Table 2. Level-3 performance for [+/- Head] V-V

4.5 Syntactic Category Filter

To test the function of the Filter-C in the model, two sets of 500 V-V compounds are randomly picked out from verbs of category VC corpus, and from verbs of category VA in Sinica Corpus.[10]. Table 3 and 4 show the performance of the system on the two kinds of verbs when evaluated to level-3. The results show that the system using the syntactic category filter (+SCF) performs slightly better than that without using the filter (-SCF) only in the precision of first ranked class in the outside test. Beside that, the use of the syntactic category filter generally undermines the performance of the system. Such a result might be explained by the fact that synonymous words in CILIN are not necessarily of the same syntactic category; it also suggests that for the entire model recall is perhaps more important than precision in Module-A.

	outside		Inside		Baseline
n	+SCF	-SCF	+SCF	-SCF	
1	**49.60%**	**47.60%**	**64.40%**	**67.20%**	**22.90%**
2	63.20%	64.00%	76.40%	78.40%	39.74%
3	70.00%	73.60%	84.40%	84.80%	50.27%

Table 3. Level-3 performance for V-V of category VC

	outside		inside		Baseline
n	+SCF	-SCF	+SCF	-SCF	
1	**41.00%**	**38.60%**	**52.00%**	**58.60%**	**15.90%**
2	52.20%	49.60%	67.40%	73.80%	26.84%
3	55.80%	55.00%	73.00%	80.20%	34.61%

Table 4. Level-3 performance for V-V of category VA

4.6 Classification Errors

An examination of the bad performing cases suggests that there are three major sources of erroneous classification in the experiments. (1) Some test compounds are just idiomatic or non semantic compositional. Naturally, it is highly difficult, if not impossible, to correctly predict their semantic classes. (2) Some compounds are from unproductive S-templates, which causes the example sparseness of the T-similar compounds. The scarcity of examples will easily lead to a poor determination result caused by a low noise tolerance of occasional bad examples. (3) Some classifications predicted by the system are reasonable to native speakers, but happen not to be the case in CILIN as the standard answers.

5. Conclusions and Further Remarks

In this paper I have proposed a character-based model of sense determination for Chinese

[10] VC (transitive action/activity) and VA (intransitive action/activity) are the two most dominant types of two-character verbs in the corpus, occupying respectively 44% and 27% around. Here the statistics does not include the VH (intransitive state) verbs, because they generally correspond to the adjectives in English, and in deed they are categorized as adjective in HowNet.

compounds using compounding template similarity. Based on this model, a system of deep semantic classification for V-V compounds is implemented, which classifies compounds according to the taxonomy of CILIN to its deep-level (level-3 and level-4) classes. The evaluation experiment reports a fairly satisfactory precision rate of the first ranked predicted semantic class (about 38% in outside test and 61% in inside test) against the baseline one (about 18%). The results also show a high inclusion rate of correct answer in the top3 ranked classes, which suggests that in the future the present non-contextual system can cooperate with a WSD module using context information. Though the model is only tested on a partial system for V-V compounds, it can be extended to work for general compounds, like V-N and N-N, with the association network further established for N characters.

The model proposed in this paper has the following advantages: (1) It proposes a similarity measure of compounding template to retrieve potential synonyms for sense approximation, which avoids the inherent difficulty of head determination in a head-oriented approach and is thus capable of handling exocentric compounds. (2) It establishes a network of character-sense association, which allows the discovery of latent senses of characters, latent synonymy, and latent polysemy, thus remedying the incompleteness effect of the MRD in use. (3) It can carry out deep semantic classification, not just shallow classification assigning general and vague categories. (4) It requires only a simple format of idealized dictionary, which facilitates the conversion from a general MRD and allows an easy enhancement of the system by adding a new MRD.

However, as can be remarked in the discussion of classification errors, the performance of the model relies much on the productivity of compounding semantic templates of the target compounds. To correctly predict the semantic class of a compound with an unproductive semantic template is no doubt very difficult due to a sparse existence of the T-similar compounds. How to remedy such an effect is thus a challenging task in the future. In addition, how to generalize the present character-based model to make it applicable to compounds with multi-character component morphemes will be another essential task to undertake. Besides, a task of automatic lexical translation for Chinese unknown compounds will also be carried out in the future. The task can be executed under the very same structure of the present model, since the only difference will be the change of working *dico*x (from dico2 to dico1) in the Module-B. A pilot experiment has already shown encouraging results.

References

Chao-Jan Chen, Ming-hong Bai, and Keh-Jiann Chen. 1997. Category Guessing for Chinese Unknown Words. In *Proceedings of the Natural Language Processing Pacific Rim Symposium* 1997, pages 35-40.

Hsin-Hsi Chen and Chi-Ching Lin. 2000. Sense-tagging Chinese corpus. In *Proceedings of ACL-2000 workshop on Chinese Language Processing*, pages 7-14.

Keh-Jiann Chen and Chao-Jan Chen. 1998. A Corpus Based Study on Computational Morphology for Mandarin Chinese. In Quantitative and Computational Studies on the Chinese Language, pages 283-306.

Keh-Jiann Chen and Chao-Jan Chen. 2000. Automatic Semantic Classification for Chinese Unknown Compound Nouns, In *Proceedings of Coling*-2000, pages 173-179.

Keh-Jiann Chen and Jia-Ming You. 2002. A Study on Word Similarity Using Context Vector Models, *Computational Linguistics & Chinese Language Processing*, 8(2):37-58.

Chu-Ren Huang et al. 1995. The Introduction of Sinica Corpus. In *Proceedings of ROCLING* VIII, pages 81-99.

Dekang Lin. 1998a. An Information-Theoretic Definition of Similarity, In *Proceedings of International Conference on Machine Learning*, pages 296-304

Dekang Lin. 1998b. Automatic retrieval and clustering of similar words. In *Proceedings of COLING/ACL-98*, pages 768–774.

Kim-Teng Lua. 1997. Prediction of Meaning of Bi-syllabic Chinese Compound Words Using Back Propagation Neural Network. In *Computer Processing of Oriental Languages*, 11(2):133-144.

Christopher Manning and Hinrich Schütze. 1999. Fondations of Statistical Natural Language Processing, MIT Press.

Jia-Ju Mei et al. 1984. TonYiCi CiLin – thesaurus of Chinese words (同義詞詞林), Shangwu Yinshuguan (商務印書館香港分館), Hong Kong.

Sabine Ploux and Bernard Victorri. 1998. Construction d'espace sémantique à l'aide de dictionnaires de synonymes. *Traitement Automatique des Langues*, 39(1):161-182.

Sabine Ploux and Hyungsuk Ji. 2003. A Model for Matching Semantic Maps Between Languages (French/English, English/French). *Computational Linguistics*, 29(2):155-178.

Philip Resnik. 1995. Using Information Content to Evaluate Semantic Similarity in a Taxonomy. In *Proceedings of the 14th International Joint Conference on Artificial Intelligence* (IJCAI), pages 448-453.

Yorick Wilks and Mark Stevenson. 1997. Sense Tagging: Semantic Tagging with a Lexicon. In *Proceedings of the SIGLEX Workshop on Tagging Text with Lexical Semantics*, pages 47-51.

David Yarowsky. 1992. Word-Sense Disambiguation Using Statistical Models of Rogets Categories Trained on Large Corpora", In *Proceedings of COLING-92*, pages 454-460.

Chinese Chunking with another Type of Spec

Hongqiao Li
Beijing Institute of Technology
Beijing 100081 China
lhqtxm@bit.edu.cn

Chang-Ning Huang
Microsoft Research Asia
Beijing 100080 China
cnhuang@msrchina.research.microsoft.com

Jianfeng Gao
Microsoft Research Asia
Beijing 100080 China
jfgao@microsoft.com

Xiaozhong Fan
Beijing Institute of Technology
Beijing 100081 China
fxz@bit.edu.cn

Abstract

Spec is a critical issue for automatic chunking. This paper proposes a solution of Chinese chunking with another type of spec, which is not derived from a complete syntactic tree but only based on the un-bracketed, POS tagged corpus. With this spec, a chunked data is built and HMM is used to build the chunker. TBL-based error correction is used to further improve chunking performance. The average chunk length is about 1.38 tokens, F measure of chunking achieves 91.13%, labeling accuracy alone achieves 99.80% and the ratio of crossing brackets is 2.87%. We also find that the hardest point of Chinese chunking is to identify the chunking boundary inside noun-noun sequences[1].

1 Introduction

Abney (1991) has proposed chunking as a useful and relative tractable median stage that is to divide sentences into non-overlapping segments only based on superficial analysis and local information. (Ramshaw and Marcus, 1995) represent chunking as tagging problem and the CoNLL2000 shared task (Kim Sang and Buchholz, 2000) is now the standard evaluation task for chunking English. Their work has inspired many others to study chunking for other human languages.

Besides the chunking algorithm, spec (the detailed definitions of all chunk types) is another critical issue for automatic chunking development. The well-defined spec can induce the chunker to perform well. Currently chunking specs are defined as some rules or one program to extract phrases from Treebank such as (Li, 2003) and (Li, 2004) in order to save the cost of manual annotation. We name it as Treebank-derived spec. However, we find that it is more valuable to compile another type of chunking spec according to the observation from un-bracketed corpus instead of Treebank.

Based on the problems of chunking Chinese that are found with our observation, we explain the reason why another type of spec is needed and then propose our spec in which the shortening and extending strategies are used to resolve these problems. We also compare our spec with a Treebank-derived spec which is derived from Chinese Treebank (CTB) (Xue and Xia, 2000). An annotated chunking corpus is built with the spec and then a chunker is also constructed accordingly. For annotation, we adopt a two-stage processing, in which text is first chunked manually and then the potential inconsistent annotations are checked semi-automatically with a tool. For the chunker, we use HMM model and TBL (Transform-based Learning) (Brill, 1995) based error correction to further improve chunking performance. With our spec the overall average length of chunks arrives 1.38 tokens, in open test, the chunking F measure achieves 91.13% and 95.45% if under-combining errors are not counted. We also find the hardest point of Chinese chunking is to identify the chunking boundary inside a noun-noun sequence.

In the remainder of this paper section 2 describes some problems in chunking Chinese text, section 3 discusses the reason why another type of spec is needed and proposes our chunking spec, section 4 discusses the annotation of our chunking corpus, section 5 describes chunking model, section 6 gives experiment results, section 7, 8 recall some related work and give our conclusions respectively.

2 Problems of Chunking Chinese Text

The purpose of Chinese chunking is to divide sentence into syntactically correlated parts of words after word segmentation and part-of-speech (POS) tagging. For example:

[NP 珠海/ns 'Zhuhai'] 的/u 'of' [NP 立体/a 'solid' 交通/n 'traffic' 框架/n 'frame'] [VP 已/d 'already' 初具规模/v 'achieve considerable scale' 了/u] 'Zhuhai has achieved considerable scale in solid traffic frame.'

According to Abney's definition, most chunks are modifier-head structures and non-overlapping. However, some syntactic structures in Chinese are very hard to be chunked correctly due to

[1] This work was done while Hongqiao Li was visiting Microsoft Research Asia.

characteristics of Chinese language, for example, less using of function words and less inflection formats. Table 1 shows the most common structural ambiguities occurred during Chinese chunking. Their occurrences and distributions of each possible structure are also reported. As can be seen in Table 1, only 77% neighboring nouns can be grouped inside one chunk; if the left word is '的/of' or a verb, this figure will ascend to 80% and 94% respectively; but if the left word is an adjective or a numeral, it will descend to 70% and 59% respectively; for 'n_c_n', only 52% are word level coordination. In contrast with English chunking, several hard problems are described in detail as following.

(1) Noun-noun compounds

Compounds formed by more than two neighboring nouns are very common in Chinese and not always all the left nouns modify the head of the compound. Some compounds consist of several shorter sub-compounds. For example:

(青年/younger 志愿者/volunteer 科技/science and technology 服务队/service team) 'young volunteer service team of science and technology'

'青年 志愿者' and '科技 服务队' are two sub-compounds and the former modifies the latter.

But sometimes it is impossible to distinguish the inner structures, for example:

世界/world 和平/peace 事业/career

It is impossible to distinguish whether it is {{世界 和平} 事业} or {世界 {和平 事业}}.

English chunking also shows such problem, and the common solution for English is not to identify their inner structure and treat them as a flat noun phrase. Following is an example in CoNLL2000 shared task:

[NP employee assistance program directors]

(2) Coordination

Coordination in all cases can be divided into two types: with conjunctions and without conjunctions. The former can be further divided into two subcategories: word-level and phrase-level coordinations. For example:

{政策性/policy 银行/bank 与/**and** 商业/commercial 银行/bank} 的/of {联系/relationship 与/**and** 合作/cooperation} 'the relationship and cooperation between policy banks and commercial banks'.

The former coordination is phrase-level and the latter is word-level. Unfortunately, sometimes it is difficult or even impossible to distinguish whether it is word-level or phrase-level at all, for example:

最低/least 工资/salary 和/and 生活费/living maintenance 'the least salary and living maintenance'

It is impossible to distinguish '最低' is a shared modifier or not. English chunking also has such kind of problems. The solution of CoNLL2000 is to leave the conjunctions outside chunks for phrase-level coordinations and to group the conjunction inside a chunk when it is word-level or impossibly distinguished phrase-level. For example:

[NP enough food and water]

In Chinese, some coordinate construction has no conjunction or punctuation inside, and also could not be distinguished from a modifier-head construction with syntactic knowledge only. For example:

整顿/order (警车/police wagon 警灯/caution light 警报器/alarm whistle) 'Order the police

Pattern[1]	No.[2]	Distributions	Examples
n_n	951	77% (modifier head) 7% (coordination) 16% (others)	(社会/society 现象/phenomenon) 'social phenomena' (语言/language 文字/wordage) 'language and wordage' (首都/capital 文艺/art *舞台/stage*) ' the stage of capital art'
v_n_n	154	6% (v_n modify the last noun) 94 % (others)	进/enter 厂/factory 工人/worker 逃避/avoid 法律/law 责任/duty 'avoid legal duties'
的_n_n	98	80% (n_n is modifier_head) 20% (others)	*执勤/watch* 的/of 交通/traffic 警察/cop 'a orderly traffic cop' *瘫痪/paralytic* 的/of 肢体/body 功能/function
a_n_n	27	70% (a modify the first n) 30% (others)	高/high 科技/technology 企业/company 'high-tech company' 老/old 新闻/news 工作者/worker 'old news worker'
m_n_n	17	41% (m modify the first n) 59% (others)	两/two 国/nation 人民/people 'our two peoples' 一些/some 农村/country 地区/area 'some rural areas'
n_c_n	88	52%(word level coordination) 48%(others)	经济/economy 和/and 社会/society 'economy and society' 质量/quality 和/and 技术/technology *要求/requirement*

[1] n, v, a, d, m, q, p, f , c are the POS tags of noun, verb, adjective, adverb, number, measure, preposition, localizer, conjunction respectively, '_' means neighboring, '的/of' is a common auxiliary word in Chinese.

[2]This statistical work is done on our test corpus whose setting is shown in Table 3.

Table 1: The observation of several common structural ambiguities during Chinese chunking

wagons, caution lights and alarm whistles'

Such problem does not exist in English because almost all coordinations have certain conjunctions or punctuations between words or phrases of the same syntactic categories in formal English.

(3) Structural ambiguities

In Chinese, some structural ambiguities in phrase level are impossible or unnecessary to be distinguished during chunking. There is an example of 'a_n_n':

现代/a 'modern' 企业/n 'industry' 制度/n 'system'

{现代 {企业 制度}} or {{现代 企业} 制度} are identically acceptable. English also has such problem. The solution of CoNLL2000 is not to distinguish inner structure and group the given sequence as a single chunk. For example, the inner structure of '[NP heavy truck production]' is '{{heavy truck} production}', whereas one reading of '[NP heavy quake damage]' is '{heavy {quake damage}}'.

Besides, 'a_n_n', 'm_n_n' and 'm_q_n_n' also have the similar problem.

3 Chinese Chunking Spec

As a kind of shallow parsing, the principles of chunking are to make chunking much more efficient and precise than full parsing. Obviously, one can shorten the length of chunks to leave ambiguities outside of chunks. For example, if we let noun-noun sequences always chunk into single word, those ambiguities listed in Table 1 would not be encountered and the performance would be greatly improved. In fact, there is an implicit requirement in chunking, no matter which language it is, the average length of chunks is as longer as possible without violating the general principle of chunking. So a trade-off between the average chunk length and the chunking performance exists.

3.1 Why another type of spec is needed

A convenient spec is to extract the lowest non-terminal nodes from a Treebank (e.g. CTB) as Chinese chunked data. But there are some problems. The trees are designed for full parsing instead of shallow parsing, thus some of these problems listed in section 2 could not be resolved well in chunking. Maybe we can compile some rules to prune the tree or break some non-terminal nodes in order to properly resolve these problems just like CoNLL2000. However, just as (Kim Sang and Buchholz, 2000) noted: "some trees are very complex and some annotations are inconsistent". So these rules are complex, the extracted data are inconsistent and manual check is also needed. In addition, the resource of Chinese Treebank is limited and the extracted data is not enough for chunking.

So we compile another type of chunking spec according to the observation from un-bracket corpus instead of Treebank. The only shortcoming is the cost of annotation, but there are some advantages for us to explore.

1) It coincides with auto chunking procedure, and we can select proper solutions to these problems without constraints of the exist Treebank. The purpose of drafting another type of chunking spec is to keep chunking consistency as high as possible without hurting the performance of auto-chunking in whole.

2) Through spec drafting and text annotating most frequent and significant syntactic ambiguities could be studied, and those observations are in turn described in the spec carefully.

3) With a proper spec and certain mechanical approaches, a large-scale chunked data could be produced without supporting from the Treebank.

3.2 Our spec

Our spec and chunking annotation are based on PK corpus[2] (Yu et al. 1996). The PK corpus is un-bracketed, but in which all words are segmented and only one POS tag is assigned to each word. We define 11 chunk types that are similar with CoNLL2000. They are NP (noun chunk), VP (verb chunk), ADJP (adjective chunk), ADVP (adverb chunk), PP (prepositional chunk), CONJP (conjunction), MP (numerical chunk), TP (temporal chunk), SP (spatial chunk), INTJP (interjection) and INDP (independent chunk).

During spec drafting we try to find a proper chunk spec to solve these problems by two ways: either merging neighboring chunks into one chunk or shortening them. Besides those structural ambiguities, we also extend boundary of the chunks with minor structural ambiguities in order to make the chunks close to the constituents.

3.2.1 Shortening

The auxiliary '的/of' is one of the most frequent words in Chinese and used to connect a pre-modifier with its nominal head. However the left boundary of such a 的-construction is quite complicated: almost all kinds of preceding clauses, phrases and words can be combined with it to form such a pre-modifier, and even one 的-construction can embed into another. So we definitely leave it outside any chunk. Similarly, conjunctions, '和/and', '或/or' and '与/and' et al., are also left outside any chunk no matter they are word-level or

[2] Can be downloaded from www.icl.pku.edu.cn

phrase-level coordinations. For instances, the examples in Section 2 are chunked as '[NP 政策性 银行] 与 [NP 商业 银行] 的 [NP 联系] 与 [NP 合作]' and '[ADJP 最低] [NP 工资] 和 [NP 生活 费]'

3.2.2 Extending

(1) NP

Similar with the shared task of CoNLL2000, we define noun compound that is formed by a noun-sequence: 'a_n_n', 'm_n_n' or 'm_q_n_n', as one chunk, even if there are sub-compounds, sub-phrase or coordination relations inside it. For instances, '[NP 青年 志愿者 科技 服务队]', '[NP 世界 和平 事业]', '[VP 整顿] [NP 警车 警灯 警报器]', '[NP 现代 企业 制度] and '[NP 立体 交通 框架]' are grouped into single chunks respectively.

However, it does not mean that we blindly bind all neighboring nouns into a flat NP. If those neighboring nouns are not in one constituent or cross the phrase boundary, they will be chunked separately, such as following two examples in Table 1: '[VP 进] [NP 厂] [NP 工人]' and '[ADJP 瘫痪] 的/u [NP 肢体] [NP 功能]'. So our solution does not break the grammatical phrase structure in a given sentence.

With this chunking strategy, we not only properly resolved these problems, but also get longer chunks. Longer chunks can make successive parsing easier based on chunking. For example, if we chunked the sentence as:

[NP 珠海] 的 [NP 立体 交通] [NP 框架] [VP 已 初具规模 了] 。/w

There would be three possible syntactic trees which are difficult to be distinguished:

1a) {{ [NP 珠海] 的 { [NP 立体 交通] [NP 框架]}} [VP 已 初具规模]}

1b) {{{ [NP 珠海] 的 [NP 立体 交通]} [NP 框架]} [VP 已 初具规模]}

1c) {{ [NP 珠海] 的 [NP 立体 交通]} { [NP 框架] [VP 已 初具规模]}}

Whereas with above chunking strategy of our spec, there is only one syntactic tree remained:

{{[NP 珠海] 的 [NP 立体 交通 框架]} [VP 已 初具规模 了]} 。/w

Another reason of the chunking strategy is that for some NLP applications such as IR, IE or QA, it is unnecessary to analyze these ambiguities at the early stage of text analysis.

(2) PP

Most PP consists of only the preposition itself because the right boundary of a preposition phrase is hard to identify or far from the preposition. But certain prepositional phrases in Chinese are formed with a frame-like construction, such as [PP 在/p 'at' …中/f 'middle'], [PP 在/p …上/f 'top'], etc. Statistics shows that more than 90% of those frame-like PPs are un-ambiguous, and others commonly have certain formal features such as an auxiliary 的 or a conjunction immediately following the localizer. Table 2 shows the statistic result. Thus with those observations, those frame-like constructions could be chunked as PP. The length of such kind of PP frames is restricted to be at most two words inside in order to keep the distribution of chunk length more even and the chunking annotation more consistent.

Pattern[1]	No.of occurrence	Ratio as a chunk
p_*_f	45	93.33%
P_*_*_f	36	97.22%
*_f	40	92.50%
*_*_f	9	77.78%

[1] This statistical work is also done on our test corpus and '*' means a wildcard for a POS tag.

Table 2: The ration of grouping these patterns as a chunk without any ambiguity

(3) SP

Most spatial chunks consist of only the localizer(with POS tag '/s' or '/f'). But if the spatial phrase is in the beginning of a sentence, or there is a punctuation (except "、") in front of it, then the localizer and its preceding words could be chunked as a SP. And the number of words in front of the localizer is also restricted to at most two for the same reason.

(4) VP

Commonly, a verb chunk VP is a pre-modifier verb construction, or a head-verb with its following verb-particles which form a morphologically derived word sequence. The pre-modifier is formed by adverbial phrases and/or auxiliary verbs. In order to keep the annotation consistent those verb particles and auxiliary verbs could be found in a closed list respectively only. Post-modifiers of a verb such as object and complement should be excluded in a verb chunk.

We find that although a head verb groups more than one preceding adverbial phrases, auxiliary verbs and following verb-particles into one VP, its chunking performance is still high. For example:

[CONJP 如果/c 'if'] **[VP 迟迟/d 'lately' 不/d 'not' 能/v 'can' 建立/v 'build' 起/v 'up']** [NP 外交/n 'diplomat 关系/n 'relation']

'If we could not build up the foreign relations soon'

3.3 Spec Comparison

We compare our spec with the Treebank-derived spec, named as S1, which is to extract the lowest non-terminal nodes from CTB as chunks from the

aspect of the solutions of these problems in section 2. Noun-noun compound and the coordination which has no conjunction are chunked identically in both specs. But for others, there are different. In S1, the conjunctions of phrase-level coordination are outside of chunks and the ones of word-level are inside a chunk, all adjective or numerical modifiers are separate from noun head. According to S1, the example in 3.2.1 should be chunked as following.

[ADJP 政策性] [NP 银行] 与 [NP 商业] [NP 银行] 的 [NP 联系 与 合作]

But these phrases that are impossible to distinguish inner structures during the early stage of text analysis are hard to be chunked and would cause some inconsistency. '[ADJP 最低] [NP 工资] 和 [NP 生活费]' or '[ADJP 最低] [NP 工资 和 生活费]', '[ADJP 现代] [NP 企业] [NP 制度]' or '[ADJP 现代] [NP 企业 制度]', are hard to make decisions with S1.

In addition, with our spec outside words are only punctuations, structural auxiliary '的 /of', or conjunctions, whereas with S1, outside words are defined as all left words after lowest non-terminal extraction.

4 Chunking Annotation

Four graduate students of linguistics were assigned to annotate manually the PK corpus with the proposed chunking spec. Many discussions between authors and those annotators were conducted in order to define a better chunking spec for Chinese. Through the spec drafting and text annotating most significant syntactic ambiguities in Chinese, such as those structural ambiguities discussed in section 2 and 3, have been studied, and those observations are carefully described in the spec in turn.

Consistency control is another important issue during annotation. Besides the common methods: manual checking, double annotation, post annotation checking, we explored a new consistency measure to help us find the potential inconsistent annotations, which is hinted by (Kenneth and Ryszard. 2000), who defined consistency gain as a measure of a rule in learning from noisy data.

The consistency of an annotated corpus in whole could be divided down into consistency of each chunk. If the same chunks appear in the same context, they should be identically annotated. So we define the consistency of one special chunk as the ratio of identical annotation in the same context.

$$\text{cons}(P, \text{context}(P)) = \frac{\text{No. of same annotation in context}(P)}{\text{No. of }(P, \text{context}(P))\text{ in corpus}} \quad (1)$$

$$\text{cons(S)} = \frac{1}{N}\sum_{i=1}^{N} cons\ (P_i, context\ (P_i)) \quad (2)$$

Where P represents a pattern of the chunk (POS or/and lexical sequence), *context*(P) represents the needed context to annotate this chunk, N represents the number of chunks in the whole corpus S.

In order to improve the efficiency we also develop a semi-automatic tool that not only check mechanical errors but also detect those potential inconsistent annotations. For example, one inputs a POS pattern: 'a_n_n', and an expected annotation result: 'B-NP_I-NP_E-NP[3]', the tool will list all the consistent and inconsistent sentences in the annotated text respectively. Based on the output one can revise those inconsistent results one by one, and finally the consistency of the chunked text will be improved step by step.

5 Chunking Model

After annotating the corpus, we could use various learning algorithms to build the chunking model. In this paper, HMM is selected because not only its training speed is fast, but also it has comparable performance (Xun and Huang, 2000). Automatic chunking with HMM should conduct the following two steps. 1) Identify boundaries of each chunk. It is to assign each word a chunk mark, named M, which contains 5 classes: B, I, E, S (a single word chunk) and O (outside all chunks). 2) Tag the chunk type, named X, which contains 11 types defined in Section 3.

So each word will be tagged with two tags: M and X (the words excluding from any chunk only have M). So the result after chunking is a sequence of triples (t, m, x), where t, m, x represent POS tag, chunk mark and chunk type respectively. All the triples of a chunk are combined as an item n_i, which also could be named as a chunk rule. Let W as the word segmentation result of a given sentence, T as POS tagging result and C ($C = n_1 n_2 \ldots n_j$) as the chunking result. The statistical chunking model could be described as following:

$$\begin{aligned} C^* &= \arg\max_C P(C \mid W, T) \\ &= \arg\max_C P(W \mid C, T) P(C, T) / P(W, T) \\ &= \arg\max_C P(W \mid C, T) P(C, T) \end{aligned} \quad (3)$$

Independent assumption is used to approximate $P(W|C,T)$, that is:

[3] B, E, I represent the left/right boundary of a chunk and inside a chunk respectively, B-NP means this word is the beginning of NP.

$$P(W \mid C,T) \approx \prod_{i=1}^{m} P(w_i \mid t_i, m_i, x_i) \quad (4)$$

If the triple is unseen, formula 5 is used.

$$P(w_i \mid t_i, m_i, x_i) = \frac{count(t_i, m_i, x_i)}{\max_{j,k}(count(t_i, m_j, x_k))^2} \quad (5)$$

For P(C, T), tri-grams among chunks and outside words are used to approximate, that is:

$$P(C,T) \approx P(n_1)P(n_2 \mid n_1)\prod_{i=3}^{k} P(n_i \mid n_{i-2}n_{i-1}) \quad (6)$$

Smoothing follows the method of (Gao et al., 2002).

In order to improve the performance we use N-fold error correction (Wu, 2004) technique to reduce the error rate and TBL is used to learn the error correction rules based on the output of HMM.

6 Data and Evaluation

The performance of chunking is commonly measured with three figures: precision (P), recall (R) and F measure that are defined in CoNLL2000. Besides these, we also use two other measurements to evaluate the performance of bracketing and labeling respectively: RCB(ratio of crossing brackets), that is the percentage of the found brackets which cross the correct brackets; LA(labeling accuracy), that is the percentage of the found chunks which have the correct labels.

$$RCB = \frac{\text{No. of the chunks crossed chunk boundaries}}{\text{No. of chunks in test data}}$$

$$LA = \frac{\text{No. of correct chunks}}{\text{No. of the chunks with correct boundaries}}$$

The average length (ALen) of chunks for each type is the average number of tokens in each chunk of given type. The overall average length is the average number of tokens in each chunk. To be more disinterested, outside tokens (including outside punctuations) are also concerned and each of them is counted as one chunk.

6.1 Chunking performance with our spec

Training and test was done on the PK corpus. Table 3 shows the detail information. We use the uni-gram of chunk POS rules as the baseline.

Data	No. of tokens	No. of chunks	No. of outside	ALen (include O)
Train	444,777	229,989	92,839	1.377
Test	28,382	13,879	5,493	1.363

Table 3:The information of data set

Table 4 shows the chunking performance of close test and open test when HMM and ten folds TBL based error correction (EC) are done respectively.

	Close Test (%)			Open Test (%)		
	F	RCB	LA	F	RCB	LA
Baseline	81.95	6.55	99.46	81.44	6.58	99.47
HMM	94.79	2.62	99.78	88.39	3.18	99.65
HMM+EC	95.11	2.38	99.91	91.13	2.87	99.80

Table 4:The overall performance of chunking

As can be seen, the performance of open test doesn't drop much. For open test, HMM achieves 6.9% F improvement, 3.4% RCB reduction on baseline; error correction gets another 2.7% F improvement, 0.3% RCB reduction. Labeling accuracy is so high even with the baseline, which indicates that the hard point of chunking is to identify the boundaries of each chunk.

Table 5 shows the performance of each type of chunks respectively. NP and VP amount to approximately 76% of all chunks, so their chunking performance dominates the overall performance. Although we extend VP and PP, their performances are much better than overall. The performance of INDP can arrive 99% although it is much longer than other types. Because its surface evidences are clear and complete owing to its definition: the meta-data of a document, all the descriptions inside a pair of parenthesis, and also certain fixed phrases which do not act as a syntactic constituent in a sentence. From the relative lower performance of NP, but the most part of all chunks, we can conclude that the hardest issue of Chinese chunking is to identify boundaries of NPs.

	Percentage(%)	ALen (tokens)	P (%)	R (%)	F (%)
NP	45.94	1.649	88.82	86.25	87.52
VP	29.82	1.416	96.60	96.49	96.55
PP	6.59	1.221	93.67	93.58	93.63
MP	3.69	1.818	89.51	86.33	87.89
ADJP	3.77	1.308	86.11	89.43	87.74
SP	2.71	1.167	84.70	84.03	84.36
TP	2.59	1.251	93.23	94.30	93.76
CONJP	2.22	1.000	97.20	98.73	97.96
INDP	1.41	4.297	99.06	99.06	99.06
ADVP	1.06	1.117	85.48	85.03	85.25
INTJP	0.23	1.016	68.75	95.65	80.00
ALL	100	1.507	91.70	90.55	91.13

Table 5:The result of each type with our spec

All the chunking errors could be classified into four types: wrong labeling, under-combining, over-combining and overlapping. Table 6 lists the number and percentage of each type of errors. Under-combining errors count about a half number of overall chunking errors, however it is not a problem in certain applications because they does not cross the brackets, thus there are still opportunities to combine them later with additional knowledge. If we evaluate the chunking result without counting those under-combining errors, the F score of the proposed chunker achieves 95.45%.

Error type	No.of the Errors	Percentage
Wrong labeling	22	2.56%
Under-combine	418	48.71%
Over-combining	339	39.51%
Overlapping	59	6.88%

Table 6:The distribution of chunking errors

With comparison we also use some other learning methods, MBL(Bosch and Buchholz, 2002), SVM(Kudoh and Matsumoto, 2001) and TBL to build the chunker. The features for MBL and SVM are the POS of current, left two and right two words, lexical of current, left one and right one word. TiMBL[4] and SVM-light[5] are used as the tools. For SVM, we convert the chunk marks BIOES to BI and the binary class SVM is used to classifier the chunk boundary, then some rules are used to identify its label. For TBL, the rule templates are all the possible combinations of the features and the initial state is that each word is a chunk. Table 7 shows the result. As seen, without error correction all these models do not perform well and our HMM gets the best performance.

	MBL	SVM	TBL	HMM
F(%)	85.31	86.25	86.92	88.39

Table 7:Comparison with different algorithms

6.2 Further applications

The length of chunks with our spec (AoL is 1.38) is longer than other Treebank-derived specs (AoL of S1 is 1.239) and closer to the constituents of sentence. Thus there are several applications benefit from the fact, such as:

1) The longest/full noun phrase identification. According to our statistics, due to including noun-noun compounds, 'a_n_n' and 'm_n_n' inside NPs, 65% noun chunks are already the longest/full noun phrases and other 22% could become the longest /full noun phrases by only one next combining step.

2) The predicate-verb identification.

By extending the average length of VPs, the main verb (or predicate-verb, also called tensed verb in English) of a given sentence could be identified based on certain surface evidences with a relatively high accuracy. With certain definition our statistics based on our test set show that 84.88% of those main verbs are located in the first longest VPs among all VPs in a sentence.

[4] http://ilk.kub.nl/software.html

[5] http://svmlight.joachims.org/

7 Related Work

For chunking spec, the CoNLL2000 shared task defines a program chunklink to extract chunks from English Treebank. (Li, 2003) defines the similar Treebank-derived spec for Chinese and she reports manual check is also needed to make data consistent. Part of the Sparkle project has concentrates on a spec based on un-bracketed corpus of English, Italian, French and German(Carroll et al., 1997). (Zhou, 2002) defines base phrase which is similar as chunk for Chinese, but his annotation and experiment are on his own corpus.

For chunking algorithm, many machine learning (ML) methods have been applied and got promising results after chunking is represented as tagging problem, such as: SVM (Kudoh and Matsumoto, 2001), Memory-based (Bosch and Buchholz, 2002), SNoW (Li and Roth), et al.. Some rule-base chunking (Kinyon, 2003) and combining rules with learning (Park and Zhang, 2003) are also reported.

For annotation, (Brants, 2000) reports the inter-annotator agreement of part-of-speech annotations is 98.57%, the one of structural annotations is 92.43% and some consistency measures. (Xue et al., 2002) also address some issues related to building a large-scale Chinese corpus.

8 Conclusion

We propose a solution of Chinese chunking with another type of spec that is based on un-bracketed corpus rather than derived from a Treebank. Through spec drafting and annotating, most significant syntactic ambiguous patterns have been studied, and those observations in turn have been described in the spec carefully. The proposed method of defining a chunking spec helps us find a proper solution for the hard problems of chunking Chinese. The experiments show that with our spec, the overall Chinese chunking F-measure achieves 91.13% and 95.45% if under-combining errors are not counted.

9 Acknowledgements

We would like to thank the members of the Natural Language Computing Group at Microsoft Research Asia. Especial acknowledgement is to the anonymous reviewers for their insightful comments and suggestions. Based on that we have revised the paper accordingly.

References

S. Abney. 1991. Parsing by chunks. In *Principle-Based Parsing*. Kluwer Academic Publishers, Dordrecht: 257–278.

L.A. Ramshaw and M.P. Marcus. 1995. Text chunkingusing transformation-based learning. In *Proceedings of the 3rd ACL/SIGDAT Workshop,* Cambridge, Massachusetts, USA: 82–94.

E. Tjong Kim Sang and S. Buchholz. 2000. Introduction to the CoNLL-2000 shared task: Chunking. In *Proceedings of CoNLL-2000 and LLL-2000*, Lisbon, Portugal: 127–132.

Sujian Li, Qun Liu and Zhifeng Yang. 2003. Chunking based on maximum entropy. *Chinese Journal of Computer*, 25(12): 1734–1738.

Heng Li, Jingbo Zhu and Tianshun Yao. 2004. SVM based Chinese text chunking. *Journal of Chinese Information Processing*, 18(2): 1–7.

Nianwen Xue and Fei Xia. 2000. The Bracketing Guidelines for the Penn Chinese Treebank(3.0). *Technical report ,University of Pennsylvania*, URL http:// www.cis.upenn.edu/~chinese/.

Eric Brill. Transformation-based error-driven learning and natural language processing: A case study in part of speech tagging. *Computational Linguistics*,21 (4):543–565.

Shiwen Yu, Huiming Duan, Xuefeng Zhu, et al. 2002. The basic processing of contemporary Chinese corpus at Peking University. *Journal of Chinese Information Processing*, 16(6): 58–65.

K.A. Kaufman and R.S. Michalski. 1999. Learning from inconsistent and noisy data: the AQ18 approach, *Proceedings of the Eleventh International Symposium on Methodologies for Intelligent Systems*, Warsaw: 411–419.

Endong Xun and Changning Huang. 2000. A unified statistical model for the identification of English baseNP, In *Proceedings of the 38th ACL*: 109–117.

Jianfeng Gao, Joshua Goodman, Mingjing Li, Kai-Fu Lee. Toward a unified approach to statistical language modeling for Chinese. *ACM Transactions on Asian Language Information Processing,* Vol. 1, No. 1, 2002: 3-33.

Dekai WU, Grace NGAI, Marine CARPUAT. N-fold Templated Piped Correction. *Proceedings of the First International Joint Conference on Natural Language Processing*, SANYA: 632–637.

Antal van den Bosch and S. Buchholz. 2002. Shallow parsing on the basis of words only: a case study, In *Proceedings of the 40th ACL*: 433–440.

Taku Kudo and Yuji Matsumoto. 2000. Use of support vector learning for chunk identification, In *Proceedings of the 4th CoNLL*: 142–144.

J. Carroll, T. Briscoe, G. Carroll et al. 1997. *Phrasal parsing software*. Sparkle Work Package 3, Deliverable D3.2.

Yuqi Zhang and Qiang Zhou. 2002. Automatic identification of Chinese base phrases. *Journal of Chinese Information Processing*, 16(6):1–8.

X. Li and D. Roth. 2001. Exploring evidence for shallow parsing. In *Proceedings of the 5th CoNLL.*

Alexandra Kinyon. 2003. A language-independent shallow-parser compiler. In *Proceedings of 10th EACL Conference*, Toulouse, France: 322-329.

S.-B. Park, B.-T. Zhang. 2003. Text chunking by combining hand-crafted rules and memory-based, In *Proceedings of the 41th ACL*: 497–504.

Thorsten Brants. 2000. Inter-annotator agreement for a German newspaper corpus, In *Second International Conference on Language Resources and Evaluation LREC-2000,* Athens, Greece: 69–76.

Nianwen Xue, Fu-Dong Chiou and M. Palmer. 2002. Building a large-scale annotated Chinese corpus, In *Proceedings of COLING.*

Combining Neural Networks and Statistics for Chinese Word sense disambiguation

Zhimao Lu Ting Liu Sheng Li

Information Retrieval Laboratory of Computer Science & Technology School,
Harbin Institute of Technology
Harbin, China, 150001
{lzm, tliu}@ir.hit.edu.cn

Abstract

The input of network is the key problem for Chinese Word sense disambiguation utilizing the Neural Network. This paper presents an input model of Neural Network that calculates the Mutual Information between contextual words and ambiguous word by using statistical method and taking the contextual words to certain number beside the ambiguous word according to (-M, +N). The experiment adopts triple-layer BP Neural Network model and proves how the size of training set and the value of M and N affect the performance of Neural Network model. The experimental objects are six pseudowords owning three word-senses constructed according to certain principles. Tested accuracy of our approach on a close-corpus reaches 90.31%,, and 89.62% on a open-corpus. The experiment proves that the Neural Network model has good performance on Word sense disambiguation.

1 Introduction

It is general that one word with many senses in natural language. According statistics, there are about 42% ambiguous words in Chinese corpus (Lu, 2001). Word sense disambiguation (WSD) is a method to determine the sense of ambiguous word given the context circumstance.

WSD, a long-standing problem in NLP, has been a very active research topic,, which can be well applied in many NLP systems, such as Information Retrieval, Text Mining, Machine Translation, Text Categorization, Text Summarization, Speech Recognition, Text to Speech, and so on.

With rising of Corpus linguistics, the machine learning methods based on statistics are booming (Yarowsky, 1992). These methods draw the support from the high-powered computers, get the statistics of large real-world corpus, find and acquire knowledge of linguistics automatically. They deal with all change by invariability, thus it is easy to trace the evaluation and development of natural language. So the statistic methods of NLP has attracted the attention of professional researchers and become the mainstream bit by bit. Corpus-based Statistical approaches are Decision Tree (Pedersen, 2001), Decision List, Genetic Algorithm, Naive-Bayesian Classifier (Escudero, 2000)、Maximum Entropy Model (Adam, 1996; Li, 1999), and so on.

Corpus-based statistical approaches can be divided into supervised and unsupervised according to whether training corpus is sense-labeled text. Supervised learning methods have the good learning ability and can get better accuracy in WSD experiments (Schütze, 1998). Obviously the data sparseness problem is a bottleneck for supervised learning algorithm. If you want to get better learning and disambiguating effect, you can enlarge the size and smooth the data of training corpus. According to practical demand, it would spend much more time and manpower to enlarge the size of training corpus. Smoothing data is merely a subsidiary measure. The sufficient large size of training corpus is still the foundation to get a satisfied effect in WSD experiment.

Unsupervised WSD never depend on tagged corpus and could realize the training of large real corpus coming from all kinds of applying field. So researchers begin to pay attention to this kind of methods (Lu, 2002). The kind of methods can overcome the sparseness problem in a degree.

It is obvious that the two kinds of methods based on statistic have their own advantages and disadvantages, and cannot supersede each other.

This paper researches the Chinese WSD using the model of artificial neural network and investigates the effect on WSD from input model of neural network constructed by the context words and the size of training corpus.

2 BP Neural Network

At the moment, there are about more than 30 kinds of artificial neural network (ANN) in the domain of research and application. Especially, BP neural network is a most popular model of ANN nowadays.

2.1 The structure of BP Neural Network

The BP model provides a simple method to calculate the variation of network performance cased by variation of single weight. This model contains not only input nodes and output nodes, but also multi-layer or mono-layer hidden nodes. Fig1.1 is a construction chart of triple-layer BP neural network. As it is including the weights modifying process from the output layer to the input layer resulting from the total errors, the BP neural network is called Error Back Propagation network.

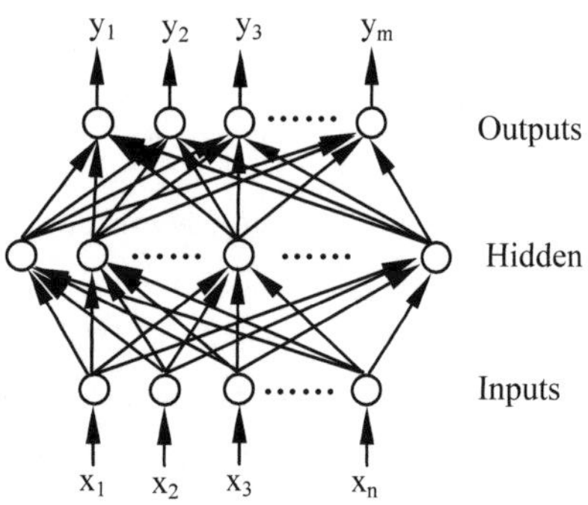

Fig. 1.1 BP Network

Fig.1.1 The structure of BP neural network Except for the nodes of input layer, all nodes of other layers are non-linear input and output. So the feature function should be differential on every part of function. General speaking, we can choose the sigmoid, tangent inspired, or linear function as the feature function because they are convenient for searching and solving by gradient technique. Formula (1) is a sigmoid function.

$$f(x) = \frac{1}{1+e^{-x}} \quad (1)$$

The output of sigmoid function ranges between 0 and 1, increasing monotonically with its input. Because it maps a very large input domain to a small range of outputs, it is often referred to as the squashing function of the unit. The output layer and hidden layer should adopt the sigmoid inspired function under the condition of intervention on the output, such as confining the output between 0 and 1.

2.2 Back Propagation function of BP neural network

The joint weights should be revised many times during the progress of the error propagating back in BP networks. The variation of joint weights every time is solved by the method of gradient descent. Because there is no objective output in hidden layer, the variation of joint weight in hidden layer is solved under the help of error back propagation in output layer. If there are many hidden layers, this method can reason out the rest to the first layer by analogy.

1) the variation of joint weights in output layer

To calculate the variation of joint weights from input *i*'th to output *k*'th is as following:

$$\Delta w_{ik} = -\eta \frac{\partial E}{\partial w_{ik}} = -\eta \frac{\partial E}{\partial O_k} \frac{\partial O_k}{\partial w_{ik}} \quad (2)$$

$$= \eta (t_k - O_k) f_2' \, O'_i = \eta \, \delta_{ik} \, O'_i$$

$$\delta_{ik} = (t_k - O_k) f_2' \quad (3)$$

$$\Delta b_{ki} = -\eta \frac{\partial E}{\partial b_{ki}} = -\eta \frac{\partial E}{\partial O_k} \frac{\partial O_k}{\partial b_{ki}} \quad (4)$$

$$= \eta (t_k - O_k) f_2' = \eta \, \delta_{ik}$$

2) the variation of joint weights in hidden layer

To calculate the variation of joint weights from input *j*'th to output *i*'th is as following:

$$\Delta w'_{ij} = -\eta \sum_{k=1}^{n} \frac{\partial E}{\partial w'_{ij}} = -\eta \sum_{k=1}^{n} \frac{\partial E}{\partial O_k} \frac{\partial O_k}{\partial O'_i} \frac{\partial O'_i}{\partial w'_{ij}} \quad (5)$$

$$= \eta \sum_{k=1}^{n} (t_k - O_k) f_2' w_{ik} f_1' p_j$$

$$= \eta \, \delta_{ij} p_j$$

where: $\delta_{ij} = e_i f_1'$, $e_i = \sum_{k=1}^{n} \delta_{ik} w_{ik}$ (6)

$$\Delta b'_{ki} = \eta \, \delta_{ij} \quad (7)$$

3. The construction of WSD model

Under the consideration of fact that only numerical data can be accepted by the input and output of neural network, if BP neural network is used on WSD, the prerequisite is to vector the part of semantic meaning (words or phrases) and sense.

In the event of training BP model, the input vector P and objective vector O of WSD should be determined firstly. And then we should choose the construction of neural network that needs to be designed, say, how many layers is network, how many neural nodes are in every layer, and the inspired function of hidden layer and output layer.

The training of model still needs the vector added weight, output, and error vector. The training is over when the sum of square errors is less than the objection of error. Or the errors of output very to adjust the joint weight back and repeat the training.

3.1 To vector the vocabulary

WSD depends on the context to judge the meaning of ambiguous words. So the input of model should be the ambiguous words and the contextual words round them. In order to vector the words in the context, the Mutual Information (MI) of ambiguous words and context should be calculated. So MI can show the opposite distance of ambiguous words and contextual words. MI can replace every contextual word. That is suitable to as the input model. The function of MI is as follow:

$$MI(w_1, w_2) = \log \frac{P(w_1, w_2)}{P(w_1)P(w_2)} \quad (8)$$

$P(w_1)$ and $P(w_2)$ are the probability of word w_1 and w_2 to appear in the corpus separately. While $P(w_1, w_2)$ is the probability of word w_1 and w_2 to appear together.

The experimental corpus in this article stems from the People Daily of 1998. The extent is 123,882 lines (10,000,000 words), including 121,400 words and phrases.

3.2 The pretreatment of BP network model

The supervised WSD need artificial mark of meaning. But it is time consuming to mark artificially. So it is difficult to get the large scope and high quality training linguistic corpus. In order to overcome this difficulty and get large enough experimental linguistic corpuses, we should turn to seek the new way.

We use pseudoword in place of the real word. That can get the arbitrary large experimental corpus according to the real demand.

3.2.1 The construction of Pseudoword

Pseudoword is the artificial combination of several real words on the basis of experimental demand to form an unreal word that possesses many features of real words and instead of real word as the experimental object in natural language research.

In the real world, one word has many meanings derives from the variation and flexible application of words. That needs a long-term natural evolution. Frankly speaking, that evolution never ceases at all times. For example, the word –'打'(da3) extends some new uses in recent years. Actually, in the endless history river of human beings, the development and variation of words meaning are rapid so far as to be more rapid than the replacement of dictionaries sometimes. Usually that makes an awkward position when you use dictionary to define the words meanings. Definitely, it is inconvenient for the research of natural linguistics based on dictionary.

But the meaning of pseudoword (Schütze, 1992) need not defined with the aid of dictionary and simulates the real ambiguous word to survey the effect of various algorithms of classified meanings.

To form a pseudoword need the single meaning word as a morpheme.

Set: $W_p = w_1 / w_2 / \ldots / w_i$

W_p is a pseudoword formed with w_i which contains i algorithms and meanings for every algorithm of pseudoword is single meaning and every living example is about equal to a pseudoword marked meaning in corpus. That is similar to the effect of artificial marked meaning. But the effect is more stable and reliable than artificial marked meaning. What's more, the scope of corpus can enlarge endless according to the demand to avoid the phenomenon of sparse data.

To define the number of algorithm, we count the average number of meanings according to the large-sized Chinese dictionaries (Table 3.1). Table 3.2 show the overall number of ambiguous word and percentage of ambiguous word having 2~4 meanings in all ambiguous word. These two charts indicate that verb is most active in Chinese and its average number of meanings is most, about 2.56. The percentage of ambiguous word having 2~4 meanings is most in all ambiguous word.

part of speech	Average sense (including single-sense word)	Average sense (only ambiguous word)
noun	1.136452	2.361200
verb	1.220816	2.558158
adjective	1.144717	2.300774
adverb	1.059524	2.078431

Table 3.1 the average number of a Chinese word's sense

3.2.2 Define the input vector

It should be based on context to determine the sense of ambiguous word. The model's input should be the vector of the ambiguous word and context words. It is well-known that the number of context words showing on the both sides of ambiguous word is not fixed in different sentences. But the number of vectors needed by BP network is fixed. In other words, the number of neural nodes of input model is fixed in the training. If the extracting method of feature vector is (-M, +N) in context, in other words there are M vectors on the left of ambiguous word and N vectors on the right, the extraction of feature vectors must span the limit of sentences. If the number of feature vectors is not enough, the ambiguous words on the left and right boundaries of whole corpus do not participate in the training.

ambiguous word	7955	/
Bi-senses word	5799	72.80%
Tri-senses word	1154	14.51%
Four-senses word	450	5.66%

Table 3.2 the distributing of ambiguous word

According to the extracting method of feature vector (-M, +N), the vector of model input is as following:

$$V_{输入} = \{MI_{11}, MI_{12}, \ldots, MI_{1i}, MI_{11}', MI_{12}', \ldots, MI_{1j}', MI_{21}, MI_{22}, \ldots, MI_{2i}, MI_{21}', MI_{22}', \ldots, MI_{2j}', MI_{31}, MI_{32}, \ldots, MI_{3i}, MI_{31}', MI_{32}', \ldots, MI_{3j}'\},\ 1 \le i \le M;\ 1 \le j \le N.$$

Where, MI_{1i} , MI_{1j}' are the MI of context and the first meaning of ambiguous word; MI_{2i} , MI_{2j}' are the MI of context and the second meaning of ambiguous word; MI_{3i} 、MI_{3j}' are the MI of context and the third meaning of ambiguous word. MI_{1i}, MI_{2i} and MI_{3i} are the feature words of ambiguous word on the left and MI of ambiguous word. MI_{1j}', MI_{2j}' and MI_{2j}' are the feature words of ambiguous word on the right and MI of ambiguous word.

pseudo-words	word ID	sample number	pseudo-words	word ID	sample number
W_1	34466	5550	W_4	84323	3773
	71345	3715		12751	2284
	31796	12098		52915	3900
	total	21363		total	9957
W_2	71072	9296	W_5	53333	1362
	78031	6024		29053	6135
	48469	1509		75941	1205
	total	16829		total	8702
W_3	7464	25925	W_6	39945	2346
	77375	2478		71335	1640
	23077	4704		51491	1012
	total	33107		total	4998

Table 3.3 the total number of the feature -vector sample of ambiguous word

Training corpus are 105,000 lines, and each line is a paragraph, totally about 10,000,000 words.

Table 3.3 shows the number of collected feature vector samples (the frequency of ambiguous word).

3.3 The definition of output model

Every ambiguous word has three meanings, totally eighteen meanings for six ambiguous words. Every ambiguous word trains a model and every model has three outputs showed by three-bit integer of binary system, such as the three meanings of ambiguous word W are showed as followed:

$s_{i1} = 100 \qquad s_{i2} = 010 \qquad s_{i3} = 001$

3.4 The definition of network structure

According to statistics, when (-M, +N) are (-8, +9) using the method of feature extraction, the cover percentage of effective information is more than 87% (Lu, 2001). However, if the sentence is very short, collecting the contextual feature words on the basis of (-8, +9) can include much useless information to the input model. Undoubtedly, that will increase more noisy effect and deduce the meaning-distinguish ability of verve network.

This article makes an on-the-spot investigation of experimental corpus, a fairly integrated meaning unit (the marks of border including comma, semicolon, ellipsis, period, question mark, exclamation mark, and the like), which average length is between 9~10 words. So this article collects the contextual feature words on the basis of (-5, +5) in the experiments, 10 feature words available that calculate MI with each meaning of ambiguous word separately to get 30 vectors. All punctuation marks should be filtered while the feature words are collected. The input layer of neural network model is regarded as 30 neural nodes. The triple-layer neural network adopts the inspired S function. From that, the number of neural nodes in hidden layer is defined as 12 on the basis of experimental contrast, and 3 neural nodes in output layer. Hence, the structure of model is 30 × 12 × 3, and the precision of differential training is defined as 0.3 based on the experimental contrast.

3.5 The test and training of model

The experimental corpus appeared in front are 123,882 lines. It is divided to three parts according to the demand of experiment, C1 (15,000 lines), C2 (60,000 lines), and C3 (105,000 lines). The open test corpus is 18,882 lines.

Table 3.3 tells us that there is a great disparity between the sample numbers of different ambiguous words in the experimental corpus of the same class. And the distribution of different meanings is not even for same ambiguous word. For the trained neural network has the good ability of differentiation for each word, the number of training sample should be about equal to each other for each meaning. So this experiment selects the least training samples. For example, there are 200 samples of the first meaning in training corpus, the second 400, and the third 500. To balance the input, each meaning merely has 200 samples to be elected for training.

Three groups of training corpus can train 3 neural networks possessing different vectors for every ambiguous word and make the unclose and open test for these networks separately.

4 The result of experiment

In order to analyze the effect that the extent of training corpus influences the meaning distinguish ability of neural network, this article trains the model of neural network using the experimental corpus individually, C_1, C2 and C_3, and makes the close and open test for 6 ambiguities separately.

The close test means the corpus are same in test and training.

The experiment is divided into two groups according to the extracting method of contextual feature words.

4.1 The first experiment one

Table 4.1 shows the result of the first experiment which extracts the contextual feature words using the method of （–5，＋5）.

In addition, the first experiment investigates that the extent of training corpus (the number of training samples big or small) influences the ability to distinguish the models. The result of test for 6

pseudo-words	close-test		open-test	
	accuracy	Training set	accuracy	Training set
W_1	0.8800	C_2	0.8951	C_3
W_2	0.8867	C_2	0.8775	C_2
W_3	0.8652	C_3	0.8574	C_3
W_4	0.8532	C_3	0.8687	C_3
W_5	0.8769	C_3	0.8745	C_3
W_6	0.8868	C_2	0.8951	C_3

Table 4.1 The contrast chat of experimental result for six ambiguities

ambiguities is showed in table 4.2 (close test), table 4.3 (open test), and table 4.4. Considering the length of this article, table 4.2 and table 4.3 shows the detailed data, and table 4.4 is brief.

pseudo-words		Training set		
		C_1	C_2	C_3
W_1	sense 1	0.9226	0.8169	0.8991
	sense 2	0.5513	0.8017	0.6872
	sense 3	0.8027	0.9564	0.9510
	average	**0.7589**	**0.8800**	**0.8720**
W_6	sense 1	0.8121	0.8780	0.9377
	sense 2	0.8389	0.8968	0.8804
	sense 3	0.7248	0.8856	0.8370
	average	**0.7919**	**0.8868**	**0.8850**

Table 4.2 The result of W_1 and W_6 in close test under the different training corpus

4.2 The second experiment

The second experiment investigates emphatically the effect that the method to collect the feature words influences the ability to distinguish BP model.

pseudo-words		Training set		
		C_1	C_2	C_3
W_1	sense 1	0.9019	0.7827	0.8942
	sense 2	0.4607	0.8097	0.7175
	sense 3	0.7792	0.9500	0.9515
	average	**0.7573**	**0.8798**	**0.8951**
W_6	sense 1	0.8233	0.9093	0.9535
	sense 2	0.8799	0.8182	0.8604
	sense 3	0.7278	0.8544	0.8038
	average	**0.8259**	**0.8683**	**0.8951**

Table 4.3 The result of W_1 and W_6 in open test under the different training corpus

There are many methods adopted in this experiment, including (–10, + 10), (–3, + 3), (–3, + 7), (–7, + 3), (–4, + 6) and (–6, + 4). Merely the ambiguous words W_1 and W_6 are regarded as the

pseudo-words		Training set		
		C_1	C_2	C_3
W_2	close	0.6628	0.8867	0.8772
W_3		0.6695	0.8453	0.8652
W_4		0.7414	0.8452	0.8532
W_5		0.8283	0.8537	0.8769
W_2	open	0.7287	0.8613	0.8700
W_3		0.8085	0.8384	0.8574
W_4		0.7920	0.8655	0.8687
W_5		0.8288	0.8775	0.8745

Table 4.4 The contrast chart of experimental result for four ambiguities

pseudo-words	feature collecting method	accuracy		Training set
		close-test	open-test	
W_1	(–10, +10)	0.8897	0.8685	C_1
	(–3, +3)	0.7917	0.7176	C_2
	(–4, +6)	0.8600	0.8888	C_3
	(–6, +4)	0.8797	0.8938	C_2
	(–3, +7)	0.8514	0.8827	C_3
	(–7, +3)	0.8431	0.8825	C_3
W_6	(–10, +10)	0.9031	0.8962	C_2
	(–3, +3)	0.8487	0.8460	C_2
	(–4, +6)	0.8982	0.8873	C_3
	(–6, +4)	0.8480	0.8772	C_2
	(–3, +7)	0.8669	0.8359	C_3
	(–7, +3)	0.8982	0.8895	C_3

Table 4.5 the experimental result under different feature collecting method

experimental objects in this group experiment. See table 4.5 for the correct percentage of WSD.

5. Analysis and discussion

See table 5.1 for the number of experimental corpus samples in experiment.

According to the table 3.3 and 5.1, the frequency of the each meaning (morpheme) of ambiguous word showing in corpus is quite different. That accords with the distribution of the every meanings of ambiguous word. However, there is one different point that the frequency of the each meaning of ambiguous word is rather high (that is the outcome selected by morpheme.). In other words, there are many examples showing for the each meaning of ambiguous word in training and test corpus. On the contrast, the difference of frequency is quite

pseudo-words	Morpheme ID	sample number	pseudo-words	Morpheme ID	sample number
W_1	34466	1040	W_4	84323	591
	71345	662		12751	484
	31796	2101		52915	829
W_2	71072	1296	W_5	53333	274
	78031	1043		29053	1153
	48469	315		75941	238
W_3	7464	4389	W_6	39945	430
	77375	469		71335	308
	23077	865		51491	158

Table 5.1 The number of experimental samples

obvious for the each meaning of real ambiguous word, because some meanings are used in oral language. But that never or seldom appears in experimental corpus.

The statistics can uncover this linguistic phenomenon. We find that the meaning of the most percentage of ambiguous word showing in the corpus is 83.54% on the whole percentage of each meaning. That illustrates the distribution of each meaning has a great disparity in real ambiguous word. Seeing that condition, to differentiate the meaning of ambiguous word is harder than that of real ambiguous word absolutely.

5.1 The analysis and discussion of the first experiment

Table 4.1 records the results of close and open tests in detail and the training materials to get these results.

Seeing from the experimental results, the correct percentage reaches 89.51% most (ambiguous word W1 and W_6) in open test of WSD, and 85.74% the least (ambiguous word W_3).

The relationship of correct percentage and the extent of training corpus can be deduced from the experimental results of table 4.2, 4.3 and 4.4.

The larger the extent of training corpus (the number of training sample), the larger the result of close test. It is obvious to see that from C1 to C2. From C2 to C3 one or two experimental results fluctuate more or less.

With the growing of training sample, the experimental results of open test increase steadily, except ambiguous word W2 (a little bit difference).

The experimental data prove the growing of training samples rise the correct percentage. However, when the rising reaches to a certain degree, more rising is not good for the improvement of model. What's more, the effect of noise is more and more remarkable. That decreases the model's ability of differentiation in a certain degree. On the other hand, after the growing of training corpus, the linguistic phenomenon around ambiguities is richer and richer, more and more complex. That makes it harder to determine the meaning.

5.2 The analysis and discussion of the second experiment

This article emphasizes on the collecting method of contextual feature words in experiment two, in other words, the effect that the different values of M and N influence the model of BP network. The experimental results (table 4.1 and 4.5) tell us that the context windows influence the correct percentage heavily. The correct percentage increases almost by leaps and bounds from (–3, + 3) to (–5, +5). The discrepancy is obvious despite close test or open test. The correct percentage increase again to(–10, + 10), in which the close test of ambiguous word W6 is more than 90% and 89.62% the close test, with the exception of W1 which open test is slightly special. That illustrates the more widely the context windows open, the more the effective information is caught to benefit the WSD more.

Comparing the four feature methods of collection, including (–3, + 7), (–7, + 3), (–4, + 6) and(–6, + 4) with(–5, + 5), the number of feature words besides the ambiguous word is various and the experimental results (table 4.1 and 4.5) are not same, although the windows are same. Among them, the correct percentage of (–5, + 5) is the highest. And that of (–4, + 6) and (–6, + 4) is better than that of (–3, + 7) and (–7, + 3) a bit. That shows the more balanceable the feature words besides ambiguous word, the more advantageous to judge meaning, and the better the experimental results.

In addition, some experimental results of open test are better than that of close test. The main reason is the experimental corpus of open test is smaller than training corpus. So the contextual meanings of ambiguous word in experimental corpus are rather explicit. Thereby, that explains why should be this kind of experimental result.

5.3 Conclusions

Considering the analysis of experimental data, the conclusions are as following:

First, the artificial model of neural network established in this article has good ability of differentiation for Chinese meaning.

Next, higher correct percentage of WSD stems from the large enough corpus.

At last, the larger the windows of contextual feature words, the more the effective information. At the same time, the more balanceable the number of feature words beside the ambiguous word, the more beneficial that for WSD.

6 Concluding remarks

Although the BP network is a classified model applied extensively, the report of research on WSD about it is seldom. Especially the report about the Chinese WSD is less, and only one report (Zhang, 2001) is available in internal reports.

Zhang (2001) uses 96 semantic classes to instead the all words in training corpus according to the *TongyiciCilin*. The input model is the codes of semantic class of contextual words and ambiguities. The experiment of WSD merely makes for one phrase '材料'(cai2liao4) in this document and the correct percentage of open test is 80.4%. '材料' has 3 meanings and that is similar to the ambiguities structured in my article.

Using BP for Chinese WSD, the key point and difficulty are on the determination of input model. The performance of input model may influence the construction of BP network and the output result directly.

We make the experiment on the input of BP network many times and finally find the input model introduced as above (table 3.1) which test result is satisfied.

Acknowledgements This work was supported by the National Natural Science Foundation of China (Grant No. 60203020).

Reference

Lu Song, Bai Shuo, et al. 2001. Supervised word sense disambiguation bassed on Vector Space Model, *Journal of Comouter Research & Development*, 38(6): 662-667.

Pedersen. 2001. *Lexical semantic ambiguous word resolution with bigram-based decision trees*, In Proceedings of the Second International Conference on Intelligent Text Processing and Computational Linguistics, pages 157-168, Mexico City, February.

Escudero, G., Marquez,L., et al, 2000. *Naive Bayes and examplar based approaches to word sense disambiguation revisited.* In Proceedings of the 14th Europear Conference on Artificial Intelligence, ECAI.

Adam,L.B. 1996. A maximum entropy approach to natural language proceeding. *Computational Linguistics*, 22(1):39-71.

Li, J. Z. 1999. An improved maximum language and its application. *Journal of software*, 3:257-263.

Yarowsky, D. *Word sense disambiguation using statistical models of Roget's categories trained on large corpora*. In: Zampolli, A., ed. Computation Linguistic'92. Nantas: Association for Computational Linguistics, 1992. 454~460.

Hinrich Schütze, 1998. Automatic word sense discrimination. *Computational Linguistics*, 24(1): 97-124.

Lu Song., Bai Shuo. 2002. An unsupervised approach to word sense disambiguation based on sense-word in vector space model. *Journal of Software*. 13(06):1082-08

Hinrich Schütze. 1992. *Context space*. In AAAI Fall Symposium on Probabilistic Approaches to Natural Language, pages 113–120, Cambridge, MA.

Lu Song Bai Shuo. 2001. *Quantitative Analysis of Context Field.* In Natural Language Processing, CHINESEJ.COMPUTERS, 24(7) , 742-747

Zhang Guoqing, Zhang Yongkui. 2001. A Neural-network Based Word Sense Disambiguation Method. *Computer Engineering*, 27(12).

Chinese Word Segmentation by Classification of Characters

Chooi-Ling GOH **Masayuki ASAHARA** **Yuji MATSUMOTO**
Graduate School of Information Science,
Nara Institute of Science and Technology
8916-5 Takayama, Ikoma,
Nara 630-0192,
Japan.
{ling-g,masayu-a,matsu}@is.naist.jp

Abstract

During the process of Chinese word segmentation, two main problems occur: segmentation ambiguities and unknown word occurrences. This paper describes a method to solve the segmentation problem. First, we use a dictionary-based approach to segment the text. We simply apply maximum matching algorithm to segment the text forwardly (FMM) and backwardly (BMM). Based on the difference between FMM and BMM, and the context, we apply a classification method based on Support Vector Machines to re-assign the word boundaries. By this way, we are using the output of a dictionary-based approach, and then applying a statistics-based approach to solve the segmentation problem. The experimental results show that our model achieves as high as 99.0 point of F-measure for overall segmentation, given the condition that no unknown word in the text, and 95.1 if unknown words exist.

1 Introduction

The first step in Chinese information processing systems is word segmentation. It is because in written Chinese, all characters are joined together, and there is no separator to mark word boundaries. A similar problem also occurs in languages like Japanese, but at least in Japanese, there exist three types of characters (hiragana, katakana and kanji), and this could be a clue for finding word boundaries. For Chinese, as there is only one type of characters (hanzi), more segmentation ambiguities may happen in a text. During the process of segmentation, two main problems occur: segmentation ambiguities and unknown word occurrences. This paper focuses on solving the segmentation ambiguity problem, and proposes a sub-model to solve the unknown word problem. There are basically two types of segmentation ambiguities: covering ambiguity and overlapping ambiguity. The definitions are given below.

Let x, y, z be some strings in Chinese which could consist of one or more characters. Subsequently, covering ambiguity is defined as follows: For string $w = xy$, $x \in W$, $y \in W$ and also $w \in W$, where W is a dictionary. As almost any single character in Chinese can be considered as a word, the definition reflexes only those cases where both word boundaries $.../xy/...$ and $.../x/y/...$ can be realized in some sentences. On the other hand, overlapping ambiguity is defined as follows: For string $w = xyz$, $w_1 = xy \in W$ and also $w_2 = yz \in W$. Although most of the time, the segmentation of one form is more preferred than the other form, but still we need to know where to use the other form. Both ambiguities depend heavily on the contexts to decide which is the correct segmentation given that particular occurrences in the texts.

(1a) and (1b) show examples of covering ambiguity. Given the string "一家", it is treated as a word in (1a), but as two words in (1b).

(1a) 胡 / 世庆 / 一家 / 三 / 口 /
Hu/ Shiqing/ whole family/ three/ member
(The whole three members of Hu Shiqing family)

(1b) 在 / 巴黎 / 一 / 家 / 杂志 / 上 /
in/ Paris/ one/ company/ magazine/ at/
(At one of the magazine company in Paris)

On the other hand, (2a) and (2b) give examples of overlapping ambiguity. The string "不可以" is segmented as "不 / 可以" in (2a) and "不可 / 以" in (2b), according to the context of the sentence.

(2a) 不 / 可以 / 淡忘 / 远在 / 故乡 / 的 / 父母 /
not/ can/ forget/ far away/ hometown/ DE/ parents/
(Cannot forget the parents who are far way at hometown)

(2b) 不可 / 以 / 营利 / 为 / 目的 /

cannot/ by/ profit/ be/ intention/
(Cannot have the intention to make profit)

We intend to solve the ambiguity problems by combining a dictionary-based approach with a statistical model. By this way, we make use of the information in a dictionary to a statistical approach. Maximum Matching (MM) algorithm, a very early and simple dictionary-based approach, is used to initially segment the text by referring to a dictionary. It tries to match the longest possible words found in the dictionary. We can either parse the sentence forwardly or backwardly. Normally, the difference between forward and backward parsing will indicate the location where overlapping ambiguities occur. Then, we use a Support Vector Machine-based (SVM) classifier to decide which output should be the correct answer. For covering ambiguity, most of the cases, forward and backward MM will give the same outputs, in this case, we will just make use of the contexts to decide whether or not to split a word into two words and etc. Our results showed that the proposed method could produce the correct answers for overlapping ambiguities up to 92%, and 52% correctly split the words for covering ambiguities.

2 Previous Work

Solving the ambiguity problems is a fundamental task in Chinese segmentation process. Although many previous researches have been done for segmentation, only a few have reported on the accuracy to solve ambiguity problems. (Li et al., 2003) suggest an unsupervised method for training the Naïve Bayes classifiers to resolve overlapping ambiguities. They achieved 94.13% accuracy with 5,759 cases of ambiguity. A variation form of TF.IDF weighting is proposed for solving covering ambiguity problem in (Luo et al., 2002). They focus on 90 ambiguous words and achieve an accuracy of 96.58%.

Most of the previous methods reported on the accuracy for overall segmentation. Recently, many researches are done by combining multiple models. Furthermore, most people have realized that working on character-based is more efficient than word-based for Chinese word segmentation. In (Xue and Converse, 2002), two classifiers are combined for Chinese word segmentation. First, a Maximum Entropy model is used to segment the text, then an error driven transformation model is used to correct the word boundaries. Similarly, they also use character-based tagging on the position of characters in words. They achieved an F-measure of 95.17. Another recent report is by (Fu and Luke, 2003), where hybrid models for integrated segmentation is proposed. Modified word juncture models and word-formation patterns are used to find the word boundaries and at the same time to identify the unknown words. They achieved 96.1 F-measure. As both methods use different corpora for the experiments, it is difficult to tell which method has done better than the other.

Solving unknown word problem is also an important process in word segmentation. An unknown word is defined as a word not found in a dictionary. Therefore, they cannot be segmented correctly by simply referring to the dictionary. Many approaches have been reported for unknown word detection such as (Chen and Bai, 1997; Chen and Ma, 2002; Fu and Wang, 1999; Lai and Wu, 1999; Ma and Chen, 2003; Nie et al., 1995; Shen et al., 1998; Zhang et al., 2002; Zhou and Lua, 1997). There are rule-based, statistics-based or even hybrid models. In other words, we cannot ignore the unknown word problem, as there always exist some unknown words (such as person names, numbers and etc) in the text even if we can get a very large dictionary. The creation of new words in Chinese is unlimited and is a continuous process. For example, the name for new diseases, technical terms, new expressions and etc. The accuracy is better if one focuses only on certain types of unknown words such as person names, place names or transliteration names, with over 80%. However, for general unknown words such as common nouns, verbs etc, the accuracy ranging from 50% to 70% only.

3 Proposed Method

The underlying concept of our proposed method is as following. We regard the problem as a character classification problem. We believe that each character in Chinese holds its characteristics to appear in a certain position in a word. In other words, it can be either used at the beginning of a word, in the middle of a word, at the end of a word, or as a single-character word. By looking at the usage of the characters, we will decide the position tag of the characters using a machine learning based model, which is the Support Vector Machines (Vapnik, 1995). This method serves as a model to solve ambiguity problem, and at the same time, embeds a model to detect unknown words. We will now describe the method in more details in the following section.

3.1 Maximum Matching Algorithm

We intend to solve the ambiguity problem by combining a dictionary-based approach with a statistical model. Maximum Matching (MM) algorithm is regarded as the simplest dictionary-based word segmentation approach. It starts from one end of a sentence, and tries to match the first longest word wherever possible. It is a greedy algorithm, but it has been empirically proved to achieve over 90% accuracy if the dictionary used is large. However, it cannot solve ambiguity problems and impossible to detect unknown words because only words exist in the dictionary can be segmented correctly. If we look at the outputs produced by segmenting the sentence forwardly (FMM), from the beginning of the sentence, and backwardly (BMM), from the end of the sentence, we will realize the places where overlapping ambiguities occur. As an example, FMM will segment the string "即将来临时" (when the time comes) into "即将/ 来临/ 时/" (immediately/ come/ when), but BMM will segment it into "即/ 将来/ 临时/" (that/ future/ temporary).

Let O_f and O_b be the outputs of FMM and BMM respectively. According to (Huang, 1997), for overlapping cases: If $O_f = O_b$, then 99% that both the MMs have the correct answer. If $O_f \neq O_b$, then 99% that either O_f or O_b has the correct answer. However, for covering ambiguity cases, even $O_f = O_b$, but both O_f and O_b could be correct or both could be wrong. If there exist unknown words, normally they will be segmented as single characters by both FMM and BMM. Based on the differences and context created by FMM and BMM, we will apply a machine learning based model to reassign the position tags which indicate the character position in the word.

3.2 Re-classification of Characters

We plan to re-classify the outputs of FMM and BMM character by character. First, we will convert the output of the MMs into character-based, where each character will be assigned with a position tag such as described in Table 1. The BIES tags are as in (Uchimoto et al., 2000) and (Sang and Veenstra, 1999) for named entity extraction. These tags show the possible character position in a word. For example, if we look at the character "本", it is used as a single character in "一/ 本/ 书/" (a book), at the end of a word in "剧本" (script), at the beginning of a word in "本来" (originally), and at the middle of a word in "基本上" (basically).

Tag	Description
S	one-character word
B	first character in a multi-character word
I	intermediate character in a multi-character word (for words longer than two characters)
E	last character in a multi-character word

Table 1: Position tags in a word

Then, based on these features, we will re-classify the tags by using a Support Vector Machine-based (SVM) chunker (Kudo and Matsumoto, 2001). The solid box in Figure 1 shows the features used to determine the class of the character "春" at location *i*. Based on the output position tags, finally, we will get the segmentation as "迎/ 新春/ 联谊会/ 上/" (welcome/ new year/ get-together party/ at/).

Position	Char.	FMM	BMM	Output
i - 2	迎	B	S	S
i - 1	新	E	B	B
i	春	B	E	E
i + 1	联	E	B	B
i + 2	谊	S	E	I
i + 3	会	B	B	E
i + 4	上	E	E	S

Figure 1: An illustration of classification process - 'At the New Year gathering party'

4 Experiments and Results

We have run our experiments with two datasets, PKU Corpus and SIGHAN Bakeoff data. The evaluation is done by using the tool provided in SIGHAN Bakeoff (Sproat and Emerson, 2003).

4.1 Experiment with PKU Corpus

4.1.1 Accuracy on Solving Ambiguity Problem

The corpus used for this experiment is from Peking University (PKU) [1], consisting of about 1 million words. It is a segmented and POS

[1] Institute of Computational Linguistics, Peking University, http://www.icl.pku.edu.cn/

tagged corpus, but we only use the segmentation information for our experiments. We divide the corpus randomly into 80% and 20%, for training and testing respectively. Since our purpose in this experiment is only for solving ambiguity problem, not the unknown word detection, we assume that all words could be found in the dictionary. We create a dictionary with all words from the corpus, which has 62,030 entries (referred to as Experiment 1). This experiment intends to show the performance of the method for solving ambiguity problem.

It is sometimes very difficult to determine how many cases of ambiguities appearing in a sentence. For example, in the sentence in Figure 1, "迎新" (welcome the new year), "新春" (new year), "春联" (a red paper that pasted on the door, written with some greeting words for celebrating new year in China), "联谊" (get-together), "联谊会" (get-together party), "会上" (at the meeting) and "上" (at) are all possible words. How many overlapping cases and covering cases are there? It is quite impossible to answer. A word candidate may cause more than one ambiguities with the alternative word candidates. Therefore, we try to represent the ambiguities by character units since our method is character based. We group each character into one of these six categories.

Let,

O_f = Output of FMM
O_b = Output of BMM
Ans = Correct answer
Out = Output from our system

Category	Conditions
Allcorrect	$O_f = O_b = Ans = Out$
Correct	$O_f \neq O_b$ and $Ans = Out$
Wrong	$O_f \neq O_b$ and $Ans \neq Out$
Match	$O_f = O_b$ and $O_f \neq Ans$ and $Ans = Out$
Mismatch	$O_f = O_b$ and $O_f \neq Ans$ and $Ans \neq Out$
Allwrong	$O_f = O_b = Ans$ and $Ans \neq Out$

Table 2: Categories for Characters

Table 2 shows the conditions for each category. Category *Allcorrect*, *Correct* and *Match* have correct answers, whereas category *Wrong*, *Mismatch* and *Allwrong* have wrong answers. We could roughly say that category *Correct* and *Wrong* belong to overlapping ambiguities and category *Match*, *Mismatch*, and *Allwrong* belong to covering ambiguities. We could also say that *Match* and *Mismatch* are cases where we need to split the words, and *Allwrong* are cases where we should not split the words but have been split by the system. Table 3 shows the results of the method for solving ambiguity problem.

Category	No. of Char.	Percentage
Allcorrect	330220	96.35%
Correct	7663	2.23%
Wrong	658	0.19%
Match	1876	0.55%
Mismatch	1738	0.51%
Allwrong	571	0.17%
Total	342726	100.00%

Table 3: Results on Disambiguation

In total, we could obtain about 99.13% that the characters are correctly tagged. If we only consider the overlapping cases (*Correct* and *Wrong*), 92.09% characters are correctly tagged. For covering cases, if we look at only those cases where we need to split the words (*Match* and *Mismatch*), 51.91% have been successfully split.

Table 4 shows the results of word segmentation. We also compare our method with a Hidden Markov Model-based (HMM) morphological analyzer, where word bi-gram is used to calculate the probability. The size of the dictionary used for HMM is the same as previous experiment, but with real POS tags. The HMM does segmentation and POS tagging simultaneously, but we only take the results of segmentation for comparison. The results show that our proposed method can achieve higher accuracy with over 99.0%. It means that our method is able to solve ambiguity problem given the information where the ambiguous locations occurred by looking at the output of FMM and BMM.

4.1.2 Accuracy on Solving Unknown Word Problem

The corpus used is the same as in Section 4.1.1, but the setting is different. In this round we divide the corpus into three sets, referring to as Set 1, Set 2 and Set 3. Set 1 plus Set 2 (80%) are used for training and Set 3 (20%) is used for testing, same as the previous experiment. The difference is the preparation of dictionary. There are two ways of preparation here. In the first case, all the words from Set 1 and Set 2 are

	FMM	BMM	SVM (char. only)	FMM + SVM	BMM + SVM	FMM + BMM + SVM (=Experiment 1)	HMM (with POS tag)
Recall	96.9	97.1	94.0	98.7	98.7	**98.9**	97.9
Precision	97.7	97.9	94.3	98.9	99.0	**99.1**	98.5
F-measure	97.3	97.5	94.1	98.8	98.9	**99.0**	98.2

Table 4: Segmentation Results

used to create the dictionary. There are 49,433 entries, and there exist 8,346 (4.0%) unknown words in the testing data (referred to as Experiment 2). This experiment intends to investigate the performance of the method if unknown words exist. In the second case, only the words from Set 1 are used to create the dictionary, making the situation that there exist unknown words in the training data (referred to as Experiment 3). The top part of Table 5 shows the proportion of Set 1 and Set 2, with the size of the dictionaries and the numbers of unknown words in Set 2 and testing data. Set 2 serves as a learning model for unknown word detection. While we segment Set 2 using FMM and BMM, most of the unknown words will be segmented into single characters (namely tag 'S'). Based on these tags and contexts, SVM-based chunker will be trained to change the tag into the correct answers. The last experiment (referred to as Experiment 4) is the reverse of Experiment 2, where nothing is used to create the dictionary. All the words are considered as unknown words. Only the characters are used as features during classification, meaning no information from FMM and BMM is available.

Bottom part of Table 5 shows the results of these experiments. Our method in fact works quite well for both solving segmentation ambiguity and unknown word detection. The problem is, while the accuracy for unknown word detection improves, at the same time, the performance degrades in solving the ambiguity problem. It is because the precision of unknown word detection is not one hundred percent. The highest recall that we can get for known words is 98.9% and for unknown words is 69.3%. However the best overall segmentation result is by dividing the training corpus into 40%/40%. This is the optimal point where a balance is found for detecting unknown words, while at the same time maintaining the accuracy of segmentation ambiguity for known words. Figure 2 shows the F-measure for segmentation, recall

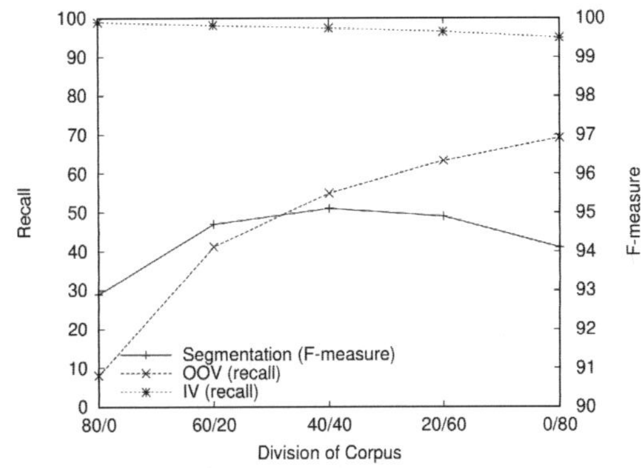

Figure 2: Accuracy by segmentation (F-measure), OOV (recall) and IV (recall)

for unknown words and known words, by different division of training corpus for creating dictionary.

4.2 Experiment with SIGHAN Bakeoff Data

As far as we know, there is no standard definition for Chinese word segmentation. The text can be segmented differently by different people depending on the linguists who decide on the rules and also the usage of the segmentation. Therefore, it is always difficult to compare the result with other methods as the data used is different. The First International Chinese Word Segmentation Bakeoff (Sproat and Emerson, 2003) intended to evaluate the accuracy of different segmenters by standardizing the training and testing data. In their closed test, only the training data is allowed to be used for training but no other material. Under this strict condition, it is possible to create a lexicon from the training data, but of course the unknown words will exist in the testing data. We have run an experiment using the bakeoff data (only the corpus from PKU and Penn Chinese

	Experiment 1	Experiment 2	Experiment 3			Experiment 4
Set1(%)/Set2(%)		80/0	60/20	40/40	20/60	0/80
# of words in Dict.	62,030	49,433	41,582	33,355	22,363	0
# of unk-words in Set 2	0	0	10,927	25,297	53,353	All
# of unk-words in Test	0	8,346	9,768	11,924	17,115	All
Recall	98.9	95.3	**95.8**	95.7	95.2	94.0
Precision	99.1	90.7	93.5	94.5	**94.7**	94.3
F-measure	99.0	92.9	94.7	**95.1**	94.9	94.1
OOV (recall)	–	8.0	41.2	54.9	63.3	**69.3**
IV (recall)	98.9	**98.9**	98.1	97.4	96.5	95.0

Table 5: Different Settings and Segmentation Results with Unknown Words

Treebank, CHTB [2]). Since our system works only on two-byte codings, some ascii codes in the data have been converted to GB codes before processing, especially numbers and alphabets. The distribution of the data is as shown in Table 6. The original dictionaries consist of 55,226 and 19,730 words respectively. According to these dictionaries, there are 1,189 and 7,216 unknown words in the testing data. After converting to GB codes, it left only 781 and 7,171 unknown words. It also means that about 34.3% and 0.6% of the unknown words automatically become known words after the conversion. The conversion reduced the number of unknown words because for example, if a numeral word "１９９８" written in GB code exists in training data, but it is written in ascii code "1998" in testing data, it is treated as unknown word at the first place. After the conversion, it will become known word.

We have set up the experiments similar to Experiment 2 and Experiment 3 above. For Experiment 2, all the words in the training data are used for creating the dictionary. For Experiment 3, it is based on our previous experiments where the division of half of the training corpus generated the best result by F-measure. Therefore, only 50% of the training corpora are used while creating the dictionaries. As a result, the new dictionaries contain 36,830 and 12,274 words respectively. Table 6 shows the details for the setting.

For PKU corpus, the best result in the bakeoff achieved 95.1 in F-measure (Zhang et al., 2003). They use hierarchical Hidden Markov Models to segment and POS tag the text. Although it is a closed test, they have used extra information such as class-based segmentation and role-based tagging models (Zhang et al., 2002), which give better result for unknown word recognition. Our method has done only slightly worse than theirs, with 94.7. The recall for unknown words is comparable, with 71.0% while the best one has 72.4%. Unfortunately, the recall for known words drops a bit, with 97.3%, while the best one is slightly better, with 97.9%, as shown in Table 7. We also compare with (Asahara et al., 2003), where similar method is used for reassigning the word boundaries, except that the words are first categorized into 5 or 10 classes (which is assumed equivalent to POS tags) using Baum-Welch algorithm, then the sentence is segmented into word sequence by a Hidden Markov Model-based segmenter. Finally, the same Support Vector Machine-based chunker is trained to correct the errors made by the segmenter. Our method which is simply a forward and backward maximum matching algorithm, has done a lot better then theirs, where complicated statistical based models are involved. They have achieved only 92.4 F-measure while we have 94.7.

On the other hand, our results for CHTB corpus are not as comparable as the best result in the bakeoff. We could only get 84.7 point of F-measure, while the best one has 88.1 (Zhang et al., 2003) and 82.9 by (Asahara et al., 2003). It may be due to the reason that the training corpus is a lot smaller than the PKU corpus and the testing data contains more unknown words.

[2]We work only on GB code, the standard coding used for simplified Chinese characters. However, it can be modified easily to suit Big5 coding for traditional Chinese characters.

	PKU Data			CHTB Data		
	# of words	# of unk-words	unk-word rate	# of words	# of unk-words	unk-word rate
Original Training	1,121,017	0	0%	250,841	0	0%
Original Testing (In GB code)	17,194	1,189 (781)	6.9% (4.5%)	39,922	7,216 (7,171)	18.1% (18.0%)
Set 1	560,649	0	0%	125,405	0	0%
Set 2	560,368	29,303	5.2%	125,436	13,976	11.1%
Testing Data	17,194	1,121	6.5%	39,922	9,769	24.5%

Table 6: Bakeoff Data

However, we still could get quite good recall for unknown words, with 57.7%, while the others have 70.5% and 41.2% respectively.

As a conclusion, our results cannot transcend the best results in the bakeoff for both corpora. However, our method is simpler. We only need a dictionary that created from a segmented corpus, FMM and BMM modules, and a classifier, without the intervention of human knowledge. We get quite comparable results for both known words and also unknown words. The result is worse when the training corpus is small and there exist a lot of unknown words such as in CHTB testing data. Therefore, we still need to investigate on the relationship between the size of training corpus and the division of corpus for training of ambiguity problem and unknown word detection.

5 Conclusion

Apparently, our proposed method has generated better result than the baseline models, FMM and BMM. We get nearly 99% accuracy if unknown words do not exist. However, in the real world, it is impossible that there is no unknown word at all even we could get a very large dictionary. Therefore, we also embedded a model to detect the unknown words. Unfortunately, while the accuracy for unknown word detection increased, the performance on solving known word ambiguity drops. As shown in the experiments with bakeoff data, our model works well only when the training corpus is large enough. As a conclusion, while our model is suited for solving segmentation ambiguity problem, it can also be used for unknown word detection. However we still need to find a balance point for solving these two problems simulteneously. We also need to research on the relationship between training corpus size and the best proportion to divide the corpus for training optimally on solving ambiguity problem and unknown word detection.

6 Acknowledgements

Thanks to Mr. Kudo for his tool on Support Vector Machine-based chunker, Yamcha. We also thank the reviewers for their invaluable comments, Peking University and SIGHAN for providing the corpora in our experiments.

References

Masayuki Asahara, Chooi Ling Goh, Xiaojie Wang, and Yuji Matsumoto. 2003. Combining Segmenter and Chunker for Chinese Word Segmentation. In *Proceedings of Second SIGHAN Workshop on Chinese Language Processing*, pages 144–147.

Keh-Jiann Chen and Ming-Hong Bai. 1997. Unknown Word Detection for Chinese By a Corpus-based Learning Method. In *Proceedings of ROCLING X*, pages 159–174.

Keh-Jiann Chen and Wei-Yun Ma. 2002. Unknown Word Extraction for Chinese Documents. In *Proceedings of COLING 2002*, volume 1, pages 169–175.

Guohong Fu and K.K. Luke. 2003. An Integrated Approach for Chinese Word Segmentation. In *Proceedings of PACLIC 17.*

Guohong Fu and Xiaolong Wang. 1999. Unsupervised Chinese Word Segmentation and Unknown Word Identification. In *Proceedings of NLPRS.*

Changning Huang. 1997. Segmentation problem in chinese processing. *Applied Linguistics*, 1:72–78.

Taku Kudo and Yuji Matsumoto. 2001. Chunking with Support Vector Machines. In *Proceedings of NAACL*, pages 192–199.

Yu-Sheng Lai and Chung-Hsien Wu. 1999. Unknown Word and Phrase Extraction Using a

	Without Unknown Word Processing (=Experiment 2)	With Unknown Word Processing (=Experiment 3)	Baum-Welch + HMM + SVM (Asahara et al., 2003)	Best Result in Bakeoff (Zhang et al., 2003)
PKU Corpus				
Recall	94.6	95.5	93.3	**96.2**
Precision	89.4	**94.1**	91.6	94.0
F-measure	92.0	94.7	92.4	**95.1**
OOV (recall)	39.7	71.0	35.7	**72.4**
IV (recall)	**98.7**	97.3	97.5	97.9
CHTB Corpus				
Recall	82.2	86.0	85.2	**88.6**
Precision	67.4	83.5	80.7	**87.5**
F-measure	74.1	84.7	82.9	**88.1**
OOV (recall)	10.1	57.7	41.2	**70.5**
IV (recall)	**98.2**	92.2	94.9	92.7

Table 7: Segmentation Results with Bakeoff Data

Phrase-Like-Unit-Based Likelihood Ratio. In *Proceeding of ICCPOL '99*, pages 5–9.

Mu Li, Jianfeng Gao, Changning Huang, and Jianfeng Li. 2003. Unsupervised Training for Overlapping Ambiguity Resolution in Chinese Word Segmentation. In *Proceedings of Second SIGHAN Workshop on Chinese Language Processing*, pages 1–7.

Xiao Luo, Maosong Sun, and Benjamin K. Tsou. 2002. Covering Ambiguity Resolution in Chinese Word Segmentation Based on Contextual Information. In *Proceedings of COLING 2002*, pages 598–604.

Wei-Yun Ma and Keh-Jiann Chen. 2003. A Bottom-up Merging Algorithm for Chinese Unknown Word Extraction. In *Proceedings of Second SIGHAN Workshop on Chinese Language Processing*, pages 31–38.

Jian-Yun Nie, Marie-Louise Hannan, and Wanying Jin. 1995. Unknown Word Detection and Segmentation of Chinese Using Statistical and Heuristic Knowledge. *Communications of COLIPS*, Vol.5:47–57.

Erik F. Tjong Kim Sang and John Veenstra. 1999. Representing Text Chunks. In *Proceedings of EACL '99*, pages 173–179.

Dayang Shen, Maosong Sun, and Changning Huang. 1998. The application & implementation of local statistics in Chinese unknown word identification. *Communications of COLIPS*, Vol.8.

Richard Sproat and Thomas Emerson. 2003. The first international chinese word segmentation bakeoff. In *Proceedings of Second SIGHAN Workshop on Chinese Language Processing*, pages 133–143.

Kiyotaka Uchimoto, Qing Ma, Masaki Murata, Hiromi Ozaku, and Hitoshi Isahara. 2000. Named Entity Extraction Based on A Maximum Entropy Model and Transformational Rules. In *Processing of the ACL 2000.*

Vladimir N. Vapnik. 1995. *The Nature of Statistical Learning Theory.* Springer.

Nianwen Xue and Susan P. Converse. 2002. Combining Classifiers for Chinese Word Segmentation. In *Proceedings of 1st SIGHAN Workshop on Chinese Language Processing*, pages 57–63.

Hua-Ping Zhang, Qun Liu, Hao Zhang, and Xue-Qi Cheng. 2002. Automatic Regcognition of Chinese Unknown Words Based on Roles Tagging. In *Proceedings of 1st SIGHAN Workshop on Chinese Language Processing.*

Hua-Ping Zhang, Hong-Kui Yu, De-Yi Xiong, and Qun Liu. 2003. HHMM-based Chinese Lexical Analyzer ICTCLAS. In *Proceedings of Second SIGHAN Workshop on Chinese Language Processing*, pages 184–187.

Guo-Dong Zhou and Kim-Teng Lua. 1997. Detection of Unknown Chinese Words Using a Hybrid Approach. *Computer Processing of Oriental Language*, 11(1):63–75.

Automated Alignment and Extraction of Bilingual Domain Ontology for Medical Domain Web Search

Jui-Feng Yeh[*+], Chung-Hsien Wu[*], Ming-Jun Chen[*] and Liang-Chih Yu[*]
[*]Department of Computer Science and Information Engineering
National Cheng Kung University, Taiwan, R.O.C.
{chwu, jfyeh, mjchen,lcyu}@csie.ncku.edu.tw
[+] Department of Computer Application Engineering
Far East College, Taiwan, R.O.C.

Abstract

This paper proposes an approach to automated ontology alignment and domain ontology extraction from two knowledge bases. First, WordNet and HowNet knowledge bases are aligned to construct a bilingual universal ontology based on the co-occurrence of the words in a parallel corpus. The bilingual universal ontology has the merit that it contains more structural and semantic information coverage from two complementary knowledge bases, WordNet and HowNet. For domain-specific applications, a medical domain ontology is further extracted from the universal ontology using the island-driven algorithm and a medical domain corpus. Finally, the domain-dependent terms and some axioms between medical terms based on a medical encyclopaedia are added into the ontology. For ontology evaluation, experiments on web search were conducted using the constructed ontology. The experimental results show that the proposed approach can automatically align and extract the domain-specific ontology. In addition, the extracted ontology also shows its promising ability for medical web search.

1 Introduction

In intelligent mining, in order to obviate the unnecessary keyword expansion, some knowledge base should be involved in the intelligent information system. In recent years, considerable progress has been invested in developing the conceptual bases for building technology that allows knowledge reuse and sharing. As information exchangeability and communication becomes increasingly global, multiple-language lexical resources that can provide transnational services are becoming increasingly important. Over the last few years, significant effort has been made to construct the ontology manually according to the domain expert's knowledge. Manual ontology merging using conventional editing tools without intelligent support is difficult, labor intensive and error prone. Therefore, several systems and frameworks for supporting the knowledge engineer in the ontology merging task have recently been proposed. To avoid the reiteration in ontology construction, the algorithm of ontology merge (UMLS http://umlsks.nlm.nih.gov/) (Langkilde and Knight 1998) and ontology alignment (Vossen and Peters 1997) (Weigard and Hoppenbrouwers 1998) (Asanoma 2001) were invested. The final ontology is a merged version of the original ontologies. The two original ontologies persist, with links established between them in alignment. Alignment usually is performed when the ontologies cover domains that are complementary to each other. In the past, domain ontology was usually constructed manually according to the knowledge or experience of the experts or ontology engineers. Recently, automatic and semi-automatic methods have been developed. OntoExtract (Fensel et al. 2002) (Missikoff et al. 2002) provided an ontology engineering chain to construct the domain ontology from WordNet and SemCor.

On the other hand, multi-lingual ontology is very important for natural language processing, such as machine translation (MT), web mining and cross language information retrieval (CLIR). Generally, a multi-lingual ontology maps the keyword set of one language to another language, or compute the co-occurrence of the words among languages. In addition, a key merit for multilingual ontology is that it can increase the relation and structural information coverage by aligning two or more language-dependent ontologies with different semantic features.

Nowadays large collections of information in various styles are available on the Internet. And finding desired information on the World Wide Web is becoming a critical issue. Some general-purpose search engine like Google (http://www.google.com) and Altavista (http://www.altavista.com/) provide the facility to mine the web. There are three major research areas about web mining: web content mining, web structure mining and web usage mining. This paper proposes a novel method to web content mining with unstructured web pages. There are many approaches in the view of natural language processing. According to the representation of web pages, there are three kinds of the content: bag of words (with order or not) (Kargupta et al. 1997) (Nahm and Mooney, 2000), phrases (Ahonen et al. 1998) (Frank et al. 1999)(Yang et al. 1999), relational terms (Cohen, 1998) (Junker 1999) and concept categories. We proposed an ontology-based web search approach. Unfortunately, there are some irrelevant pages obtained and these pages result in low precision rate and recall rate due to the problem of polysemy. To solve this problem, domain knowledge becomes necessary. The domain-specific web miners like SPIRAL, Cora (Cohen, 1998), WebKB (Martin and Eklund 2000) and HelpfulMed (Chen et al. 2003) are employed as the special search engine for the interesting topic. These ones dedicated to recipes are less likely to return irrelevant web pages when the query is entered.

In this paper, WordNet and HowNet knowledge bases are aligned to construct a bilingual universal ontology based on the co-occurrence of the words in a parallel corpus. For domain-specific applications, a medical domain ontology is further extracted from the universal ontology using the island-driven algorithm (Lee et al. 1995) and a medical domain corpus. Finally, the axioms between medical terms are derived based on semantic relations. A web search system for medical domain based on the extracted domain ontology is realized to demonstrate the feasibility of the methods proposed in this paper.

The rest of the paper is organized as follows. Section 2 describes ontology construction process and the web searching system framework. Section 3 presents the experimental results for the evaluation of our approach. Section 4 gives some concluding remarks.

2 Methodologies

Figure 1 shows the block diagram for ontology construction and the framework of the domain-specific web search system. There are four major processes in the proposed system: bilingual ontology alignment, domain ontology extraction, knowledge representation and domain-specific web search.

2.1 Bilingual Ontology Alignment

In this approach, the cross-lingual ontology is constructed by aligning the words in WordNet with their corresponding words in HowNet. First, the Sinorama (Sinorama 2001) database is adopted as the bilingual language parallel corpus to compute the conditional probability of the words in WordNet, given the words in HowNet. Second, a bottom up algorithm is used for relation mapping.

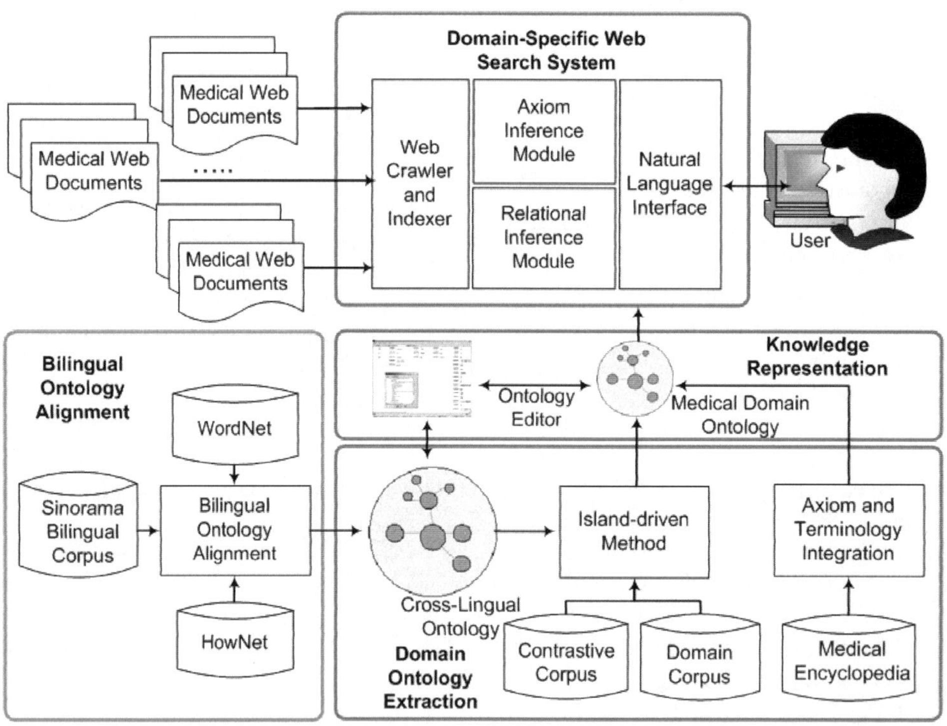

Figure 1 Ontology construction framework and the domain-specific web search system

In WordNet a word may be associated with many synsets, each corresponding to a different sense of the word. When we look for a relation between two different words we consider all the synsets associated with each word (Christiane 1998). In HowNet, each word is composed of primary features and secondary features. The primary features indicate the word's category. The purpose of this approach is to increase the relation and structural information coverage by aligning the above two language-dependent ontologies, WordNet and HowNet, with different semantic features.

The relation "is-a" defined in WordNet corresponds to the primary feature defined in HowNet. Equation (1) shows the mapping between the words in HowNet and the synsets in WordNet. Given a Chinese word, CW_i, the probability of the word related to synset, $synset^k$, can be obtained via its corresponding English synonyms, $EW_j^k, j=1,...,m$, which are the elements in $synset^k$. The probability is estimated as follows.

$$
\begin{aligned}
&\Pr(synset^k \mid CW_i) \\
&= \sum_{j=1}^{m} \Pr(synset^k, EW_j^k \mid CW_i) \\
&= \sum_{j=1}^{m} (\Pr(synset^k \mid EW_j^k, CW_i) \times \Pr(EW_j^k \mid CW_i))
\end{aligned}
\quad (1)
$$

where

$$
\Pr\left(synset^k \mid EW_j^k, CW_i\right) = \frac{N\left(synset_j^k, EW_j^k, CW_i\right)}{\sum_l N\left(synset_j^l, EW_j^k, CW_i\right)} \quad (2)
$$

In the above equation, $N\left(synset_j^k, EW_j^k, CW_i\right)$ represents the number of co-occurrences of CW_i, EW_j^k and $synset_j^k$. The probability $\Pr\left(EW_j^k \mid CW_i\right)$ is set to one when at least one of the primary features, $PF_i^l(CW_i)$, of the Chinese word defined in the HowNet matches one of the ancestor nodes of synset, $synset_j^k\left(EW_j\right)$ except the root nodes in the hierarchical structures of the noun and verb; Otherwise set to zero. That is,

$$
\Pr\left(EW_j \mid CW_i\right) = \begin{cases} 1 & \text{if } \left(\bigcup_l PF_i^l(CW_i) - \{entity, event, act, play\}\right) \\ & \cap \left(\bigcup ancestor(\bigcup_k synset_j^k(EW_j)) - \{entity, event, act, play\}\right) \neq \varnothing \\ 0 & otherwise \end{cases}
$$

(3)

where {enitity,event,act,play} is the concept set in the root nodes of HowNet and WordNet.

Finally, the Chinese concept, CW_i, has been integrated into the synset, $synset_j^k$, in WordNet as long as the probability, $\Pr(synset^k \mid CW_i)$, is not zero. Figure 2 shows the concept tree generated by aligning WordNet and HowNet.

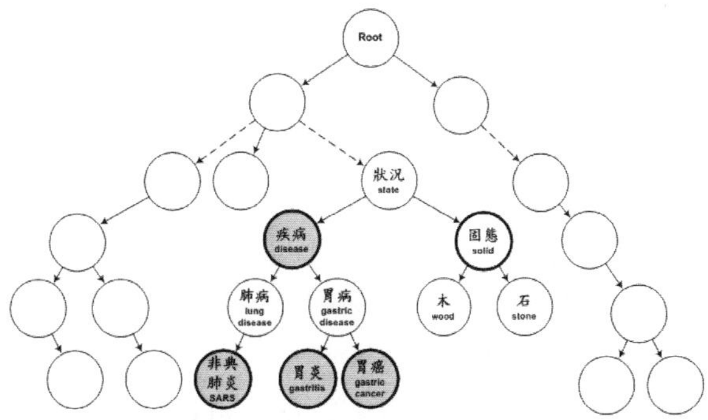

Figure 2. Concept tree generated by aligning WordNet and HowNet. The nodes with bold circle represent the operative nodes after concept extraction. The nodes with gray background represent the operative nodes after relation expansion.

2.2 Domain ontology extraction

There are two phases to construct the domain ontology: 1) extract the ontology from the cross-language ontology by island-driven algorithm, and 2) integrate the terms and axioms defined in a medical encyclopaedia into the domain ontology.

2.2.1 Extraction by island-driven algorithm

Ontology provides consistent concepts and world representations necessary for clear communication within the knowledge domain. Even in domain-specific applications, the number of words can be expected to be numerous. Synonym pruning is an effective alternative to word sense disambiguation. This paper proposes a corpus-based statistical approach to extracting the domain ontology. The steps are listed as follows:

Step 1: Linearization: This step decomposed the tree structure in the universal ontology shown in Figure 2 into the vertex list that is an ordered node sequence starting at the leaf nodes and ending at the root node.

Step 2: Concept extraction from the corpus: The node is defined as an operative node when the Tf-idf value of word W_i in the domain corpus is higher than that in its corresponding contrastive (out-of-domain) corpus. That is,

$$operative\_node(W_i) = \begin{cases} 1, & if\ Tf-idf_{Domain}(W_i) > Tf-idf_{Contrastive}(W_i) \\ 0, & Otherwise \end{cases} \quad (4)$$

where

$$Tf-idf_{Domain}(W_i) = freq_{i,Domain} \times \log \frac{n_{i,Domain} + n_{i,Contrastive}}{n_{i,Domain}}$$

$$Tf-idf_{Contrastive}(W_i) = freq_{i,Contrastive} \times \log \frac{n_{i,Domain} + n_{i,Contrastive}}{n_{i,Contrastive}}$$

In the above equations, $freq_{i,Domain}$ and $freq_{i,Contrastive}$ are the frequencies of word W_i in the domain documents and its contrastive (out-of-domain) documents, respectively. $n_{i,Domain}$ and $n_{i,Contrastive}$ are the numbers of the documents containing word W_i in the domain documents and its contrastive documents, respectively. The nodes with bold circle in Figure 2 represent the operative nodes.

Step 3: Relational expansion using the island-driven algorithm: There are some domain concepts not operative after the previous steps due to the problem of insufficient data. From the observation in ontology construction, most of the inoperative concept nodes have operative hypernym nodes and hyponym nodes. Therefore, the island-driven algorithm is adopted to activate these inoperative concept nodes if their ancestors and descendants are all operative. The nodes with gray background shown in Figure 2 are the activated operative nodes.

Step 4: Domain ontology extraction: The final step is to merge the linear vertex list sequence into a hierarchical tree. However, some noisy concepts not belonging to this domain ontology are operative after step 3. These noisy nodes with inoperative noisy concepts should be filtered out automatically. Finally, the domain ontology is extracted and the final result is shown in Figure 3.

After the above steps, a dummy node is added as the root node of the domain concept tree.

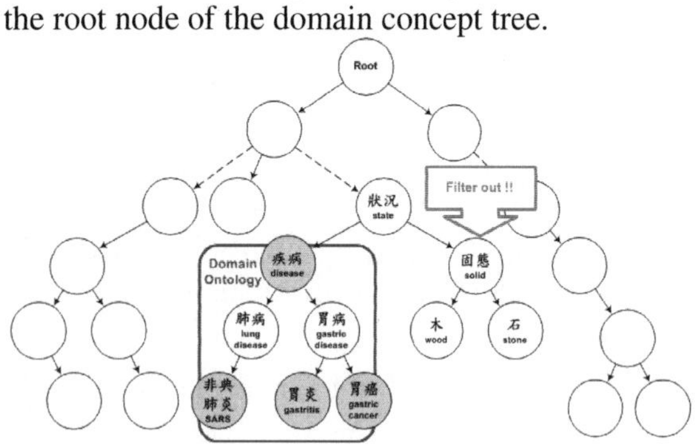

Figure 3 The domain ontology after filtering out the isolated concepts

2.2.2 Axiom and terminology integration

In practice, specific domain terminologies and axioms should be derived and introduced into the ontology for domain-specific applications. In our approach, 1213 axioms derived from a medical encyclopaedia have been integrated into the domain ontology. Figure 4 shows an example of the axiom. In this example, the disease "diabetes" is tagged as level "A" which represents that this disease is frequent in occurrence. And the degrees for the corresponding syndromes represent the causality between the disease and the syndromes. The axioms also provide two fields "department of the clinical care" and "the category of the disease" for medical information retrieval.

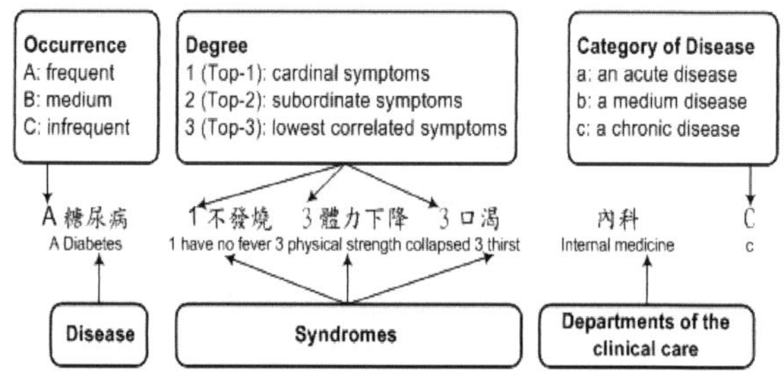

Figure 4 axiom example

2.3 Domain-specific web search

This paper proposed a medical web search engine based on the constructed medical domain ontology. The engine consists of natural language interface, web crawler and indexer, relation inference module and axiom inference module. The functions and techniques of these modules are described as follows.

2.3.1 Natural language interface and web crawler and indexer

Natural language interface is generally considered as an enticing prospect because it offers many advantages: it would be easy to learn and easy to remember, because its structure and vocabulary are already familiar to the user; it is particularly powerful because of the multitude of ways in which to accomplish a search action by using the natural language input. A natural language query is transformed to obtain the desired representation after the word segmentation, removing the stop words, stemming and tagging process.

The web crawler and indexer are designed to seek medical web pages from Internet, extract the content and establish the indices automatically.

2.3.2 Concept inference module

For semantic representation, traditionally, the keyword-based systems will introduce two problems. First, ambiguity usually results from the polysemy of words. The domain ontology will give a clear description of the concepts. In addition, not all the synonyms of the word should be expanded without constraints. Secondly, relations between the concepts should be expanded and weighted in order to include more semantic information for semantic inference. We treat each of the user's input and the content of web pages as a sequence of words. This means that the sequence of words is treated as a bag of words regardless of the word order. For the word sequence of the user's input,

$$q=W_q=w_{q1}, w_{q2}, ..., w_{qK},$$

and the word sequence of the web page,

$$A=W_A=w_{A1}, w_{A2}, ..., w_{AL},$$

The similarity between input query and the page is defined as the similarity between the two bags of words. The similarity measure based on key concepts in the ontology is defined as follows.

$$\begin{aligned} & Sim_{relation}(A_i,q) \\ & = Sim_{relation}(W_{A_i},W_q) \\ & = Sim_{relation}(w_{A_i1},w_{A_i2},...,w_{A_iL},w_{q1},w_{q2},...,w_{qK}) \\ & = \sum_{k=1,l=1}^{K,L} H_{kl} \end{aligned} \tag{5}$$

where H_{kl} is concept similarity of w_{Al} and w_{qk}. Most of the keyword expansion approaches use the extension of scope by the synonyms. In this paper the similarity, H_{kl}, is defined as

$$H_{kl} = \begin{cases} 1 & w_{Al} \text{ and } w_{qk} \text{ are identical} \\ \frac{1}{2^r} & w_{Al} \text{ and } w_{qk} \text{ are hypernyms,} \\ & r \text{ is the number of levels in between} \\ \left(1-\frac{1}{2^r}\right)^2 & w_{Al} \text{ and } w_{qk} \text{ are synonyms,} \\ & r \text{ is the number of their common concepts} \\ 0 & \text{others} \end{cases} \tag{6}$$

2.3.3 Axiom inference module

Some axioms, such as "result in" and "result from," that are expected to affect the performance of a web search system in a technical domain are defined to describe the relationship between syndromes and diseases. This aspect is the use of specific terms used in the medical domain. We collected the data about syndromes and diseases from a medical encyclopedia and tagged the diseases with three levels according to its occurrence and syndromes with four levels according to its significance to the specific disease. The "result in" relation score is defined as $RI(A_i,q)$ if a disease occurs in the input query and its corresponding syndromes appear in the web page. Similarly, if syndrome occurs in the input query and its corresponding disease appears in the web page, the "result from" relation score is defined as $RF(A_i,q)$. The relation score is estimated as follows.

$$\begin{aligned} Axiom(A_i,q) &= \max\{RI(A_i,q),RF(A_i,q)\} \\ &= \max\{RI(w_{A_i1},w_{A_i2},...,w_{A_iP},w_{q1},w_{q2},...,w_{qR}), \\ &\quad RF(w_{A_i1},w_{A_i2},...,w_{A_iP},w_{q1},w_{q2},...,w_{qR})\} \\ &= \max\{\sum_{p=1,r=1}^{P,R} d_{pr}^{RI}, \sum_{p=1,r=1}^{P,R} d_{pr}^{RF}\}, \end{aligned} \tag{7}$$

where $d_{pr}^{RI}=1/2^{n-1}$ if disease w_{Ap} results in syndrome w_{qr} and w_{qr} is the top-n feature of w_{Ap}. Similarly, $d_{pr}^{RF}=1/2^{n-1}$ if syndrome w_{Ap} results from disease w_{qr} and w_{Ap} is the top-n feature of w_{qr}. The conditional probability of the i-th web pages with respect to aspect $s_{A,2}$ and query q is defined as

$$Sim_{axiom}(A_i,q)=\frac{Axiom(A_i,q)}{\sum_i Axiom(A_i,q)}.$$

3 Evaluation

To evaluate the proposed approach, a medical web search system was constructed. The web pages were collected from several Websites and totally 2322 web pages for medical domain and 8133 web pages for contrastive domain were collected.

On the other hand, the training and test queries for training and evaluating the system performance were also collected. Forty users, who do not take part in the system development, were asked to provide a set of queries given the collected web pages. After post-processing, the duplicate queries and the queries out of the medical domain are removed. Finally, 3207 test queries mixed Chinese with English words using natural language were obtained.

3.1 Keyword-Based VSM Approach: A baseline system for comparison

In recent years, most of the information retrieval approaches were based on the Vector-Space Model (VSM). Assuming that the query is denoted as a vector $q=(q_1,q_2,...,q_n)$ and the web page is represented as a vector $A = (a_1, a_2, ..., a_n)$. The Tf-idf measure is employed and the similarity can be measured by the cosine function defined as follows.

$$Sim_{keyword-based}(A_i, q) = \cos(a, q) = \frac{\sum_{i=1}^{n} a_i q_i}{\sqrt{\sum_{i=1}^{n} a_i^2} \times \sqrt{\sum_{i=1}^{n} q_i^2}} \quad (8)$$

where $\|a\| = 1$. This approach for key term expansion based on synonym set is also adopted in the baseline system. The results and discussions are described in the following sections.

3.2 Weight determination using 11-avgP score

The medical domain web search system is modeled by the linear combination of relational inference model and axiom inference model. The normalized weight factor, α, is employed for concept expansion as follows.

$$Sim(A_i, q) = (1-\alpha)Sim_{relation}(A_i, q) + \alpha \times Sim_{axiom}(A_i, q) \quad (9)$$

This experiment is conducted on the estimation of the combination weights for each model. The results are shown in Figure 5. The performance measure called 11-AvgP [Eichmann and Srinivasan 1998] was used to summarize the precision and recall rates. The best 11-AvgP score will be obtained when the weight $\alpha = 0.428$.

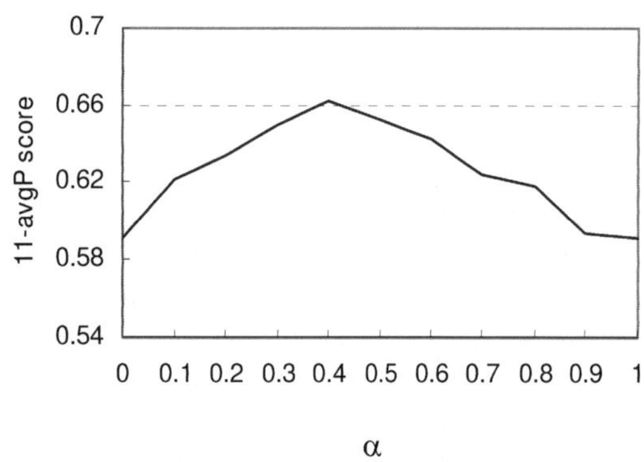

Figure 5 The 11-avgP score with different values of α

3.3 Evaluation on different inference modules

In the following experiments, web pages were separately evaluated by focusing on one inference module based on the domain-specific ontology at a time. That is, the mixture weight is set to 1 for one inference module and the other is set to 0 in each evaluation. For comparison, the keyword-based VSM approach and the ontology-based system are also evaluated and shown in Figure 6. The precision and recall rates are used as the evaluation measures. And the ontology based approach means the combination of concept inference and axiom inference described in the section 3.2.

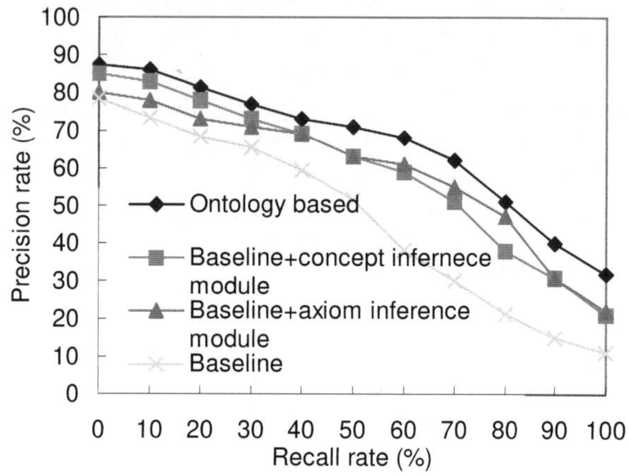

Figure 6 The precision rates and recall rates of the proposed method and the baseline system

4 Conclusion

This paper has presented an approach to automated ontology alignment and domain ontology extraction from two knowledge bases. In this approach, a bilingual ontology is developed using a corpus-based statistical approach from two well established language-dependent knowledge bases, WordNet and HowNet. A domain-dependent ontology is further extracted from the universal ontology using the island-driven algorithm and a domain corpus. In addition, domain-specific terms and axioms are also added into the domain ontology. We have applied the domain-specific ontology to the web page search in medical domain. The experimental results show that the proposed approach outperformed the keyword-based and synonym expansion approaches.

References

N. Asanoma. 2001 Alignment of Ontologies: WordNet and Goi-Taikei. WordNet and Other Lexical Resources Workshop Program, NAACL2001. 89-94

Christiane Fellbaum, 1998 WordNet an electronic Lexical Database, The MIT Press 1998. pp307-308

Fensel, D., Bussler, C., Ding, Y., Kartseval, V., Klein, M., Korotkiy, M., Omelayenko, B. and Siebes R. 2002 Semantic Web Application Areas, the 7th International Workshop on Applications of Natural Language to Information Systems (NLDB02).

M. Missikoff,, R. Navigli, and P. Velardi. 2002 Integrated approach to Web ontology learning and engineering, Computer , Volume: 35 Issue: 11 . 60 –63

N.F. Noy, and M. Musen,. 2000 PROMPT: Algorithm and Tool for Automated Ontology Merging and Alignment, Proceedings of the National Conference on Artificial Intelligence. AAAI2000. 450-455

Sinorama Magazine and Wordpedia.com Co. 2001 Multimedia CD-ROMs of Sinorama from 1976 to 2000, Taipei.

P. Vossen, and W. Peters, 1997 Multilingual design of EuroWordNet, Proceedings of the Delos workshop on Cross-language Information Retrieval.

H. Weigard, and S. Hoppenbrouwers, 1998, Experiences with a multilingual ontology-based lexicon for news filtering, Proceedings in the 9th International Workshop on Database and Expert Systems Applications. 160-165

H. Kargupta, I. Hamzaoglu, and B. Stafford. 1997. Distributed data mining using an agent based architecture. In Proceedings of Knowledge Discovery and Data Mining, 211-214.

U. Y. Nahm and R. J. Mooney. 2000. A mutually beneficial integration of data mining and information extraction. In Proceeding of the AAAI-00.

H. Ahonen, O. Heinoen, M. Klemettinen, and A. Verkamo. 1998. Applying data mining techniques for descriptive phrase extraction in digital document collections. In Advence in Digital Libraries.

E. Frank, G. W. Paynter, I. H. Witten, C. Gutwin, and C. G. Nevill-Manning. 1999. Domain-specific keyphrase extraction. In proceding of IJCAI-99, 668-673.

Y. Yang, J. Carbonell, R. Brown, T. Pierce, B. T. Archibald, and X. Liu. 1999. Learning approaches for detecting and tracking news events. IEEE Intelligent Systems, 14(4):32-43.

W. W. Cohen. 1998. A web-based information system that reasons with structured collocations of text. In Proceedings of 2nd Agent'98

M. Junker, M. Sintek, and M. Rinck. 1999 Learning for text categorization and information extraction with ilp. In Proceedings of the Workshop on Learning Language in Logic, Bled, Slovenia

S. Oyama, T. Kokubo, and T. Ishida. 2004 Domain-Specific Web Search with Keyword Spice. IEEE Transactions on Knowledge and Data Engineering, Vol 16,NO. 1, 17-27.

Sankar K. Pal, Varun Talwar, and Pabitra Mitra. 2002. Web Minging in Soft Computing Framework: Relevance, State of the Art and Future Directions. IEEE Transactions on Neural Networks, Vol. 13, NO. 5.

T. Hofmann. 1999. The cluster-abstraction model: Unsupervised learning of topic hierarchies from text data. In Proceedings of 16th IJCAI, 682-687,

P. Martin and P. Eklund. 2000. Knowledge Indexation and Retrieval and the Word Wide Web. IEEE Intelligent Systems, special issue "Knowledge Management and Knowledge Distribution over the Internet"

H. Chen, A. M. Lally, B. Zhu, and M. Chau. ,2003 HelpfulMed: Intelligent Searching for Medical Information over the internet. Journal od the American Society for Information Science and Technology, 54(7):683-694.

D. Eichmann, , Ruiz, M., Srinivasan, P., 1998 Cross-language information retrieval with the UMLS Metathesaurus, Proceeding of ACM Special Interest Group on Information Retreival (SIGIR), ACM Press, NY (1998), 72-80.

A Statistical Model for Hangeul-Hanja Conversion in Terminology Domain

Jin-Xia HUANG, Sun-Mee BAE, Key-Sun CHOI
Department of Computer Science
Korea Advanced Institute of Science and Technology/KORTERM/BOLA
373-1 Guseong-dong, Yuseong-gu, Daejeon, 305-701
{hgh, sbae, kschoi}@world.kaist.ac.kr

Abstract

Sino-Korean words, which are historically borrowed from Chinese language, could be represented with both Hanja (Chinese characters) and Hangeul (Korean characters) writings. Previous Korean Input Method Editors (IMEs) provide only a simple dictionary-based approach for Hangeul-Hanja conversion. This paper presents a sentence-based statistical model for Hangeul-Hanja conversion, with word tokenization included as a hidden process. As a result, we reach 91.4% of character accuracy and 81.4% of word accuracy in terminology domain, when only very limited Hanja data is available.

1 Introduction

More than one half of the Korean words are Sino-Korean words (Chang, 1996). These words are historically borrowed from Chinese language, could be represented with both Hanja and Hangeul writings. Hanja writing is rarely used in modern Korean language, but still plays important roles in the word sense disambiguation (WSD) and word origin tracing, especially in the terminology, proper noun and compound noun domain.

Automatic Hangeul-Hanja conversion is very difficult for system because of several reasons. There are 473 Hangeul characters (syllables) have Hanja correspondences, map to 4888 common Hanja characters (Kim, 2003). Each of these Hangeul characters could correspond to from one to sixty-four Hanja characters, so it is difficult to system to select the correct Hanja correspondence. Besides that, the sino-Korean Hangeul characters/words could be also native Korean characters/words according to their meaning. For example, "수술(*susul*): stamen, operation, fringe") could correspond to a native Korean word "수술 (stamen)", a sino-Korean word "手術 (operation)", and a mixed word "繡술 (fringe)" (Bae, 2000). It means in Hangeul-Hanja conversion, the same word may be either converted to Hanja or remain as Hangeul writing. In addition, compound sino-Korean words could be written in both with-space and without-space formats even after part of speech (POS) tagging, because the space using is very flexible in Korean language. For example, "한자변환 (*Hanja bienhuan*) (Hanja conversion)" could be in both "한자변환" and "한자 변환" writing formats. It means a compound word tokenization should be included as a pre-processing in Hangeul-Hanja conversion. Automatic Hangeul-Hanja conversion also suffers from another problem, that there are no enough Hanja corpora for statistical approach. In modern Korean language, only few sino-Korean words are written in Hanja writing generally, and the same sino-Korean word with the same meaning could be in either Hangeul or Hanja writing even in the same text.

This paper presents a sentence-based statistical model for Hangeul-Hanja conversion. The model includes a transfer model (TM) and a language model (LM), in which word tokenization is included as a hidden process for compound word tokenization. To find answer for the issues like adapt the model to character or word level, or limit the conversion target to only noun or expand it to other Part of Speech (POS) tags, a series of experiments has been performed. As a result, our system shows significant better result with only very limited Hanja data, when we compare it to the dictionary-based conversion approach used in commercial products.

In the following of this paper: Section 2 discusses related works. Section 3 describes our model. Section 4 discusses several factors considered in the model implementation and experiment design. Section 5 gives the evaluation approaches and a series of experiment results. Section 6 presents our conclusion.

2 Related Works

There are several related areas according to the tasks and approaches. First is previous Korean Hanja, Japanese Kanji (Chinese characters in Japanese language) and Chinese Pinyin input methods, the second one is English-Korean transliteration.

Korean IME (Haansoft, 2002; Microsoft, 2002)

supports word-based Hangeul-to-Hanja conversion. It provides all possible Hanja correspondences to all Hanja-related-Hangeul words in user selected range, without any candidate ranking and sino-Korean word recognition. User has to select sino-Korean words and pick out the correct Hanja correspondence. Word tokenization is performed by left-first longest match method; no context nor statistical information is considered in the correspondence providing, except last-used-first approach in one Korean IME (Microsoft, 2002).

A multiple-knowledge-source based Hangeul-Hanja conversion method was also proposed (Lee, 1996). It was a knowledge based approach which used case-frame, noun-noun collocation, co-occurrence pattern between two nouns, last-used-first and frequency information to distinguish the sense of the sino-Korean words and select the correct Hanja correspondence for the given Hangeul writing. Lee (1996) reported that for practical using, there should be enough knowledge base, including case-frame dictionary, collocation base and co-occurrence patterns to be developed.

There are several methods were proposed for Japanese Kana-Kanji conversion, including last-used-first, most-used-first, nearby character, collocation and case frame based approaches. The word co-occurrence pattern (Yamashita, 1988) and case-frame based approach (Abe, 1986) were reported with a quite high precision. The disadvantages include, there should be enough big knowledge-base developed before, and syntactic analyzer was required for the case frame based approach.

Chinese Pinyin conversion is a similar task with Hangeul-Hanja conversion, except that all Pinyin syllables are converted to Chinese characters. To convert Pinyin P to Chinese characters H, Chen and Lee (2000) used Bayes law to maximize $\Pr(H|P)$, in which a LM $\Pr(H)$ and a typing model $\Pr(P|H)$ are included. The typing model reflects online typing error, and also measures if the input is an English or Chinese word. As the report, the statistical based Pinyin conversion method showed better result than the rule and heuristic based Pinyin conversion method.

Hangeul-Hanja conversion normally does not need to convert online input. So we assume the user input is perfect, and employ a transfer model instead of the typing model in Chen and Lee (2000).

The third related work is transliteration. In statistical based English-Korean transliteration, to convert English word E to Korean word K, a model could use Korean LM $\Pr(K)$ and TM $\Pr(E|K)$ (Lee, 1999; Kim et.al, 1999) to maximize $\Pr(K|E)$, or use English LM $\Pr(E)$ and TM $\Pr(K|E)$ to maximize $\Pr(E,K)$ (Jung et, al., 2000).

3 The Model

Different from previous Hangeul-Hanja conversion method in Korean IMEs, our system uses statistical information in both sino-Korean word recognition and the best Hanja correspondence selection. There are two sub-models included in the model, one is Hangeul-Hanja TM, and the other one is Hanja LM. They provide a unified approach to the whole conversion processing, including compound word tokenization, sino-Korean word recognition, and the correct Hanja correspondence selection.

Let S be a Hangeul string (block) not longer than a sentence. For any hypothesized Hanja conversion T, the task is finding the most likely T^*, which is a most likely sequence of Hanja and/or Hangeul characters/words, so as to maximize the highest probability $\Pr(S, T)$: $T^* = \text{argmax}_T \Pr(S, T)$.

$\Pr(S, T)$ could be transfer probability $\Pr(T|S)$ itself. And like the model in Pinyin IME (Chen and Lee, 2000), we also try to use a Hanja LM $\Pr(T)$, to measure the probabilities of hypothesized Hanja and/or Hangeul sequences. The model is also a sentence-based model, which chooses the probable Hanja/Hangeul word according to the context. Now the model has two parts, TM $\Pr(T|S)$, and LM $\Pr(T)$. We have:

$$T^* = \Pr(S,T) = \underset{T}{\text{argmax}} \Pr(T \mid S) \Pr(T) \quad (1)$$

T is a word sequence which composed by t_1, t_2, …, t_n, where t_i could be either Hanja or Hangeul word/character. We can see the model in equation (1) does not follow the bayes law. It is only a combination model of TM and LM, in which TM reflects transfer probability, and LM reflects context information. Using linear interpolated bigram as LM, the model in equation (1) can be rewritten as equation 2.

$$\Pr(S,T) \approx \prod_{i=1}^{n} \Pr(t_i \mid s_i)\{\beta \Pr(t_i \mid t_{i-1}) + (1-\beta)\Pr(t_i)) \quad (2)$$

Word tokenization is also a hidden process in model (2), so both $T=t_1, t_2, \ldots, t_n$ and $T'=t'_1, t'_2, \ldots t'_m$ can be the correspondences of given source sentence S. In practice, a Viterbi algorithm is used to search the best T^* sequence.

We do not use the noisy channel model $\Pr(T|S) = \text{argmax}_T \Pr(S|T)\Pr(T)$ to get T^*, because most of the Hanja characters has only one Hangeul writing, so that most of the $\Pr(S|T)$ tend to be 1. So if we use the noisy channel model in Hangeul-Hanja conversion, the model would be weakened to Hanja LM $\Pr(T)$ in most of the cases.

4 Implementation

There are several factors should be considered in the model implementation. For example, we could adapt the model to character-level or word-level; we could adopt a TM weight as an interpolation coefficient, and find out the suitable weight for best result; we can also consider about utilizing Chinese corpus to try to overcome the sparsness problem of Hanja data. We can also limit the sino-Korean candidates to only noun words, or expand the candidates to noun, verb, modifier and affix and so on, to see what kind of POS-tag-restriction is better for the Hangeul-Hanja conversion.

We adopt previous dictionary-based approach as our base-line system. To get the higher precision in the base-line experiments, we also want to check if the big dictionary or small dictionary would be better for the Hangeul-Hanja conversion.

4.1 Word Level or Character Level

There are two kinds of levels in the model implementation. In word level implementation, the s_i in equation (2) is a Hangeul word. In character level implementation, s_i is a sequence of Hangeul characters.

In word level implementation, there is no word tokenization after POS tagging, so unknown word or compound word is considered as one word without further tokenization. The advantage of word level implementation is, there is no noisy caused by tokenization error. Its disadvantage is that, the system is weak for the unknown and compound word conversion.

To the contrary, in character level implementation, word tokenization are performed as a hidden process of the model. There are several reasons for why word tokenization is required even after POS tagging. First, it is because the morph analysis dictionary is different from the Hangeul-Hanja word dictionary, so the compound word in the morph dictionary still could be unknown word in Hangeul-Hanja dictionary. Second, there are some unknown words even after POS tagging, and this situation is quite serious in terminology or technical domain. Character level implementation will tokenize a given word to all possible character strings, and try to find out the best tokenization way by finding the most likely T^* via equation (2).

Obviously, character level implementation is better than word level implementation for unknown and compound word conversion, but it also raises the risk of bringing too much noise because of the tokenization error. We have to distinguish which one is better through the experiment.

4.2 Transfer Model Weight

Our model in equation 2 is not derived from Bayes law. We just use the conditional probability $Pr(T|S)$ to reflect the Hangeul-Hanja conversion possibility, and assume Hanja LM $Pr(S)$ would be helpful for the output smoothing. The model is only a combination model, so we need a interpolation coefficient α - a TM weight, to get the best combination way of the model. Get the log of the equation, the equation (2) can be rewritten as equation (3).

$$\begin{aligned} T^* \approx \arg\max_T \sum_{i=1}^{n} \{ & \alpha \log(\Pr(t_i \mid s_i)) \\ & + (1-\alpha)\log\{\beta \Pr(t_i \mid t_{i-1}) + (1-\beta)\Pr(t_i)\}\} \end{aligned} \quad (3)$$

where, $\alpha = [0,1]$ is the TM weight.

When α takes a value between 0 to 1, it's a combination model. When α=1, the model is a TM; and when α=0, the model is a LM.

To the LM, we test both unigram and bigram in word level experiment. The interpolated bigram in equation (3) is used for character level implementation.

4.3 Language Resource Utilization

There is no much Hanja data could be used for Hangeul-Hanja conversion. So we treat Hangeul-Hanja word dictionary as a Dictionary corpus, which is 5.3Mbytes in our experiment, to get unigram, bigram and transfer probability. The extracted data from dictionary is called dictionary data D.

Second, we extract user data U from a very small user corpus (0.28Mbytes in our open test), which is in the same domain with the testing data.

Finally, we assume that Chinese corpus is helpful for the Hangeul-Hanja conversion because of the historical relation between them, although they may not exactly the same words in the two language. We convert the code of the Hanja words to Chinese ones (GB in our experiment) to get Chinese data D (unigram and bigram) for the Hanja words from Chinese corpus, which is 270Mbytes corpus in news domain (TREC9, 2000).

We want to know how much these different data D, U, C can help for Hangeul-Hanja conversion, and testify that through experiment.

4.4 POS Tag Constraint

We compare two cases to see the influence of the POS tag constraint in sino-Korean recognition. The first case is only treat Noun as potential sino-Korean, and in the other case we extend noun to other possible POS tags, including noun, verb, modification, suffix, and affix. The sign, foreign, junction words are excluded from the potential sino-Korean candidates. It is because these words would never be sino-Korean in practice. A POS tagger is employed for the pre-processing of our system.

Actually, most of the sino-Korean words that need Hanja writing are noun words, but in practice, the POS tagger normally shows tagging errors. Such kind of tagging error is much more serious in terminology and technical domain. It is one of the reasons why we want to expand the noun words to other possible POS tags. Another reason is, the more restricted the POS tag constraint is, the lower the coverage is, although the higher precision could be expected. So we should have a test to see if the constraint should be more restrict or less.

4.5 Dictionary Size

We develop a dictionary-based conversion system as our base line system. This dictionary-based system follows the approach used in the previous Korean IMEs. The difference is our system uses POS tagger, and gives the best candidate for all sino-Korean words, when previous IMEs only provide all possible candidates without ranking and let user to select the correct one.

Intuitively, the bigger the dictionary is, the better the conversion result would be. But generally, the word in bigger dictionary has more candidates, so it is still possible that bigger dictionary will low down the conversion performance. So we want to distinguish which one is better for Hangeul-Hanja in practical using.

We used two dictionaries in the experiments, one contains 400k Hangeul-Hanja word entries, and one contains 60k Hangeul-Hanja word entries.

5 Experiment

This chapter shows the experiments on the model in equation 3 and some different implementations we have discussed above.

There are two parts in the experiments, first one is mostly related to word level model implementation, in which the basic issues like language resource utilization and POS tag restriction, and some word level related issues like bigram or unigram for LM in word level are tested. The second part is mostly character level related.

Several evaluation standards are employed in the experiments. The adopted standards and evaluation approaches are reported in the first section of the experiments.

5.1 Evaluation Standard and Approach

We use several evaluation standards in the experiments. To reflect the readability from the user viewpoint, we adopt word and phrase (sentence) level accuracy, precision and recall; to compare the automatic conversion result with the standard result – from the developer viewpoint, Dice-coefficient based similarity calculation is employed also; to compare with previous Chinese Pinyin input method, a character based accuracy evaluation is also adopted.

An automatic evaluation and analysis system is developed to support large scale experiments. The system compares the automatic result to the standard one, and performs detailed error analysis using a decision tree.

5.2 Word Level Experiment

In this part, the basic issues like language resource utilization and POS tag restriction, and the word level related issues, like bigram or unigram for LM are performed.

The objects of **the first experiment** are, firstly, compare a simple LM based statistical approach with the base line - dictionary based approach; secondly, see if large dictionary is better than small dictionary in dictionary based conversion; thirdly, see if Chinese corpus does help to the Hangeul-Hanja conversion.

A small dictionary based conversion (Dic), large dictionary based conversion (BigDic), a unigram (Unigram) and a bigram based (Bigram) word level conversion, are performed to compared to the each other.

The small dictionary Dic has 56,000 Hangeul-Hanja entries; while the large dictionary BigDic contains 280,000 Hangeul-Hanja entries. The unigram and bigram are extracted from Chinese data C. The test set is a small test set with 90 terms (180 content words) from terminology domain. Word level precision and recall with F1-measure are employed as evaluation standard.

	Dic	BigDic	unigram	bigram
P	57.1%	50.0%	78.6%	78.6%
R	25.7%	44.0%	70.6%	70.6%
F1	35.4%	46.8%	74.4%	74.4%

Table 1. Base line (small dic vs. large dic) vs. Statistical approach (unigram vs. bigram)

From the result shows in table 1, we can get the conclusions that, 1) compare to the small dictionary, large dictionary reaches better F1-measure because of the enhancement in recall, although the precision is slightly low downed because of more Hanja candidates for given Hangeul entry; 2) Statistical approach shows obvious better result than the dictionary based approach, although it is only a very simple LM; 3) Chinese data does help to the Hangeul-Hanja conversion. We have to evaluation its impact by comparing it with other Hanja data in further experiments. 4) Bigram shows similar result with unigram in word level conversion, it shows that data sparseness problem is still very serious.

The objects of **the second experiment** include the evaluation on different POS tag constraints and the comparison between different language resources.

First is evaluation on different POS tag constraints. Let the system employs unigram based Hangeul-Hanja conversion approach, which uses dictionary data D (word unigram from large dictionary at here). Our experiment wants to compare the case of only considering noun as potential sino-Korean words ("Dn" in table 2), with the case of extending the POS tags to verb, modification and affix ("De" in table 2). Second evaluation is comparison on different language resources. As we have mentioned above, D is data from large dictionary (word unigram is used at here), U is data from very small user corpus, and C is data from Chinese corpus. We want to compare the different combination of these language resources. In the second evaluation, extended POS tag constraint is employed.

The experiment uses a test set with 5,127 terms (12,786 content words, 4.67 Hanja candidates per sino-Korean word in average) in computer science and electronic engineering domain. User data U is from user corpus, which is the same with the test set at here (so it is a closed test). In evaluation, a dice-coefficient based similarity evaluation standard is employed.

	Dn	De	U	C	DC	DU	UC	DUC
Sim	0.71	0.75	0.81	0.72	0.75	0.82	0.82	0.81

Table 2. POS tag constraint and language resource evaluation

From the table 2, we can see that, 1) the extended POS tag constraint ("De" in table 2) shows better result than the noun POS tag constraint ("Dn"); 2) User data U shows better result than dictionary data D ("U" ⇔ "De", "UC" ⇔ "DC" in table 2), and dictionary data D shows better result than Chinese data C ("De" ⇔ "C"), although Chinese corpus (where C is from) is 270MB, and much larger than the Hangeul-Hanja dictionary (5.3MB here, where D is from). It shows that the effect of Chinese data is quite limited in despite of its usefulness.

The object of the third experiment is to find out which TM weight α is better for the word model.

	α=0	α=0.5	α=1
P	78.6%	76.52%	84.80%
R	70.6%	70.70%	77.31%
F1	74.4%	73.4%	80.8%

Table 3. TM weight in word model

Let α to be 0, 0.5, 1, and so the model in equation (3) is LM, combined model, and TM, with the same environment of the second experiment, we get the result in table 3. Word level precision and recall with F1-measure is evaluated. We can see the TM with α=1 shows the best result.

5.3 Character Level Experiment

In the character level experiments, first, we compare the character level model with base line dictionary based approach; Second, compare the character level model with the word level model; Third, to find out the best TM weight for the character level model.

This part of experiments uses a new test set, which has 1,000 terms in it (2,727 content words; 3.9 Hanja candidates per sino-Korean word in average). The user data U has 12,000 Hangeul-Hanja term pairs in it. U is from the same domain of the test set (computer science and electronic engineering domain at here), but there is no overlap with the test set (so it is a opened test).

Several different evaluation standards are employed. As the first column of table 4, "CA", "WA" and "SA" mean character, word, sentence (terms) accuracy, respectively. "Sim" is the similarity based evaluation, and F1 is the value of word level F1-measure which is from word precision/recall evaluation.

%	Dic	wD1	wDUC1	D.5	DU0	DU.2	DU.5	DU.8	DU1
CA	62.9	69.1	75.0	73.1	81.0	89.3	90.2	91.0	91.4
WA	49.9	73.8	75.3	64.6	72.4	77.1	82.3	82.1	81.4
SA	18.8	43.4	51.2	34.7	48.2	67.0	67.5	67.1	68.1
Sim	68.4	75.5	79.7	77.9	82.5	90.4	91.2	91.7	92.1
F1	39.0	65.6	69.7	51.2	60.8	75.7	75.9	75.9	76.2

Table 4: Character level model vs. word level model vs. base line (dictionary based approach)

The first row of table 4 shows the Hangeul-Hanja conversion approach with the employed data and TM weight α. "Dic" is the base line dictionary based approach; "w" means word level model; "D" means dictionary data (extracted from the large dictionary with 400,000 Hangeul-Hangeul and Hangeul-Hanja entries), U means user data described above, C means Chinese data. The digital value like ".5" is TM weight. So, as an example, "wDUC1" means word model with α=1 and using all data resources D, U and C; "DU.2" means character model with α=0.2 and using data D and U.

From the table 4, we can get the conclusions that, 1) all statistical model based approaches shows obviously better performance than the base line dictionary based approach "Dic" (Dic ⇔ others). 2) In most cases, character models show better results than word model (DUx ⇔ wDUCw1). But when there is no user data, word mode is better than character model (wD1⇔D.5). 3) Among character models, the TM with α=1 shows the best result ("DU1" ⇔ "DU.x"). 4) User data has positive impact on the performance ("Dw1 ⇔ DUCw1", "D.5 ⇔ DU.5"), and it is especially important to the character model ("D.5 ⇔ DU.5"). It is because character model may cause more noise because of word tokenization error when there is no user data.

From the table 4, we can see the best result is gotten from character based TM with using dictionary and user data D, U ("DU1"). The best character accuracy is 91.4%, when the word accuracy is 81.4%. The character accuracy is lower than the typing and language model based Chinese Pinyin IME, which was 95% in Chen & Lee (2000). But consider that in our experiment, there is almost no Hanja data except dictionary, and also consider the extra difficulty from terminology domain, this comparision result is quite understandable. Our experiment also shows that, compare to using only LM like it in Chen & Lee (2000), TM shows significantly better result in character accuracy (from 81.0% to 91.4% in our experiment: "DU0" ⇔ "DU1", table 4). Our user evaluation also shows that, to the terminology domain, the automatic conversion result from the system shows even better quality than the draft result from untrained human translator.

5.4 Different Evaluation Standards

Figure 1 shows the trends of different evaluation standards in the same experiment shown in table 4. We can see character accuracy "CA" shows similar trend with similarity based standard "Sim", while word accuracy "WA" and sentence (terms) accuracy "SA" show similar trends with F1-measure "F1", in which "F1"is based on word precision and recall.

From the user viewpoint, word/sentence accuracy and F1-measure reflects readability better than character accuracy. It is because, if there is a character wrongly converted in a word, it affects the readability of whole word but not only that character's. However, character accuracy is more important to the system evaluation, especially for the character level model implementation. It is because the character accuracy can reflect the system performance in full detail than the word or sentence (term) based one.

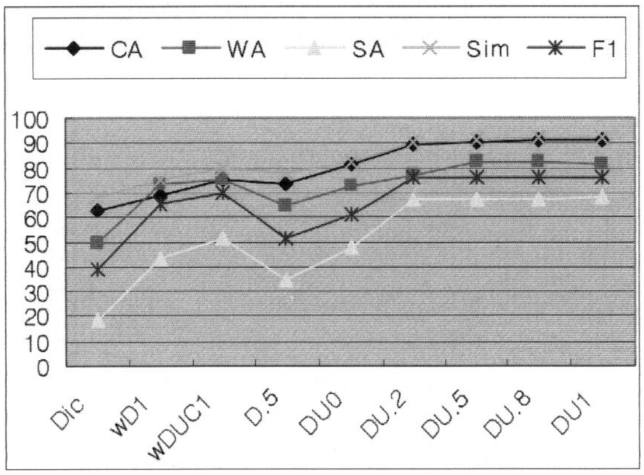

Figure1.The trends of different evaluation standards

6 Conclusion

This paper proposes a sentence based statistical model for Hangeul-Hanja conversion in Korean language. This model provides a unified approach to the whole conversion processing, which includes word tokenization, sino-Korean word recognition and the correct Hanja correspondence selection. A series of experiments have been done for the issues in model and system implementation. Including, adapting the model to character-level or word-level, the influence of the TM weight, the different POS tag constraints on the sino-Korean word recognition, etc.

The experiments show that best result is achieved from character based TM with using both dictionary and user data. The best character accuracy in computer science and electronic engineering terminology domain is 91.4%, which is even better than the draft result from untrained human translator.

This paper also uses several different evaluation standards to see which method is the most suitable one. As a result, we found that the word/term accuracy and word based precision/recall can reflect the user readability well, when the character accuracy is more suitable to the system performance evaluation in full detail.

We are doing further research on general domain, especially about utilizing the concept hierarchy of thesaurus to solve data sparseness problem. We are also considering about use Japanese corpus for Hangeul-Hanja, because the Kanji in Japanese language also has some overlap with the Hanja in Korean language.

7 Acknowledgements

This work was supported in part by Ministry of Science & Technology of Korean government and Korea Science & Engineering Foundation.

References

Abe, M. & Y. Oshima, 1986. *A Kana-Kanji Translation System for Non-segmented Input Sentences Based on Syntactic and Semantic Analysis*, in the Proceedings of COLING-86, 280-285, 1986.

Chen, Zheng and Kai-Fu Lee. 2002. *A New Statistical Approach To Chinese Pinyin Input.* The 38th Annual Meeting of the Association for Computational Linguistics (ACL-2000.)

Dice, L.R. 1945. *Measures of the amount of ecologic association between species.* Journal of Ecology, 26:297-302

Gao, Jianfeng, Hai-Feng Wang, Mingjing Li and Kai-Fu Lee. 2000. *A Unified Approach to Statical Language Modeling for Chinese.* ICASSP-2000, Istanbul, Turkey, June 5 - 9, 2000

Haansoft. 2002. Hangeul 2002. Haansoft Inc.

Kim, Kyongsok. 2003. *Hangeul correspondence for Hanja character in KSX1001.* http://asadal.cs.pusan.ac.kr/hangeul/code/ksx1001-name-hj-v02.txt

Kim J.J., J.S. Lee, and K-S. Choi., 1999. *Pronunciation unit based automatic English-Korean transliteration model using neural network*, In Proceedings of Korea Cognitive Science Association (in Korean).

Lee, Jaeseong. 1999. *An English-Korean Transliterationand retransliteration model for cross-lingual information retrieval.* Ph.D Dissertation. KAIST

Lee, Jong-Hyeok, 1996. *A Sense-analysis-based Hangeul-Hanja conversion System. In Computational Semantics and Application, Meanum Company*, 1996. pp247-278. (in Korean)

Microsoft, 2002. *Korean Input Method 2002.* Microsoft Corporation.

Chang, Suk-Jin. 1996. *Korean.* London Oriental and African Language Library 4. Philadelphia, PA.: John Benjamins. pp.2

Jung , SungYoung, SungLim Hong & EunOk Paek. 2000. *An English to Korean Transliteration Model of Extended Markov Window.* 18th International Conference on Computational Linguistics

TREC9. 2001. http://trec.nist.gov/

Yamashita, M. & F. Obashi, 1988. *Collocational Analysis in Japanese Text Input*, in the Proceedings of COLING-88, 770-772, 1988.

Chinese Term Extraction from Web Pages Based on Compound word Productivity

Hiroshi Nakagawa
Information Technology Center, The University of Tokyo
7-3-1 Hongou, Bunkyo
Tokyo, JAPAN, 113-0033
nakagawa@dl.itc.u-tokyo.ac.jp

Hiroyuki Kojima*, **Akira Maeda****
Faculty of Economics, The University of Tokyo
7-3-1 Hongou, Bunkyo
Tokyo, JAPAN, 113-0033
* kojima@e.u-tokyo.ac.jp,
**maeda@lib.u-tokyo.ac.jp

Abstract

In this paper, we propose an automatic term recognition system for Chinese. Our idea is based on the relation between a compound word and its constituents that are simple words or individual Chinese character. More precisely, we basically focus on how many words/characters adjoin the word/character in question to form compound words. We also take into account the frequency of term. We evaluated word based method and character based method with several Chinese Web pages, resulting in precision of 75% for top ten candidate terms.

1 Introduction

Automatic term recognition, ATR in short, aims at extracting domain specific terms from a corpus or Web pages. Domain specific terms are terms that express the concept specifically defined in the given domain. They are required to have a unique meaning in order for efficient communication about the topic of the domain. It is, however, difficult to decide automatically whether they are unique. So we put this issue aside. In terms of feasibility, their grammatical status is important, for instance part of speeches. Although they are not necessarily confined to simple words where "simple word" means a word which could not be further divided into shorter and more basic words, the majority of them are actually compound words,. Thus, we here focus on both of simple and compound words.

In terms of text length, even one Web page which is not long gives us a number of domain specific vocabulary like "national library", "library policy" if the Web page is about libraries. If we expand domain specific terms to this extent, the big portion of domain specific terms are compound words. Obviously, the majority of compound words consist of relatively small number of distinct simple words. In this situation, it is natural to pay attention to the relation among compound words and their constituent simple words.

(Kageura and Umino 1996) proposed an important feature of domain specific terms called *termhood* which refers to the degree that a linguistic unit is related to a domain-specific concept. Presumably, it is necessary to develop an ATR method that calculates termhood of each term candidate extracted from a domain corpus that usually consists of a number of documents. Many works of ATR use statistics of term candidate distribution in a corpus such as term frequency to calculate the termhood of every term candidate.

This frequency based methods, however, heavily depend on the size of corpus. Thus we do not expect a good result if we extract domain specific terms from one or a few Web pages. If we shift our focus from a corpus based statistics like frequency to **term space** that consists of all term candidates, we expect better result of extracted terms even from one Web page because of the following reason: A set of term candidates has its own structure like relations between compound words and their constituent simple words as stated before. The statistical information about these relations comes from more microscopic structure than term frequency. Thus, if we utilize more information from term space, it is reasonable to expect better performance in extracting from a small text like one Web page. Without this kind of information, we will be suffering from the shortage of information for ATR.

Now look at frequency based information and information inherent with term space more closely. Even though several kinds of statistics about actual use in a corpus such as term frequency give a good approximation of termhood. They are not necessarily meanings in a writer's mind. On the contrary, the statistics of term space can reflect the meaning in a writer's mind because it is up to a writer's decision how to make a compound word term to express a complicated concept using simple word terms as its components. More precisely, if a certain simple word, say *N*, expresses the basic concept of a domain that the document treats, the writer of the document, we expect, uses *N* not only many times but in various ways. One of typical way of this kind is that he/she composes quite a few compound words using *N* and uses these compound words in documents he/she writes. For this reason, we have to focus on the relation among simple words and compound words when pursuing new ATR methods.

One of the attempts to make use of this relation has been done by Nakagawa and Mori (2003). Their method is based on the number of distinct simple words that come left or right of a simple word term to make up compound word terms. In this paper, we apply their method to deal with Web pages written in Chinese.

In this paper, section 2 gives the background of ATR methods. In section 3 we introduce ATR method developed by Nakagawa and Mori(2003). Section 4, 5 and 6 are for how to apply their method to Chinese language and evaluation of two proposed method: 1) Word based method using Chinese morphological analyzer ICTCLAS(Zhang, Yu, Xiong and Liu. 2003), 2) Stop character based method.

2 Background

2.1 Typical Procedures of Automatic Term Recognition

An ATR procedure consists of two procedures in general. The first one is a procedure of extracting term candidates from a corpus. The second procedure is to assign each term candidate a score that indicates how likely the term candidate is a term to be recognized. Then all candidates are ranked according to their scores. In the remaining part of this section, we describe the background of a candidate extraction procedure and a scoring procedure respectively.

2.2 Candidates Extraction

In term candidates extraction from the given text corpus, we mainly focus on compound words as well as simple words. To extract compound words which are promising term candidates and at the same time to exclude undesirable strings such as "*is a*" or "*of the*", the frequently used method is to filter out the words that are the member of a *stop-word-list*.

The structure of complex term is another important factor for automatic term candidate extraction. A syntactic structure that is the result of parsing is focused on in many works. Since we focus on these complex structures, the first task in extracting term candidates is a morphological analysis including part of speech (POS) tagging. There are no explicit word boundary marker in Chinese, we first have to do morphological analysis which segments out words from a sentence and does POS tagging at the same time.

After POS tagging, the complex structures mentioned above are extracted as term candidates. Previous studies have proposed many promising ways for this purpose, for instance, Smadja and McKeown (1990), and Frantzi and Ananiadou (1996) tried to treat more general structures like collocations.

2.3 Scoring

The next step of ATR is to assign each term candidate its score in order to rank them in descending order of termhood. Many researchers have sought the definition of term candidate's score which approximates termhood. In fact, many of those proposals make use of statistics of actual use in a corpus such as term frequency which is so powerful and simple that many researchers directly or indirectly have used it. The combination of term frequency and inverse document frequency is also well studied i.e. (Uchimoto et al 2000), (Fukushige and Noguchi 2000). On the other hand, several scoring methods that are neither directly nor heavily based on frequency of term candidates have been proposed. Among those, Ananiadou et al. proposed C-value (Frantzi and Ananiadou 1996) which counts how independently the given compound word is used in the given corpus. Hisamitsu (2000) proposes a way to measure termhood which estimates how far the document containing given term is different from the distribution of documents not containing the given term. However, the method proposed by Nakagawa and Mori (2003) outperforms these methods in terms of NTCIR1 TMREC task(Kageura, et al, 1999).

2.4 Chinese Term Extraction

As for Chinese language NLP, very many works about word segmentation were published i.e. (Ma and Xia 2003). Nevertheless the term "Term extraction" has not yet been used for Chinese NLP, key words extraction have been a target for a long time. For instance, key words extraction from news articles (Li. et al. 2003) is the recent result which uses frequency and length of character string for scoring. Max-duplicated string based method (Yang and Li. 2002) is also promising. In spite of previous research efforts, there have been no attempt so far to apply the relation between simple and compound words to Chinese term extraction, and that is exactly what we propose in this paper.

3 Scoring methods with Simple word Bigrams

3.1 Simple word Bigrams

The relation between a simple word and complex words that include the simple word is very important in terms of term space structure. Nevertheless, to my knowledge, this relation has not been paid enough attention so far except for the method proposed by Nakagawa and Mori (2003). In this paper, taking over their works, we focus on compound words among the various types of complex terms. In technical documents, the majority of domain-specific terms are noun phrases or compound words consisting of small size vocabulary of simple words. This observation leads to a new scoring methods that measures how many distinct compound words contain the simple word in question as their part in a given document or corpus. Here, suppose the situation where simple word: N occurs with other simple words as a part of many compound words shown in Figure 1 where [N M] means bigram of noun N and M.

[LN1 N] (#L1)	[N RN1](#R1)
[LN2 N] (#L2)	[N RN2](#R2)
:	:
[LNn N](#Ln)	[N RNm](#Rm)

Figure 1. Noun Bigram and their Frequency

In Figure 1, [LNi N] (i=1,..,n) and [N RNj] (j=1,...,m) are simple word bigrams which make (a part of) compound words. #Li and #Rj (i=1,..,n and j=1,..,m) mean the frequency of the bigram [LNi N] and [N RNj] in the corpus respectively. Note that since we depict only bigrams, compound words like [LNi N RNj] which contains [LNi N] and/or [N RNj] as their parts might actually occur in a corpus. Note that this noun trigram might be a part of longer compound words. We show an example of a set of noun bigrams. Suppose that we extract compound words including "trigram" as term candidates from a corpus as shown in the following example.

Example 1.
trigram statistics, word trigram, class trigram, word trigram, trigram acquisition, word trigram statistics, character trigram

Then, noun bigrams consisting of a simple word "trigram" are shown in Figure 2 where the number between (and) shows the frequency in the corpus.

word trigram (3)	trigram statistics (2)
class trigram (1)	trigram acquisition (1)
character trigram(1)	

Figure 2. An example of noun bigram

Now we focus on and utilize simple word bigrams to define the scoring function. Note that we are only concerned with simple word bigrams and not with a simple word per se because, as stated before, we are concerned with the relation between a compound word and its component simple words.

3.2 Scoring Function

3.2.1 Score of simple word

Since there are infinite number of scoring functions based on [LNi N] or [N RNj], we here consider the following simple but representative scoring functions.

#LDN(N) and **#RDN(N) :** These are the number of distinct simple words which directly precede or succeed **N**. These coincide with "n" and "m" in Figure 1 respectively. For instance, in an example shown in Figure 2, #LDN(trigram)=3, #RDN(trigram)=2.

Using #LDN and #RDN we define **LN(N)** and **RN(N):** These are based on the number of occurrence of each noun bigram, and defined for [LNi N] and [N RNj] as follows respectively.

$$LN(N) = \sum_{i=1}^{\#LDN(N)} (\#Li) \quad (1)$$

$$RN(N) = \sum_{j=1}^{\#RDN(N)} (\#Rj) \quad (2)$$

LN(N) and **RN(N)** are the frequencies of nouns that directly precede or succeed **N**. For instance, in an example shown in Figure 2, LN(trigram)=5, and RN(trigram)=3.

Let's think about the background of these scoring functions. #LDN(N) and #RDN(N), where we do not take into account the frequency of each noun bigram but take into account the number of distinct nouns that adjoin to N to make compound words. That indicates how linguistically and domain dependently productive the noun:N is in a given corpus. That means that if N presents a key and/or basic concept of the domain treated by the corpus, writers in that domain work out many distinct compound words with N to express more complicated concepts. On the other hand, as for **LN(N)** and **RN(N)**, we also focus on frequency of each noun bigram as well. In other words, statistic bias in actual use of noun:N is, this time, one of our main concern. For example, in Figure 2, LN(trigram,2)=11, and RN(trigram,2)=5. In conclusion, since **LN(N)** and **RN(N)** convey more information than #LDN(N) and #RDN(N), we adopt **LN(N)** and **RN(N)** in this research.

3.2.2 Score of compound words

The next thing to do is expanding those scoring functions for simple word to the scoring functions for compound words. We adopt a geometric mean for this purpose. Now think of a compound word : CN = $N_1 N_2 \ldots N_L$, where N_i (i= 1,.., L) is a simple word. Then a geometric mean: **LR** of CN is defined as follows.

$$LR(CN)=\left(\prod_{i=1}^{L}(LN(N_i)+1)(RN(N_i)+1)\right)^{\frac{1}{2L}} \qquad (3)$$

For instance, if we use LN(N) and RN(N) in example 1, LR(trigram) = $\sqrt{(3+1)\times(5+1)}$ = 4.90. LR does not depend on the length of CN where "length" means the number of simple words that consist of CN. This is because since we have not yet had any idea about the relation between the importance of a compound word and a length of the compound word, it is fair to treat all compound words, including simple words, equally no matter how long or short each compound word is.

3.2.3 Combining LR and Frequency of Nouns

We still have not fully utilized the information about statistics of actual use in a corpus in the bigram based methods described in 3.2.1 and 3.2.2. Among various kinds of information about actual use, the important and basic one is the frequency of single-and compound words that occur independently. The term "independently" means that the left and right adjacent words are not nouns. For instance, "word patterns" occurs independently in "we use the word patterns which occur in this sentence." Since the scoring functions proposed in 3.2.1 is noun bigram statistics, the number of this kind of independent occurrences of nouns themselves have not been used so far. If we take this information into account, the better results are expected. Thus, if a simple word or a compound word occurs independently, the score of the noun is simply multiplied by the number of its independent occurrences. We call this new scoring function as **FLR(CN)** which is defined as follows.

if N occurs independently
then $FLR(CN) = LR(CN) \times f(CN)$
where f(CN) means the number of independent occurrences of noun CN (4)

4 Term Extraction for Chinese based on Morphological Analysis

If we try to apply the scoring method proposed in section 3 directly to a Chinese text, every word should be POS tagged because we extract multi-word unit of several types of POS tag sequences as candidates of domain specific terms. For this we need a Chinese morphological analyzer because Chinese is an agglutinative language. Actually, we use Chinese morphological analyzer: ICTCLAS(Zhang and Liu 2004). As term candidates, we extract compound word: MWU having the following POS tag sequence expressed in (5). A multi-word-unit: MWU is defined by the following CFG rules where the right hand sides are expressed as a regular expression.

MWU <-- [ag a]* [ng n nr ns nt nz nx vn an i j]+
MWU <-- MWU$^?$b [ng n nr ns nt nz nx vn an i j]$^+$
MWU <-- [ag a]$^+$ [u k] MWU
MWU <-- MWU (u|k|*he-2*|*yu-3*) MWU
(5)

where "ag", "a", "n"..., "u" are all tags used in ICTCLAS.

Roughly speaking (5) means an adjective followed by the repetition of [adjective noun particle] followed by a noun. The problem is the ambiguity of POS tagging because the same word is very often used verb as well as noun. In addition, unknown words like newly appeared proper names also impairs the accuracy. Due to this problem caused by morphological analyzer, the accuracy is degraded.

Once we segment out word sequences conforming the above POS tag sequences, we calculate LN and RN of each component word. In calculation of LN and RN, a word whose POS is c, u or k is omitted. In other words, if a word sequence "w1 w2 w3" where POS of w2 is c u or k, then we calculate RN of w1 and LN of w3 by regarding the word sequence as "w1 w3."

Then we combine LN and RN of each word to calculate FLR by definition of (3) and (4) to sort all extracted candidates in descending order of FLR.

We apply the proposed methods to 30 Web pages from People's Daily news. The areas are social, international and IT related news. The average length is 592.6 characters. Firstly, we extract relevant terms by hand from each news article and use it as the gold standard. The average number of gold standard terms per one news particle is 15.9 words. Secondly, we extract terms from each news article and sort them in descending order by the proposed method and evaluate them by a precision of top N terms defined as follows.

$CT(K)$= 1 if Kth term is one of the gold standard terms.
0 otherwise

$$precision(K) = \frac{\sum_{i=1}^{K} CT(i)}{K} \quad (6)$$

where N is the number of the gold standard terms, and in our experiment, N=20. *Precision(K)*, where K=1,..,20, are shown in Figure 3 as "Strict."

We also use another precision rate *precision'* which is not strict and defined as follows.

$CTpart(K)$= 1 if one of gold standard terms. is a part of Kth term
0 otherwise

$$precision'(K) = \frac{\sum_{i=1}^{K} CTpart(i)}{K} \quad (7)$$

These are also shown in Figure 3 as "Partly."

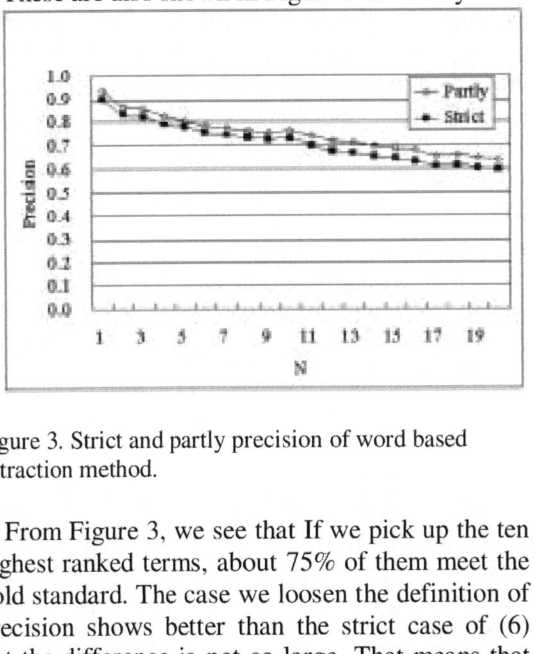

Figure 3. Strict and partly precision of word based extraction method.

From Figure 3, we see that If we pick up the ten highest ranked terms, about 75% of them meet the gold standard. The case we loosen the definition of precision shows better than the strict case of (6) but the difference is not so large. That means that the proposed word based ranking method works very well to extract important Chinese terms from news articles.

5 Character based Term Extraction

There are several reasons why we would like to develop a term extraction system without morphological analyzer.

The first reason is that the accuracy of morphological analyzer is, in spite of the great advancement of these years, still around 95% (GuoDong and Jian 2003).

The second reason is that there possibly exist terminologies with unexpected POS sequences. If we deal only with academic papers or technical documents, we expect POS sequences of terminologies with high accuracy. However, if we consider terminology extraction from Web pages, the possibility of unexpected POS sequence may rise.

The third reason is language independency. Currently proposed and/or used morphological analyzers heavily depend either upon the sophisticated linguistic knowledge about the target language or upon a big size corpus of the target language if machine learning is employed. These linguistic resources, however, are not always available.

Due to these reasons, we also developed term candidate extraction system which does not use a morphological analyzer. Instead of morphological analyzer, we try to employ a stop word list. In Chinese, as stop words, we find many character unigrams and bigrams because one Chinese character conveys larger amount of information than a character of Latin alphabet. They are partly shown in Appendix A.

As term candidates, we simply extract character strings between two stop words that are nearest each other within a sentence. Obviously, the character strings thus extracted are not necessarily meaningful compound words. Therefore we cannot directly use these strings as words to calculate LN and RN function. Back to the idea that Chinese characters are ideograms, we come up to the idea that we calculate LN and RN of each character appearing within every character strings extracted as candidates. An example is shown in Figure 4.

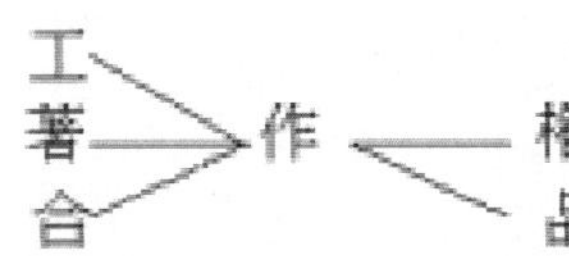

LN(*zuo-4*)=3 RN(*zuo-4*)=2

Figure 4. LN and RN of Chinese character *zuo-4*

In calculation of LN and RN, we neglect characters whose POS are c ,u or k as same as we did in morphological analyzer based method.

Once we calculate LN and RN of each character, FLR of every character string is calculated as defined by (3) and (4) to sort them in descending order of FLR.

Actually this idea is very similar with left and right entropy used to extract two character Chinese words from a corpus (Luo and Sun. 2003). However what we would like to extract is a set of longer compound words or even phrases used in a Web page. Moreover we only use the Web page and do not use any other language resources such as a big corpus at all due to the reason described above in this section.

We evaluate the proposed character based extraction method against the same Web pages from People's Daily news used in Morphological Analysis based method described in Section 4. We also use the same gold standard terms described in Section 4 for evaluation. The strict and partly precision defined by (6) and (7) are used. The result is shown in Figure 5.

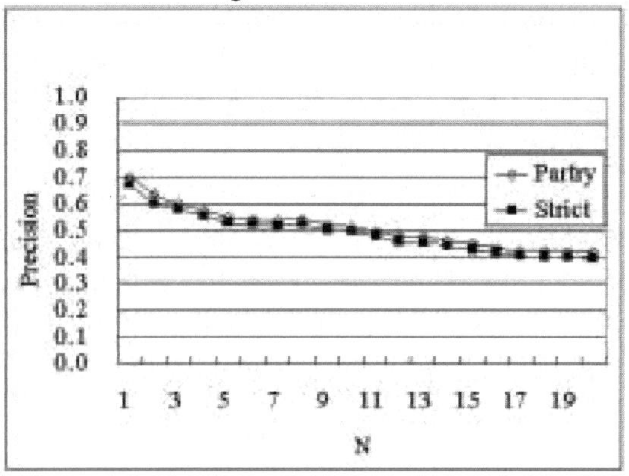

Figure 5. Strict and partly precision of character based extraction method.

Comparing Figure 3 with Figure 5, apparently the result of extracted terms of word based method is better than that of character based method. However, it does not necessarily mean that the character based term extraction is inferior.

If you take a glance at the stop word list of Appendix A, it seems that several of the stop words are selected mainly from words in auxiliary verbs, pronouns, adverbs, particles, prepositions, conjunctions, exclamations, onomatopoeic words and punctuation marks. However, in reality, our selection is based rather on meaning, usage and generally frequency of use than parts of speech. Thus some of them are not function words but content words in order to exclude non-domain-specific words. Actually, the stop words are not only character unigram but character bigram. Because Chinese character is ideograph and each character may have plural meanings, it is difficult only to use character unigram as a stop word in Chinese.

Our method based on these viewpoints resulted in getting an interesting consequence. We show an example of news article and extracted terms from it by this method in Appendix B and Appendix C. This news article is entitled "The Culture of Tibetan Web Site is formally created." Let's take a look at an underlined sentence in this short article and underlined terms extracted from there. This sentence says: According to the introduction, The Culture of Tibetan Web Site is a site of special pure culture for the purpose of "investigating the essence of Tibetan culture, showing the scale of Tibetan culture and raising the spirit of Tibetan culture". In the case of method based on stop word list, we can extract compound term of "investigating the essence of Tibetan culture (盘点藏族文化精英)", "showing the scale of Tibetan culture (展示藏族文化规模)", "raising the spirit of Tibetan culture (弘扬藏族文化精神)" and so on from this sentence. On the contrary, by the term extraction method based on morphological analysis, gerund , for example, "showing(展示)" and "raising (弘扬), can not be extracted.

We said that the majority of domain specific terms are noun phrases or compound words consisting of small size vocabulary of simple words as stated in section 3. So we especially have paid attention to relation among nouns. However most of Chinese nouns can also be used as verbs. Moreover inflection of Chinese verbs can hardly be recognized visually. It is difficult to distinguish verb from noun by morphological analysis. Certainly ICTCLAS classifies the character that has meaning of both verb and noun into the category of vn (verb and noun). But gerunds and verbal noun infinitives are not contained in vn. For instance, "写信" means not only "write a letter" but "writing letter." Thus we have to pay attention to verbs in Chinese too. Only by tuning up stop word list, we can take gerunds and verbal noun infinitives into account to some extent. Appendix C shows one of the evidence of this observation.

6 Conclusion

In this paper, we apply automatic term recognition system based on FLR proposed by Nakagawa and Mori (2003) to Chinese Web pages because the term extraction from small text like one Web page is the future oriented topic. We proposed two methods: word based and character based extraction and ranking using the compound word productivity of simple words. Since the accuracies of term recognition are around 60% for top 1,000 term candidates in NTCIR TMREC task(Kageura et al 1999), the result of 75% accuracy of top ten candidates is a good start.

References

Ananiadou, S. 1994. A Methodology for Automatic Term Recognition. In *Proceedings of 14th International Conference on Computational Linguistics* :1034 - 1038.

GuoDong Zhou and Jian Su. 2003. A Chinese Efficient Analyser Integrating Word Segmentation, Part-Of-Speech Tagging, Partial Parsing and Full Parsing, *In*

Proceedings of The Second SIGHAN Workshop, on Chinese Language Processing .ACL2003 :78-83

Frantzi, T.K. and Ananiadou, S. 1996. Extracting nested collocations. In *Proceedings of 16th International Conference on Computational Linguistics* :41-46.

Fukushige, Y. and N. Nogichi. 2000. Statistical and linguistic approaches to automatic term recognition NTCIR experiments at Matsushita. *Terminology* 6(2) :257-286

Hua-PingZhang, Hong-KuYu, De-Yi Xiong and Qun Liu. 2003. HHMM-based Chinese Lexical Analyzer ICTCLAS. In *Proceedings of The Second SIGHAN Workshop, on Chinese Language Processing .ACL2003* :184-187

Hisamitsu, T, 2000. A Method of Measuring Term Representativeness. In *Proceedings of 18th International Conference on Computational Linguistics* :320-326.

Kageura, K. and Umino, B. 1996. Methods of automatic term recognition: a review. *Terminology* 3(2) :259-289.

Kageura, K. et al, 1999. TMREC Task: Overview and Evaluation. In *Proceedings of the First NTCIR Workshop on Research in Japanese Text Retrieval and Term Recognition* :411-440.

Shengfen Luo and Maosong Sun. 2003. Two-Character Chinese Word Extraction Based on Hybrid of Internal and Contextual Measures. In *Proceedings of The Second SIGHAN Workshop, on Chinese Language Processing .ACL2003* :24-30

Qing Ma and Fei Xia. 2003. Proceedings of The Second SIGHAN Workshop, on Chinese Language Processing .ACL2003, Sappro

Sujian Li,Houfeng Wang,Shiwen Yu and Chengsheng Xin. 2003. News-Oriented Automatic Chinese Keyword Indexing. In *Proceedings of The Second SIGHAN Workshop, on Chinese Language Processing .ACL2003* :92-97

Nakagawa, H. and Tatsunori Mori. 2003. Automaic Term Recognition based on Statistics of Compound words and their Components, Terminology 9(2) :201-219

Smadja, F.A. and Mckeown, K.R. 1990. Automatically extracting and representing collocations for language generation. In *Proceedings of the 28th Annual Meetings of the Association for Computational Linguistics* :252-259.

Uchimoto, K., S.Sekine, M. Murata, H.Ozaku and H. Isahara. 2000. Term recognition using corpora from different fields. *Terminology* 6(2) :233-256

Wenfeng Yang and Xing Li. 2002. Chinese keyword extraction based on max-duplicated strings of the documents. In *Proceedings of the 25th annual international ACM SIGIR conference on Research and develop-ment in information retrieval*, pp. 439-440.

Kevin Zhang and Qun Liu. 2004. ICTCLAS. *http://www.nlplab.cn/zhangle/morphix-nlp /manual /node12.html*

Appendix A: A part of stop word list

本月 乒乓 扑通 比较 毕竟 必定 必然 嘻嘻
也不 别看 别说 何必 哎呀 我国 起来 来着
啊 按 吧 把 被 比 彼 必 边 便 别 并 不
到 得 等 点 顶 都 对 吨 多 俄 而 耳 尔

Appendix B: An example of news article

藏人文化网站正式启动

本报兰州电 记者阿旦增报道：由甘肃雪域藏人文化传播有限责任公司创办的藏人文化网站（www．tibetcul．com），经过近一年的筹建，日前在兰州正式启动。

据介绍，以"盘点藏族文化精英、整合藏族文化队伍、展示藏族文化规模、弘扬藏族文化精神"为宗旨的藏人文化网是一个纯文化专业网站。网站设有唐古拉风、藏人之友等 9 个频道。网站总监旺秀才丹表示，藏人文化网将倾力关注当代藏族人的文化和生活，反映当代藏族人的精神世界以及他们在 21 世纪社会转型和文化重建时期崭新的精神、文化、生活风貌。

Appendix C: Terms extracted from Appendix B.

Word Based (Top 10 terms with score of equation (4))

文化(12.49), 藏人文化网站(12.36), 藏人文化网(5.47), 藏族人的文化和生活(4.94), 藏族文化精神(4.33), 甘肃雪域藏人文化(4.29), 宗旨的藏人文化网(4.17), 藏人之友(3.88), 藏族文化精英(3.60), 藏族文化规模(3.60)

Character Based(Top 11 terms with score equation (4))

文化(13.49), 藏人文化网(10.00), 藏人(9.58), 藏族文化精英(6.78), 宗旨的藏人文化网(6.01), 代藏族人的文化和生活(5.76), 藏人文化网站正式启动(5.45), 弘扬藏族文化精神(5.22), 展示藏族文化规模(4.38), 纯文化专业网站(4.37), 整合藏族文化队伍(4.27)

Using Synonym Relations In Chinese Collocation Extraction

Wanyin Li
Department of Computing,
The Hong Kong Polytechnic University,
Hung Hom, Kowloon, Hong Kong
cswyli@comp.polyu.edu.hk

Qin Lu
Department of Computing,
The Hong Kong Polytechnic University,
Hung Hom, Kowloon, Hong Kong
csluqin @comp.polyu.edu.hk

Ruifeng Xu
Department of Computing, The Hong Kong Polytechnic University,
Hung Hom, Kowloon, Hong Kong
csrfxu@comp.polyu.edu.hk

Abstract

A challenging task in Chinese collocation extraction is to improve both the precision and recall rate. Most lexical statistical methods including Xtract face the problem of unable to extract collocations with lower frequencies than a given threshold. This paper presents a method where HowNet is used to find synonyms using a similarity function. Based on such synonym information, we have successfully extracted synonymous collocations which normally cannot be extracted using the lexical statistical approach. We applied synonyms mapping to each headword to extract more synonymous word bi-grams. Our evaluation over 60MB tagged corpus shows that we can extract synonymous collocations that occur with very low frequency, sometimes even for collocations that occur only once in the training set. Comparing to a collocation extraction system based on Xtract, we have reached the precision rate of 43% on word bi-grams for a set of 9 headwords, almost 50% improvement from precision rate of 30% in the Xtract system. Furthermore, it improves the recall rate of word bi-gram collocation extraction by 30%.

1 Introduction

A Chinese collocation is a recurrent and conventional expression of words which holds syntactic and semantic relations. A widely adopted definition given by Benson (Benson 1990) stated that "*a collocation is an arbitrary and recurrent word combination.*" For example, we say "warm greetings" rather than "hot greetings", "broad daylight" rather than "bright daylight". Similarly, in Chinese "行李" "包裹" "包袱" are three nouns with similar meanings, however, we say "思想包袱" rather than "思想行李", "托运行李"rather than "托运包袱".

Study in collocation extraction using lexical statistics has gained some insights to the issues faced in collocation extraction (Church and Hanks 1990, Smadja 1993, Choueka 1993, Lin 1998). As the lexical statistical approach is developed based on the "recurrence" property of collocations, only collocations with reasonably good recurrence can be extracted. Collocations with low occurrence frequency cannot be extracted, thus affecting the recall rate. The precision rate using the lexical statistics approach can reach around 60% if both word bi-gram extraction and n-gram extractions are taking into account (Smadja 1993, Lin 1997 and Lu et al. 2003). The low precision rate is mainly due to the low precision rate of word bi-gram extractions as only about 30% - 40% precision rate can be achieved for word bi-grams.

In this paper, we propose a different approach to find collocations with low recurrences. The main idea is to make use of synonym relations to extract synonymous collocations. Lin (Lin 1997) described a distributional hypothesis that if two words have similar set of collocations, they are probably similar. In HowNet, Liu Qun (Liu et al. 2002) defined the word similarity as two words that can substitute each other in the context and keep the sentence consistent in syntax and semantic structure. That means, naturally, two similar words are very close to each other and they can be used in place of the other in certain context. For example, we may either say "买书"or "订书" as "卖" and "订" are semantically close to each other. We apply this lexical phenomenal after the lexical statistics based extractor to find the low frequency synonymous collocations, thus increasing recall rate.

The rest of this paper is organized as follows. Section 2 describes related existing collocation extraction techniques based on both lexical statistics and synonymous collocation. Section 3 describes our approach on collocation extraction. Section 4 evaluates the proposed method. Section 5 draws our conclusion and presents possible future work.

2 Related Work

Methods have proposed to extract collocations based on lexical statistics. Choueka (Choueka 1993) applied quantitative selection criteria based on frequency threshold to extract adjacent n-grams (including bi-grams). Church and Hanks (Church and Hanks 1990) employed mutual information to extract both adjacent and distant bi-grams that tend to co-occur within a fixed-size window. But the method did not extend to extract n-grams. Smadja (Smadja 1993) proposed a statistical model by measuring the spread of the distribution of co-occurring pairs of words with higher strength. This method successfully extracted both adjacent and distant bi-grams and n-grams. However, the method failed to extract bi-grams with lower frequency. The precision rate on bi-grams collocation is very low, only around high 20% and low 30%. Even though, it is difficult to measure recall rate in collocation extraction (almost no report on recall estimation), It is understood that low occurrence collocations cannot be extracted. Our research group has further applied the Xtract system to Chinese (Lu et al. 2003) by adjusting the parameters to optimize the algorithm for Chinese and a new weighted algorithm was developed based on mutual information to acquire word bi-grams with one higher frequency word and one lower frequency word. The result has achieved an estimated 5% improvement in recall rate and a 15% improvement in precision comparing to the Xtract system.

All of the above techniques do not take advantage of the wide range of lexical resources available including synonym information. Pearce (Pearce 2001) presented a collocation extraction technique that relies on a mapping from a word to its synonyms for each of its senses. The underlying intuitions is that if the difference between the occurrence counts of one synonyms pair with respect to a particular word was at least two, then this was deemed sufficient to consider them as a collocation. To apply this approach, knowledge in word (concept) semantics and relations to other words must be available such as the use of WordNet. Dagan (Dagan 1997) applied similarity-based smoothing method to solve the problem of data sparseness in statistical natural language processing. The experiments conducted in his later works showed that this method achieved much better results than back-off smoothing methods in word sense disambiguation. Similarly, Hua Wu (Wu and Zhou 2003) applied synonyms relationship between two different languages to automatically acquire English synonymous collocation. This is the first time that the concept synonymous collocation is proposed. A side intuition raised here is that nature language is full of synonymous collocations. As many of them have low occurrences, they are failed to be retrieved by lexical statistical methods. Even though there are Chinese synonym dictionaries, such as 《同义辞林》(Tong Yi Ci Lin), the dictionaries lack structured knowledge and synonyms are too loosely defined to be used for collocation extraction.

HowNet developed by Dong et al (Dong and Dong 1999) is the best publicly available resource on Chinese semantics. By making use of semantic similarities of words, synonyms can be defined by the closeness of their related concepts and the closeness can be calculated. In Section 3, we present our method to extract synonyms from HowNet and using synonym relations to further extract collocations.

Sun (Sun 1997) did a preliminary *Quantitative* analysis on Chinese collocations based on their arbitrariness, recurrence and the syntax structure. The purpose of this study is to help differentiate if a collocation is true or not according to the quantitative factors. By observing the existence of synonyms information in natural language use, we consider it possible to identify different types of collocations using more semantic and syntactic information available. We discuss the basic ideas in section 5..

3 Our Approach

Our method of extracting Chinese collocations consists of three steps.

Step 1: Take the output of any lexical statistical algorithm which extracts word bi-gram collocations. The data is then sorted according to each headword , W_h, with its co-word, W_c, listed.

Step 2: For each headword W_h used to extract bi-grams, we acquire its synonyms based on a similarity function using HowNet. Any word in HowNet having similarity value over a threshold value is chosen as a synonym headword W_s for additional extractions.

Step 3: For each synonym headword, W_s, and the co-word W_c of W_h, as its synonym, if the bi-gram (W_s , W_c) is not in the output of the lexical statistical algorithm in Step one, take this bi-gram (W_s , W_c) as a collocation if the pair co-occurs in the corpus by additional search to the corpus.

3.1 Structure of HowNet

Different from WordNet or other synonyms dictionary, HowNet describes words as a set of concepts(义项) and each concept is described by a set of primitives(义元). The following lists for the word "打", one of its corresponding concepts

NO.=017144
W_C=打
G_C=V
E_C=~网球，~牌，~秋千，~太极，球~得很棒
W_E=play
G_E=V
E_E=
DEF=exercise|锻练,sport|体育

In the above record, DEF is where the primitives are specified. DEF contains up to four types of primitives: the *basic independent primitive* (基本独立义元), the *other independent primitive*(其他独立义元), the *relation primitive* (关系义元), and the *symbol primitive*(符号义元), where the basic independent primitive and the other independent primitive are used to indicate the semantics of a concept and the others are used to indicate syntactical relationships. The similarity model described in the next subsection will consider both of these relationships.

The primitives are linked by a hierarchical tree to indicate the parent-child relationships of the primitives as shown in the following example:

```
entity|实体
  └ thing|万物
      └ physical|物质
          └ animate|生物
              └ AnimalHuman|动物
                  ├ human|人
                  │   └ humanized|拟人
                  └ animal|兽
                      └ beast|走兽
```

This hierarchical structure provides a way to link one concept with any other concept in HowNet, and the closeness of concepts can be simulated by the distance between two concepts.

3.2 Similarity Model Based on HowNet

Liu Qun (Liu 2002) defined word similarity as two words which can substitute each other in the same context and still maintain the sentence consistent syntactically and semantically. This is very close to our definition of synonyms. Thus we directly used their similarity function, which is stated as follows.

A word in HowNet is defined as a set of concepts and each concept is represented by primitives. Thus, HowNet can be described by W, a collection of n words, as:

$W = \{ w_1, w_2, \ldots w_n\}$Each word w_i is, in turn, described by a set of concepts S as:

$W_i = \{ S_{i1}, S_{i2,\ldots} S_{ix}\}$,

And, each concept S_i is, in turn, described by a set of primitives:

$S_i = \{ p_{i1}, p_{i2} \ldots p_{iy}\}$

For each word pair, w_1 and w_2, the similarity function is defined by

$$Sim(w_1, w_2) = \max_{i=1..n,\, j=1...m} Sim(S_{1i}, S_{2j}) \quad (1)$$

where S_{1i} is the list of concepts associated with W_1 and S_{2j} is the list of concepts associated with W_2.

As any concept S_i is presented by its primitives, the similarity of primitives for any p_1, and p_2 of the same type, can be expressed by the following formula:

$$Sim(p_1, p_2) = \frac{\alpha}{Dis(p_1, p_2) + \alpha} \quad (2)$$

where α is an adjustable parameter set to 1.6, and $Dis(p_1, p_2)$ is the path length between p_1 and p_2 based on the semantic tree structure. The above formula where α is a constant does not indicate explicitly the fact that the depth of a pair of nodes in the tree affects their similarity. For two pairs of nodes (p_1, p_2) and (p_3, p_4) with the same distance, the deeper the depth is, the more commonly shared ancestros they would have which should be semantically closer to each other. In following two tree structures, the pair of nodes (p_1, p_2) in the left tree should be more similar than (p_3 , p_4) in the right tree.

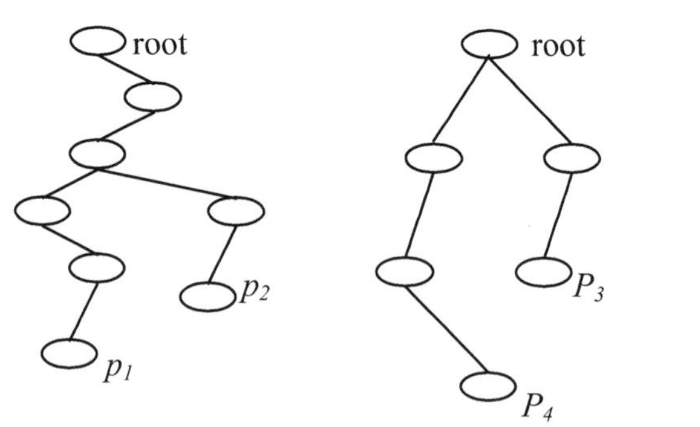

To indicate this observation, α is modified as a function of tree depths of the nodes using the formula $\alpha = min(d(p_1), d(p_2))$. Consequently, the formula (2) is rewritten as formular (2^a) during the experiment.

$$Sim(p_1, p_2) = \frac{\min(d(p_1), d(p_2))}{Dis(p_1, p_2) + \min(d(p_1), d(p_2))} \quad (2^a)$$

where $d(p_i)$ is the depth of node p_i in the tree. The comparison of calculating the word similarity by applying the formula (2) and (2^a) is shown in Section 4.4.

Based on the DEF description in HowNet, different primitive types play different roles only some are directly related to semantics. To make use of both the semantic and syntactic information included in HowNet to describe a word, the similarity of two concepts should take into consideration of all primitive types with weighted considerations and thus the formula is defined as

$$Sim(S_1, S_2) = \sum_{i=1}^{4} \beta_i \prod_{j=1}^{i} Sim_j(p_{1j}, p_{2j}) \quad (3)$$

where β_i is a weighting factor given in (Liu 2002) with the sum of $\beta_1 + \beta_2 + \beta_3 + \beta_4$ being 1, and $\beta_1 \geq \beta_2 \geq \beta_3 \geq \beta_4$. The distribution of the weighting factors is given for each concept a priori in HowNet to indicate the importance of primitive p_i in defining the corresponding concept S.

3.3 Collocation Extraction

In order to extract collocations from a corpus, and to obtain result for **Step 1** of our algorithm, we used the collocation extraction algorithm developed by the research group at the Hong Kong Polytechnic University(Lu et al. 2003). The extraction of bi-gram collocation is based on the English Xtract(Smaja 1993) with improvements. Based on the three Steps mentioned earlier, we will present the extractions in each step in the subsections.

3.3.1 Bi-gram Extraction

Based on the lexical statistical model proposed by Smadja in Xtract on extracting English collocations, an improved algorithm was developed for Chinese collocation by our research group and the system is called CXtract. For easy of understanding, we will explain the algorithm briefly here. According to Xtract, word cooccurence is denoted by a tripplet (w_h, w_i, d) where w_h is a given headword, w_i is a co-word appeared in the corpus in a distance d within the window of [-5, 5]. The frequency f_i of the co-word w_i in the window of [-5, 5] is defined as:

$$f_i = \sum_{j=-5}^{5} f_{i,j} \quad (4)$$

where $f_{i,j}$ is the frequency of the co-word at distance j in the corpus within the window. The average frequency of f_i, denoted by $\overline{f}_i$, is given by

$$\overline{f_i} = \sum_{j=-5}^{5} f_{i,j} / 10 \quad (5)$$

Then, the average frequency $\overline{f}$, and the standard deviation σ are defined by

$$\overline{f} = \frac{1}{n}\sum_{i=1}^{n} f_i \,;\ \sigma = \sqrt{\frac{1}{n}\sum_{i=1}^{n}(f_i - \overline{f})^2} \quad (6)$$

The *Strength* of the co-occurrence for the pair (w_h, w_i,), denoted by k_i, is defined by

$$k_i = \frac{f_i - \overline{f}}{\sigma}, \quad (7)$$

Furthermore, the *Spread* of (w_h, w_i,),, denoted as U_i, which characterizes the distribution of w_i around w_h is define as:

$$U_i = \frac{\sum (f_{i,j} - \overline{f_i})^2}{10}; \quad (8)$$

To eliminate the bi-grams with unlikely co-occurrence, the following sets of threshold values is defined:

$$C1: k_i = \frac{f_i - \overline{f}}{\sigma} \geq K_0 \quad (9)$$

$$C2: U_i \geq U_0 \quad (10)$$

$$C3: f_{i,j} \geq \overline{f_i} + (K_1 \cdot \sqrt{U_i}) \quad (11)$$

However, the above statistical model given by Smadja fails to extract the bi-grams with a much higher frequency of w_h but a relatively low frequency word of w_i,. For example, in the bi-gram棘手问题, freq (棘手) is much lower than the freq (问题). Therefore, we further defined a weighted mutual information to extract this kind of bi-grams:

$$R_i = \frac{f(w_h, w_i)}{f(w_i)} \geq R_0, \quad (12)$$

As a result, the system should return a list of triplets (w_h, w_i, d), where (w_h, w_i,) is considered collocations.

3.3.2 Synonyms Set

For each given headword w_h, before taking it as an input to extract its bi-grams directly, we fist apply the similarity formula described in Equation (1) to generate a set of synonyms headwords W_{syn}:

$$W_{syn} = \{w_s : Sim(w_h, w_s) > \theta\} \quad (13)$$

Where $0 < \theta < 1$ is an algorithm parameter which is adjusted based on experience. We set it as 0.85 from the experiment because we would like to balance the strength of the synonyms relationship and the coverage of the synonyms set. The setting of the parameter $\theta < 0.85$ weaks the similarity strength of the extracted synonyms. For example, for a given collocation "改善关系", that is unlikely to include the candidates "改善护照", "改善契据", "改善通连". On the other hand, by setting the parameter $\theta > 0.85$ will limit the coverage of the synonyms set and hence lose valuable synonyms. For example, for a given bi-gram "重大贡献", we hope to include the candidate synonymous collocations such as "重大成果", "重大成绩", "重大成就". We will show the test of θ in the section 4.2.

This synonyms headwords set provides the possibility to extract the synonymous collocation with the lower frequency that failed to be extracted by lexical statistic.

3.3.3 Synonymous Collocations

A phenomenal among the collocations in natural language is that there are many synonymous collocations exist. For example, 'switch on light' and 'turn on light', "财务问题" and "财政问题". Due to the domain specification of the corpus, some of the synonymous collocations may fail to be extracted by the lexical statistic model because of their lower frequency. Based on this observation, this paper takes a further step. The basic idea is for a bi-gram collocation (w_h, w_c, d) we select the synonyms w_s of w_h with the maximum similarity respect to all the concepts contained by w_h, we deem (w_s, w_c, d) as a collocation if its occurrence is greater than 1 in the corpus. There are similar works discussed by Pearce (Pearce 2001). .

For a given collocation (w_s, w_c, d), if $w_s \in W_{syn}$, then we deem the triple (w_s, w_c, d) as a synonymous collocation with respect to the collocation (w_h, w_c, d) if the co-occurrence of (w_s, w_c, d) in the corpus is greater than one. Therefore, we define the collection of synonymous collocations C_{syn} as:

$$C_{syn} = \{(w_s, w_c, d) : Freq(w_s, w_c, d) > 1\} \quad (14)$$

where $w_s \in W_{syn}$.

4 Evaluation

The performance of collocation is normally evaluated by precision and recall as defined below.

$$precision = \frac{number\ of\ correct\ Extracted\ Collocations}{total\ number\ of\ extracted\ Collocations} \quad (15)$$

$$recall = \frac{number\ of\ correct\ Extracted\ Collocations}{total\ number\ of\ actual\ Collocations} \quad (16)$$

To evaluate the performance of our approach, we conducted a set of experiments based on 9 selected headwords. A baseline system using only lexical statistics given in 3.3.1 is used to get a set of baseline data called Set A. The output using our algorithm is called Set B. Results are checked by hand for validation on what is true collocation and what is not a true collocation.

F_5	F_4	F_3	F_2	F_1	Headwo	F1	F2
*	*	*	*	*	重大	突破	*
*	*	*	*	*	重大	问题	*
*	*	*	*	*	重大	貢獻	*
*	*	*	*	*	重要	成果	*
*	*	*	*	*	重要	問題	*
*	*	*	*	*	重要	指示	*
*	*	*	*	*	重要	论述	*
*	*	*	*	*	重要	批示	*
*	*	*	作出	了	重要	贡献	*
*	*	*	*	占有	重要	地位	*
*	*	*	*	*	根本	改观	*
*	*	*	*	*	根本	好转	*
*	两	国	人民	的	根本	利益	*
*	*	*	*	*	基本	原则	*
*	*	*	*	*	基本	国策	*
*	*	*	*	*	基本	生活费	*
*	*	*	党	的	基本	路线	*
*	*	*	党	的	基本	理论	*

Table 1. Sample table for the true collocation with headword "重要"

F_5	F_4	F_3	F_2	F_1	Head	F1	F2	F3	F4	F5
*	*	*	*	个	重要	*	*	*	*	*
*	*	工作	*	*	重要	*	*	*	*	*
*	*	关系	*	*	重要	*	*	*	*	*
国	*	*	*	*	重要	*	*	*	*	*
*	*	工作	*	*	重大	*	*	*	*	*
*	*	关系	*	*	重大	*	*	*	*	*
*	*	*	*	国家	重大	*	*	*	*	*
*	*	*	*	进行	重大	*	*	*	*	*
我国	*	*	*	*	重大	*	*	*	*	*
我们	*	*	*	*	重大	*	*	*	*	*
*	*	*	*	有	重大	*	*	*	*	*
*	*	*	*	*	根本	*	是	*	*	*
*	两	国	人民	的	根本	利益	*	*	*	*
*	*	*	*	最	根本	的	*	*	*	*
*	*	交通	*	的	根本	出路	在于	科学化	*	*
*	关系	*	*	*	基础	*	*	*	*	*
*	社会	*	*	*	基础	*	*	*	*	*
*	*	*	*	原则	基础	上	*	*	*	*
*	*	*	*	*	基础	打	牢	*	*	*

Table 2. Sample table for the bi-grams that are not true collocations

Table 1 shows samples of extracted word bi-grams using our algorithm that are considered synonymous collocations for the headword "重要". **Table 2** shows extracted bi-grams by our algorithm that are not considered true collocations.

4.1 Test Set

Our experiment is based on a corpus of six months tagged People Daily with 11 millions number of words. For word bi-gram extractions, we consider only content words, thus headwords are selected from noun, verb and adjective only. For evaluation purpose, we selected randomly 3 nouns, 3 verbs and 3 adjectives with frequency of low, medium and high. Thus, in **Step 1** of the algorithm, 9 headwords were used to extract bi-gram collocations from the corpus, and 253 pairs of collocations were extracted. Evaluation by hand has identified 77 true collocations in Set A test set. The overall precision rate is 30% (see Table 3).

	Noun+Verb +Adjective
Headword	9
Extracted Bi-grams	253
True collocations using lexical statistics only	77
Precision rate	30%

Table 3: Statistics in test set for set A

Using **Step 2** of our algorithm, where $\theta=0.85$ is used, we have obtained 55 synonym headwords (include the 9 headwords). Out of these 55 synonyms, 614 bi-gram pairs were then extracted from the lexical statistics based algorithm, in which 179 are consider true collocations. Then, by applying **Step 3** of our algorithm, we extracted an additional 201 bi-gram pairs, among them, 178 are considered true collocations. Therefore, using our algorithm, the overall precision rate has achieved 43%, an improvement of almost 50%. The data is summarized in **Table 4.**

	n., v, and adj.
Synonyms headword	55
Bi-grams (lexical statistics)	614
Non-synonym collocations (lexical statistics only)	179
Extracted synonym collocations Step 2	201
True synonym collocations using Step 2	178
Overall precision rate	43%

Table 4: Statistics in test set for mode B

4.2 The choice of θ

We also conducted a set of experiments to choose the best value for the similarity function's threshold θ. We tested the best value of θ with both the precision rate and the estimated recall rate using the so called remainder bi-grams. The remainder bi-grams is the total number of bi-grams extracted by the algorithm. When precision goes up, the size of the result is smaller, which in a way is an indicator of less recalled collocations. **Figure 1** shows the precision rate and the estimated recall rate in testing the value of θ.

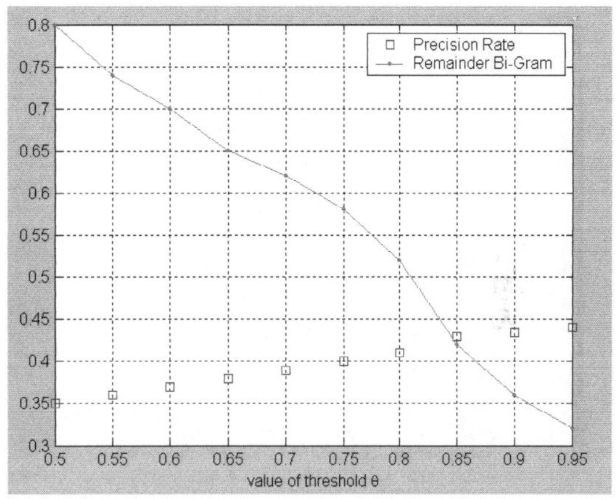

Figure 1. Precision Rate vs. value of θ

From Figure 1, it is obvious that at $\theta=0.85$ the recall rate starts to drop more drastically without much incentive for precision.

	Extracted Bi-grams using lexical statistics	Extracted Synonyms Collocations using Step 2
(1.2,1.4,12)	465	328
(1.4,1.4,12)	457	304
(1.4,1.6,12)	394	288
(1.2,1.2,12)	513	382
(1.2,1.2,14)	503	407
(1.2,1.2,16)	481	413

Table 5: Value of (K_0, K_1, U_0).

4.3 The test of (K_0, K_1, U_0)

The original threshold for CXtract is *(1.2, 1.2, 12)* for the parameters (K_0, K_1, U_0). However, with synonyms collocations, we have also conducted some experiments to see whether the parameters should be adjusted. **Table 5** shows the statistics to test the value of (K_0, K_1, U_0). The similarity threshold θ was fixed at 0.85 throughout the experiments.

The experimental shows that varying the value of (k_0, k_1) does not bring any benefit to our algorithm. However, increasing the value of u_0 did improve the extraction of synonymous collocations. **Figure 2** shows that $U_0 = 14$ is a good trade-off for the precision rate and the remainder Bi-grams. The basic meaning behind the result is reasonable. According to Smadja, U_0 defined in the formula (8) represents the co-occurrence distribution of the candidate collocation (w_h, w_c) in the position of d ($-5 \leqslant d \leqslant 5$). For a true collocation (w_h, w_c, d), its co-occurrence in the position d is much higher than in other positions which leads to a peak in the co-occurrence distribution. Therefore, it is selected by the statistical algorithm based on the formula (10). Based on the physical meaning behind, one way to improve the precision rate is to increase the value of the threshold U_0. A side effect to an increased value of U_0 is that the recall is decreased because some true collocations do not meet the condition of co-occurrence greater than U_0. Step 2 of the new algorithm regains some true collocations lost because of a higher U_0 in Step 1.

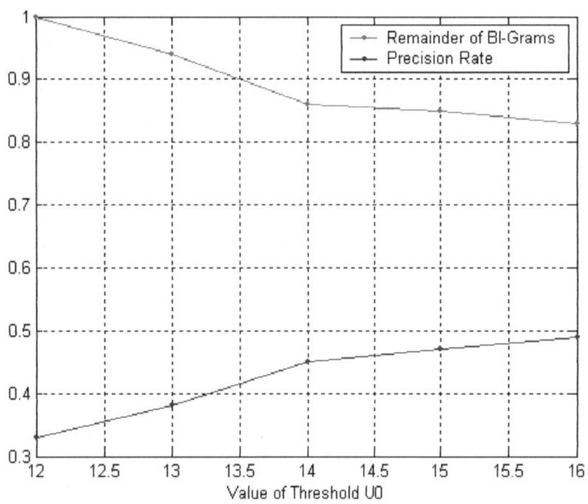

Figure 2. Precision Rate vs. Value of U_0

4.4 The comparison of similarity calculation based on formula (2) and (2^a)

Table 6 shows the similarity value given by formula (2) where α is a constant given the value 1.6 and by formula (2^a) where α is replaced by a function of the depths of the nodes. Results show that (2^a) is more fine tuned and reflects the nature of the data better. For example, 工人 and 农民 are more similar than 工人 and 运动员. 粉红 and 红 are much similar but not the same.

Word 1	Word 2	Formula (2)	Formula (2^a)
男人	女人	0.86	0.95
男人	父亲	1.00	1.00
男人	和尚	0.86	0.95
男人	高兴	0.05	0.10
工人	农民	0.72	0.88
工人	运动员	0.72	0.88
中国	美国	0.94	0.92
粉红	红	1.00	0.92
粉红	红色	1.00	0.92
十分	非常	1.00	1.00
十分	特别	0.62	0.95
考虑	思想	0.70	1.00
思考	考虑	1.00	1.00

Table 6: comparison of similarity calculation

5 Conclusion and Further Work

In this paper, we have presented a method to extract bi-gram collocations using lexical statistics model with synonyms information. Our method reaches the precision rate of 43% for the tested data. Comparing to the precision of 30% using lexical statistics only, our improvement is close to 50%. In additional, the recall improved 30%. The contribution is that we have made use of synonym information which is plentiful in the natural language use and it works well to supplement the shortcomings of lexical statistical method.

Manning claimed that the lack of valid substitution for a synonym is a characteristics of collocations in general (Manning and Schutze 1999). To extend our work, we consider the use of synonym information can be further applied to help identify collocations of different types.

Our preliminary study has suggested that collocation can be classified into 4 types:

Type 0 Collocation: Fully fixed collocation which include some idioms, proverbs and sayings such as "缘木求鱼" "釜底抽薪" and so on.

Type 1 Collocation: Fixed collocation in which the appearance of one word implies the co-occurrence of another one such as "裁减 员额".

Type 2 Collocation: Strong collocation which allows very limited substitution of the components, for example, "裁减 职位", "减少职位", "缩减职位" and so on.

Type 3 Collocation: Normal collocation which allows more substitution of the components, however a limitation is still required. For example, "减少 开支" "缩减 开支" "压缩开支" "消减开支".

By using synonym information and define substitutability, we can validate whether collocations are fixed collocations, strong collocations with very limited substitutions, or general collocations that can be substituted more freely.

6 Acknowledgements

Our great thanks to Dr. Liu Qun of the Chinese Language Research Center of Peking University for letting us share their data structure in the Synonyms Similarity Calculation. This work is partially supported by the Hong Kong Polytechnic University (Project Code A-P203) and CERG Grant (Project code 5087/01E)

References

M. Benson, 1990. *Collocations and General Purpose Dictionaries.* International Journal of Lexicography, 3(1): 23-35

Y. Choueka, 1993. *Looking for Needles in a Haystack or Locating Interesting Collocation Expressions in Large Textual Database.* Proceedings of RIAO Conference on User-oriented Content-based Text and Image Handling: 21-24, Cambridge.

K. Church, and P. Hanks, 1990. *Word Association Norms, Mutual Information,and Lexicography.* Computational Linguistics, 6(1): 22-29.

I. Dagan, L. Lee, and F. Pereira. 1997. *Similarity-based method for word sense disambiguation.* Proceedings of the 35th Annual Meeting of ACL: 56-63, Madrid, Spain.

Z. D. Dong and Q. Dong. 1999. *Hownet*, http://www.keenage.com

D. K. Lin, 1997. *Using Syntactic Dependency as Local Context to Resolve Word Sense Ambiguity.* Proceedings of ACL/EACL-97: 64-71, Madrid, Spain

Q. Liu, 2002. *The Word Similarity Calculation on <<HowNet>>.* Proceedings of 3rd Conference on Chinese lexicography, TaiBei

Q. Lu, Y. Li, and R. F. Xu, 2003. *Improving Xtract for Chinese Collocation Extraction.* Proceedings of IEEE International Conference on Natural Language Processing and Knowledge Engineering, Beijing

C. D. Manning and H. Schutze, 1999. *Foundations of Statistical Natural Language Processing.* The MIT Press, Cambridge, Massachusetts

D. Pearce, 2001. *Synonymy in Collocation Extraction.* Proceedings of NAACL'01 Workshop on Wordnet and Other Lexical Resources: Applications, Extensions and Customizations

F. Smadja, 1993. *Retrieving collocations from text: Xtract.* Computational Linguistics, 19(1): 143-177

H. Wu, and M. Zhou, 2003. *Synonymous Collocation Extraction Using Translation Information.* Proceeding of the 41st Annual Meeting of ACL

D. K. Lin, 1998. *Extracting collocations from text corpora.* In Proc. First Workshop on Computational Terminology, Montreal, Canada.

M. S. Sun, C. N. Huang and J. Fang, 1997. *Preliminary Study on Quantitative Study on Chinese Collocations.* ZhongGuoYuWen, No.1, 29-38, (in Chinese).

The Construction of A Chinese Shallow Treebank

Ruifeng Xu
Dept. Computing,
The Hong Kong Polytechnic University,
Kowloon, Hong Kong
csrfxu@comp.polyu.edu.hk

Qin Lu
Dept. Computing,
The Hong Kong Polytechnic University,
Kowloon, Hong Kong
csluqin@comp.polyu.edu.hk

Yin Li
Dept. Computing,
The Hong Kong Polytechnic University,
Kowloon, Hong Kong
csyinli@comp.polyu.edu.hk

Wanyin Li
Dept. Computing,
The Hong Kong Polytechnic University,
Kowloon, Hong Kong
cswyli@comp.polyu.edu.hk

Abstract

This paper presents the construction of a manually annotated Chinese shallow Treebank, named *PolyU Treebank*. Different from traditional Chinese Treebank based on full parsing, the PolyU Treebank is based on shallow parsing in which only partial syntactical structures are annotated. This Treebank can be used to support shallow parser training, testing and other natural language applications. Phrase-based Grammar, proposed by Peking University, is used to guide the design and implementation of the PolyU Treebank. The design principles include good resource sharing, low structural complexity, sufficient syntactic information and large data scale. The design issues, including corpus material preparation, standard for word segmentation and POS tagging, and the guideline for phrase bracketing and annotation, are presented in this paper. Well-designed workflow and effective semiautomatic and automatic annotation checking are used to ensure annotation accuracy and consistency. Currently, the PolyU Treebank has completed the annotation of a 1-million-word corpus. The evaluation shows that the accuracy of annotation is higher than 98%.

1 Introduction

A Treebank can be defined as a syntactically processed corpus. It is a language resource containing annotations of information at various linguistic levels such as words, phrases, clauses and sentences to form a 'bank of linguistic trees'. There are many Treebanks built for different languages such as the Penn Treebank (Marcus 1993), ICE-GB (Wallis 2003), and so on. The Penn Chinese Treebank is an important resource (Xia et al. 2000; Xue et al. 2002). Its annotation is based on Head-driven Phrase Structure Grammar (HPSG). The corpus of 100,000 Chinese words has been manually annotated with a strict quality assurance process. Another important work is the Sinica Treebank at the Academic Sinica, Taiwan (Chen et al. 1999; Chen et al. 2003). Information-based Case Grammar (ICG) was selected as the language framework. A head-driven chart parser was performed to do phrase bracketing and annotating. Then, manual post-editing was conducted. According to the report, The Sinica Treebank contains 38,725 parsed trees with 329,532 words.

Most reported Chinese Treebanks, including the two above, are based on full parsing which requires complete syntactical analysis including determining syntactic categories of words, locating chunks that can be nested, finding relations between phrases and resolving the attachment ambiguities. The output of full parsing is a set of complete syntactic trees. Automatic full parsing, however, is difficult to achieve good performance. Shallow parsing (or partial parsing) is usually defined as a parsing process aiming to provide a limited amount of local syntactic information such as non-recursive noun phrases, V-O structures and S-V structures etc. Since shallow parsing can recognize the backbone of a sentence more effectively and accurately with lower cost, people has in recent years started to work using results from shallow parsing. A shallow parsed Treebank can be used to extract information for different applications especially for training shallow parsers.

Different from full parsing, annotation to a shallow Treebank is only targeted at certain local structures in a sentence. The depth of "shallowness" and the scope of annotation vary from different reported work. Thus, two issues in shallow Treebank annotation is (1) what information and (2) to what depths the syntactic information should be annotated. Generally speaking, the degree of "shallowness" and the syntactical labeling are determined by the requirement of the serving applications. The choice of full parsing or shallow parsing is dependent on the need of the application including resources and the capability of system to be developed (Xia et al. 2000; Chen et al. 2000; Li et al. 2003). Currently, there is no large-scale shallow annotated Treebank available as a publicly resource for training and testing.

In this paper, we present a manually annotated shallow Treebank, called the *PolyU Treebank*. It is targeted to contain 1-million-word contemporary Chinese text. The whole work on the PolyU Treebank follows the Phrase-based Grammar proposed by Peking University (Yu et al. 1998). In this language framework, a phrase, lead by a lexical word(or sometimes called a content word) as a head, is considered the basic syntactical unit in a Chinese sentence. The building of the PolyU Treebank was originally designed as training data for a shallow parser used for Chinese collocation extraction. From linguistics viewpoint, a collocation occurs only in words within a phrase, or between the headwords of related phrases (Zhang and Lin 1992). Therefore, the use of syntactic information is naturally considered an effective way to improve the performance of collocation extraction systems. The typical problems like *doctor-nurse* (Church and Hanks 1990) could be avoided by using such information. When employing syntactical information in collocation extraction, we restrict ourselves to identify the stable phrases in the sentences with certain levels of nesting. Thus it has motivated us to produce a shallow Treebank.

A natural way to obtain a shallow Treebank is through extracting shallow structures from a fully parsed Treebank. Unfortunately, all the available fully parsed Treebank, such as the Penn Treebank and the Sinica Treebank, are annotated using different grammars than our chosen Phrase-based Grammar. Also, the sizes of these Treebank are much smaller in scale to be useful for training our shallow parser.

This paper presents the most important design issues of the PolyU Treebank and the quality control mechanisms. The rest of this paper is organized as follows. Section 2 introduces the overview and design principles. Section 3 to Section5, present the design issues on corpus material preparation, the standard for word segmentation and POS tagging, and the guideline for phrase bracketing and labeling, respectively. Section 6 discusses the quality assurance mechanisms including a carefully designed workflow, parallel annotation, and automatic and semi-automatic post-annotation checking. Section 7 gives the current progress and future work.

2 Overview and Design Principles

The objective of this project is to manually construct a large shallow Treebank with high accuracy and consistency.

The design principles of The PolyU Treebank are: high resource sharing ability, low structural complexity, sufficient syntactic information and large data scale. First of all, the design and construction of The PolyU Treebank aims to provide as much a general purpose Treebank as possible so that different applications can make use of it as a NLP resource. With this objective, we chose to follow the well-known Phrase-based Grammar as the framework for annotation as this grammar is widely accepted by Chinese language researchers, and thus our work can be easily understood and accepted.

Due to the lack of word delimitation in Chinese, word segmentation must be performed before any further syntactical annotation. High accuracy of word segmentation is very important for this project. In this project, we chose to use the segmented and tagged corpus of People Daily annotated by the Peking University. The annotated corpus contains articles appeared in the People Daily Newspaper in 1998. The segmentation is based on the guidelines, given in the Chinese national standard GB13715, (Liu et al. 1993) and the POS tagging specification was developed according to the 'Grammatical Knowledge-base of contemporary Chinese'. According to the report from Peking University, the accuracy of this annotated corpus in terms of segmentation and POS tagging are 99.9% and 99.5%, respectively (Yu et al. 2001). The use of such mature and widely adopted resource can effectively reduce our cost, ensure syntactical annotation quality. With consistency in segmentation, POS, and syntactic annotation, the resulting Treebank can be readily shared by other researchers as a public resource.

The second design principle is low structural complexity. That means, the annotation framework should be clear and simple, and the labeled syntactic and functional information should be commonly used and accepted. Considering the characteristics of shallow annotation, our project has focused on the annotation of phrases and headwords while the sentence level syntax are ignored.

Following the framework of Phrase-based Grammar, a *base-phrase* is regarded as the smallest unit where a base-phrase is defined as a 'stable' and 'simple' phrase without nesting components. Study on Chinese syntactical analysis suggests that phrases should be the fundamental unit instead of words in a sentence. This is because, firstly, the usage of Chinese words is very flexible. A word may have different POS tags serving for different functions in sentences. On the contrary, the use of Chinese phrases is much more stable. That is, a phrase has very limited functional use in a sentence. Secondly, the construction rules of Chinese phrases are nearly the same as that of Chinese sentences. Therefore, the analysis of phrases can help identifying POS and grammatical functions of words. Naturally, it should be regarded as the basic syntactical unit. Usually, a base-phrase is driven by a lexical word as its headword. Examples of base-phrases include base NP, base VP and so on, such as the sample shown below.

[市场/n 经济/n]NP [团体/n 旅客/n]NP

Using base-phrases as the start point, nested levels of phrases are then identified, until the maximum phrases (will be defined later) are identified. Since we do not intend to provide full parsing information, there has to be a limit on the level of nesting. For practical reasons, we choose to limit the nesting of brackets to 3 levels. That means, the depth of our shallow parsed Treebank will be limited to 3. This restriction can limit the structural complexity to a manageable level.

Our nested bracketing is not strictly bottom up. That is we do not simply extend from base-phrase and move up until the 3rd level. Instead, we first identify the *maximal-phrase* which is used to identify the backbone of the sentence. The maximal-phrase provides the framework under which the base-phrases of up to 2 levels can be identified. The principles for the identification of scope and depth of phrase bracketing are briefly explained below and the operating procedure is indicated by the given order in which these principles are presented. More details is given in Section 5.

Step 1: Annotation of maximal-phrase which is the shortest word sequence of maximally spanning non-overlapping edges which plays a distinct semantic role of a predicate. A maximal-phrase contains two or more lexical words.

Step 2: Annotation of base-phrases within a maximal-phrase. In case a base-phrase and a maximal-phrase are identical and the maximal-phrase is already bracketed in Step 1, no bracketing is done in this step. For each identified base-phrase, its headword will be marked.

Step 3: Annotation of next level of bracketing, called mid-phrase which is expended from a base-phrase. A mid-phrase is annotated only if it is deemed necessary. The process starts from the identified base-phrase. One more level of syntactical structure is then bracketed if it exists within the maximal-phrase.

The third design principle is to provide sufficient syntactical information for natural language application even though shallow annotation does not necessarily contain complete syntactic information at sentence level. Some past research in Chinese shallow parsing were on single level base-phrases only (Sun 2001). However, for certain applications, such as for collocation extraction, identification of base-phrases only are not very useful. In this project, we have decided to annotate phrases within three levels of nesting within a sentence. For each phrase, a label is be given to indicate its syntactical information, and an optional semantic or structural label is given if applicable. Furthermore, the headword of a base-phrase is annotated. We believe these information are sufficient for many natural language processing research work and it is also manageable for this project within its working schedule.

Fourthly, aiming to support practical language processing, a reasonably large annotated Treebank is expected. Studies on English have shown that Treebank of word size 500K to 1M is reasonable for syntactical structure analysis (Leech and Garside 1996). In consideration of the resources available and the reference of studies on English, we have set out our Treebank size to be one million words. We hope such a reasonably large-scale data can effectively support some language research, such as collocation extraction.

We chose to use the XML format to record the annotated data. Other information such as original article related information (author, date, etc.), annotator name, and other useful information are also given through the meta-tags provided by XML. All the meta-tags can be removed by a program to recover the original data.

We have performed a small-scale experiment to compare the annotation cost of shallow annotation and full annotation (followed Penn Chinese Treebank specification) on 500 Chinese sentences by the same annotators. The time cost in shallow annotation is only 25% of that for full annotation. Meanwhile, due to the reduced structural complexity in shallow annotation, the accuracy of first pass shallow annotation is much higher than full annotation.

3 Corpus Materials Preparation

The People Daily corpus, developed by PKU, consists of more than 13k articles totaling 5M words. As we need one million words for our Treebank, we have selected articles covering different areas in different time span to avoid duplications due to short-lived events and news topics. Our selection takes each day's news as one single unit, and then several distant dates are randomly selected among the whole 182 days in the entire collection. We have also decided to keep the original articles' structures and topics indicators as they may be useful for some applications.

4 Word Segmentation and Part-of-Speech Tagging

The articles selected from PKU corpus are already segmented into words following the guidelines given in GB13715. The annotated corpus has a basic lexicon of over 60,000 words. We simply use this segmentation without any change and the accuracy is claimed to be 99.9%.

Each word in the PKU corpus is given a POS tag. In this tagging scheme, a total of 43 POS tags are listed (Yu et al. 2001). Our project takes the PKU POS tags with only notational changes explained as follows:

The morphemes tags including *Ag* (Adjectives morphemes), *Bg, Dg, Ng, Mg, Rg, Tg, Qg,* and *Ug* are re-labeled as lowercase letters, *ag, bg, dg, ng, mg, rg, tg, qg* and *ug*, respectively. This modification is to ensure consistent labeling in our system where the lower cases are used to indicate word-level tags and upper cases are used to indicate phrase-level labels.

5 Phrase Bracketing and Annotation

Phrase bracketing and annotation is the core part of this project. Not only all the original annotated files are converted to XML files, results of our annotations are also given in XML form. The meta tags provided by XML are very helpful for further processing and searching to the annotated text. .

Note that in our project, the basic phrasal analysis looks at the context of a clause, not a sentence. Here, the term *clause* refers the text string ended by some punctuations including comma (,), semicolon (;), colon (:), or period (.). Certain punctuation marks such as ‘、’, ‘<’, and ’>’ are not considered clause separators. For example,

经过严密侦查，警方锁定了 2 个嫌疑人。

is considered having two clauses and thus will be bracketed separately. It should be pointed out that he set of Chinese punctuation marks are different from that of English and their usage can also be different. Therefore, an English sentence and their Chinese translation may use different punctuation marks. For example, the sentence

汤姆、约翰、和杰克一起回学校

is the translation of the English ‘*Tom, John, and Jack go back to school together*’ , which uses ‘、’ rather than comma(,) to indicate parallel structures, and is thus considered one clause.

Each clause will then be processed according to the principles discussed in Section 2. The symbols ‘[’ and ‘]’ are used to indicate the left and right boundaries of a phrase. The right bracket is appended with syntactic labels as described in the general form of [Phrase]SS-FF, where SS is a mandatory syntactic label such as *NP*(noun phrase) and *AP*(adjective phrase), and FF is an optional label indicating internal structures and semantic functions such as *BL*(parallel), *SB*(a noun is the object of verb within a verb phrase). A total of 21 SS labels and 20 FF labels are given in our phrase annotation specification. For example, the functional label *BL* identifies parallel components in a phrase as indicated in the example [荣誉/n 与/c 尊严/n]NP-BL.

As in another example shown below,

[美国/ns 科学家/n]NP [绘制/v# 出/v]VP-SBU
[X 染色体/n 的/u [高/a 精度/n 图谱/n]NP]NP

the phrase [绘制/v 出/v] is a verb phrase, thus it is labeled as *VP*. Furthermore, the verb phrase can be further classified as a verb-complement type. Thus an additional SBU function label is marked. We should point out that since the FF labels are not syntactical information and are thus not expected to be used by any shallow parsers. The FF labels carry structural and/or semantic information which are of help in annotation. We consider it useful for other applications and thus decide to keep them in the Treebank. **Appendix 1** lists all the FF labels used in the annotation.

5.1 Identification of Maximal-phrase:

The maximal-phrases are the main syntactical structures including subject, predicate, and objects in a clause. Again, maximal-phrase is defined as the phrase with the maximum spanning non-overlapping length, and it is a predicate playing a distinct semantic role and containing more than one lexical word. That means a maximal-phrase contains at least one base-phrase. As this is the first stage in the bracketing process, no nesting should occur. In the following annotated sentence,

[中国/ns 旅游年/n]NP 是/v [一/m 次/q 国家级/b 的/u 宣传/vn 促销/vn 活动/vn]NP (Eg.1)

there are two separate maximal-phrases, [中国/ns 旅游年/n]NP , and [一/m 次/q 国家级/b 的/u 宣传/vn 促销/vn 活动/vn]NP. Note that 是/v is considered a base-phrase, but not a maximal-phrase because it contains only one lexical word. Unlike many annotations where the object of a sentence is included as a part of the verb phrase, we treat them as separate maximal-phrases both due to our requirement and also for reducing nesting.

If a clause is completely embedded in a larger clause, it is considered a special clause and given a special name called an *internal clause* . We will bracket such an internal clause as a maximal phrase with the tag *‘IC’* as shown in the following example,

[极大/a 地/u 鼓舞/v]VP [全党/n 和/c 全国/n 各族/r 人民/n 更加/d 紧密/a 地/u 团结/v 起来/v]IC

5.2 Annotation of Base-phrases:

A base-phrase is the phrase with stable, close and simple structure without nesting components. Normally a base-phrase contains a lexical word as headword. Taking the maximal-phrase [一/m 次/q 国家级/b 的/u 宣传/vn 促销/vn 活动/vn]NP in Eg.1 as an example, [一/m 次/q]QP and [宣传/vn 促销/vn 活动/vn]NP, are base-phrases in this maximal-phrase. Thus, the sentence is annotated as

[中国/ns 旅游年/n]NP 是/v

[[一/m 次/q]QP-ML 国家级/b 的/u [宣传/vn 促销/vn 活动/vn]NP]NP

In fact, [中国/ns 旅游年/n]NP and 是/v are also base-phrases. 是/v is not bracketed because it is a single lexical word as a base-phrase without any ambiguity and it is thus by default not being bracketed. [中国/ns 旅游年/n]NP is not further bracketed because it overlaps with a maximal-phrase. Our annotation principle here is that if a base-phrase overlaps with a maximal-phrase, it will not be bracketed twice.

The identification of base-phrase is done only within an already identified maximal-phrase. In other words, if a base-phrase is identified, it must be nested inside a maximal-phrase or at most overlaps with it. It should be pointed out that the identification of a base-phrase is the most fundamental and most important goal of Treebank annotation. The identification of maximal-phrases can be considered as parsing a clause using a top-down approach. On the other hand, the identification of a base-phrase is a bottom up approach to find the most basic units within a maximal-phrase.

5.3 Mid-Phrase Identification:

Due to the fact that sometimes there may be more syntactic structures between the base-phrases and maximal-phrases, this step uses base-phrase as the starting point to further identify one more level of the syntactical structure in a maximal-phrase. Takes Eg.1 as an example, it is further annotated as

[中国/ns 旅游年/n]NP 是/v [[一/m 次/q]QP-ML
[国家级/b 的/u [宣传/vn 促销/vn 活动/vn]NP]NP]NP

where the underlined text shows the additional annotation.

As we only limit our nesting to three levels, any further nested phrases will be ignored. The following sentence shows the result of our annotation with three levels of nesting:

[目前/t [企业/n 集团/n 发展/vn]NP [值得/v 注意/v
的/u [[几/m 个/q]QP 问题/n]NP]NP]NP

However, a full annotation should have 4 levels of nesting as shown below. The underlined text is the 4th level annotation skipped by our system.

[目前/t [企业/n 集团/n 发展/vn [值得/v 注意/v 的/u
[[几/m 个/q]QP 问题/n]NP]NP]NP]NP

5.4 Annotation of Headword

In our system, a '#' tag will be appended after a word to indicate that it is a headword of the base-phrase. Here, a headword must be a lexical word rather than a function word.

In most cases, a headword stays in a fixed position of a base-phrase. For example, the headword of a noun phrase is normally the last noun in this phrase. Thus, we call this position the default position. If a headword is in the default position, annotation is not needed. Otherwise, a '#' tag is used to indicate the headword.

For example, in a clause,

[美国/ns 科学家/n]NP [绘制/v 出/v]VP-SBU,

[绘制/v 出/v] is a verb phrase, and the headword of the phrase is 绘制/v, which is not in the default position of a verb phrase. Thus, this phrase is further annotated as:

[美国/ns 科学家/n]NP [绘制/v# 出/v]VP-SBU

Note that 科学家/n is also a headword, but since it is in the default position, no explicit annotation is needed.

6 Annotation and Quality Assurance

Our research team is formed by four people at the Hong Kong Polytechnic University, two linguists from Beijing Language and Culture University and some research collaborators from Peking University. Furthermore, the annotation work has been conducted by four post-graduate students in language studies and computational linguistics from the Beijing Language and Culture University.

The annotation work is conducted in 5 separate stages to ensure quality output of the annotation work. The preparation of annotation specification and corpus selection was done in the first stage. Researchers in Hong Kong invited two linguists from China to come to Hong Kong to prepare for the corpus collection and selection work. A thorough study on the reported work in this area was conducted. After the project scope was defined, the SS labels and the FF labels were then defined. A Treebank specification was then documented. The Treebank was given the name PolyU Treebank to indicate that it is produced at the Hong Kong Polytechnic University. In order to validate the specifications drafted, all the six members first manually annotated 10k-word material, separately. The outputs were then compared, and the problems and ambiguities occurred were discussed and consolidated and named Version 1.0. Stage 1 took about 5 months to complete. Details of the specification can be downloaded from the project website www.comp.polyu.edu.hk/~cclab.

In Stage 2, the annotators in Beijing were then involved. They had to first study the specification and understand the requirement of the annotation. Then, the annotators under the supervision of a team member in Stage 1 annotated 20k-word materials together and discussed the problems occurred.

During this two-month work, the annotators were trained to understand the specification. The emphasis at this stage was to train the annotators' good understanding of the specification as well as consistency by each annotator and consistency by different annotators. Further problems occurred in the actual annotation practice were then solved and the specification was also further refined or modified.

In Stage 3, which took about 2 months, each annotator was assigned 40k-word material each in which 5k-words material were duplicate annotated to all the annotators. Meanwhile, the team members in Hong Kong also developed a post-annotation checking tool to verify the annotation format, phrase bracketing, annotation tags, and phrase marks to remove ambiguities and mistakes. Furthermore, an evaluation tool was built to check the consistency of annotation output. The detected annotation errors were then sent back to the annotators for discussion and correction. Any further problems occurred were submitted for group discussion and minor modification on the specification was also done.

In stage 4, each annotator was dispatched with one set of 50k-word material each time. For each distribution, 15k-word data in each set were distributed to more than two annotators in duplicates so that for any three annotators, there would be 5K duplicated materials. When the annotators finished the first pass annotation, we used the post-annotation checking tool to do format checking in order to remove the obvious annotation errors such as wrong tag annotation and cross bracketing. However, it was quite difficult to check the difference in annotation due to different interpretation of a sentence. What we did was to make use of the annotations done on the duplicate materials to compare for consistency. When ambiguity or differences were identified, discussions were conducted and a result used by the majority would be chosen as the accepted result. The re-annotated results were regarded as the Golden Standard to evaluate the accuracy of annotation and consistency between different annotators. The annotators were required to study this Golden Standard and go back to remove similar mistakes. The annotated 50k data was accepted only after this. Then, a new 50k-word materials was distributed and repeated in the same way. During this stage, the ambiguous and out-of-tag-set phrase structures were marked as *OT* for further process. The annotation specification was not modified in order to avoid frequent revisit to already annotated data. About 4 months were spent on this stage.

In Stage 5, all the members and annotators were grouped and discuss the *OT* cases. Some typical new phrase structure and function types were appended in the specification and thus the final formal annotation specification was established. Using this final specification, the annotators had to go back to check their output, modify the mistakes and substitute the *OT* tags by the agreed tags. Currently, the project was already in Stage 5 with 2 months of work finished. A further 2 months was expected to complete this work.

Since it is impossible to do all the checking and analysis manually, a series of checking and evaluating tools are established. One of the tools is to check the consistency between text corpus files and annotated XML files including checking the XML format, the filled XML header, and whether the original txt material is being altered by accident. This program ensures that the XML header information is correctly filled and during annotation process, no additional mistakes are introduced due to typing errors.

Furthermore, we have developed and trained a shallow parser using the Golden Standard data. This shallow parser is performed on the original text data, and its output and manually annotated result are compared for verification to further remove errors

Now, we are in the process of developing an effective analyzer to evaluate the accuracy and consistency for the whole annotated corpus. For the exactly matched bracketed phrases, we check whether the same phrase labels are given. Abnormal cases will be manually checked and confirmed. Our final goal is to ensure the bracketing can reach 99% accuracy and consistency.

7 Current Progress and Future Work

As mentioned earlier, we are now in Stage 5 of the annotation. The resulting annotation contains 2,639 articles selected from PKU People Daily corpus. These articles contains 1, 035, 058 segmented Chinese words, with on average, around 394 words in each article. There are a total of 284, 665 bracketed phrases including nested phrases. A summary of the different SS labels used are given in Table 1.

NP	NT	NS	NR	NZ	TP	FP
117799	7899	1452	10137	339	5216	2431
S	V	VP	AP	DP	PP	QP
4910	4827	71000	16688	154	25672	9143
DE	SU	XD	IC	BA	BEI	RP
1252	125	178	3889	1010	373	171

Table 1. Statistics of annotated syntactical phrases

For each bracketed phrase, if its FF label does not fit into the corresponding default pattern, (like for the noun phrase(*NP*), the default grammatical structure is that the last noun in the phrase is the headword and other components are the modifiers, using *PZ* tags), its FF labels should then be explicitly labeled. The statistics of annotated FF tags are listed in Table 2.

BL	FZ	ZZ	SBI	SBU	SD	DU
12341	5792	1253	14519	8805	5096	810
FJ	JY	DL	ML	SL	YY	DX
263	2699	26	160	352	507	10172
DD	FS	MD	GJ	SJ	OT	
583	1161	1091	102	2932	5255	

Table 2. Statistics of function and structure tags

For the material annotated by multiple annotators as duplicates, the evaluation program has reported that the accuracy of phrase annotation is higher than 99.5% and the consistency between different annotators is higher than 99.8%. As for other annotated materials, the quality evaluation program preliminarily reports the accuracy of phrase annotation is higher than 98%. Further checking and evaluation work are ongoing to ensure the final overall accuracy achieves 99%.

Up to now, the FF labels of 5,255 phrases are annotated as *OT.* That means about 1.8% (5,255 out of a total of 284,665) of them do not fit into any patterns listed in Table 2. Most of them are proper noun phrase, syntactically labeled as PP. We are investigating these cases and trying to identify whether some of them can be in new function and structure patterns and give a new label.

It is also our intention to further develop our tools to improve the automatic annotation analysis and evaluation program to find out the potential annotation error and inconsistency. Other visualization tools are also being developed to support keyword searching, context indexing, and annotation case searching. Once we complete Stage 5, we intend to make the PolyU Treebank data available for public access. Furthermore, we are developing a shallow parser and using The PolyU Treebank as training and testing data.

Acknowledgement

This project is partially supported by the Hong Kong Polytechnic University (Project Code A-P203) and CERG Grant (Project code 5087/01E)

References

Baoli Li, Qin Lu and Yin Li. 2003. Building a Chinese Shallow Parsed Treebank for Collocation Extraction, *Proceedings of CICLing 2003*: 402-405

Fei Xia, et al. 2000. Developing Guidelines and Ensuring Consistency for Chinese Text Annotation *Proceedings of LREC-2000*, Greece

Feng-yi Chen, et al. 1999. Sinica Treebank, *Computational Linguistics and Chinese Language Processing,* 4(2):183-204

G. N. Leech, R.Garside. 1996. *Running a grammar factory: the production of syntactically analyzed corpora or "treebanks",* Johansson and Stenstron.

Honglin Sun, 2001. *A Content Chunk Parser for Unrestricted Chinese Text,* Ph.D Thesis, Peking University, 2001

Keh-jiann Chen et al. 2003. *Building and Using Parsed Corpora* (Anne Abeillé ed. s) KLUWER, Dordrecht

Kenneth Church, and Patrick Hanks. 1990. Word association norms, mutual information, and lexicography, *Computational Linguistics*, 16(1): 22-29

Marcus, M. et al. 1993. Building a Large Annotated Corpus of English: The Penn Treebank, *Computational Linguistics*, 19(1): 313-330.

Nianwen Xue, et al. 2002. Building a Large-Scale Annotated Chinese Corpus, *Proceedings of COLING 2002*, Taipei, Taiwan

Sean Wallis, 2003. *Building and Using Parsed Corpora* (Anne Abeillé eds) KLUWER, Dordrecht

Shiwen Yu, et al. 1998. *The Grammatical Knowledge- base of contemporary Chinese: a complete specification.* Tsinghua University Press, Beijing, China

Shiwen Yu, et al. 2001. Guideline of People Daily Corpus Annotation, Technical report, Beijing University

Shoukang Zhang and Xingguang Lin, 1992. *Collocation Dictionary of Modern Chinese Lexical Words*, Business Publisher, China

Yuan Liu, et al. 1993. *Segmentation standard for Modern Chinese Information Processing and automatic segmentation methodology.* Tsinghua University Press, Beijing, China

Appendix 1 The structural and semantic FF labels

BL	并列关系	[中国/ns 与/c 南非/ns]NP-BL
FZ	复指关系	[[祖国/n 的/u 心脏/n]NP [天安门/ns 广场/n]NS]NP-FZ
PZ	偏正关系	[稚嫩/a 的/u 娃娃脸/n]NP-PZ
ZZ	状中结构	[全力/n 组织/v]V-ZZ
SBI	述宾关系	[帮助/v 群众/n]V-SBI
SBU	述补关系	[负担/v [过/d 重/a]AP]VP-SBU
SD	顺递关系	[审核/v 发放/v]V-SD
JY	兼语关系	[[切实/ad 帮助/v]VP 群众/n [解决/v 各种/r 实际/a 困难/an]VP-SBI]VP-JY
PO	时间信息	[7 月/t 1 日/t]TP-PO
DU	时段信息	[今后/t 3 /m 年/q]TP-DU
FJ	附加信息	[代表/n 们/k]NP-FJ
DL	动量信息	[十/m 下/v 江南/ns]VP-DL
ML	名量信息	[5 /m 次/q]QP-ML
SL	时量信息	[[第二/m 天/q]QP-SL 4 时/t]TP
YY	原因信息	[因/p 冻/v]PP-YY [因/p 饿/a]PP-YY 死亡/v
DX	对象信息	[向/p [受灾/vn 地区/n]NP]PP-DX
DD	地点信息	[在/p 深圳/ns]PP-DD [参观/v 考察/v]V-BL
FS	方式信息	[通过/p [股票/n 上市/v]S]PP-FS
MD	目的信息	[为/p [发展/v 两岸/n 关系/n]VP-SBI]PP-MD
GJ	工具信息	[用/p 公款/n]PP-GJ 请客/v
SJ	时间信息	[于/p [3 1 日/t 上午/t]TP]PP-SJ
OT	其他	

Appendix 2 Example of an Annotated Article

```
XW_RM_19980402-07-009.xml
<?xml version="1.0" encoding="GB2312" ?>
<!DOCTYPE SPFILE SYSTEM "spfile.dtd">
<SPFILE><!--SPFILE stands for shallow parsed file.  -->
    <metadata>
    <filename>XW_RM_19980402-07-009.xml</filename>
    <source>RENMINRIBAO_19980402</source>
    <annotators>
        <drafter name="Zhang Qian" date="2003-4-26" />
        <reviser name="Linda Li" date="2003-5-2" />
        <reviser name="Ruifeng Xu" date="2003-10-12" />
    </annotators>
    </metadata>
<head><title>[[四千/m 年/q 前/f]TP [尸体/n 防腐/vn 技术/n]NP]NP </title>
    <subtitle> </subtitle> <authors>
    <author name="作者姓名 1" affiliation="作者单位 1" />
    <author name="作者姓名 2" affiliation="作者单位 2" email="a@b.c" /> </authors></head>
<body>
<![CDATA[
19980402-07-009-001/m [[四千/m 年/q 前/f]TP [尸体/n 防腐/vn 技术/n]NP]NP
19980402-07-009-002/m 考古学家/n [[对/p 4 0 0 0/m 多/m 年/q 前/f 的/u 一/m
具/q 埃及/ns 木乃伊/n 进行/v 研究/vn]VP 后/f]TP 发现/v ，/w [[古/a 埃及/ns]NP
人/n]NP [早/a 在/p 那时/r]AP-SBU [就/d 利用/v 香料/n 进行/v [尸体/n 防腐
/vn]VP]VP 。/w
19980402-07-009-003/m [据/p [《/w 华盛顿/ns 邮报/n 》/w 报道/v]S]PP-DX ，/w [[德
国/ns 塔宾根/nz 大学/n]NT 的/u [乌里奇·韦塞尔/nr 等/u 人/n]NP-FZ]NP [对/p [1 9
1 4 年/t 在/p 埃及/ns 基扎/ns 出土/v 的/u [伊杜/nr 的/u 木乃伊/n]NP]NP]PP-DX
进行/v 了/u 检验/vn 。/w
19980402-07-009-004/m 他们/r 发现/v ，/w [其/r 骨骼/n]NP [已经/d [用/p 松脂/n 和
/c 以/p 钠/n 为主/v 的/u 化合物/n]PP-GJ [处理/v 过/u 了/y]VP-SBU]VP 。/w [松脂
/n 和/c [钠/n 化合物/n]NP]NP-BL 具有/v [[防腐/v 和/c 保存/v 尸体/n]VP-BL 的/u
功效/n]NP 。/w 另外/c ，/w 他们/r [还/d 发现/v]VP [[伊杜/nr 遗体/n 的/u 骨骼
/n]NP 浸透/v 了/u [具有/v 保护/vn 作用/n 的/u [粘性/n 物质/n]NP]NP]IC 。/w
19980402-07-009-005/m 伊杜/nr 是/v [[大约/d 公元前/t 2 1 5 0年/t 时/Ng 古/a 埃
及王国/ns 时期/n]TP 的/u [松木/n 贸易/vn 官员/n]NP]NP 。/w
]]></body>
</SPFILE>
```

Combining Prosodic and Text Features for Segmentation of Mandarin Broadcast News

Gina-Anne Levow
University of Chicago
levow@cs.uchicago.edu

Abstract

Automatic topic segmentation, separation of a discourse stream into its constituent stories or topics, is a necessary preprocessing step for applications such as information retrieval, anaphora resolution, and summarization. While significant progress has been made in this area for text sources and for English audio sources, little work has been done in automatic, acoustic feature-based segmentation of other languages. In this paper, we consider exploiting both prosodic and text-based features for topic segmentation of Mandarin Chinese. As a tone language, Mandarin presents special challenges for applicability of intonation-based techniques, since the pitch contour is also used to establish lexical identity. We demonstrate that intonational cues such as reduction in pitch and intensity at topic boundaries and increase in duration and pause still provide significant contrasts in Mandarin Chinese. We build a decision tree classifier that, based only on word and local context prosodic information without reference to term similarity, cue phrase, or sentence-level information, achieves boundary classification accuracy of 84.6-95.6% on a balanced test set. We contrast these results with classification using text-based features, exploiting both text similarity and n-gram cues, to achieve accuracies between 77-95.6%, if silence features are used. Finally we integrate prosody, text, and silence features using a voting strategy to combine decision tree classifiers for each feature subset individually and all subsets jointly. This voted decision tree classifier yields an overall classification accuracy of 96.85%, with 2.8% miss and 3.15% false alarm rates on a representative corpus sample, demonstrating synergistic combination of prosodic and text features for topic segmentation.

1 Introduction

Natural spoken discourse is composed of a sequence of utterances, not independently generated or randomly strung together, but rather organized according to basic structural principles. This structure in turn guides the interpretation of individual utterances and the discourse as a whole. Formal written discourse signals a hierarchical, tree-based discourse structure explicitly by the division of the text into chapters, sections, paragraphs, and sentences. This structure, in turn, identifies domains for interpretation; many systems for anaphora resolution rely on some notion of locality (Grosz and Sidner, 1986). Similarly, this structure represents topical organization, and thus would be useful in information retrieval to select documents where the primary sections are on-topic, and, for summarization, to select information covering the different aspects of the topic.

Unfortunately, spoken discourse does not include the orthographic conventions that signal structural organization in written discourse. Instead, one must infer the hierarchical structure of spoken discourse from other cues. Prior research (Nakatani et al., 1995; Swerts, 1997) has shown that human labelers can more sharply, consistently, and confidently identify discourse structure in a word-level transcription when an original audio recording is available than they can on the basis of the transcribed text alone. This finding indicates that substantial additional information about the structure of the discourse is encoded in the acoustic-prosodic features of the utterance. Given the often errorful transcriptions available for large speech corpora, we choose to focus here on fully exploiting the prosodic cues to discourse structure present in the original speech. We then compare the effectiveness of a pure prosodic classification to text-based and mixed text and prosodic based classification.

In the current set of experiments, we concentrate on sequential segmentation of news broadcasts into individual stories. While a richer hierarchical segmentation is ultimately desirable, sequential story segmentation provides a natural starting point. This level of segmentation can also be most reliably performed by human labelers and thus can be considered most robust, and segmented data sets are publicly available.

Furthermore, we apply prosodic-based segmentation to Mandarin Chinese, in addition to textual features. Not only is the use of prosodic cues to topic segmentation much less well-studied in general than is the use of text cues, but the use of prosodic cues has been largely limited to English and other European languages.

2 Related Work

Most prior research on automatic topic segmentation has been applied to clean text only and thus used textual features. Text-based segmentation approaches have utilized term-based similarity measures computed across candidate segments (Hearst, 1994) and also discourse markers to identify discourse structure (Marcu, 2000).

The Topic Detection and Tracking (TDT) evaluations focused on segmentation of both text and speech sources. This framework introduced new challenges in dealing with errorful automatic transcriptions as well as new opportunities to exploit cues in the original speech. The most successful approach (Beeferman et al., 1999) produced automatic segmentations that yielded retrieval results approaching those with manual segmentations, using text and silence features. (Tur et al., 2001) applied both a prosody-only and a mixed text-prosody model to segmentation of TDT English broadcast news, with the best results combining text and prosodic features. (Hirschberg and Nakatani, 1998) also examined automatic topic segmentation based on prosodic cues, in the domain of English broadcast news, while (Hirschberg et al., 2001) applied similar cues to segmentation of voicemail.

Work in discourse analysis (Nakatani et al., 1995; Swerts, 1997) in both English and Dutch has identified features such as changes in pitch range, intensity, and speaking rate associated with segment boundaries and with boundaries of different strengths. They also demonstrated that access to acoustic cues improves the ease and quality of human labeling.

3 Prosody and Mandarin

In this paper we focus on topic segmentation in Mandarin Chinese broadcast news. Mandarin Chinese is a tone language in which lexical identity is determined by a pitch contour - or *tone* - associated with each syllable. This additional use of pitch raises the question of the cross-linguistic applicability of the prosodic cues, especially pitch cues, identified for non-tone languages. Specifically, do we find intonational cues in tone languages? The fact that emphasis is marked intonationally by expansion of pitch range even in the presence of Mandarin lexical tone (Shen, 1989) suggests encouragingly that prosodic, intonational cues to other aspects of information structure might also prove robust in tone languages.

4 Data Set

We utilize the Topic Detection and Tracking (TDT) 3 (Wayne, 2000) collection Mandarin Chinese broadcast news audio corpus as our data set. Story segmentation in Mandarin and English broadcast news and newswire text was one of the TDT tasks and also an enabling technology for other retrieval tasks. We use the segment boundaries provided with the corpus as our gold standard labeling. Our collection comprises 3014 news stories drawn from approximately 113 hours over three months (October-December 1998) of news broadcasts from the Voice of America (VOA) in Mandarin Chinese, with 800 regions of other program material including musical interludes and teasers. The transcriptions span approximately 750,000 words. Stories average approximately 250 words in length to span a full story. No subtopic segmentation is performed. The audio is stored in NIST Sphere format sampled at 16KHz with 16-bit linear encoding.

5 Prosodic Features

We consider four main classes of prosodic features for our analysis and classification: pitch, intensity, silence and duration. Pitch, as represented by f0 in Hertz was computed by the "To pitch" function of the Praat system (Boersma, 2001). We selected the highest ranked pitch candidate value in each voiced region. We then applied a 5-point median filter to smooth out local instabilities in the signal such as vocal fry or small regions of spurious doubling or halving. Analogously, we computed the intensity in decibels for each 10ms frame with the Praat "To intensity" function, followed by similar smoothing.

For consistency and to allow comparability, we compute all figures for word-based units, using the automatic speech recognition transcriptions provided with the TDT Mandarin data. The words are used to establish time spans for computing pitch or intensity mean or maximum values, to enable durational normalization and the pairwise comparisons reported below, and to identify silence or non-speech duration.

It is well-established (Ross and Ostendorf, 1996) that for robust analysis pitch and intensity should be normalized by speaker, since, for example, average pitch is largely incomparable for male and female speakers. In the absence of speaker identification software, we approximate speaker normalization with story-based normalization, computed as $\frac{val-mean}{mean}$, assuming one speaker per topic[1]. For duration, we consider both absolute and normalized word duration, where average word duration is used as the mean in the calculation above.

6 Prosodic Analysis

To evaluate the potential applicability of prosodic features to story segmentation in Mandarin Chinese, we performed some initial data analysis to determine if words in story-final position differed from the same words used throughout the story in news stories. This lexical match allows direct pairwise comparison. We anticipated that since words in Mandarin varied not only in phoneme sequence but also in tone sequence, a direct comparison might be particularly important to eliminate sources of variability. Features that differed significantly would form the basis of our classifier feature set.

We found significant differences for each of the features we considered. Specifically, word duration, normalized mean pitch, and normalized mean intensity all differed significantly for words in topic-final position relative to occurrences throughout the story (paired t-test, two-tailed, $p < 0.05, p < 0.0025, p < 0.0025$, respectively) . Word duration increased, while both pitch and intensity decreased. A small side experiment using 15 hours of English broadcast news from the TDT collection shows similar trends, though the magnitude of the change in intensity is smaller than that observed for the Chinese. Furthermore, comparison of average pitch and average intensity for 1, 5, and 10 word windows at the beginning and end of news stories finds that pitch and intensity are both significantly higher ($p < 0.001$) at the start of stories than at the end.

These contrasts are consistent with, though in some cases stronger than, those identified for English (Nakatani et al., 1995) and Dutch (Swerts, 1997). The relatively large size of the corpus enhances the salience of these effects. We find, importantly, that reduction in pitch as a signal of topic finality is robust across the typological contrast of tone and non-tone languages. These findings demonstrate highly significant intonational effects even in tone languages and suggest that prosodic cues may be robust across wide ranges of languages.

[1] This is an imperfect approximation as some stories include off-site interviews, but seems a reasonable choice in the absence of automatic speaker identifi cation.

7 Classification

7.1 Prosodic Feature Set

The results above indicate that duration, pitch, and intensity should be useful for automatic prosody-based identification of topic boundaries. To facilitate cross-speaker comparisons, we use normalized representations of average pitch, average intensity, and word duration. We also include absolute word duration. These features form a word-level context-independent feature set.

Since segment boundaries and their cues exist to contrastively signal the separation between topics, we augment these features with local context-dependent measures. Specifically, we add features that measure the change between the current word and the next word.[2] This contextualization adds four contextual features: change in normalized average pitch, change in normalized average intensity, change in normalized word duration, and duration of following silence or non-speech region.

7.2 Text Feature Set

In addition to the prosodic features which are our primary interest, we also consider a set of features that exploit textual similarity to identify segment boundaries. Motivated by text and topic similarity measures in the vector space model of information retrieval (Salton, 1989), we compute a vector representation of the words in 50 word windows preceding and following the current potential boundary position. We compute the cosine similarity of these two vectors. We employ a $tf * idf$ weighting; each term is weighted by the product of its frequency in the window (tf) and its inverse document frequency (idf) as a measure of topicality. We also consider the same similarity measure computed across 30 word windows. The final text similarity measure we consider is simple word overlap, counting the number of words that appear in both 50 word windows defined above. We did not remove stopwords, and used the word-based units from the ASR transcription directly as our term units. We expect that these measures will be minimized at topic boundaries where changes in topic are accompanied by changes in topical terminology.

Finally we identified a small set of word unigram features occuring within a ten-word window immediately preceding or following a story boundary that

[2] We have posed the task of boundary detection as the task of fi nding segment-fi nal words, so the technique incorporates a single-word lookahead. We could also repose the task as identifi cation of topic-initial words and avoid the lookahead to have a more on-line process. This is an area for future research.

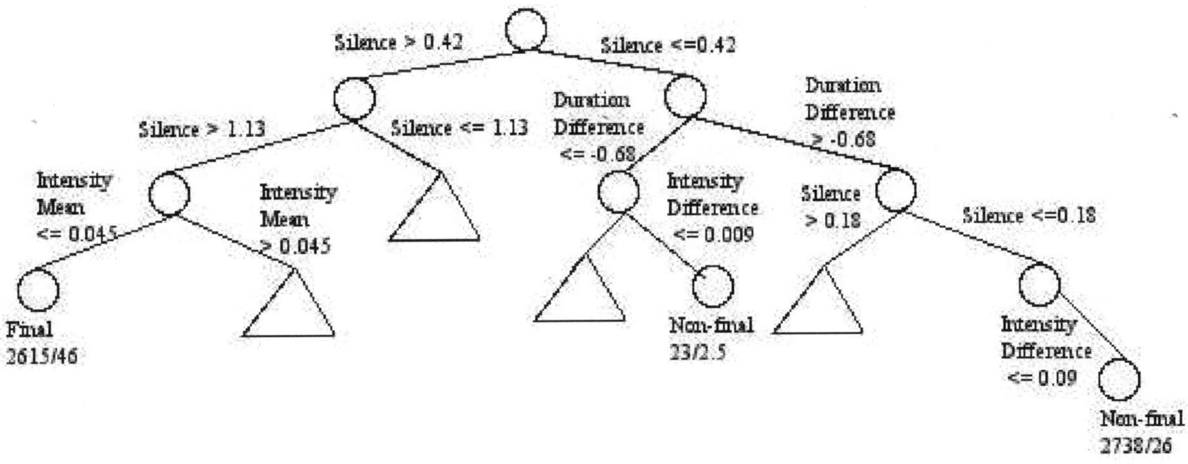

Figure 1: Prosody-based decision tree classifier labeling words as segment-final or non-segment-final

were indicative of such a boundary.[3] These features include the Mandarin Chinese words for "audience", "reporting", and "Voice of America." We used a boolean feature for each such word corresponding to its presence or absence in the current word's environment in the classifier formulation.

7.3 Classifier Training and Testing Configuration

We employed Quinlan's C4.5 (Quinlan, 1992) decision tree classifier to provide a readily interpretable classifier. Now, the vast majority of word positions in our collection are non-segment-final. So, in order to focus training and test on segment boundary identification and to assess the discriminative capability of the classifier, we downsample our corpus to produce a 50/50 split of segment-final and non-final words. We train on 3500 segment-final words[4] and 3500 non-final words, not matched in any way, drawn randomly from the full corpus. We test on a similarly balanced test set of 500 instances.

7.4 Classifier Evaluation

7.4.1 Prosody-only classification

The resulting classifier achieved 95.6% accuracy, with 2% missed boundaries and 7% false alarms. This effectiveness is a substantial improvement over the sample baseline of 50%. A portion of the decision tree is reproduced in Figure 1. Inspection of the tree indicates the key role of silence as well as the use of both contextual and purely local features of pitch, intensity, and duration. The classifier relies on the theoretically and empirically grounded features of pitch, intensity, duration, and silence, where it has been suggested that higher pitch and wider range are associated with topic initiation and lower pitch or narrower range is associated with topic finality.

We performed a set of contrastive experiments to explore the impact of different lexical tones on classification accuracy. We grouped words based on the lexical tone of the initial syllable into high, rising, low, and falling. We found no tone-based differences in classification with all groups achieving 94-96% accuracy. Since the magnitude of the difference in pitch based on discourse position is comparable to that based on lexical tone identity, and the overlap between pitch values in non-final and final positions is relatively small, we obtain consistent results.

7.4.2 Text and Silence-based Classification

In a comparable experiment, we employed only the text similarity, text unigram, and silence duration features to train and test the classifier. These features similarly achieved a 95.6% overall classification accuracy, with 3.6% miss and 5.2% false alarms. Here the best classification accuracy was achieved by the $tf * idf$ weighted 50 word window based text similarity measure. The text unigram features also contributed to overall classifier effectiveness. A portion of the decision tree classifier using text-based features is reproduced in Figure 2.

7.4.3 Combined Prosody and Text Classification

Finally we built a combined classifier integrating all prosodic, textual, and silence features. This classi-

[3] We used the ngram functionality to Boostexter (Schapire and Singer, 2000) to identify these units.

[4] We excluded a small proportion of words for which the pitch tracker returned no results.

fier yielded an accuracy of 96.4%, somewhat better effectiveness, still with more than twice as many false alarms as missed detections. The decision tree utilized all prosodic features. $tf * idf$ weighted cosine similarity alone performed as well as any of the other text similarity or overlap measures. The text unigram features also contributed to overall classifier effectiveness. A portion of the decision tree classifier using prosodic, textual, and silence features is reproduced in Figure 3.

7.5 Feature Comparison

We also performed a set of contrastive experiments with different subsets of available features to assess the dependence on these features.[5] We grouped features into 5 sets: pitch, intensity, duration, silence, and text-similarity. For each of the prosody-only, text-only, and combined prosody and text-based classifiers, we successively removed the feature class at the root of the decision tree and retrained with the remaining features (Table 1).

We observe that although silence duration plays a very significant role in story boundary identification for all feature sets, the richer prosodic and mixed text-prosodic classifiers are much more robust to the absence of silence information. Further we observe that intensity and then pitch play the next most important roles in classification. This behavior can be explained by the observation that, like silence or non-speech regions, pitch and intensity changes provide sharp, local cues to topic finality or initiation. Thus the prosodic features provide some measure of redundancy for the silence feature. In contrast, the text similarity measures apply to relatively wide regions, comparing pairs of 50 word windows.

7.6 Further Feature Integration

Finally we considered effectiveness on a representative test sampling of the full data set, rather than the downsampled, balanced set, adding a proportional number of unseen non-final words to the test set. We observed that although the overall classification accuracy was 95.6% and we were missing only 2% of the story boundaries, we produced a high level of false alarms (4.4%), accounting for most of the observed classification errors. Given the large predominance of non-boundary positions in the real-word distribution, we sought to better understand and reduce this false alarm rate, and hopefully reduce the overall error rates. At the same time, we hoped to avoid a dramatic increase in the miss rate.

To explore this question, we considered the contribution of each of the three main feature types - prosody, text, and silence - and their combined effects on false alarms. We constructed independent feature-set-specific decision tree classifiers for each of the feature types and compared their independent classifications to those of the integrated classifier. We found that while there was substantial agreement across the different feature-based classifiers in the cases of correct classification, erroneous classifications often occured when the assignment was a minority decision. Specifically, one-third of the false alarms were based on a minority assignemnt, where only the fully integrated classifier deemed the position a boundary or where it agreed with only one of the feature-set-specific classifiers.

Based on these observations, we completed our multi-feature integration by augmenting the decision tree based classification with a voting mechanism. In this configuration, a boundary was only assigned in cases where the integrated classifier agreed with at least two of the feature-set-specific classifiers. This approach reduced the false alarm rate by one-third, to 3.15%, while the miss rate rose only to 2.8%. The overall accuracy on a representative sample distribution reached 96.85%.

8 Conclusion and Future Work

We have demonstrated the utility of prosody-only, text-only, and mixed text-prosody features for automatic topic segmentation of Mandarin Chinese. We have demonstrated the applicability of intonational prosodic features, specifically pitch, intensity, pause and duration, to the identification of topic boundaries in a tone language. We find highly significant decreases in pitch and intensity at topic final positions, and significant increases in word duration. Furthermore, these features in both local form and contextualized form provide the basis for an effective decision tree classifier of boundary positions that does not use term similarity or cue phrase information, but only prosodic features.

We observe similar effectiveness for all feature sets when all features are available, with slightly better classification accuracy for the text and hybrid text-prosody approach. We further observe that the prosody-only and hybrid feature sets are much less sensitive to the absence of individual features, and, in particular, to silence features, as pitch and intensity provide comparable sharp cues to the position of topic boundaries. These findings indicate that prosodic features are robust cues to topic boundaries, both with and without textual cues.

Finally, we demonstrate the joint utility of the dif-

[5]For example, VOA Mandarin has been observed stylistically to make idiosyncratically large use of silence at story boundaries. (personal communication, James Allan).

	Prosody-only		Text+Silence		Text+Prosody	
	Accuracy	Pct. Change	Accuracy	Pct. Change	Accuracy	Pct. Change
All	95.6%	0	95.6%	0	96.4%	0
Silence	84.6%	-11.5%	77.4%	-19%	89.6%	-6.9%
Intensity	80.4%	-15.9%			85.4%	-11.4%
Pitch	63.6%	-33.4%			78.6%	-18.5%

Table 1: Reduction in classification accuracy with removal of features. Each row is labeled with the feature that is newly removed from the set of available features.

ferent feature sets - prosodic, textual, and silence. The use of a simple voting mechanism exploits the different contributions of each of the feature-set-specific classifiers in conjunction with the integrated classifier. This final combination allows a substantial reduction of the false alarm rate, reduction in the overall error rate, and only a small increase in the miss rate. Further tuning of relative miss and false alarm rates is certainly possible, but should be tied to a specific task application.

There is still substantial work to be done. We would like to integrate speaker identification for normalization and speaker change detection. We also plan to explore the integration of text and prosodic features for the identification of more fine-grained sub-topic structure, to provide more focused units for information retrieval, summarization, and anaphora resolution. We also plan to explore the interaction of prosodic and textual features with cues from other modalities, such as gaze and gesture, for robust segmentation of varied multi-modal data.

References

D. Beeferman, A. Berger, and J. Lafferty. 1999. Statistical models for text segmentation. *Machine Learning*, 34((1-3)):177–210.

P. Boersma. 2001. Praat, a system for doing phonetics by computer. *Glot International*, 5(9–10):341–345.

B. Grosz and C. Sidner. 1986. Attention, intention, and the structure of discourse. *Computational Linguistics*, 12(3):175–204.

M. Hearst. 1994. Multi-paragraph segmentation of expository text. In *Proceedings of the 32nd Annual Meeting of the Association for Computational Linguistics*.

Julia Hirschberg and Christine Nakatani. 1998. Acoustic indicators of topic segmentation. In *Proceedings on ICSLP-98*.

J. Hirschberg, M. Bacchiani, D. Hindel, P. Isenhour, A. Rosenberg, L. Stark, L. Stead, S. Whittaker, and G. Zamchick. 2001. Scanmail: Browsing and searching speech data by content. In *Proceedings of EUROSPEECH 2001*.

D. Marcu. 2000. *The Theory and Practice of Discourse Parsing and Summarization*. MIT Press.

C. H. Nakatani, J. Hirschberg, and B. J. Grosz. 1995. Discourse structure in spoken language: Studies on speech corpora. In *Working Notes of the AAAI Spring Symposium on Empirical Methods in Discourse Interpretation and Generation*, pages 106–112.

J.R. Quinlan. 1992. *C4.5: Programs for Machine Learning*. Morgan Kaufmann.

K. Ross and M. Ostendorf. 1996. Prediction of abstract labels for speech synthesis. *Computer Speech and Language*, 10:155–185.

Gerard Salton. 1989. *Automatic Text Processing: The Transformation, Analysis and Retrieval of Information by Computer*. Addison-Wesley, Reading, MA.

Robert E. Schapire and Yoram Singer. 2000. BoosTexter: A boosting-based system for text categorization. *Machine Learning*, 39((2/3)):135–168.

X.-N. Shen. 1989. *The Prosody of Mandarin Chinese*, volume 118 of *University of California Publications in Linguistics*. University of California Press.

Marc Swerts. 1997. Prosodic features at discourse boundaries of different strength. *Journal of the Acoustical Society of America*, 101(1):514–521.

G. Tur, D. Hakkani-Tur, A. Stolcke, and E. Shriberg. 2001. Integrating prosodic and lexical cues for automatic topic segmentation. *Computational Linguistics*, 27(1):31–57.

C. Wayne. 2000. Multilingual topic detection and tracking: Successful research enabled by corpora and evaluation. In *Language Resources and Evaluation Conference (LREC) 2000*, pages 1487–1494.

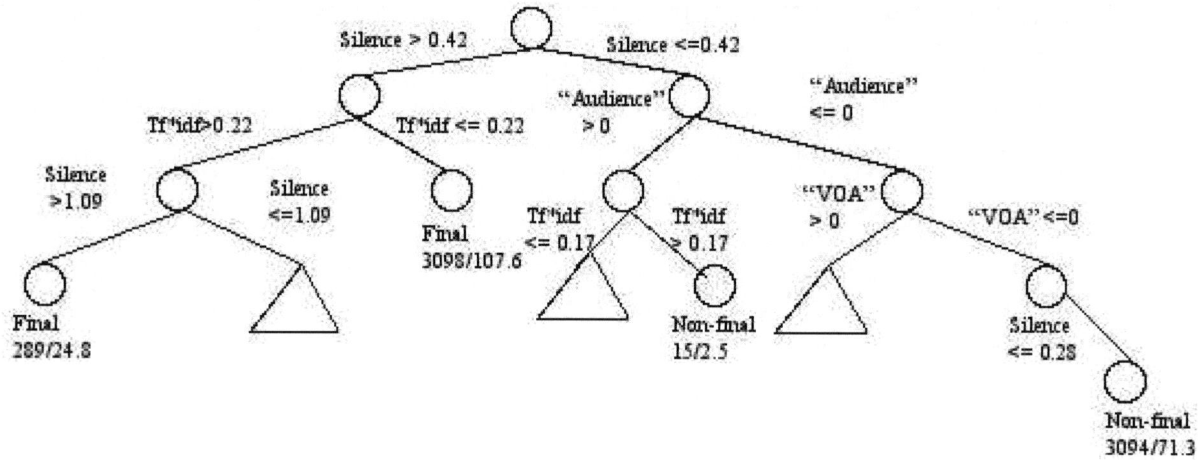

Figure 2: Text-feature-based decision tree classifier labeling words as segment-final or non-segment-final

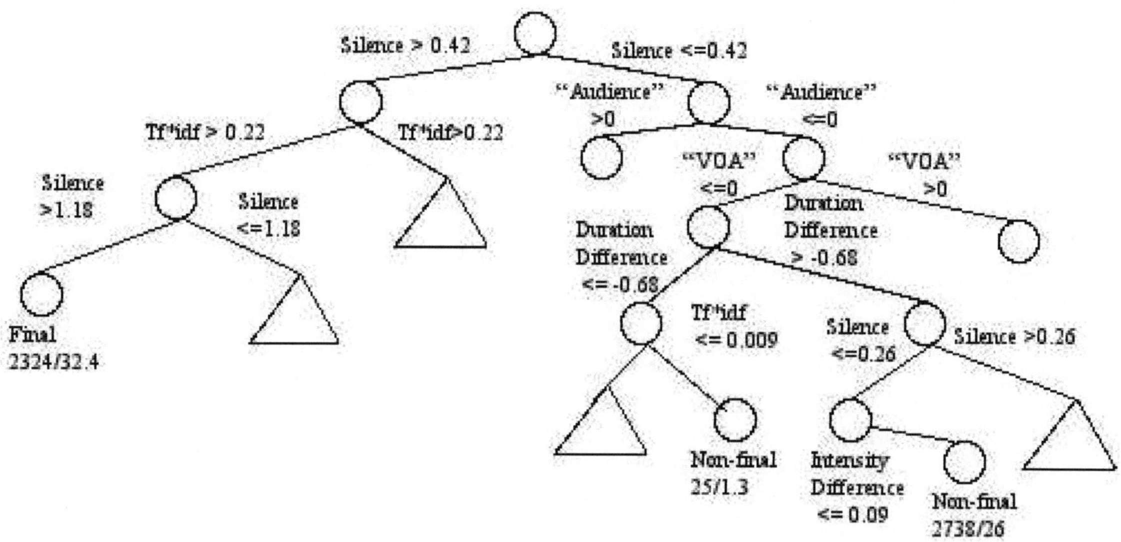

Figure 3: Prosody, text, and silence based decision tree classifier labeling words as segment-final or non-segment-final

Automatic Semantic Role Assignment for a Tree Structure

Jia-Ming You
Institute of Information Science
Academia Sinica
swimming@hp.iis.sinica.edu.tw

Keh-Jiann Chen
Institute of Information Science
Academia Sinica
Kchen@iis.sinica.edu.tw

Abstract

We present an automatic semantic roles labeling system for structured trees of Chinese sentences. It adopts dependency decision making and example-based approaches. The training data and extracted examples are from the Sinica Treebank, which is a Chinese Treebank with semantic role assigned for each constituent. It used 74 abstract semantic roles including thematic roles, such as 'agent'; 'theme', 'instrument', and secondary roles of 'location', 'time', 'manner' and roles for nominal modifiers. The design of role assignment algorithm is based on the different decision features, such as head-argument/modifier, case makers, sentence structures etc. It labels semantic roles of parsed sentences. Therefore the practical performance of the system depends on a good parser which labels the right structures of sentences. The system achieves 92.71% accuracy in labeling the semantic roles for pre-structure- bracketed texts which is considerably higher than the simple method using probabilistic model of head-modifier relations.

1. Introduction

For natural language understanding, the process of fine-grain semantic role assignment is one of the prominent steps, which provides semantic relations between constituents. The sense and sense relations between constituents are core meaning of a sentence.

Conventionally there are two kinds of methods for role assignments, one is using only statistical information (Gildea and Jurafsky, 2002) and the other is combining with grammar rules (Gildea and Hockenmaier, 2003). However using only grammar rules to assign semantic roles could lead to low coverage. On the other hand, performance of statistical methods relies on significant dependent features. Data driven is a suitable strategy for semantic roles assignments of general texts. We use the Sinica Treebank as information resource because of its various domains texts including politics, society, literature…etc and it is a Chinese Treebank with semantic role assigned for each constituent (Chen etc., 2003). It used 74 abstract semantic roles including thematic roles, such as 'agent'; 'theme', 'instrument', and secondary roles of 'location', 'time', 'manner' and modifiers of nouns, such as 'quantifier', 'predication', 'possessor', etc. The design of role assignment algorithm is based on the different decision features, such as head-argument/modifier, case makers, sentence structures etc. It labels semantic roles of parsed sentences by example-based probabilistic models.

1.1 Sinica Treebank

The Sinica Treebank has been developed and released to public since 2000 by Chinese Knowledge Information Processing (CKIP) group at Academia Sinica. The Sinica Treebank version 2.0 contains 38944 structural trees and 240,979 words in Chinese. Each structural tree is annotated with words, part-of-speech of words, syntactic structure brackets, and semantic roles. For conventional structural trees, only syntactic information was annotated. However, it is very important and yet difficult for Chinese to identify word relations with purely syntactic constraints (Xia et al., 2000). Thus, partial semantic information, i.e. semantic role for each constituent, was annotated in Chinese structural trees. The grammatical constraints are expressed in terms of linear order of semantic roles and their syntactic and semantic restrictions. Below is an example sentence of the Sinica Treebank.

Original sentence:
他 'Ta' 要 'yao' 張三 'ZhangSan' 撿 'jian' 球 'qiu' 。
He ask Zhang San to pick up the ball.

Parsed tree:
S(agent:NP(Head:Nhaa:他'He')|Head:VF2:要'ask' |goal:NP(Head:Nba:張三'Zhang San') |theme:VP(Head:VC2:撿'pick'|goal:NP(Head:Nab:球 ''ball')))

Figure 1: An example sentence of Sinica Treebank

In the Sinica Treebank, not only the semantic relations of a verbal predicate but also the modifier head relations were marked. There are 74 different semantic roles, i.e. the task of semantic role assignment has to establish the semantic relations among phrasal heads and their arguments/modifiers within 74 different choices.

The set of semantic roles used in the Sinica Treebank is listed in the appendix.

2. Example-based Probabilistic Models for Assigning Semantic Roles

The idea of example-based approaches is that semantic roles are preserved for the same event frames. For a target sentence, if we can find same examples in the training corpus, we can assign the same semantic role for each constituent of the target sentence as the examples. However reoccurrence of exact same surface structures for a sentence is very rare, i.e. the probability of finding same example sentences in a corpus is very low. In fact, by observing structures of parsed trees, we find that most of semantic roles are uniquely determined by semantic relations between phrasal heads and their arguments/modifiers and semantic relations are determined by syntactic category, semantic class of related words. For example:

Original sentence:
我們 'wo men' 都 'du' 喜歡 'xi huan' 蝴蝶 'hu die'。

We all like butterflies.

Parsed tree:
S(experiencer:NP(Head:Nhaa:我們 'we')|quantity:Dab:都 'all'|Head:VK1:喜歡 'like' |goal:NP(Head:Nab:蝴蝶 'butterflies'))。

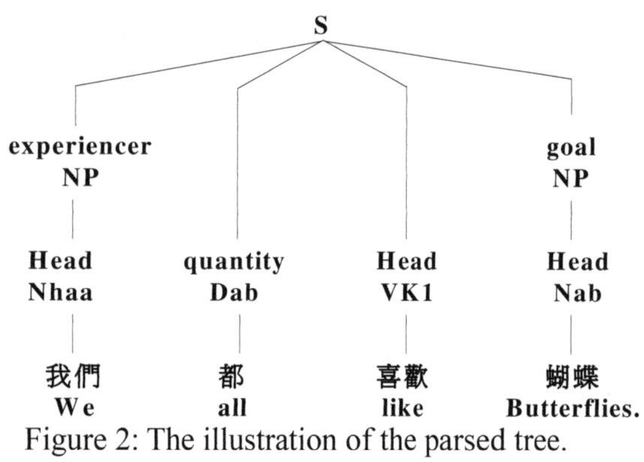

Figure 2: The illustration of the parsed tree.

In Figure2, 喜歡 'like' is the sentential head; 我們 'we' and 蝴蝶 'butterflies' are the arguments; 都 'all' is the modifier. As a result, the semantic role 'experiencer' of 我們 'we' is deduced from the relation between 我們 'we' and 喜歡 'like', since the event frame of 喜歡 'like' has the two arguments of experiencer and goal and the experiencer usually takes the subject position. The semantic roles of 蝴蝶 'butterflies' and 都 'all' are assigned by the same way. For the task of automatic role assignment, once phrase boundaries and phrasal head are known, the semantic relations will be resolved by looking for similar head-argument/modifier pairs in training data.

2.1 Example Exaction

To extract head-argument/modifier examples from the Sinica Treebank is trivial, since phrase boundaries and semantic roles, including phrasal head, are labeled. The extracted examples are pairs of head word and target word. The target word is represented by the head of the argument/modifier, since the semantic relations are established between the phrasal head and the head of argument/modifier phrase. An extracted word pair includes the following features.

Target word:
The head word of argument/modifier.

Target POS:
The part-of-speech of the target word.

Target semantic role:
Semantic role of the constituent contains the target word as phrasal head.

Head word:
The phrasal head.

Head POS:
The part-of-speech of the head word.

Phrase type:
The phrase which contains the head word and the constituent containing target word.

Position:
Shows whether target word appears before or after head word.

The examples we extracted from Figure 2 are listed below.

Target thematic Role	experiencer	quantify	goal
Target word	我們 'we'	都 'all'	蝴蝶 'butterflies'
Target POS	Nhaa	Dab	Nab
Head word	喜歡 'like'	喜歡 'like'	喜歡 'like'
Head POS	VK1	VK1	VK1
Phrase type	S	S	S
Position	before	before	after

Table 1: The three head-argument/modifier pairs extracted from Figure 2.

Classifiers	Coverage	Accuracy	Performance
P(r| h, h_pos, t, t_pos, pt, position)	23.02%	96.60%	22.24%
P(r| h_pos, t, t_pos, pt, position)	56.11%	95.53%	53.60%
P(r| h, h_pos, t_pos, pt, position)	52.98%	91.45%	48.45%
P(r| h_pos, t_pos, pt position)	97.38%	89.87%	87.52%

Table 2: Coverage and accuracy of different features combinations

2.2 Probabilistic Model for Semantic Role Assignment

It is possible that conflicting examples (or ambiguous role assignments) occur in the training data. We like to assign the most probable roles. The probability of each semantic role in a constituent with different features combinations are estimated from extract examples.

$$
\begin{aligned}
&P(r \mid constituent) \\
&= P(\mathrm{r} \mid \mathrm{h}, \mathrm{h\_pos}, \mathrm{t}, \mathrm{t\_pos}, \mathrm{pt}, \mathrm{position})^{1} \\
&= \frac{\#(\mathrm{r}, \mathrm{h}, \mathrm{h\_pos}, \mathrm{t}, \mathrm{t\_pos}, \mathrm{pt}, \mathrm{position})}{\#(\mathrm{h}, \mathrm{h\_pos}, \mathrm{t}, \mathrm{t\_pos}, \mathrm{pt}, \mathrm{position})}
\end{aligned}
$$

Due to the sparseness of the training data, it's not possible to have example feature combinations matched all input cases. Therefore the similar examples will be matched. A back off process will be carried out to reduce feature constraints during the example matching. We will evaluate performances for various features combinations to see which features combinations are best suited for semantic roles assignments.

We choose four different feature combinations. Each has relatively high accuracy. The four classifiers will be back off in sequence. If none of the four classifiers is applicable, a baseline model of assigning the most common semantic role of target word is applied.

if # of (h,h_pos,t,t_pos,pt,position) > threshold
P(r|constituent)=P(r|h,h_pos,t,t_pos,pt,position)

Else
if # of (h_pos,t,t_pos,pt,position) > threshold
P(r|constituent)=P(r|h_pos,t,t_pos,pt,position)

Else
if # of (h,h_pos,t_pos,pt,position) > threshold
P(r|constituent)=P(r|h,h_pos,t_pos,pt,position)

Else
if # of (h_pos,t_pos,pt,position) > threshold
P(r|constituent)=P(r|h_pos,t_pos,pt,position)

Else
Baseline model:
P(r|constituent)=P(r| t, t_pos,pt)

3. Experiments

We adopt the Sinica Treebank as both training and testing data. It contains about 40,000 parsed sentences. We use 35,000 sentences as training data and the rest 5,000 as testing data. The table 2 shows the coverage of each classifier, their accuracies, and performance of each individual classifier without back off process. The table 3 shows combined performance of the four classifiers after back off processes in sequence. The baseline algorithm is the simple unigram approach to assign the most common role for the target word. Because the accuracy of the four classifiers is considerably high, instead of using linear probability combinations we will rather use the most reliable classifier for each different features combination.

Method	Accuracy
Backoff	90.29%
Baseline:	68.68%

Table 3: The accuracy of our backoff method and the base line (the most common semantic roles)

3.1 Error Analyses

Although the accuracy of back off model is relatively high to the baseline model, it still has quite a room for improvement. After analyzed the errors, we draw following conclusions.

---

1 r: semantic role; h: the head word;
h_pos: part-of-speech of head word;
t: the target word;
t_pos: part-of-speech of target word;
pt: the phrase type.

a) Semantic head vs. syntactic head

A semantic role for a prepositional phrase (PP) is mainly determined by the syntactic head of PP, i.e. preposition, and the semantic head of PP, i.e. the head word of the DUMMY-argument of PP. For example, in Figure 3, the two sentences are almost the same, only the contents of PP are different. Obviously, the semantic roles of PP (在 'in' 印尼 'Indonesia') is location, and the semantic role of PP (在 'in' 今年 'this year') is time. Therefore the semantic roles of the two PPs should be determined only within the scope of PP and not relevant to matrix verb.

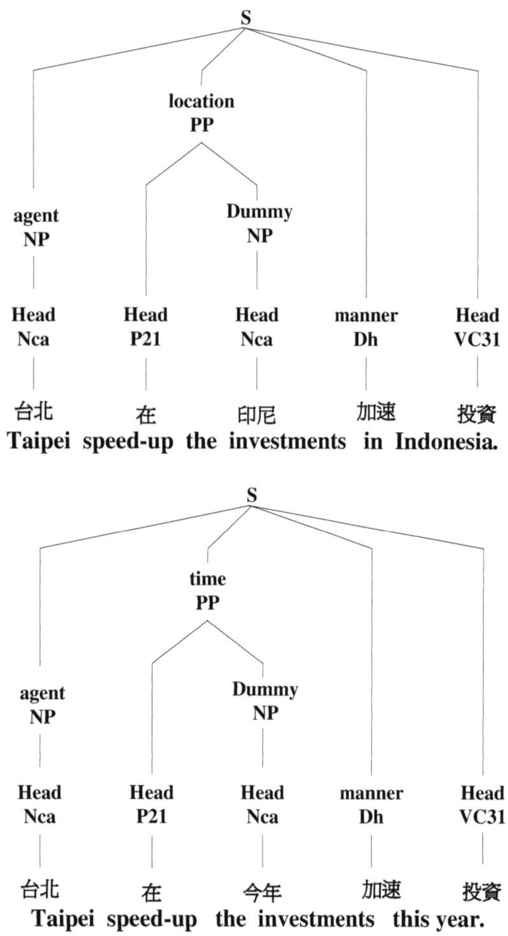

Figure 3: Parsed trees of "台北在印尼加速投資" and "台北在今年加速投資"

b) Structure-dependent semantic roles assignments

Complex structures are always the hardest part of semantic roles assignments. For example, the sentences with passive voice are the typical complex structures. In Figure 4, the semantic role of 蝴蝶 'Butterflies' is not solely determined by the head verb 吸引 'attracted' and itself. Instead we should inspect the existence of passive voice and then reverse the roles of subject and object.

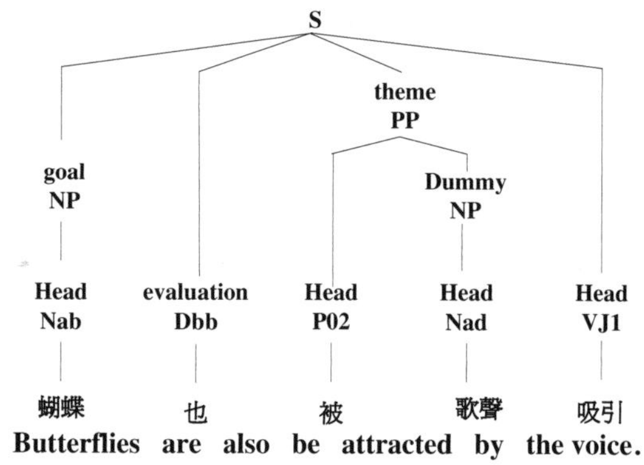

Figure 4: A parsed tree of passive sentence "蝴蝶也被歌聲吸引"

4 Refined Models

Chen & Huang (1996) had studied the task of semantic assignment during Chinese sentence parsing. They concluded that semantic roles are determined by the following 4 parameters.

1. Syntactic and semantic categories of the target word,
2. Case markers, i.e. prepositions and postpositions
3. Phrasal head, and
4. Sub-categorization frame and its syntactic patterns.

Therefore head-modifier/argument examples only resolve most of semantic role assignments. Some of complex cases need other parameters to determine their semantic roles. For instance, the argument roles of Bei sentences (passive sentence) should be determined by all four parameters.

The refined model contain two parts, one is the refinements of features data which provide more precisely information and the other is the improvements of back off process to deal with special semantic roles assignments.

4.1 Refinement of Features Extractions

The refinements of features extractions focus on two different cases, one is the features extractions of case-marked structures, such as PP and GP (postpositional phrases), and the other is the general semantic class identifications of synonyms.

The features of PP/GP include two different

feature types: the internal and the external features. The internal features of phrases compose of phrasal head and Dummy-head; the external features are heads (main verbs) of the target phrases.

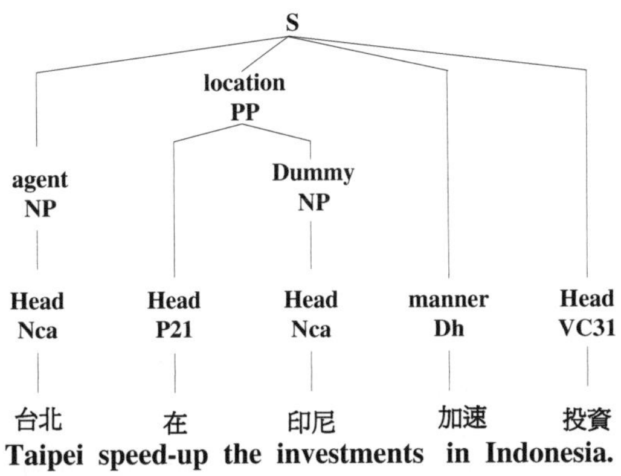

Figure 5: A parsed tree for demonstrating features extractions of PP

	Internal relation	External relation
Target thematic role	Dummy	location
Target word	印尼 'Indonesia'	在..印尼 'in..Indonesia'
Target POS	Nca	P21
Head word	在 'in'	投資 'invest'
Head POS	P21	VC31
Phrase type	PP	S
Position	after	before

Table 4: The internal/external relations of Figure 5.

The semantic class identifications of synonyms are crucial for solving data sparseness problems. Some type of words are very productive, such as numbers, DM (determinative measurement), proper names. They need to be classified into different semantic classes. We use some tricks to classify them into specific word classes. For example we label 1 公斤 'one kilogram', 2 公斤 'two kilograms' as their canonical form 某公斤 'n kilograms'; 第一天 'the first day', 第二天 'the second day ' as 第某天 'the nth days'; 張三 'Zhang San', 李四 'Li Si' as a personal name…etc. With this method, we can increase the number of matched examples and resolve the problem of occurrences of unknown words in a large scale.

4.2 Dependency Decisions and Refined Back off Processes

The refined back off model aimed to solve semantic roles assignments for certain special structures. Using only head-modifier features could result into decision making with insufficient information. As illustrated before, the semantic role of 蝴蝶 'butterflies' in Figure 4 is 'agent' observed from the head-argument feature. But in fact the feature of passive voice 被 'passive' tells us that the subject role of 蝴蝶 'butterflies' should be the semantic role 'goal' instead of the usual role of 'agent'.

Therefore we enhanced our back off process by adding some dependency decisions. The dependency conditions include special grammar usage like passive form, quotation, topical sentences… etc. In the refined back off process, first we have to detect which dependency condition is happened and resolved it by using dependency features. For example, if the feature word 被 'passive' occurs in a sentence, we realize that the subjective priority of semantic roles should be reversed. For instance, 'goal' will take subject position instead of 'agent' ('goal' appears before 'agent').

4.3 Experiment Results

The experiments were carried out for the refined back off model with the same set of training data and testing data as in the previous experiments. Table 5 shows that the refined back off model gains 2.4 % accuracy rate than the original back off model. However most of the improvement is due to the refinements of features extractions and canonical representation for certain classes of words. A few improvements were contributed to the decision making on the cases of structure dependency.

Method	Accuracy
Refined Backoff	92.71%
Backoff	90.29%
Baseline	68.68%

Table 5: Role assignment accuracies of refined backoff, backoff, and baseline models.

5 Conclusion and Future Works

Semantic roles are determined by the following 4 parameters.

1. Syntactic and semantic categories of the target word,
2. Case markers, i.e. prepositions and postpositions,
3. Phrasal head, and
4. Sub-categorization frame and its syntactic patterns.

We present an automatic semantic roles labeling system. It adopts dependency decision making and example-based approaches, which makes decision on the amount of parameters by observing the occurrence of dependency features and to utilize the minimal amount of feature combinations to assign semantic roles. It labels semantic roles of parsed sentences. Therefore the practical performance of the system depends on a good parser which labels the right structures of sentences. The system achieves 92.71% accuracy in labeling the semantic roles for pre-structure- bracketed texts which is considerably higher than the simple method using probabilistic model of head-modifier relations.
In the future, we will consider fine-grain semantic role assignment problems. The current semantic roles assignment is focus on one sentence. However, the occurrences of frame elements are not limited to a single sentence. For instance, "John bought the books from Mary". The semantic roles of 'John' and 'Mary' are agent and theme respectively. According to Fillmore's FrameNet, the frame element assignment for the above sentence should be 'John' the buyer, 'Mary' the seller, 'the books' the goods. The precondition of buy-frame says that the seller should be the owner of the goods. Therefore after the sentence parsing and logical reasoning, the following semantic relations should be established.

Event frame: Commerce-buy
Buyer: John
Seller: Mary
Goods: books
Additional frame: Own

Before the buy event
Owner: Mary
Possession: books
After the buy event
Owner: John
Possession: books

The semantic roles assignment is a process of crossing phrasal and sentential boundaries. Some semantic roles of an event might occur at left or right context. Therefore we have to analyze the relation between two consecutive events. The relations include causal relation, temporal relation, resultant relation, etc. How to resolve the above problems will be our future studies.

References

Chen, Keh-Jiann, Chu-Ren Huang. 1996. *Information-based Case Grammar: A Unification-based Formalism for Parsing Chinese. Journal of Chinese Linguistics Monograph* Series No. 9.

Chen, Keh-Jiann, Chu-Ren Huang, Feng-Yi Chen, Chi-Ching Luo,Ming-Chung Chang, Chao-Jan Chen, and Zhao-Ming Gao, 2003. *Sinica Treebank: Design Criteria, Representational Issues and Implementation*. In Anne Abeille (Ed.) *Treebanks Building and Using Parsed Corpora*. Language and Speech series. Dordrecht:Kluwer, pp231-248.

Chu-Ren Huang, Keh-Jiann Chen, and Benjamin K. T'sou Eds. *Readings in Chinese Natural Language Processing*. 23-45. Berkeley: JCL.

Daniel Gildea and Daniel Jurafsky. 2002. *Automatic Labeling of Semantic Roles*. *Computational Linguistics*, 28(3):245-288

Daniel Gildea and Julia Hockenmaier. 2003. *Identifying Semantic Roles Using Combinatory Categorial Grammar.* Conference on Empirical Methods in Natural Language Processing (EMNLP).

Xia, Fei, 2000, *The Part-of-Speech Tagging Guidelines for the Penn Chinese Treebank (3.0)*. IRCS Report 00-07. Philadelphia, PA: University of Pennsylvania.

Appendix:

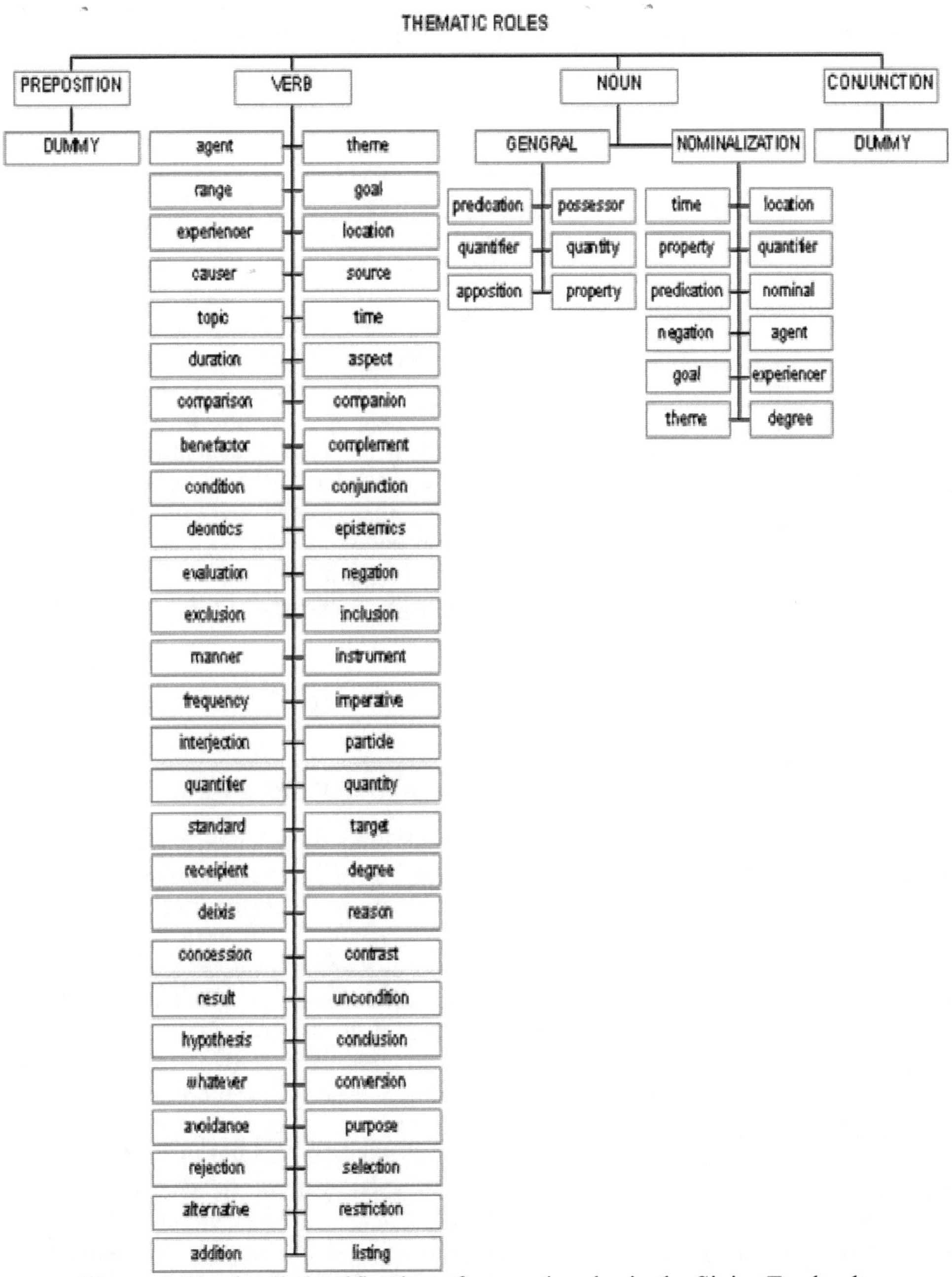

Figure 6: The detail classification of semantic roles in the Sinica Treebank

A Large-Scale Semantic Structure for Chinese Sentences

Tang Li
Institutue for Infocomm Research
21 Heng Mui Keng Terrace
Singapore119613
Tangli@I2R.a-star.edu.sg

Ji Donghong, Yang Lingpeng
Institutue for Infocomm Research
21 Heng Mui Keng Terrace
Singapore119613
{dhji, lpyang}@I2R.a-star.edu.sg

Abstract

Motivated by a systematic analysis of Chinese semantic relationships, we constructed a Chinese semantic framework based on surface syntactic relationships, deep semantic relationships and feature structure to express dependencies between lexical meanings and conceptual structures, and relations that underlie those lexical meanings. Analyzing the semantic representations of 10000 Chinese sentences, we provide a model of semantically and syntactically annotated sentences from which reliable information on combinatorial possibilities of each semantic item targeted for analysis can be displayed. We also propose a semantic argument – head relation, 'basic conceptual structure' and the 'Head-Driven Principle'. Our results show that we can successfully disambiguate some troublesome sentences, and minimize the redundancy in language knowledge descriptions for natural language processing.

1 Introduction

To enable computer-based analysis of Chinese sentences in natural language texts we have developed a semantic framework, taking into account concepts used in the Berkeley FrameNet Project (Baker, Fillmore, & Lowe 1998; Fillmore & Baker 2001) and the Penn Chinese Tree Bank (Nianwen Xue; Fei Xia et al. 2000). The FrameNet Project, as a computational project, is creating a lexical resource for English, based on the principle of semantic frames. It has tried to concentrate on frames which help to explain the meanings of groups of words, rather than frames that cover just one word. The representation of the valences of its target words and descriptions of the semantic frames underlying the meanings of the words described are the mainly part of the database. The Penn Chinese Tree Bank analyzed the syntactic structure of a phrase or sentence for selected text, based on the current research in Chinese syntax and the linguistic expertise of those involved in this project. Different from Pan's syntactic structures and FrameNet's semantic frames, our object is to record exactly how the semantic features relates frames to those syntactic constituents. The key task is to determine the relationship between the two direct constituents in terms of the semantic relationship. The grammar functions are also considered for primarily identifying the relation. Here, we use methods developed for the analysis of semantic relationships to produce a framework based on the direct component link. Our framework is largely a semantic one, but it has adopted some crucial principles of syntactic analysis in the semantic structure analysis.

In this paper, we present our model of semantically and synactically annotated 10000 Chinese sentences. The focus is on the analysis of the semantic relationships between one word to another in a sentence. We also briefly discuss the annotation process.

2 Theoretical Framework and Case Study

The basic assumption of Frame Semantics (Fillmore 1976;1977; Fillmore & Atkins 1992; Petruck 1996) as it applies to the description of lexical meanings is that each word (in a given meaning) evokes a particular frame and possibly profiles some element or aspect of that frame. By being linked to frames, each word is directly connected with other words in its frame(s). where word dependence association are needed from surface syntactic structures which actually reflect the grammatical relationship to the deep semantics structure whereby semantic content are put into natural language. The meaning of a word, in most cases, is best demonstrated by reference to a semantic network. Referential meaning on its own is insufficient. Word meaning would include the other dimensions concerning the structure and function of words. Unlike English, in which there are two major types of evidence that help to determine the syntactic structure of a phrase or sentence: morphological information and distributional information (such as word order) , in Chinese the lack of conclusive morphological cues makes ambiguity analyses for one sentence more likely. Moreover, most Chinese sentences order are very flexible. Phrase omission, word movement, ellipsis and binding also make it difficult to characterize their grammatical relation. So the semantic information provides important clues for Chinese sentence analyse. We have to rely on semantic knowledge to guide role assignment. Thus, we propose a method allowing a syntactic and semantic-based analysis of sequences and relationship of semantic items to obtain the common distribution of the relationship order.

3 Method

The analysis method that will be presented here is logically equivalent to the parsing of syntax and semantic dependency with feature constraints.

The key idea in our method is to avoid the complexity hierarchical tree sturcture. We are concerned with building structures that reflect basic relationships between one word and other in a single sentence. We use methods developed for the analysis of semantic relationships to produce a framework based on the order link. We started from an initial analysis based on the surface syntactics, then we analyzed deep semantic relationships, and attempted to improve it by removing the semantic order from the syntactic structure and reconnecting them in different places. Since many word phrase patterns are difficult for computers to recognize, trying to compromise between linguistic correctness and engineering convenience, we link the difference semantic roles on the flat level, while employing a few template rules. All semantic words are linked on the same level. They are non-hierarchical constructs. This flatted representation allows access to various levels of syntactic description tree simultaneously. In fact, the purpose of generalization is to get a regular expression from the original sentence.

We manually tagged two kind of relationship among our large-scale frameworks: 1. syntax-semantic relationship; 2. semantic feature relationship.

Our framework consists of a set of nodes and a set of arcs that join the nodes, with each word or concept corresponding to a node and links between any two nodes that are directly associated. The basic links in the framework are between one word item to another based on immediate semantic deperdency order. We summarized the immediate semantic relationship through a variety of semantic relation features such as agent, reason, result and so on. The feature of relationship between two nodes are labeled on the arc.

We developed the first fully instantiated semantic structure by manually labeling semantic representations in a machine-readable format. To make sure that our model can deal with various kinds of texts in real life situations, we have analysed 10000 sentences from large Web site corpora based on our formal model. Our aim is not to describe in detail any specific, but to capture at an abstract level the semantic relations between the direct components in a sentence. Our model's most important domain of application is to Chinese sentence analysis, but it may also be applicable to different languages. This semantic framwork constructs a model on the basis of a few rules.

The present paper indicates how situation types are represented, how these representations are composed from semantic representations of linguistic constituents, and how these type differences affect the expression of sentences.

3.1 Syntax-Semantics Relationship Labeling

This work flow includes linking and labeling of each relation between direct semantic items in single sentences, which reflects different semantic representation, and descriptions of the relations of each frame's basic conceptual structure in terms of semantic actions. A semantic representation is a feature that allows one word in the sentence to point at some other word to which it is related. A word in a sentence may have much direct representation, these are differentiated by the semantic action. By analyzing the direct se mantic representation, we can capture semantic relationships between words, reconstructing a framework for the order of Chinese sentences.

In most cases syntactic relationships are consistent with semantic relationships. The following framework shows show some important similarities between the structure of syntactic and semantic structure. For example, in

我在看电视.（'I am watching TV.'）

Syntactically, '我'（I）is subject, directly relating to the verbal predicate '看'（watch）, '电视'（TV）is object , also links to the verbal predicate directly. '在'（be doing）as a adverb is an adjoined predicate '看'（watch）, there is a direct relationship between the two nodes. Semantically, '我'（I）is the agent and '电视'（TV）is the recipients, both of them have a direct relationship with the activity '看'（watch）. So we link the different nodes as follows:

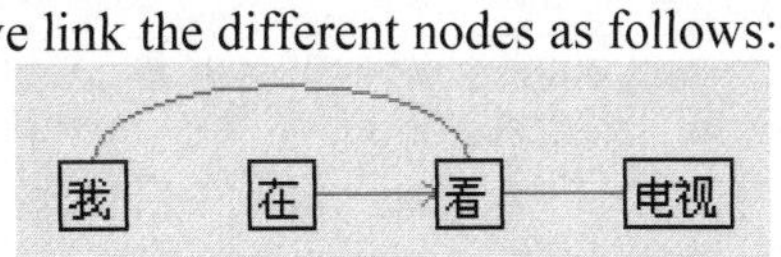

In cases where the relationship between syntax and semantics is inconsistent, by syntactic analysis, if there are multiple syntactic analyses among a sentence, we always choose the analysis

relationship that is consistent with the semantic relationship. For example, the Chinese sentence

街边坐着许多人。

（many people sit beside the street.）

The above sentence can be analyzed either of the following two syntactic structures.

type 1:

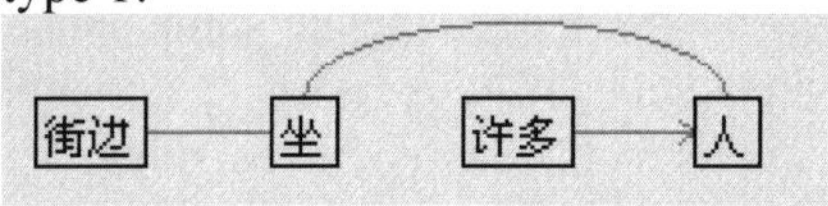

type 2:

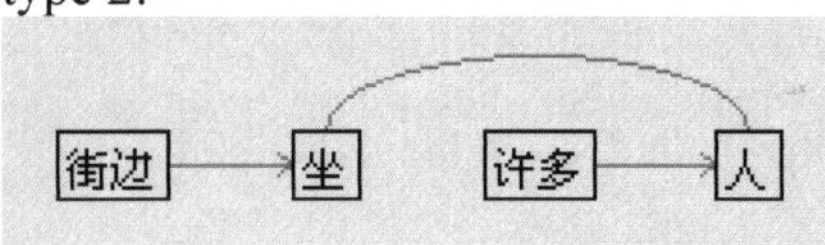

The two syntactic structures are analyzed with difference in the first node and the second node. In type 1, '街边'（beside of the street）is analyzed as subject, for type2, the linguist also analyzed it as adverb modifier, adjuncting to the predicate '坐'（seat）. But when this sentence is analyzed in terms of semantics, there is only one relationship structure similar as type 2. '人'（people）is analyzed as agent, '街边'（beside of the street）as localizer, attached to the activity '坐'（seat）. This semantic structure is consistent with the syntactic structure type 2. Only one structure can display both syntax and semantic relationship simultaneously. So we choose the second analysis.

If the syntactic relationship is different from the semantic relationship, we take no account of the syntactic order. In the Chinese sentence

她哭红了眼睛。

（she cry so much that her eyes become red.）

Within the surface syntactic structure, adjective '红'（red）will be analyzed as complementation and directly associated with main verb '哭'（cry）, which indicate result of predicate. Underlying the syntactic structure, '红'（red）actually point to '眼睛'（eyes）in semantic representation. There is no direct semantic relationship between '哭'（cry）and '红'（red）. The semantic network can be analyzed as: she cry + her eyes become red, the immediate relationship between 'he' as a possessor and 'belly' as a possession and that between 'belly' as entity and 'painful' as description. In this case we link the node '红'（red）to '眼睛'（eyes）directly based on semantic relationship.

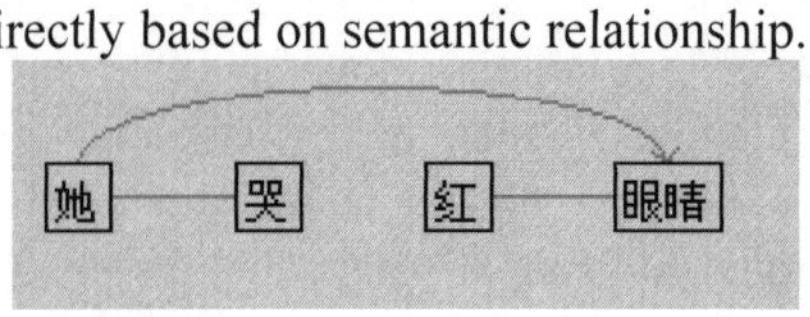

3.2 'Head' Determination

The basic link is the direct link between two semantic units. In addition, a set of general rules for determining the directions has been identified.

1. That between Head and Its Modifier as a Case of Direct Relationship

The head (see below), and the modifiers that come before it, constitute a type of modification relationship, which is one of the typical cases of direct relationships, e.g,

A. Gao zige de ren
  tall body DE person
  the person with tall body

B. (to be compared with the above sentence)
  ren de gezi gao
  person DE body tall
  'The person's body is tall.'

In the above sentence, *ren* 'person' and *gezi* 'body' hold a modification relationship, but *gao* 'tall' and *ren*'person' are related indirectly as the relationship between the two words is realized through that of *gezi* 'body'. Therefore, we say that the relationship that *ren* 'person' holds with *gezi* 'body' is a direct one, but that with *gao* is a rather indirect one.

2. That between An Action Verb and Its Patient as a Case of a Direct relationship

In case a head noun is an AGENT of an action verb within a modifying phrase, then the relationship between the Head none and the action verb is a direct one. The following sentences illustrate the point.

C. chi pingguo de nuhai.
  Eat apples DE girl
  'the girl who is eating apples.'

D. (to be compared with the above sentence)
  nuhai chi pingguo
  girl eat apples
  'The girl is eating apples.'

In the above sentence, *nuhai* 'girl' is an AGENT of the action verb *chi* 'eat', the two words have a direct semantic relationship, therefore we link them directly and annotate 'girl' as a head. In contrary, the relationship between *nuhai* 'girl' and *pingguo* 'apples' is of an indirect type.

3. Other Cases of Direct Relationships

In case there is neither a modification nor an AGENT/PATIENT relationship, the whole phrase, which is still directly related to a following describing phrase, has to be embedded. E.g.,

E. ban shiqing yinggai guquan daju.
Handle problem should care-about overall situation
'People should care about the overall situation when they handle problems.'

F. chouyan hai shenti.
  Smoke harm health

'Smoking harms health.'

G. ta neng daying de shiqing wo ye neng daying.

He can accept DE event I also can accept

'The event that he can accept are also acceptable to me.'

3.3 'Head' Determination

Since Chinese lacks morphological cues, the grammatical markers (such as 的，把，被) and word order are comparatively important cues for the relationship determination. We have to rely on grammatical and semantic knowledge to guide role assignment.

In this study, we have proposed an approach that combines 'basic conceptual structure' and our 'Head-Driven Principle'. According to the 'Head-Driven Principle', most structures are analyzed as having a 'Head' which is connected to various types of modifiers, such as Head-NP (adjective-noun, noun-adverbial pairs 我们都), Head-VP (adverbial-verb, verb-adverbial, adjective-verb…). In our framework, modification is represented by attaching tags with arrows to the core semantic item whereve the type of modification can be clearly identified. Since the SVO is the basic order in Chinese, there is no modifier relationship among the level of SVO. In our model, 'Subject-Predicate Structures' and 'Verb-Object Structures' are represented as non-head. In above example, the relation linking the 'core' noun and verb with their 'adjunct' is tagged with an arrow to indicate that it is a 'head'. Both A and B label the 'head' as the core noun. E labels the 'head' as the core verb. Employing the 'Head-Driven Principle' for the construction of semantic models. Some ambiguous sentences can be clearly represented. The different meaning among sentence or phrase containing same words can also be described . Conside the following sentence and phrases:

学生喜欢老师。

（The students like the teachers.）

喜欢老师的学生

(the students who like the teachers)

学生喜欢的老师

(the teachers who the students like)

All of above examples containing same meaning words can have very different meaning, depending on the different word order and grammatical marker '的'（DE）. We use head tagging to construct different frameworks for these structures:

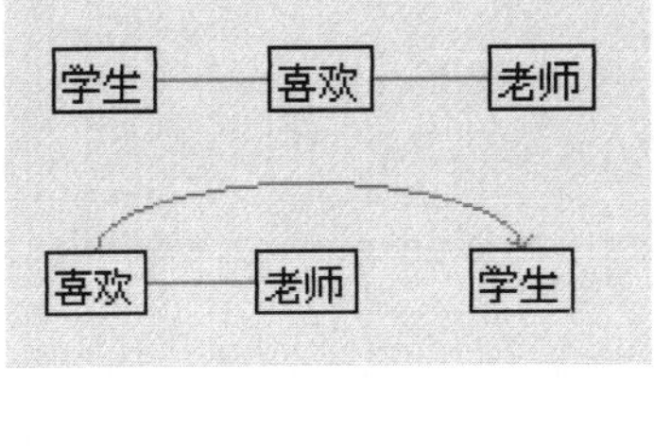

The above three head semantic structures clearly show us the different relationships among sentence and noun phrases with different meaning. The head words are connected to their modifier through arrow arcs. The first SVO relationship is also represented by non-head tagging.

3.4 Feature Abstracting and Labeling

Based on the analysis of semantic relationships, we have been parsing feature structures to express dependencies between semantic features. In our analysis model, semantic feature means a variety of detailed semantic relationships. Most of the time, semantic features are not so easy to define. Some feature typologies have been provided, but there is still much discussions about the nature of a feature in a text. To avoid the confusion of feature classification, we proposed a method to abstract the semantic feature directly from sentences that contain the natural feature word. For those sentences without semantic features insert , we'll labeling the semantic features refer to the categorys include in other sentences, attached on the relationship arcs. Thus we constructed a semantic framework based on multi-profile dimension. For example:

Ta gezi bu gao.

His stature isn't tall.

He isn't tall.

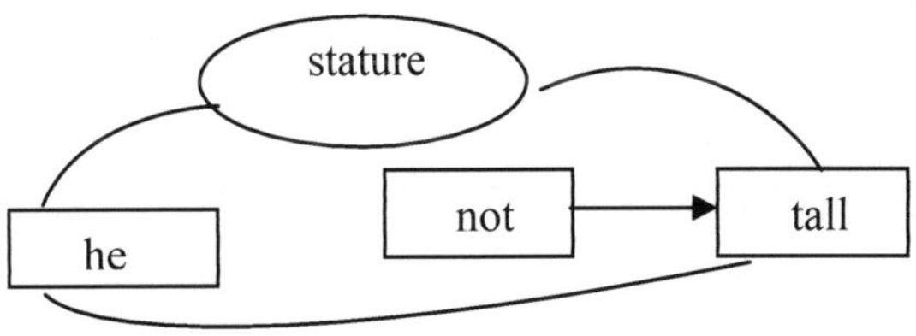

In traditional analysis, 'stature' is just a syntactic constituent in a sentence. However, the essential meaning of the sentence is 'he is not tall', 'stature' is semantic feature linking 'he' and 'tall' together, thus in our semantic analysis we link only 'he' and 'tall' semantically, 'stature' is taken as feature marking a semantic relationship, rather than an immediate constituent. This Chinese semantic structure, after feature abstraction, is very similar to its English counterpart. It facilitates the translation from one language into another.

In some sentences , there are not only semantic features but also their particular values included. Similarly we abstracted the values attached on the features. Thus we can expand the feature structures to express this level of detail. For example

Ta liang mi gao.

he two meters tall

'He is two meters tall.'

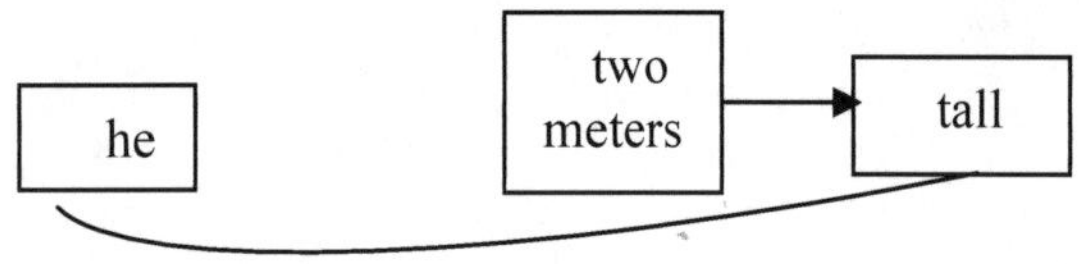

In the above framework, 'tall' is the semantic feature describing staturs of the agent 'he' , and 'two meters' express the value of the feature. They provid different information at different level, constructing a feature sturcture.

4 The Advantages of Our Semantic Model

In developing our semantic frameworks, we also have articulated a framework of 'Noun-Centrality' as a supplement to the widely assumed 'Verb-Centrality' practice. We can successfully disambiguate some troublesome sentences, and minimize the redundancy in language knowledge description for natural language processing. We automatically learn a simpler, less redundant representation of the same information.

First, comparing syntactic order and semantic order, we used the reconstructed original order, giving some different order sentences similar results. Thus, variations of order in the same sentence can reveal the same relationships.

One semantic structure may correspond to more syntactic structures in Chinese, and this correspondence can be made specifically clear using our approach.

1.Ta da-le wo	2.Ta ba wo da-le	3.Wo BEI Ta da-le
She beat me	She BA me beat	I BEI she beat
'She beat me.'	'She beat me.'	'I have been beaten by her.'

The above three sentences, their syntactic structures are clearly different from each other. That is, the direct object *wo* 'me' appears right after the main verb in (1) whereas the same logical object has moved to a pre-verbal position with the help of a special Chinese preposition *BA* in (2) and to a sentence-initial position with the help of *BEI* in (3). But underlying the difference syntactic structures, they share the same basic semantic structure, using semantic represented expression, the three sentences of above example can be described in below.

AGENT	*Ta* 'she'
PATIENT	*Wo'me'*
ACTION	*Da* 'beat'

Several different sentences which should be analyzed as having the same syntactic structure may have fundamentally different semantic structures. The following three sentences S1, S2and S3, for example, should be analyzed as having the syntactic structure, but their semantic structures are nevertheless represented as S1', S2' and S3' respectively in our framework.

NP + V + Adj + NP

S1=Ta xiao-tong le duzi

he laugh-painful ASP belly

'He laughed so much that his belly was painful.'

S2=Wo kan-tou le ni

I see- through ASP you

'I understand you thoroughly.'

S3=Ta da po-le beizi

She broke up the cup

She broke up the cup.

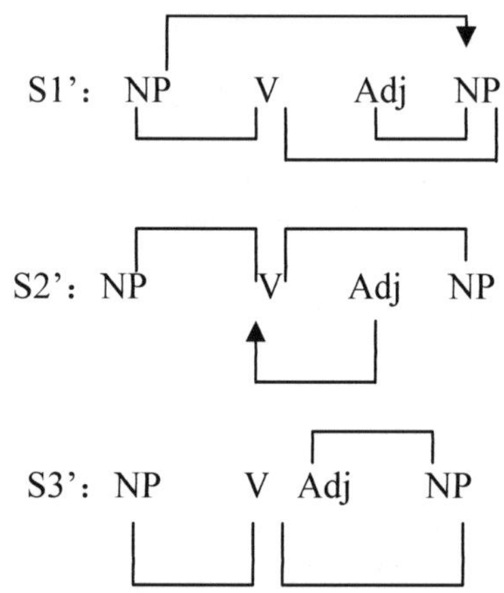

On the other hand, many structural ambiguities in Chinese sentences are one of the major problems in Chinese syntactic analyses. One syntactic structure may correspond to two or more semantic structures, that is, various forms of structural ambiguity are widely observed in Chinese. Disregarding the semantic types will cause syntactic ambiguity. If this type of information is not available during parsing, important clues will be missing, and loss of accuracy will result. Consider the Chinese sentence

Ta de yifu zuo de piaoliang.

Her cloth do DE beautiful

Reading 1: 'She has made the cloth beautifully

Reading 2: (Somebody) has made her cloth beautifully.'

Syntactically, the sentence, with either one of the above two semantic interpretations, should be analyzed as

```
                  S
               /     \
          NP            VP
       /     \        /    \
   NP          N    V       Adj (Complement)
   |           |    |       |
   Ta de    yifu   zuo de piaoliang
   Her    cloth     make DE beautiful
```

But the two semantic structures have to be properly represented in a semantics-oriented framework. We do so as in type A and type B respectively.

Type A: Ta de yifu zuo de piaoliang.

Her cloth do DE beautiful

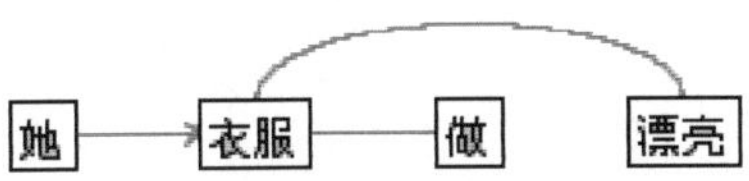

Type B: Ta de yifu zuo de piaoliang.

Her cloth do DE beautiful

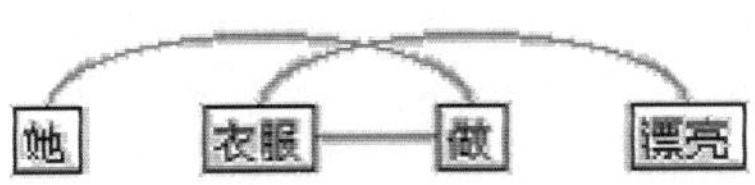

So under our proposal, the above two different types of semantic relations can be clearly represented..

5 Conclusion

In this paper we have demonstrated how our semantic model can be created to analyze and represent the semantic relationships of Chinese sentence structures. The semantic model project is producing a structured tree bank with a richer set of semantic and syntactic relationships of different words on the basis of the analysis of lexical meanings and conceptual structures that underlie those lexical meanings. We developed some methods for determining the relationship between direct semantic items based on the analysis of syntactic and semantic order. The key advantages of our semantic model are:

a) many ambiguous sentences can be clearly represented.

b) minimal redundancy in language knowledge description for natural language processing.

We hope to use the minimum analysis method to find the semantic order with equal relationship among new sentence. We then used the partition relationship as a training database to recognize new order as similar as these order structures.

We also have been creating feature sets parsing feature structures to expressing dependencies between semantic features. Furthermore, we abstracted the values attached to the features. Thus we can expand the feature structures to express this level of detail.

References

Baker C, Fillmore C, Lower J 1998 The Berkeley FrameNet Project, In *Proc. of ACL/COLING 1998.*

Daniel Gildea and Daniel Jurafsky 2002 Automatic Labeling of Semantic Roles. In *Proc. of ACL 2000.*

Nianwen Xue, Fei Xia 2000 The Bracketing Guidelines for the Pann Chinese Treebank, IRCS Report 00-08 University of Pennsylvania, Oct 2000

Dominique Dutoit, Thierry Poibeau 2002 Inferring Knowledge from a Large Semantic Network, In *Proc. of COLING 2000*

James Henderson, Paola Merlo, Ivan Petroff 2002 Using Syntactic Analysis to Increase Efficiency in Visualizing Text Collections, In *Proc. of ACL/COLING 2002.*

Do We Need Chinese Word Segmentation for Statistical Machine Translation?

Jia Xu and **Richard Zens** and **Hermann Ney**
Chair of Computer Science VI
Computer Science Department
RWTH Aachen University, Germany
{xujia,zens,ney}@cs.rwth-aachen.de

Abstract

In Chinese texts, words are not separated by white spaces. This is problematic for many natural language processing tasks. The standard approach is to segment the Chinese character sequence into words. Here, we investigate Chinese word segmentation for statistical machine translation. We pursue two goals: the first one is the maximization of the final translation quality; the second is the minimization of the manual effort for building a translation system.

The commonly used method for getting the word boundaries is based on a word segmentation tool and a predefined monolingual dictionary. To avoid the dependence of the translation system on an external dictionary, we have developed a system that learns a domain-specific dictionary from the parallel training corpus. This method produces results that are comparable with the predefined dictionary.

Further more, our translation system is able to work without word segmentation with only a minor loss in translation quality.

1 Introduction

In Chinese texts, words composed of single or multiple characters, are not separated by white spaces, which is different from most of the western languages. This is problematic for many natural language processing tasks. Therefore, the usual method is to segment a Chinese character sequence into Chinese "words".

Many investigations have been performed concerning Chinese word segmentation. For example, (Palmer, 1997) developed a Chinese word segmenter using a manually segmented corpus. The segmentation rules were learned automatically from this corpus. (Sproat and Shih, 1990) and (Sun et al., 1998) used a method that does not rely on a dictionary or a manually segmented corpus. The characters of the unsegmented Chinese text are grouped into pairs with the highest value of mutual information. This mutual information can be learned from an unsegmented Chinese corpus.

We will present a new method for segmenting the Chinese text without using a manually segmented corpus or a predefined dictionary. In statistical machine translation, we have a bilingual corpus available, which is used to obtain a segmentation of the Chinese text in the following way. First, we train the statistical translation models with the unsegmented bilingual corpus. As a result, we obtain a mapping of Chinese characters to the corresponding English words for each sentence pair. By using this mapping, we can extract a dictionary automatically. With this self-learned dictionary, we use a segmentation tool to obtain a segmented Chinese text. Finally, we retrain our translation system with the segmented corpus.

Additionally, we have performed experiments without explicit word segmentation. In this case, each Chinese character is interpreted as one "word". Based on word groups, our machine translation system is able to work without a word segmentation, while having only a minor translation quality relative loss of less than 5%.

2 Review of the Baseline System for Statistical Machine Translation

2.1 Principle

In statistical machine translation, we are given a source language ('French') sentence $f_1^J = f_1 \ldots f_j \ldots f_J$, which is to be translated into a target language ('English') sentence $e_1^I = e_1 \ldots e_i \ldots e_I$. Among all possible target language sentences, we will choose the sentence with the highest probability:

$$\hat{e}_1^I = \underset{e_1^I}{\operatorname{argmax}} \left\{Pr(e_1^I|f_1^J)\right\} \quad (1)$$

$$= \underset{e_1^I}{\operatorname{argmax}} \left\{Pr(e_1^I) \cdot Pr(f_1^J|e_1^I)\right\} \quad (2)$$

The decomposition into two knowledge sources in Equation 2 is known as the source-channel approach to statistical machine translation (Brown et al., 1990). It allows an independent modeling of target language model $Pr(e_1^I)$ and translation model $Pr(f_1^J|e_1^I)$[1]. The target language model describes the well-formedness of the target language sentence. The translation model links the source language sentence to the target language sentence. The argmax operation denotes the search problem, i.e. the generation of the output sentence in the target language. We have to maximize over all possible target language sentences.

The resulting architecture for the statistical machine translation approach is shown in Figure 1 with the translation model further decomposed into lexicon and alignment model.

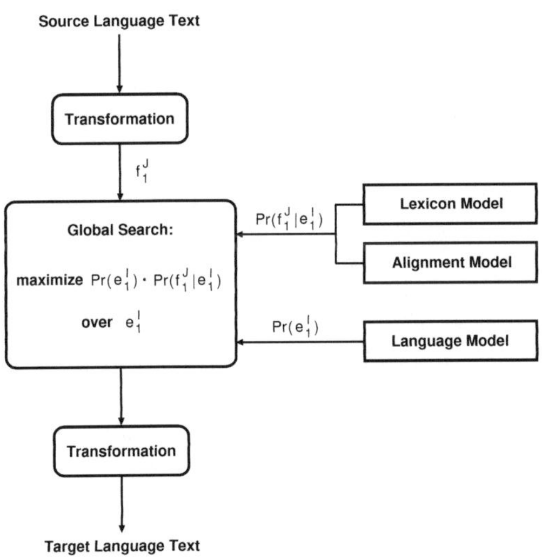

Figure 1: Architecture of the translation approach based on Bayes decision rule.

2.2 Alignment Models

The alignment model $Pr(f_1^J, a_1^J|e_1^I)$ introduces a 'hidden' alignment $\mathbf{a} = a_1^J$, which describes a mapping from a source position j to a target position a_j. The relationship between the translation model and the alignment model is given by:

$$Pr(f_1^J|e_1^I) = \sum_{a_1^J} Pr(f_1^J, a_1^J|e_1^I) \quad (3)$$

In this paper, we use the models IBM-1, IBM-4 from (Brown et al., 1993) and the Hidden-Markov alignment model (HMM) from (Vogel et al., 1996). All these models provide different decompositions of the probability $Pr(f_1^J, a_1^J|e_1^I)$. A detailed description of these models can be found in (Och and Ney, 2003).

A *Viterbi alignment* $\hat{a}_1^J$ of a specific model is an alignment for which the following equation holds:

$$\hat{a}_1^J = \underset{a_1^J}{\operatorname{argmax}}\ Pr(f_1^J, a_1^J|e_1^I). \quad (4)$$

The alignment models are trained on a bilingual corpus using GIZA++(Och et al., 1999; Och and Ney, 2003). The training is done iteratively in succession on the same data, where the final parameter estimates of a simpler model serve as starting point for a more complex model. The result of the training procedure is the Viterbi alignment of the final training iteration for the whole training corpus.

2.3 Alignment Template Approach

In the translation approach from Section 2.1, one disadvantage is that the contextual information is only taken into account by the language model. The single-word based lexicon model does not consider the surrounding words. One way to incorporate the context into the translation model is to learn translations for whole word groups instead of single words. The key elements of this translation approach (Och et al., 1999) are the *alignment templates*. These are pairs of source and target language phrases with an alignment within the phrases.

The alignment templates are extracted from the bilingual training corpus. The extraction algorithm (Och et al., 1999) uses the word alignment information obtained from the models in Section 2.2. Figure 2 shows an example of a word aligned sentence pair. The word alignment is represented with the black boxes. The figure also includes some of the possible alignment templates, represented as the larger, unfilled rectangles. Note that the extraction algo-

[1]The notational convention will be as follows: we use the symbol $Pr(\cdot)$ to denote general probability distributions with (nearly) no specific assumptions. In contrast, for model-based probability distributions, we use the generic symbol $p(\cdot)$.

rithm would extract many more alignment templates from this sentence pair. In this example, the system input was the sequence of Chinese characters *without* any word segmentation. As can be seen, a translation approach that is based on phrases circumvents the problem of word segmentation to a certain degree. This method will be referred to as *"translation with no segmentation"* (see Section 5.2).

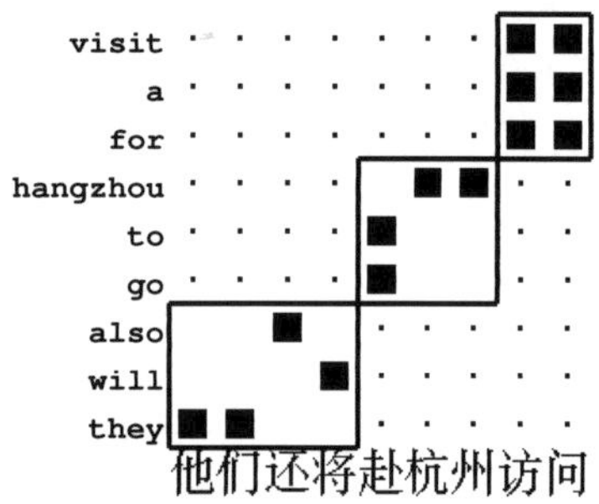

Figure 2: Example of a word aligned sentence pair and some possible alignment templates.

In the Chinese–English DARPA TIDES evaluations in June 2002 and May 2003, carried out by NIST (NIST, 2003), the alignment template approach performed very well and was ranked among the best translation systems.

Further details on the alignment template approach are described in (Och et al., 1999; Och and Ney, 2002).

3 Task and Corpus Statistics

In Section 5.3, we will present results for a Chinese–English translation task. The domain of this task is news articles. As bilingual training data, we use a corpus composed of the English translations of a Chinese Treebank. This corpus is provided by the Linguistic Data Consortium (LDC), catalog number LDC2002E17. In addition, we use a bilingual dictionary with 10K Chinese word entries provided by Stephan Vogel (LDC, 2003b).

Table 1 shows the corpus statistics of this task. We have calculated both the number of words and the number of characters in the corpus. In average, a Chinese word is composed of 1.49 characters. For each of the two languages, there is a set of 20 special characters, such as digits, punctuation marks and symbols like "()%$..."

The training corpus will be used to train a word alignment and then extract the alignment templates and the word-based lexicon. The resulting translation system will be evaluated on the test corpus.

Table 1: Statistics of training and test corpus. For each of the two languages, there is a set of 20 special characters, such as digits, punctuation marks and symbols like "()%$..."

		Chinese	English
Train	Sentences	4 172	
	Characters	172 874	832 760
	Words	116 090	145 422
	Char. Vocab.	3 419 + 20	26 + 20
	Word Vocab.	9 391	9 505
Test	Sentences	993	
	Characters	42 100	167 101
	Words	28 247	26 225

4 Segmentation Methods

4.1 Conventional Method

The commonly used segmentation method is based on a segmentation tool and a monolingual Chinese dictionary. Typically, this dictionary has been produced beforehand and is independent of the Chinese text to be segmented. The dictionary contains Chinese words and their frequencies. This information is used by the segmentation tool to find the word boundaries. In the LDC method (see Section 5.2) we have used the dictionary and segmenter provided by the LDC. More details can be found on the LDC web pages (LDC, 2003a). This segmenter is based on two ideas: it prefers long words over short words and it prefers high frequency words over low frequency words.

4.2 Dictionary Learning from Alignments

In this section, we will describe our method of learning a dictionary from a bilingual corpus.

As mentioned before, the bilingual training corpus listed in Section 3 is the only input to the system. We firstly divide every Chinese characters in the corpus by white spaces, then train the statistical translation models with this unsegmented Chinese text and its English translation, details of the training method are described in Section 2.2.

To extract Chinese words instead of phrases as in Figure 2, we configure the training parameters in GIZA++, the alignment is then restricted to a multi-source-single-target relationship, i.e. one or more Chinese characters are translated to one English word.

The result of this training procedure is an alignment for each sentence pair. Such an alignment is represented as a binary matrix with $J \cdot I$ elements.

An example is shown in Figure 3. The unsegmented Chinese training sentence is plotted along the horizontal axes and the corresponding English sentence along the vertical axes. The black boxes show the Viterbi alignment for this sentence pair. Here, for example the first two Chinese characters are aligned to "industry", the next four characters are aligned to "restructuring".

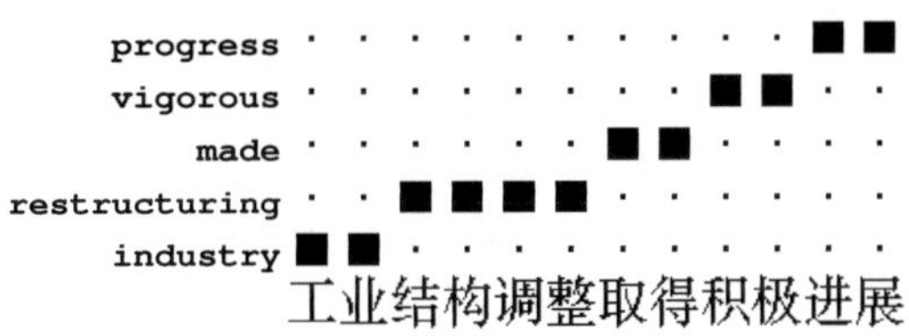

Figure 3: Example of an alignment without word segmentation.

The central idea of our dictionary learning method is: *a contiguous sequence of Chinese characters constitute a Chinese word, if they are aligned to the same English word.* Using this idea and the bilingual corpus, we can automatically generate a Chinese word dictionary. Table 2 shows the Chinese words that are extracted from the alignment in Figure 3.

Table 2: Word entries in Chinese dictionary learned from the alignment in Figure 3.

Nr.	Entry
1	工业
2	结构调整
3	取得
4	积极
5	进展

We extract Chinese words from all sentence pairs in the training corpus. Therefore, it is straightforward to collect word frequency statistics that are needed for the segmentation tool. Once, we have generated the dictionary, we can produce a segmented Chinese corpus using the method described in Section 4.1. Then, we retrain the translation system using the segmented Chinese text.

4.3 Word Length Statistics

In this section, we present statistics of the word lengths in the LDC dictionary as well as in the self-learned dictionary extracted from the alignment.

Table 3 shows the statistics of the word lengths in the LDC dictionary as well as in the learned dictionary. For example, there are 2 368 words consisting of a single character in learned dictionary and 2 511 words in the LDC dictionary. These single character words represent 16.9% of the total number of entries in the learned dictionary and 18.6% in the LDC dictionary.

We see that in the LDC dictionary more than 65% of the words consist of two characters and about 30% of the words consist of a single character or three or four characters. Longer words with more than four characters constitute less than 1% of the dictionary. In the learned dictionary, there are many more long words, about 15%. A subjective analysis showed that many of these entries are either named entities or idiomatic expressions. Often, these idiomatic expressions should be segmented into shorter words. Therefore, we will investigate methods to overcome this problem in the future. Some suggestions will be discussed in Section 6.

Table 3: Statistics of word lengths in the LDC dictionary and in the learned dictionary.

word	LDC dictionary		learned dictionary	
length	frequency	[%]	frequency	[%]
1	2 334	18.6	2 368	16.9
2	8 149	65.1	5 486	39.2
3	1 188	9.5	1 899	13.6
4	759	6.1	2 084	14.9
5	70	0.6	791	5.7
6	20	0.2	617	4.4
7	6	0.0	327	2.3
≥8	11	0.0	424	3.0
total	12 527	100	13 996	100

5 Translation Experiments

5.1 Evaluation Criteria

So far, in machine translation research, a single generally accepted criterion for the evaluation of the experimental results does not exist. We have used three automatic criteria. For the test corpus, we have four references available. Hence, we compute all the following criteria with respect to multiple references.

- WER (word error rate):
  The WER is computed as the minimum number of substitution, insertion and deletion operations that have to be performed to convert the generated sentence into the reference sentence.
- PER (position-independent word error rate):
  A shortcoming of the WER is that it requires a perfect word order. The word order of an acceptable sentence can be different from that of the target sentence, so that the WER measure alone could be misleading. The PER compares the words in the two sentences ignoring the word order.
- BLEU score:
  This score measures the precision of unigrams, bigrams, trigrams and fourgrams with respect to a reference translation with a penalty for too short sentences (Papineni et al., 2001). The BLEU score measures accuracy, i.e. large BLEU scores are better.

5.2 Summary: Three Translation Methods

In the experiments, we compare the following three translation methods:

- Translation with **no segmentation**: Each Chinese character is interpreted as a single word.
- Translation with **learned segmentation**: It uses the self-learned dictionary.
- Translation with **LDC segmentation**: The predefined LDC dictionary is used.

The core contribution of this paper is the method we called *"translation with learned segmentation"*, which consists of three steps:

- The input is a sequence of Chinese characters without segmentation. After the training using GIZA++, we extract a monolingual Chinese dictionary from the alignment. This is discussed in Section 4.2, and an example is given in Figure 3 and Table 2.
- Using this learned dictionary, we segment the sequence of Chinese characters into words. In other words, the LDC method is used, but the LDC dictionary is replaced by the learned dictionary (see Section 4.1).
- Based on this word segmentation, we perform another training using GIZA++. Then, after training the models IBM1, HMM and IBM4, we extract bilingual word groups, which are referred as alignment templates.

5.3 Evaluation Results

The evaluation is performed on the LDC corpus described in Section 3. The translation performance of the three systems is summarized in Table 4 for the three evaluation criteria WER, PER and BLEU. We observe that the translation quality with the learned segmentation is similar to that with the LDC segmentation. The WER of the system with the learned segmentation is somewhat better, but PER and BLEU are slightly worse. We conclude that it is possible to learn a domain-specific dictionary for Chinese word segmentation from a bilingual corpus. Therefore the translation system is independent of a predefined dictionary, which may be unsuitable for a certain task.

The translation system using no segmentation performs slightly worse. For example, for the WER there is a loss of about 2% relative compared to the system with the LDC segmentation.

Table 4: Translation performance of different segmentation methods (all numbers in percent).

method	error rates		accuracy
	WER	PER	BLEU
no segment.	73.3	56.5	27.6
learned segment.	70.4	54.6	29.1
LDC segment.	71.9	54.4	29.2

5.4 Effect of Segmentation on Translation Results

In this section, we present three examples of the effect that segmentation may have on translation quality. For each of the three examples in

Figure 4, we show the segmented Chinese source sentence using either the LDC dictionary or the self-learned dictionary, the corresponding translation and the human reference translation.

In the first example, the LDC dictionary leads to a correct segmentation, whereas with the learned dictionary the segmentation is erroneous. The second and third token should be combined ("Hong Kong"), whereas the fifth token should be separated ("stabilize in the long term"). In this case, the wrong segmentation of the Chinese source sentence does not result in a wrong translation. A possible reason is that the translation system is based on word groups and can recover from these segmentation errors.

In the second example, the segmentation with the LDC dictionary produces at least one error. The second and third token should be combined ("this"). It is possible to combine the seventh and eighth token to a single word because the eighth token shows only the tense. The segmentation with the learned dictionary is correct. Here, the two segmentations result in different translations.

In the third example, both segmentations are incorrect and these segmentation errors affect the translation results. In the segmentation with the LDC dictionary, the first Chinese characters should be segmented as a separate word. The second and third character and maybe even the fourth character should be combined to one word.[2] The fifth and sixth character should be combined to a single word. In the segmentation with the learned dictionary, the fifth and sixth token (seventh and eighth character) should be combined ("isolated"). We see that this term is missing in the translation. Here, the segmentation errors result in translation errors.

6 Discussion and Future Work

We have presented a new method for Chinese word segmentation. It avoids the use of a predefined dictionary and instead learns a corpus-specific dictionary from the bilingual training corpus.

The idea is extracting a self-learned dictionary from the trained alignment models. This method has the advantage that the word entries in the dictionary all occur in the training data, and its content is much closer to the training text as a predefined dictionary, which can never cover all possible word occurrences. Here, if the content of the test corpus is closer to that of the

[2]This is an example of an ambiguous segmentation.

Example 1

LDC dictionary:
有利 香港 经济 长期 繁荣 稳定 。
It will benefit Hong Kong's economy to prosper and stabilize in the long term.

Learned dictionary:
有利 香 港 经济 长期繁荣 稳定 。
It will benefit Hong Kong's economy to prosper and stabilize in the long term.

Reference:
It will be benificial for the stability and prosperity of Hong Kong in the long run.

Example 2

LDC dictionary:
但是 这 次 会议 呢 还是 取得 了 一定 的 进展 。
but this meeting down or achieved certain progress.

Learned dictionary:
但是 这次 会议 呢 还是 取得了 一定 的 进展 。
however, this meeting straight down still achieved certain progress.

Reference:
Neverless, this meeting has achieved some progress.

Example 3

LDC dictionary:
... 在世 界 上面 临 孤立 的 又 一个 证明 ...
... the unification of the world carried adjacent isolate of proof, ...

Learned dictionary:
... 在 世界 上 面临 孤 立 的 又一个 证明 ...
... in the world faced with a became another proof, ...

Reference:
... another proof that ... is facing isolation in the world ...

Figure 4: Translation examples using the learned dictionary and the LDC dictionary.

training corpus, the quality of the dictionary is higher and the translation performance would be better.

The experiments showed that the translation quality with the learned segmentation is competitive with the LDC segmentation. Additionally, we have shown the feasibility of a Chinese–English statistical machine translation system that works without any word segmentation. There is only a minor loss in translation performance. Further improvements could be possible by tuning the system toward this specific task.

We expect that our method could be improved by considering the word length as discussed in Section 4.3. As shown in the word length statistics, long words with more than four characters occur only occasionally. Most of them are named entity words, which are written in English in upper case. Therefore, we can apply a simple rule: we accept a long Chinese word only if the corresponding English word is in upper case. This should result in an improved dictionary. An alternative way is to use the word length statistics in Table 3 as a prior distribution. In this case, long words would get a penalty, because their prior probability is low.

Because the extraction of our dictionary is based on bilingual information, it might be interesting to combine it with methods that use monolingual information only.

For Chinese–English, there is a large number of bilingual corpora available at the LDC. Therefore using additional corpora, we can expect to get an improved dictionary.

References

P. F. Brown, J. Cocke, S. A. Della Pietra, V. J. Della Pietra, F. Jelinek, J. D. Lafferty, R. L. Mercer, and P. S. Roossin. 1990. A statistical approach to machine translation. *Computational Linguistics*, 16(2):79–85, June.

P. F. Brown, S. A. Della Pietra, V. J. Della Pietra, and R. L. Mercer. 1993. The mathematics of statistical machine translation: Parameter estimation. *Computational Linguistics*, 19(2):263–311, June.

LDC. 2003a. LDC Chinese resources home page. http://www.ldc.upenn.edu/Projects/Chinese/LDC_ch.htm.

LDC. 2003b. LDC resources home page. http://www.ldc.upenn.edu/Projects/TIDES/mt2004cn.htm.

NIST. 2003. Machine translation home page. http://www.nist.gov/speech/tests/mt/index.htm.

F. J. Och and H. Ney. 2002. Discriminative training and maximum entropy models for statistical machine translation. In *Proc. of the 40th Annual Meeting of the Association for Computational Linguistics (ACL)*, pages 295–302, Philadelphia, PA, July.

F. J. Och and H. Ney. 2003. A systematic comparison of various statistical alignment models. *Computational Linguistics*, 29(1):19–51, March.

F. J. Och, C. Tillmann, and H. Ney. 1999. Improved alignment models for statistical machine translation. In *Proc. of the Joint SIGDAT Conf. on Empirical Methods in Natural Language Processing and Very Large Corpora*, pages 20–28, University of Maryland, College Park, MD, June.

D. D. Palmer. 1997. A trainable rule-based algorithm for word segmentation. In *Proc. of the 35th Annual Meeting of ACL and 8th Conference of the European Chapter of ACL*, pages 321–328, Madrid, Spain, August.

K. A. Papineni, S. Roukos, T. Ward, and W. J. Zhu. 2001. Bleu: a method for automatic evaluation of machine translation. Technical Report RC22176 (W0109-022), IBM Research Division, Thomas J. Watson Research Center, September.

R. W. Sproat and C. Shih. 1990. A statistical method for finding word boundaries in Chinese text. *Computer Processing of Chinese and Oriental Languages*, 4:336–351.

M. Sun, D. Shen, and B. K. Tsou. 1998. Chinese word segmentation without using lexicon and hand-crafted training data. In *Proc. of the 36th Annual Meeting of ACL and 17th Int. Conf. on Computational Linguistics (COLING-ACL 98)*, pages 1265–1271, Montreal, Quebec, Canada, August.

S. Vogel, H. Ney, and C. Tillmann. 1996. HMM-based word alignment in statistical translation. In *COLING '96: The 16th Int. Conf. on Computational Linguistics*, pages 836–841, Copenhagen, Denmark, August.

A Semi-Supervised Approach to Build Annotated Corpus for Chinese Named Entity Recognition

Xiaoshan FANG[#], Jianfeng GAO[*], Huanye SHENG[#]
[*]Microsoft Research Asia, jfgao@microsoft.com
[#]Shanghai Jiaotong University, China, {fang-xs, hysheng}@sjtu.edu.cn

Abstract

This paper presents a semi-supervised approach to reduce human effort in building an annotated Chinese corpus. One of the disadvantages of many statistical Chinese named entity recognition systems is that training data may be in short supply, and manually building annotated corpus is expensive. In the proposed approach, we construct an 80M hand-annotated corpus in three steps: (1) Automatically annotate training corpus; (2) Manually refine small subsets of the automatically annotated corpus; (3) Combine small subsets and whole corpus in a bootstrapping process. Our approach is tested on a state-of-the-art Chinese word segmentation system (Gao et al., 2003, 2004). Experiments show that only a small subset of hand-annotated corpus is sufficient to achieve a satisfying performance of the named entity component in this system.

1 Introduction

The success of applying statistical methods to natural language processing tasks depends to a large degree upon the quality and amount of available training data.

This paper presents our method of creating training data for the statistical Chinese word segmenter proposed in Gao *et al.* (2003). The segmenter is based on improved source-channel models, which are trained on a large amount of annotated training data. Whereas the hand-annotation is a very expensive task, creating the training data automatically remains an open research problem. Our approach falls somewhere between the two extremes of the spectrum. We try to minimize the human effort while keeping the quality of the annotation reasonably good for model estimation. The method to be presented has been discussed briefly in Gao *et al.* (2003). This paper presents an extended description with more details and experimental results.

The training data refer to a set of Chinese sentences where word boundaries and types have been annotated. Our basic solution is the bootstrapping approach described in Gao *et al.* (2002). It consists of three steps: (1) Initially, we use a greedy word segmenter to annotate the corpus, and obtain initial models based on the initial annotated corpus; (2) We re-annotate the corpus using the obtained models; (3) Re-train the models using the re-annotated corpus. Steps 2 and 3 are iterated until the performance of the system converges.

In this approach, the quality of the resulting models depends to a large degree upon the quality of the initial annotated corpus. Because there are many named entities that are not stored in a dictionary, traditional dictionary-based forward maximum matching (FMM) algorithm is not sufficient to create a good initial corpus. We thus manually annotate named entities on a small subset (call *seed set*) of the training data. Then, we obtain a model on the seed set (called *seed model*). We thus improve the initial model which is trained on the initial annotated training corpus by interpolating it with the seed model. Our experiments show that a relatively small seed set (e.g., 10 million characters, which takes approximately three weeks for 4 persons to annotate the NE tags) is enough to get a good improved model for initialization.

The remainder of this paper is organized as follows: Section 2 summarizes the related work. Section 3 deals with our approach to improve model estimation for Chinese word segmentation. The experiments are presented at Section 4. Finally we conclude in Section 5.

2 Related work

Traditional statistical approaches use a parametric model with maximum likelihood estimation (MLE), usually with smoothing methods to deal with data sparseness problems. These approaches have been introduced for the task of Chinese word segmentation. According to the training data used (word-segmented or not), the Chinese word segmentation can be achieved in a supervised or unsupervised manner.

As an example of unsupervised training, Ge *et al.* (1999) presents a simple zero-th order Markov

[1] This work was done while the author was visiting Microsoft Research Asia.

model of the words in Chinese text. They developed an efficient algorithm to train their model on an unsegmented corpus. Their basic assumption is that Chinese words are usually 1 to 4 characters long. They however did not take into account a large amount of named entities (e.g. Chinese organization name, transliterate name and some person names) most of which are longer than 4 characters (e.g., 微软亚洲研究院 Microsoft Research Asia, 加利福尼亚 California, 陈欧阳晓彤 a woman's name which puts her husband's surname ahead).

An and Wong used Hidden Markov Models (HMM) for segmentation. Their system is solely trained on a corpus which has been manually annotated with word boundaries and Part-of-Speech tags. Wu (2003) also used the training data to tune the segmentation parameters of their MSR-NLP Chinese system. He used the annotated training data to deal with the morphologically derived words.

In this paper we present a semi-supervised training method where we use both an auto-segmented training corpus and a small hand-annotated subset of it. Comparing to unsupervised approaches, our approach leads to a better segmenter that can identify much more named entities which are not in the dictionary. Comparing to supervised approaches, our method requires much less human effort for data annotation.

The Chinese word segmenter used in this study is described in Gao *et al.* (2003). The segmenter provides a unified approach to word segmentation and named entity (NE) recognition. This unified approach is based on the improved source-channel models of Chinese sentence generation, with two components: a source model and a set of channel models. For each word class (e.g. a person name), there is a channel model (referred to as *class model* afterwards) that estimates the generative probability of a character string given the word type. The source model is used to estimate the generative probability of a word sequence, in which each word belongs to one word class (e.g. a word in a lexicon or a named entity). In another word, it indicates, given a context, how likely a word occurs. So the source model is also referred to as *context model* afterwards. This paper focuses the discussion on how to create annotated corpus for context model estimation.

3 A semi-supervised approach to improve context model estimation

In this study the context model is a trigram model which estimates the probability of a word class.

Ideally, given an annotated corpus, where each sentence is segmented into words which are tagged by their word types, the trigram word class probabilities can be calculated using MLE, together with a backoff schema (Katz, 1987) to deal with the sparse data problem. Unfortunately, building such annotated training corpora is very expensive.

Our basic solution is the bootstrapping approach described in Gao et al. (2002). It consists of three steps: (1) Initially, a greedy word segmenter (i.e. FMM) is used to annotate the corpus, and an initial context model is obtained based on the initial annotated corpus; (2) Re-annotate the corpus using the obtained models; (3) Re-train the context model using the re-annotated corpus. Steps 2 and 3 are iterated until the performance of the system converges.

In the above approach, the quality of the context model depends to a large degree upon the quality of the initial annotated corpus, which is however not satisfied due to the fact that many named entities cannot be identifying using the greedy word segmenter which is based on the dictionary. As a consequence, the above approach achieves a low accuracy in detecting Chinese named entities.

A straightforward solution to the above problem is to obtain large amount of high-quality annotated corpus for context model estimation. Unfortunately, manually creating such annotated corpus is very expensive. For example, Douglas (1999) pointed out that at least up to about 1.2 million words of training data are necessary to train an HMM name recognizer. To guarantee a high degree of accuracy (e.g. 90% F-measure), it requires about 800 hours, or 20 person*weeks of labor to annotate and check the amount of data. This is almost certainly more time than would be required by a skilled rule writer to write a rule-based name recognizer achieving the same level of performance, assuming all the necessary resources, such as lexicons and name lists, are already available.

Our training data contains approximately 80 million Chinese characters from various domains of text. We are facing three questions in annotating the training data. (1) How to generate a high quality hand-annotated corpus? (2) How to best use the valuable hand-annotated corpus so as to achieve a satisfying performance? (3) What is the optimal size of the hand-annotated corpus, considering the tradeoff between the cost of human labor and the performance of the resulting segmenter?

We leave the answers to the first and third questions to Section 4. In what follows, we describe our method of using small set of human-annotated corpus to boost the quality of the annotation of the entire corpus. It consists of 6 steps.

Step 1: Manually annotate named entities on a small subset (call seed set) of the training data.

Step 2: Obtain a context model on the seed set (called seed model).

Step 3: Re-annotate the training corpus using the seed model and then train an improved context model using the re-annotated corpus.

Step 4: Manually annotate another small subset of the training data. Repeat Steps (2) and (3) until the entire training data have been annotated.

Step 5: Repeat steps 1 to 4 using different seed sets (we used three seed sets in our experiments, as we shall describe in Section 4).

Step 6: Combine all context models obtained in step 5 via linear interpolation:

$$P(xyz) = \Sigma\, \lambda_i \times P_i(xyz) \quad (1)$$

Here $P_i(xyz)$ is the trigram probability of the i-th context model. λ_s is the interpolation weights which vary from 0 to 1.

4 Experiments

In this section, we first present our experiments on the generation and evaluation of hand-annotated corpus to answer the first two questions. Then, the answer to the third question is given in subsection 4.2.

4.1 The generation and evaluation of hand-annotated corpus

4.1.1 The generation of hand-annotated corpus

Four students, whose major is Chinese language, annotate the corpus according to a pre-defined MSRA's guideline of Chinese named entities. We find that we have to revise the guideline when they were annotating the corpus. For example, Chinese character string "申城博览会 (Shanghai Exposition)"can be tagged as either "[L 申]城博览会" or "[L 申城]博览会". Here "申" is the abbreviation of "上海(Shanghai)". "城" is the abbreviation of "城市(city)". L is the tag of location name. It is not clearly described in the guideline where the named entity's right boundary is.

We obtain in total three manually annotated subsets (i.e. seed sets) by the following process:

1. Annotate the training data using a greedy word segmenter. Highlight the NEs and their tags.
2. Randomly select 10 million characters from the annotated training data and then ask the students to manually refine these 10 million characters. The refinement includes correcting the wrong NE tags and adding missing NE tags.
3. Repeat the second step, and then combine the obtained new 10-million-character subset with the first one. Hence, a 20-million-character subset of the training data is obtained.
4. Repeat the second step, and then combine the obtained new 10-million-character subset with the 20-million-character subset. Hence, a 30-million-character subset of the training data is obtained.

A manually annotated test set was developed as well. The text corpus contains approximately a half million Chinese characters that have been proofread and balanced in terms of domain, styles, and times.

4.1.2 The evaluation of hand-annotated corpus

To evaluate the quality of our annotated corpus, we trained a context model using the method described in Section 3, with the first-obtained 10-million-character seed set. We then compare the performance of the resulting segmenter with those of other state-of-the-art segmenters and the FMM segmenter.

4.1.2.1 Evaluation metrics

We conduct evaluations in terms of precision (P) and recall (R).

$$P = \frac{number \cdot of \cdot correctly \cdot identified \cdot NEs}{number \cdot of \cdot identified \cdot NEs} \quad (2)$$

$$R = \frac{number \cdot of \cdot correctly \cdot identified \cdot NEs}{number \cdot of \cdot all \cdot NEs} \quad (3)$$

4.1.2.2 Segmenters in Comparison

1. The **MSWS** system is one of the best available products. It is released by Microsoft® (as a set of Windows APIs). **MSWS** first conducts the word-breaking using MM (augmented by heuristic rules for disambiguation), and then conducts factoid detection and NER using rules.
2. The **LCWS** system is one of the best research systems in mainland China. It is released by Beijing Language University. The system works similarly to **MSWS**, but has a larger dictionary containing more PNs and LNs.
3. The **PBWS** system is a rule-based Chinese parser which can also output the word segmentation results. It explores high-level linguistic knowledge, such as syntactic structure for Chinese word segmentation and NER.

4.1.2.3 Results

The performance of the resulting segmenter is compared with those of three state-of-the-art segmenters and FMM segmenter in Table 1. Here PN, LN and ON stand for person name, location name and organization name respectively. The first column lists the segmenters.

As can be seen from Table 1, the resulting segmenter (SSSC.10m) achieves comparable results with those of the other three state-of-the-art word segmenters. From Table 1 we also find that our semi-supervised approach makes a 2.4%-49% improvement over FMM.

Segmenter	PN		LN		ON	
	R %	P %	R %	P %	R %	P %
MSWS	74.4	90.7	44.2	93.5	46.9	64.2
LCWS	78.1	94.5	72.0	85.4	13.1	71.3
PBWS	78.7	78.0	73.6	76.7	21.6	81.7
FMM	65.7	84.4	82.7	76.0	56.6	38.6
SSSC.10m	73.6	86.6	80.7	89.5	84.3	56.8
Impr. (%)	12.0	2.6	2.4	17.7	49.0	47.1

Table 1: Results on different Chinese word segmenters

The results show a moderate amount of hand-annotated corpus leads our segmenter to a state-of-the-art performance.

4.2 The optimal size of the hand-annotated corpus

Regarding the third question: what is the optimal size of the hand-annotated subset, considering the tradeoff between the cost of human labor and the performance of the resulting segmenter? We obtain a series of results using 10-30-million-character subsets as seed sets, and then plot three graphs showing the relationship between the performances and their corresponding human efforts of constructing the seed set.

4.2.1 Baselines

We use two baselines.

One is the FMM method, which does not use annotated training data. It is used to evaluate the performances using 10-30-million-character subsets (see Figure 1).

The other is to use all the human effort of annotating the whole training data, which takes about 1920 person*hours human effort. It is used to calculate how much labor we would save by using the semi-supervised approach described in section 3.

4.2.2 Results

The relationship between the performances and their corresponding human efforts of constructing the seed sets is shown in Figure 1. The X-axes give the human efforts on building 10, 20, and 30-million-character subsets. They are 360, 720, and 1080 person*hours. The Y-axes show the recall and precision results on person name, location name and organization name, separately.

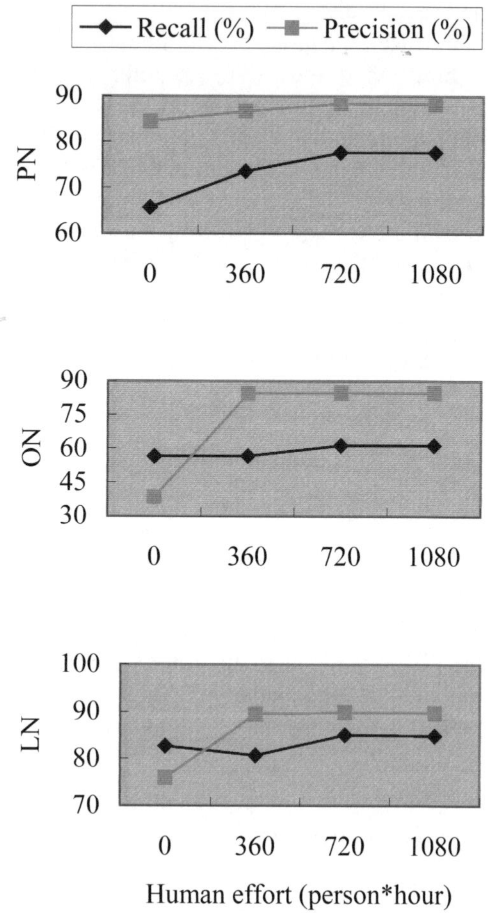

Figure 1: The relationship between the performances and their corresponding human efforts

We observe that both the recall and precision results first go upwards, and level off after the use of 720 person*hours, which is the corresponding human effort of constructing 20 million characters. This means that 20 million characters is a saturation point, because more human effort does not lead to any improvement in performance, and less human effort leads to lower performance.

From the fact that manually annotating the whole training data costs 1920 person*hours, we indicate that by using our semi-supervised approach we save 62.5% human labor in corpus annotation.

5 Conclusion

This paper presents a semi-supervised method to save human effort in building annotated corpus. This method uses a small set of human-annotated corpus to boost the quality of the annotation of the entire corpus. We test this method on Gao's Chinese word segmentation system, which achieves a state-of-the-art performance on SIGHAN backoff data sets (Gao et al, 2004).

Several conclusions can be drawn from our experiments:

- The obtained corpus is of high quality.
- 20-million-characters is the optimal size of hand-annotated subset to boost the 80-million-character training data, considering the trade-off between the cost of human labor and the performance of the resulting segmenter.
- We save 62.5% human labor in corpus annotation.

References

An, Q. and Wong, W. S. 1996. *Automatic segmentation and tagging of Hanzi text using a hybrid algorithm.* In Proceedings of the 9th International Conference on Indus-trial & Engineering Applications of AI & Expert Systems.

Borthwick, Andrew. 1999. *A Maximum Entropy Approach to Named Entity Recognition.* Ph.D. thesis, New York University.

Douglas Appelt. 1999. *Introduction to Information Extraction Technology.* A Tutorial Prepared for IJCAI-99.

Gao, Jianfeng, Joshua Goodman, Mingjing Li and Kai-Fu Lee. 2002. *Toward a unified approach to statistical language modeling for Chinese.* ACM TALIP, 1(1): 3-33.

Gao, Jianfeng, Mu Li and Changning Huang. 2003. *Improved source-channel models for Chinese word segmentation.* In ACL-2003. Sapporo, Japan.

Gao, Jianfeng, Andi Wu, Mu Li, Chang-Ning Huang, Hongqiao Li, Haowei Qin and Xinsong Xia. 2004. *Adaptive Chinese Word Segmentation.* In proceedings of ACL 2004. Barcelona, Spain.

Ge, X., Pratt, W. and Smyth, P. 1999. *Discovering Chinese Words from Unsegmented Text.* SIGIR-99, pages 271-272.

Hockenmaier, J. and Brew, C. 1998. *Error-driven learning of Chinese word segmentation.* In J. Guo, K. T. Lua, and J. Xu, editors, 12th Pacific Conference on Language and Information, pp. 218229, Singapore. Chinese and Oriental Languages Processing Society.

Katz, S. M. 1987. *Estimation of probabilities from sparse data for the language model component of a speech recognizer.* IEEE Trans. Acoustics, Speech Signal Process. ASSP-35, 3 (March), 400-401.

Palmer, David. 1997. *A Trainable Rule-Based Algorithm for Word Segmentation.* In Proceedings of the 35th Annual Meeting of the Association for Computational Linguistics (ACL '97), Madrid.

Sun, Jian, Jianfeng Gao, Lei Zhang, Ming Zhou, and Changning Huang. 2002. *Chinese named entity identification using class-based language model.* In: COLING 2002. Taipei, Taiwan.

Wu, Andi. 2003. *Chinese Word Segmentation in MSR-NLP.* In Proceedings of the Second SIGHAN Workshop on Chinese Language Processing, Sapporo, Japan.

A New Chinese Natural Language Understanding Architecture Based on Multilayer Search Mechanism

Wanxiang Che **Ting Liu** **Sheng Li**
School of Computer Science and Technology
Harbin Institute of Technology
P.O. Box 321, HIT
Harbin China, 150001
{car, tliu, ls}@ir.hit.edu.cn

Abstract

A classical Chinese Natural Language Understanding (NLU) architecture usually includes several NLU components which are executed with some mechanism. A new Multilayer Search Mechanism (MSM) which integrates and quantifies these components into a uniform multilayer treelike architecture is presented in this paper. The mechanism gets the optimal result with search algorithms. The components in MSM affect each other. At last, the performance of each component is enhanced. We built a practical system – CUP (Chinese Understanding Platform) based on MSM with three layers. By the experiments on Word Segmentation, a better performance was achieved. In theory the normal cascade and feedback mechanism are just some special cases of MSM.

1 Introduction

At present a classical Chinese NLU architecture usually includes several components, such as Word Segmentation (Word-Seg), POS Tagging, Phrase Analysis, Parsing, Word Sense Disambiguation (WSD) and so on. These components are executed one by one from lower layers (such as Word-Seg, POS Tagging) to higher layers (such as Parsing, WSD) to form a kind of cascade mechanism. But when people build a NLU system based on these complex language analysis, it is a very serious problem since the errors of each layer component are multiplied. With more and more analysis components, the final result becomes too bad to be applicable.

Another problem is that the components in the system affect each other when people build a practical but toy NLU system. Here the toy system means that each component is ideal enough with perfect input. But in fact, on the one hand the lower layer components need the information of higher layer components; on the other hand the incorrect analysis of lower layers must reduce the accuracy of higher layers. In Chinese Word-Seg component, many segmentation ambiguities which cannot be solved using only lexical information. In order to improve the performance of Word-Seg, we have to use some syntax and even semantic information. Without correct Word-Seg results, however the syntax and semantic parser cannot obtain a correct analysis. It is a chain debts problem.

People have tried to solve the error-multiplied problem by integrating multi-layers into a uniform model (Gao et al., 2001; Nagata, 1994). But with the increasing number of integrated layers, the model becomes too complex to build or solve.

The feedback mechanism (Wu and Jiang, 1998) helps to use the information of high layers to control the final result. If the analysis at feedback point cannot be passed, the whole analysis will be denied. This mechanism places too much burden on the function of feedback point. This leads to the problems that a correct lower layer result may be rejected or an error result may be accepted.

We propose a new Multilayer Search Mechanism (MSM) to solve the problems mentioned above. Based on the mechanism, we build a practical Chinese NLU platform – CUP (Chinese Understanding Platform). Section 2 introduces the background and architecture of the new mechanism and how to build it up. Experimental results with CUP is given in Section 3. In Section 4, we discuss why the new mechanism gets better results than the old ones. Conclusions and the some future work follow in Section 5.

2 Multilayer Search Mechanism

The novel Multilayer Search Mechanism (MSM) integrates and quantifies NLU components into a uniform multilayer treelike platform, such as Word-Seg, POS Tagging, Parsing and so on. These components affect each other by computing the final score and then get better results.

2.1 Background

Considering a Chinese sentence, the sentence analysis task can be formally defined as finding a set of word segmentation sequence (W), a POS tagging sequence (POS), a syntax dependency parsing tree (DP) and so on which maximize their joint probability $P(W, POS, DP, \cdots)$. In this paper, we assume that there are only three layers W, POS and DP in MSM. It is relatively straightforward, however, to extend the method to the case for which there are more than three layers. Therefore, the sentence analysis task can be described as finding a triple $< W, POS, DP >$ that maximize the joint probability $P(W, POS, DP)$.

$$< W, POS, DP >= \arg\max_{W,POS,DP} P(W, POS, DP)$$

The joint probability distribution $P(W, POS, DP)$ can be written in the following form using the chain rule of probability:

$$\begin{aligned} & P(W, POS, DP) \\ & = P(W)P(POS|W)P(DP|W, POS) \end{aligned}$$

Where $P(W)$ is considered as the probability of the word segmentation layer, $P(POS|W)$ is the conditional probability of POS Tagging with a given word segmentation result, $P(DP|W, POS)$ is the conditional probability of a dependency parsing tree with a given word segmentation and POS Tagging result similarly. So the form of $< W, POS, DP >$ can be transformed into:

$$\begin{aligned} & < W, POS, DP > \\ & = \arg\max_{W,POS,DP} P(W, POS, DP) \\ & = \arg\max_{W,POS,DP} P(W)P(POS|W)P(DP|W, POS) \\ & = \arg\max_{W,POS,DP} \log P(W) + \log P(POS|W) \\ & \quad + \log P(DP|W, POS) \\ & = \arg\min_{W,POS,DP} -\log P(W) - \log P(POS|W) \\ & \quad - \log P(DP|W, POS) \end{aligned}$$

We consider that each inversion of probability's logarithm at the last step of the above equation is a score given by a component (Such as Word-Seg, POS Tagging and so on). So at last, we find an n-tuple $< W, POS, DP, \cdots >$ that minimizes the last score S_n of a sentence analysis result with n layers. S_n is defined as:

$$S_n = s_1 + s_2 + \cdots + s_n \tag{1}$$

s_i denotes the score of the ith layer component.

2.2 The Architecture of Multilayer Search Mechanism

Because there are lots of analysis results at each layer, it's a combinatorial explosion problem to find the optimal result. Assuming that each component produces m results for an input on average and there are n layers in a NLU system, the final search space is m^n. With the increasing of n, it's impossible for a system to find the optimal result in the huge search space.

The classical cascade mechanism uses a greedy algorithm to solve the problem. It only keeps the optimal result at each layer. But if it's a fault analysis result for the optimal result at a layer, it's impossible for this mechanism to find the final correct analysis result.

To overcome the difficulty, we build a new Multilayer Search Mechanism (MSM). Different from the cascade mechanism, MSM maintains a number of results at each component, so that the correct analysis should be included in these results with high probability. Then MSM tries to use the information of all layer components to find out the correct analysis result. Different from the feedback mechanism, the acceptance of an analysis is not based on a higher layer components alone. The lower layer components provide some information to help to find the correct analysis result as well.

According to the above idea, we design the architecture of MSM with multilayer treelike structure. The original input is root and the several analysis results of the input become branches. Iterating this progress, we get a bigger analysis tree. Figure 1 gives an analysis example of a Chinese sentence "他喜爱美丽的鲜花。" (He likes beautiful flowers). For the input sentence, there are several Word-Seg results with scores (the lower the better). Then for each of Word-Seg results, there are several POS Tagging results, too. And for each of POS Tagging result, the same thing happens. So we get a big tree structure and the correct analysis result is a path in the tree from the root to the leaf except for there is no correct analysis result in some analysis components.

A search algorithm can be used to find out the correct analysis result among the lowest score in the tree. But because each layer cannot give the exact score in Equation 1 as the standard score and the ability of analysis are different with different layers, we should weight every score. Then the last score is the linear weighted sum (Equation 2).

$$S_n = w_1 s_1 + w_2 s_2 + \cdots + w_n s_n \qquad (2)$$

s_i denotes the score of the ith layer component which we will introduce in Section 3; w_i denotes the weight of the ith layer components which we will introduce in the next section.

In order to get the optimal result, all kinds of tree search algorithms can be used. Here the BEST-FIRST SEARCH Algorithm (Russell and Norvig, 1995) is used. Figure 2 shows the main algorithm steps.

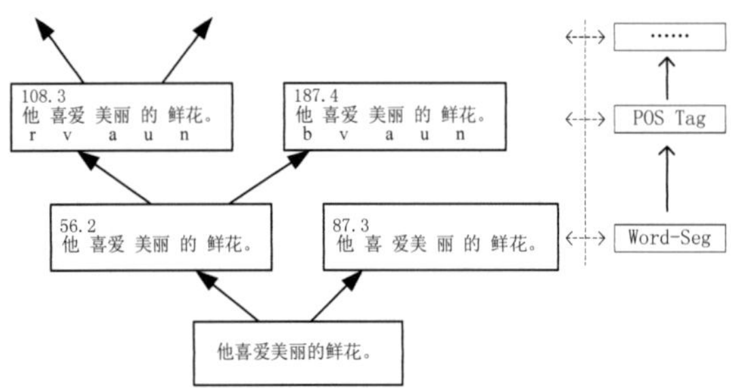

Figure 1: An Example of Multilayer Search Mechanism

1. Add the initial node (starting point) to the queue.
2. Compare the front node to the goal state. If they match then the solution is found.
3. If they do not match then expand the front node by adding all the nodes from its links.
4. If all nodes in the queue are expanded then the goal state is not found (e.g.there is no solution). Stop.
5. According to Equation 2 evaluate the score of expanded nodes and reorder the nodes in the queue.
6. Go to step 2.

Figure 2: BEST-FIRST SEARCH Algorithm

2.3 Layer Weight

We should find out a group of appropriate $w_1, w_2, \cdots, w_n$ in Equation 2 to maximize the number of the optimal paths in MSM which can get the correct results. They are expressed by W^*.

$$W^* = \arg\max_{W} ObjFun(\min S_n) \qquad (3)$$

Here W^* is named as Whole Layer Weight. $ObjFun(*)$ denotes a function to value the result that a group of W can get. Here we can consider that the performance of each layer is proportional to the last performance of the whole system in MSM. So it maybe the F-Score of Word-Seg, precision of POS Tagging and so on. $\min S_n$ returns the optimal analysis results with the lowest score.

Here, the F-Score of Word-Seg can be defined as the harmonic mean of recall and precision of Word-Seg. That is to say:

$$Seg.F\text{-}Score = \frac{2 * Seg.Pre * Seg.Rec}{Seg.Pre + Seg.Rec}$$

$$Seg.Pre = \frac{\#\text{words correctly segmented}}{\#\text{words segmented}}$$

$$Seg.Rec = \frac{\#\text{words correctly segmented}}{\#\text{words in input texts}}$$

Finding out the most suitable group of W is an optimization problem. Genetic Algorithms (GAs) (Mitchell, 1996) is just an adaptive heuristic search algorithm based on the evolutionary ideas of natural selection and genetics to solve optimization problems. It exploits historical information to direct the search into the region of better performance within the search space.

To use GAs to solve optimization problems (Wall, 1996) the following three questions should be answered:

1. How to describ genome?
2. What is the objective function?
3. Which controlling parameters to be selected?

A solution to a problem is represented as a genome. The genetic algorithm then creates a population of solutions and applies genetic operators such as mutation and crossover to evolve the solutions in order to find the best one(s) after several generations. The numbers of population and generation are given by controlling parameters. The objective function decides which solution is better than others.

In MSM, the genome is just the group of W which can be denoted by real numbers between 0 and 1. Because the result is a linear weighted sum, we should normalize the weights to let $w_1 + w_2 + \cdots + w_n = 1$. The objective function is just $ObjFun(*)$ in Equation 3. Here the F-Score of Word-Seg is used to describe it. We set the genetic generations as 10 and the populations in one generation as 30. The Whole Layer Weight shows in the row of WLW in Table 4. The F-Score of Word-Seg shows as Table 3.

We can see that the Word-Seg layer gets an obviously large weight. So the final result is inclined to the result of Word-Seg.

2.4 Self Confidence

Our analysis indicates that the method of weighting a whole layer uniformly cannot reflect the individual information of each sentence to some component. So the F-Score of Word-Seg drops somewhat comparing with using Only Word-Seg. For example, the most sentences which have ambiguities in Word-Seg component are still weighted high with Word-Seg layer weight. Then the final result may still be the same as the result of Word-Seg component. It is ambiguous, too. So we must use a parameter to decrease the weight of a component with ambiguity. It is used to describe the analysis ability of a component for an input. We name it as Self Confident (SC) of a component. It is described by the difference between the first and the second score of a component. Then the bigger SC of a component, the larger weight of it.

There are lots of methods to value the difference between two numbers. So there are many kinds of definitions of SC. We use A and B to denote the first and the second score of a component respectively. Then the SC can be defined as $B - A$, $\frac{B}{A}$ and so on. We must select the better one to represent SC. The *better* means that a method which gets a lower Error Rate with a threshold t^* which gets the Minimal Error Rate.

$$t^* = \arg\min_t ErrRate(t)$$

$ErrRate(t)$ denotes the Error Rate with the threshold t. An error has two definitions:

- SC is higher than t but the first result is fault
- SC is lower than t but the first result is right

Then the Error Rate is the ratio between the error number and the total number of sentences.

Table 2 is the comparison list between different definitions of SC and their Minimal Error Rate of Word-Seg. By this table we select $B - A$ as the last SC because it gets the minimal Minimal Error Rate within the different definitions of SC.

SC is added into Equation 2 to describe the individual information of each sentence intensively. Equation 4 shows the new score method of a path.

$$S_n = w_1 sc_1 s_1 + w_2 sc_2 s_2 + \cdots + w_n sc_n s_n \quad (4)$$

sc_i denotes the SC of a component in the ith layer.

3 Experimental Results

3.1 Score of Components

We build a practical system CUP (Chinese Understanding Platform) based on MSM with three layers – Word-Seg, POS Tagging and Parsing. Each component not only provides the n-best analysis result, but also the score of each result.

In the Word-Seg component, we use the unigram model (Liu et al., 1998) to value different results of Word-Seg. So the score of a result is:

$$Score_{Word\text{-}Seg} = -\log P(W) = -\sum \log P(w_i)$$

w_i denotes the ith word in the Word-Seg result of a sentence.

In the POS Tagging component the classical Markov Model (Manning and Schütze, 1999) is used to select the n-best POS results of each Word-Seg result. So the score of a result is:

$$\begin{aligned} Score_{POS} &= -\log P(POS|W) \\ &= -\log \frac{P(W|POS)P(POS)}{P(W)} \\ &= -\sum \log P(w_i|t_i) - \sum \log P(t_i|t_{i-1}) \\ &\quad + \log P(W) \end{aligned}$$

t_i denotes the POS of the ith word in a Word-Seg result of a sentence.

In the Parsing component, we use a Chinese Dependency Parser System developed by HIT-IRLab[1]. The score of a result is:

$$\begin{aligned} Score_{Parsing} &= -\log P(DP|W, POS) \\ &= -\log \frac{P(W, POS, DP)}{P(W, POS)} \\ &= -\sum \log P(l_{ij}) \\ &\quad + \log P(W, POS) \end{aligned}$$

l_{ij} denotes a link between the ith and jth word in a Word-Seg and POS Tagging result of a sentence.

Table 1 gives the one and five-best results of each component with a correct input. The test data comes from Beijing Univ. and Fujitsu Chinese corpus (Huiming et al., 2000). The F-Score is used to value the performance of the Word-Seg, Precision to POS Tagging and the correct rate of links to Parsing.

Table 1: The five-best results of each component

	1-best	5-best
Word-Seg	87.83%	94.45%
POS Tag	85.34%	93.28%
Parsing	80.25%	82.13%

3.2 Self Confidence Selection

In order to select a better SC, we test all kinds of definition form to calculate their Minimal Error Rate. For example $B-A$, $\frac{B}{A}$ and so on. A and B denote the first and the second score of a component respectively. Table 2 shows the relationship between definition forms of SC and their Minimal Error Rate. Here, we experimented with the first and the second Word-Seg results of more than 7100 Chinese sentences.

3.3 F-Score of Word-Seg

The result of Word-Seg is used to test our system's performance, which means that the $ObjFun(*)$ returns the F-Score of Word-Seg.

There are 1,500 sentences as training data and 500 sentences as test data. Among these data about 10% sentences have ambiguities and the others come from Beijing Univ. and Fujitsu Chinese corpus (Huiming et al., 2000). In CUP the five-best results of each component are selected. Table 3 lists the F-Score of Word-Seg. They use Only Word-Seg (OWS), Whole Layer Weight (WLW), SC (SC) and FeedBack mechanism (FB) separately. Using the feedback mechanism means that the last analysis result of a sentence is decided by the Parsing. We select the result which has the lowest score of Parsing. Table 4 shows the weight distributions in WLW and SC weighting methods.

3.4 The Efficiency of CUP

The efficiency test of CUP was done with 7112 sentences with 20 Chinese characters averagely. It costs 58.97 seconds on a PC with PIV 2.0 CPU and 512M memory. The average cost of a sentence is 0.0083 second.

4 Discussions

According to Table 1, we can see that the performance of each component improved with the increasing of the number of results. But at the same time, the processing time must increase. So we should balance the efficiency and effectiveness with an appropriate number of results. Thus, it's more possible for CUP to find out the correct analysis than the original cascade mechanism if we can invent an appropriate method.

We define SC as $B-A$ which gets the minimal Minimal Error Rate with the analysis of the

Table 2: SC and Minimal Error Rate

Definition Form of SC	**Minimal Error Rate**
$\frac{1}{A} - \frac{1}{B}$	23.85%
$B - A$	21.07%
$\frac{B}{A}$	23.98%
$\frac{B}{A} - \frac{A}{B}$	23.98%
$\frac{B-A}{\text{length of a sentence}}$	24.12%
$\frac{B-A}{\text{length of a sentence}+100}$	23.71%

Table 3: F-Score of Word-Seg

	OWS	WLW	SC	FB
F-Score	86.99%	85.80%	88.13%	80.72%

Table 4: Layer Weight

	1-layer	2-layer	3-layer
In WLW	0.84	0.12	0.04
In SC	0.44	0.40	0.16

[1]The Parser has not been published still.

Table 2. Take the case of Word Segmentation:

$$B - A = \sum_i \log P(w_i^A) - \sum_j \log P(w_j^B)$$

It's just the difference between logarithms of different word results' probability of the first and the second result of Word Segmentation.

Table 3 shows that MSM using SC gets a better performance than other methods. For a Chinese sentence "桌子下放着几坛酒。". (There are some drinks under the table). The CUP gets the correct analysis – "桌子/n 下/nd 放/v 着/u 几/m 坛/q 酒/n 。/w". But the cascade and feedback mechanism's result is "桌子/n 下放/v 着/u 几/m 坛/q 酒/n 。/w".

The cascade mechanism uses the Only Word-Seg result. In this method $P(\text{下放})$ is more than $P(\text{下}) * P(\text{放})$. At the same time, the wrong analysis is a grammatical sentence and is accepted by Parsing. These create that these two mechanisms cannot get the correct result. But the MSM synthesizes all the information of Word-Seg, POS Tagging and Parsing. Finally it gets the correct analysis result.

Now, CUP integrates three layers and its efficiency is high enough for practical applications.

5 Conclusions and Future Work

A new Chinese NLU architecture based on Multilayer Search Mechanism (MSM) integrates almost all of NLU components into a uniform multilayer treelike platform and quantifies these components to use the search algorithm to find out the optimal result. Thus any component can be added into MSM conveniently. They only need to accept an input and give several outputs with scores. By experiments we can see that a practical system – CUP based on MSM improves the performance of Word-Seg to a certain extent. And its efficiency is high enough for most practical applications.

The cascade and the feedback mechanism are *JUST* the special cases of MSM. If greedy algorithm is used at each layer to expand the result with the lowest score, MSM becomes the cascade mechanism. If the weight of each layer except the feedback point is set 0, the MSM becomes the feedback mechanism.

In the future we are going to add the Phrase Analysis, WSD (Word Sense Disambiguation) and Semantic Analysis components into CUP, because it is impossible to analyze some sentences correctly without semantic understanding and the Phrase Analysis helps to enhance the performance of Parsing. At last, CUP becomes a whole Chinese NLU platform with Word-Seg, POS Tagging, Phrase Analysis, Parsing, WSD and Semantic Analysis, six components from lower layers to higher layers. Under the framework of MSM, it becomes very easy to add these components.

With the increasing of layers the handle speed must decrease. So some heuristic search algorithms will be used to improve the speed of searching while enhancing the speed of each component. Under the MSM framework, we can do these easily.

The performance of each component should be improved in the future. At least, it is impossible for MSM to find out the correct analysis result if there is a component which cannot give a correct result within n-best results with a correct input. In addition, we are going to evaluate the performance of each component not just Word-Seg only.

6 Acknowledgements

We thank Liqi Gao and Zhuoran Wang provide the Word Segmentation tool, Wei He provide the POS Tagging tool and Jinshan Ma provide the Parser tool for us. We acknowledge Dekang Lin for his valuable comments on the earlier versions of this paper. This work was supported by NSFC 60203020.

References

Shan Gao, Yan Zhang, Bo Xu, ChengQing Zong, ZhaoBing Han, and RangShen Zhang. 2001. The research on integrated chinese words segmentation and labeling based on trigram statistic model. In *Proceedings of IJCL-2001*, Tai Yuan, Shan Xi, China.

Duan Huiming, Song Jing, Xu Guowei, Hu Guoxin, and Yu Shiwen. 2000. The development of a large-scale tagged chinese corpus and its applications. *Applied Linguistics*, (2):72–77.

Ting Liu, Yan Wu, and Kaizhu Wang. 1998. The problem and algorithm of maximal probability word segmentation. *Journal of Harbin Institute of Technology*, 30(6):37–41.

Christopher D. Manning and Hinrich Schütze. 1999. *Foundations of Statistical Natural Language Processing.* The MIT Press, Cambridge, Massachusetts.

Melanie Mitchell. 1996. *An Introduction to Genetic Algorithms.* The MIT Press, Cambridge, Massachusetts.

Masaaki Nagata. 1994. A stochastic japanese morphological analyzer using a forward-dp backward-A* n-best search algorithm. In *Proceedings of the 15th International Conference on Computational Linguistics*, pages 201–207.

Stuart Russell and Peter Norvig. 1995. *Artificial Intelligence: A Modern Approach*. Prentice Hall Series in Artificial Intelligence, Englewood Cliffs, NJ, USA.

Matthew Wall. 1996. GAlib: A C++ Library of Genetic Algorithms components. http://lancet.mit.edu/ga/.

Andi Wu and Zixin Jiang. 1998. Word segmentation in sentence analysis. In *Proceedings of the 1998 International Conference on Chinese Information Processing*, pages 169–180, Beijing, China.

Aligning Bilingual Corpora Using Sentences Location Information*

Li Weigang Liu Ting Wang Zhen Li Sheng
Information Retrieval Lab, Computer Science & Technology School,
Harbin Institute of Technology 321#
Harbin, China, 150001
{LEE, tliu, wangzhen, lis}@ir.hit.edu.cn

Abstract

Large amounts of bilingual resource on the Internet provide us with the probability of building a large scale of bilingual corpus. The irregular characteristics of the real texts, especially without the strictly aligned paragraph boundaries, bring a challenge to alignment technology. The traditional alignment methods have some difficulties in competency for doing this. This paper describes a new method for aligning real bilingual texts using sentence pair location information. The model was motivated by the observation that the location of a sentence pair with certain length is distributed in the whole text similarly. It uses (1:1) sentence beads instead of high frequency words as the candidate anchors. The method was developed and evaluated through many different test data. The results show that it can achieve good aligned performance and be robust and language independent. It can resolve the alignment problem on real bilingual text.

1 Introduction

There have been a number of papers on aligning parallel texts at the sentence level in the last century, e.g., (Brown et al. 1991; Gale and Church, 1993; Simard et al. 1992; Wu DeKai 1994). On clean inputs, such as the Canadian Hansards and the Hong Kang Hansards, these methods have been very successful.

(Church, Kenneth W, 1993; Chen, Stanley, 1993) proposed some methods to resolve the problem in noisy bilingual texts. Cognate information between Indo-European languages pairs are used to align noisy texts. But these methods are limited when aligning the language pairs which are not in the same genre or have no cognate information. (Fung, 1994) proposed a new algorithm to resolve this problem to some extent. The algorithm uses frequency, position and recency information as features for pattern matching. (W. Bin, 2000) adapted the similar idea with (Fung, 1994) to align special domain bilingual texts. Their algorithms need some high frequency word pairs as anchor points. When processing the texts that include less high-frequency words, these methods will perform weakly and with less precision because of the scarcity of the data problem.

(Haruno and Yamazaki, 1996) tried to align short texts without enough repeated words in structurally different languages, such as English and Japanese. They applied the POS information of content words and an online dictionary to find matching word pairs. But this is only suitable for the short texts.

The real text always includes some noisy information. It has the following characteristics as follows:

1) There are no strict aligned paragraph boundaries in real bilingual text;

2) Some paragraphs may be merged into a larger paragraph because of the translator's individual idea;

3) There are many complex translation patterns in real text;

4) There exist different styles and themes;

5) Different genres have different inherent characteristics.

The tradition approaches to alignment fall into two main classes: lexical and length. All these methods have limitations when facing the real text according to the characteristics mentioned above.

* This research was supported by National Natural Science Foundation (60203020) and Science Foundation of Harbin Institute of technology (hit.2002.73).

We proposed a new alignment method based on the sentences location information. Its basic idea is that the location of a sentence pair with certain length is distributed in the whole text similarly. The local and global location information of a sentence pair is fully combined together to determine the probability with which the sentence pair is a sentence bead.

In the first of the following sections, we describe several concepts. The subsequent section reports the mathematical model of our alignment approach. Section 4 presents the process of anchors selection and algorithm implementation is shown in section 5. The experiment results and discussion are shown in section 6. In the final section, we conclude with a discussion of future work.

2 Several conceptions

1) Alignment anchors: (Brown, 1991) firstly introduced the concept of alignment anchors when he aligned Hansard corpus. He considered that the whole texts were divided into some small fragments by these alignment anchors. Anchors are some aligned sentence pairs.

2) Sentence bead: and at the same time, (Brown, 1991) called each aligned sentence pair a sentence bead. Sentence bead has some different styles, such as (0:1), (1:0), (1:1), (1:2), (1: more), (2:1), (2:2), (2: more), (more: 1), (more: 2), (more: more).

3) Sentence pair: Any two sentences in the bilingual text can construct a sentence pair.

4) Candidate anchors: Candidate anchors are those that can be possible alignment anchors. In this paper, all (1:1) sentence beads are categorized as candidate anchors.

3 Mathematical Model of Alignment

The alignment process has two steps: the first step is to integrate all the origin paragraphs into one large paragraph. This can eliminate the problem induced by the vague paragraph boundaries. The second step is the alignment process. After alignment, the bilingual text becomes sequences of translated fragments. The unit of a fragment can be one sentence, two sentences or several sentences. The traditional alignment method can be used with the fragment with several sentences to improve the alignment granularity. In this paper the formal description of the alignment task was given by extending the concepts of bipartite graph and matching in graph theory.

3.1 Bipartite graph

Bipartite graph: Here, we assumed G to be an undirected graph, then it could be defined as G=<V, E>. The vertex+ set of V has two finite subsets: V_1 and V_2, also $V_1 \cup V_2=V$, $V_1 \cap V_2=\phi$. Let E be a collection of pairs, when $e \in E$, then $e=\{v_i, v_j\}$, where $v_i \in V_1, v_j \in V_2$. The triple G was described as, $G=<V_1, E, V_2>$, called bipartite graph. In a bipartite graph G, if each vertex of V_1 is joined with each vertex of V_2, or vice versa, here an edge represents a sentence pair. The collection E is the set of all the edges. The triple $G=<V_1, E, V_2>$ is called complete bipartite graph. We considered that: $|V_1|=m$, $|V_2|=n$, where the parameters m and n are respectively the elements numbers of V_1 and V_2. The complete bipartite graph was usually abbreviated as Km, n (as shown in figure 1).

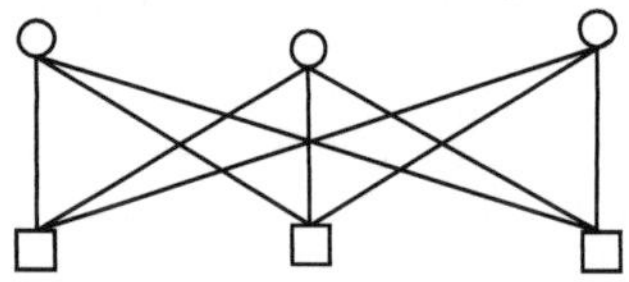

Figure 1 $K_{3,3}$ complete bipartite graph

3.2 Matching

Matching: Assuming $G=<V_1, E, V_2>$ was a bipartite graph. A matching of G was defined as M, a subset of E with the property that no two edges of M have a common vertex.

3.3 Best Alignment Matching

The procedure of alignment using sentence location information can be seen as a special matching. We defined this problem as "Best Alignment Matching" (BAM).

BAM: If $M=<S, E_M, T>$ is a best alignment matching of $G=<S, E, T>$, then M must meet the following conditions:

1) All the vertexes in the complete bipartite graph are ordered;

2) The weight of any edges in E_M $d(s_i, t_j)$ has: $d(s_i, t_j)< D$ (where D is alignment threshold); at the same time, there are no edges $\{s_k, t_r\}$ which made $k<i$ and $r>j$, or $k>i$ and $r<j$;

3) If we consider: |S|=m and |T|=n, then the edge $\{s_m, t_n\}$ belonged to E_M;

Best alignment matching can be attained by searching for the smallest weight of edge in collection E, until the weight of every edge $d(s_i, t_j)$ is equal or more than the alignment threshold D. Generally, the alignment threshold D is determined according to experience because different texts have different styles.

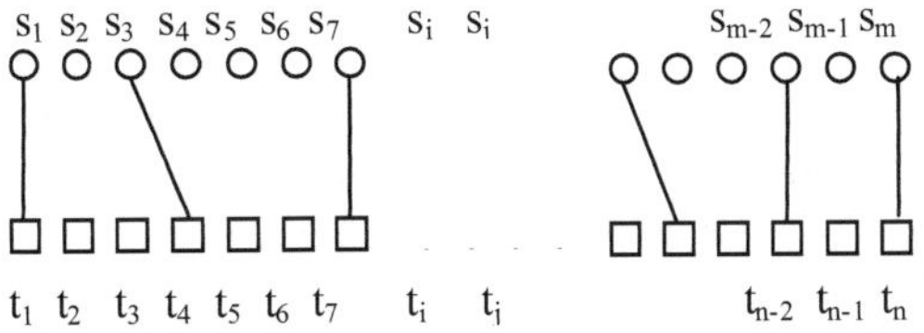

Figure 2 Sketch map of $K_{m,n}$ BAM under alignment threshold D

If each sentence in the text S (or T) corresponds with a vertex in V_1(or V_2), the text S or T can be denoted by $S(s_1, s_2, s_3, \ldots s_i, \ldots s_j, \ldots s_m)$ or $T(t_1, t_2, t_3 \ldots t_i, \ldots t_j, \ldots t_n)$. Considering the form merely, each element in S combined with any element in T can create a complete bipartite graph. Thus the alignment task can be seen as the process of searching for the BAM in the complete bipartite graph. As shown in figure 2, the edge $e = \{s_i, t_j\}$ belongs to M; this means that the i-th sentence in text S and the j-th sentence in text T can make an alignment anchor. Each edge is corresponding to an alignment value. In order to ensure the bilingual texts are divided with the same fragment number, we default that the last sentence in the bilingual text is aligned. That is to say, $\{s_m, t_n\} \in E_M$ was correct, if |S|=m and |T|=n in the BAM mathematical model.

We stipulated the smaller the alignment value is, the more similar the sentence pair is to a candidate anchor. The smallest value of the sentence pair is found from the complete bipartite graph. That means the selected sentence pair is the most probable aligned (1:1) sentence bead. Alignment process is completed until the alignment anchors become saturated under alignment threshold value.

Sentence pairs extracted from all sentence pairs are seen as alignment anchors. These anchors divide the whole texts into short aligned fragments. The definition of BAM ensures that the selected sentence pairs cannot produce cross-alignment errors, and some cases of (1: more) or (more: 1) alignment fragments can be attained by the fragments pairs between two selected alignment anchors.

4 Anchors Selection during Alignment

All (1:1) sentence beads are extracted from different styles of bilingual texts. The distribution states that all of them are similar as presented in figure 3. The horizontal axis denotes the sentence number in Chinese text, and the vertical axis denotes the sentence number in English text.

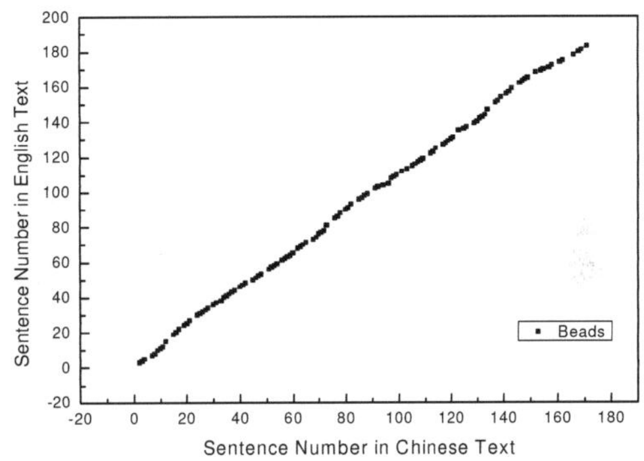

Figure 3 Distribution of (1:1) sentence beads in bilingual texts

Statistical results show that more than 85% sentence beads are (1:1) sentence beads in bilingual texts and their distributions obey an obvious law well. (DeKai Wu, 1994) offered that (1:1) sentence beads occupied 89% in English-Chinese as well. If we select these style sentence beads as candidate anchors, the alignment method will be general on any other language pairs. The main points of our alignment method using sentences location information are: locating by the whole text, collocating by sentence length and checking by a bilingual dictionary. Location information of any sentence pair is used fully. Three lengths are used: are sentence length, upper context length above the sentence pair and nether context length below the sentence. All this information is considered to calculate the alignment weight of each sentence pair. Finally, the sentence pair with high weight will be checked by a English-Chinese bilingual dictionary.

In order to study the relationship between every sentence pair of $\{s_i, t_j\}$, four parameters are defined:

Whole text length ratio: $P0 = Ls / Lt$;

Upper context length ratio: $Pu[i, j] = Us_i / Ut_j$;

Nether context length ratio: $Pd[i, j] = Ds_i / Dt_j$

Sentence length ratio: $Pl[i, j] = Ls_i / Lt_j$;

Where

s_i the i-th sentence of S;

t_j the j-th sentence of T;

Ls the length of source language text S;

Lt the length of target language text T;

Ls_i the length of s_i;

Lt_j the length of t_j;

Us_i the upper context length above sentence s_i;

Ut_j the upper context length above sentence t_j;

Ds_i the nether context length below sentence s_i;

Dt_j the nether context length below sentence t_j;

Figure 4 illustrates clearly the relationship of all variables.

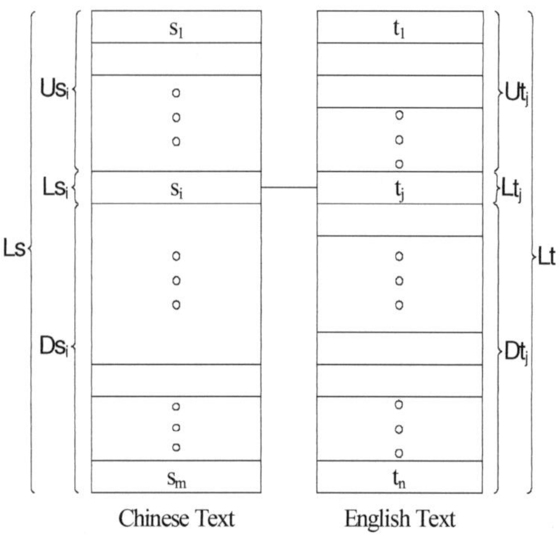

Figure 4 Sketch map of variables relationship

If s_i and t_j can construct a (1:1) alignment anchor, P[i, j] must be less than the alignment threshold, where P[i,j] denotes the integrated alignment value between s_i and t_j. We assume that the weight coefficient of Pl[i, j] is 1. Only considering the form, Pu[i, j] and Pd[i, j] must have the same weight coefficient. Here the weight coefficient is set α. We constructed a formal alignment function on every sentence pair:

$$P[i,j] = \alpha(Pu[i, j]-P0)^2 + (Pl[i, j] -P0)^2 +\alpha(Pd[i, j] -P0)^2$$

Where, the parameter α is the weight coefficient, if can adjust the weight of sentence pair length and the weight of context lengths well. The longer the text is, the more insensitive the effect of the context-length is. So α's value should increase in order to balance the whole proportion. The short text is vice versa. In this paper we define:

$$\alpha= (Ls/Ls_i + Lt/Lt_j)/2$$

According to the definition of BAM, the smaller the alignment function value of P[i, j] is, the more the probability of sentence pair $\{s_i, t_j\}$ being a (1:1) sentence bead is. In this paper, we adopt a greedy algorithm to select alignment anchors according to all the alignment function values of P[i, j] which are less than the alignment threshold. This procedure can be implemented with a time complexity of O(m*n).

To obtain further improvement in alignment accuracy requires calculation of the similarity of the sentence pairs. An English-Chinese bilingual dictionary is adopted to calculate the semantic similarity between the two sentences in a sentence pair. The similarity formula based on a bilingual dictionary is followed:

$$H = \frac{L|Match(S)|+L|Match(T)|}{L|S|+L|T|}$$

Where L| | is the bytes number of all elements, Match (T) is (according to English-Chinese dictionary) the English words which have Chinese translation in the Chinese sentence, Match (S) is the matched Chinese fragments.

According to the above dictionary check, alignment precision is improved greatly. We take a statistic on all the errors and find that most errors are partial alignment errors. Partial alignment means that the alignment location is correct, but a half pair of the alignment pairs is not integrated. It is very difficult to avoid these errors when only taking into account the sentence location and length information. Thus in order to reduce this kind of error, we check the semantic similarity of the context-adjacent sentence pairs also. Because these pairs could be other alignment patterns, such as (1:2) or (2:1), the similarity formulas have some difference from the (1:1) sentence pair formula. Here, a simple judgement is performed. It is shown as:

If（Ls_{i-1} * P0 > Lt_{j-1}）

$$H_{\text{adjacent}} = \frac{L|Match(S)|+L|Match(T)|}{(1+P0)*Ls_{\text{adjacent}}}$$

else

$$H_{\text{adjacent}} = \frac{L|Match(S)|+L|Match(T)|}{(1+1/P0)*Lt_{\text{adjacent}}}$$

Here, those alignment anchors whose similarities exceed the similarity threshold based on the bilingual dictionary will become the final alignment anchors. These final anchors divide the whole bilingual texts into aligned fragments.

5 Algorithm Implementation

According to the definition of BAM, the first selected anchor will divide the whole bilingual texts into two parts. We stipulated that the sentences in the upper part of source text cannot match any sentence in the nether part of target text. As shown in Fig 5, after the first alignment anchors were selected, the second candidate anchors must be selected in the first quadrant or the third quadrant and exclusive from the boundary. It is obvious that if the candidate anchors exist in the second quadrant or fourth quadrant, the cross alignment will happen. For example, if the (i, j) is the first selected alignment anchor, and the (i-1, j+1) is the second selected alignment anchor, the cross alignment appears. We can limit the anchors selection field to prevent the cross-alignment errors.

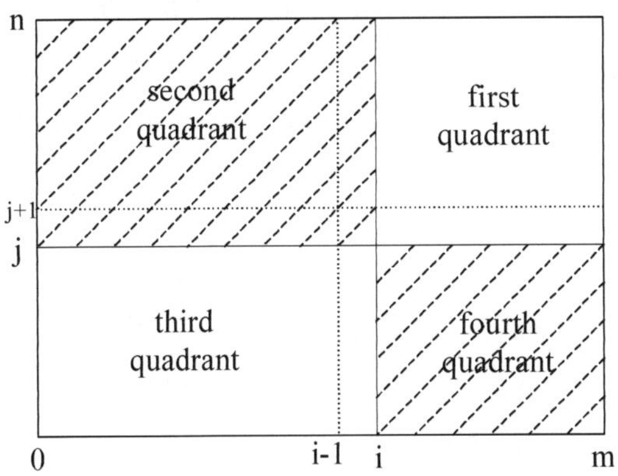

Figure 5 Anchors selection in Bilingual Texts

In addition, in order to resolve the problem that the first sentence pair is not a (1:1) sentence bead, we use a virtual sentence length as the origin alignment sentence bead when we initialize the alignment process.

The implementation of alignment algorithm is described as followed:

1) Load the bilingual text and English-Chinese dictionary;

2) Identify the English and Chinese sentences boundaries and number each sentence;

3) Default the last sentence pair to be aligned and calculate every sentence pair's alignment value;

4) Search for sentence pair that is corresponding to the smallest alignment function value;

5) If the smallest alignment function value is less than the alignment threshold and the go to step 6), and if the smallest value is equal to or more than the threshold, then go to step 7);

6) If the similarity of the sentence pair is more than a certain threshold, the sentence pair will become an alignment anchor and divide the bilingual text into two parts respectively, then limit the search field of the next candidate anchors and go to the step 4)

7) Output the aligned texts, and go to the end.

6 Results and Discussion

We use the real bilingual texts of the seventeenth chapter in the literary masterpiece "Wuthering Heights" as our test data. The basic information of the data is shown in the table 1.

English text size	38.1K
Chinese text size	25.1K
English sentence number	273
Chinese sentence number	277

Table 1 Basic information of the test data

In order to verify the validity of our algorithm, we implement the classic length-based sentence alignment method using dynamic programming. The precision is defined:

Precision = The correct aligned sentence pairs / All alignment sentence pairs in bilingual texts

The comparison results are presented in table 2.

Method	Precision (%)
Length-based alignment method	20.3
Location-based alignment method	87.8

Table 2 Comparison results between two methods

Because the origin bilingual texts have no obvious aligned paragraph boundaries, the error extension phenomena happen easily in the length-based alignment method if the paragraphs are not strictly aligned correctly. Its alignment results are so weaker that it cannot be used. If we omit all of the origin paragraphs information, we merge all the paragraphs in the bilingual text into one larger paragraph respectively. The length-based alignment method rated the precision of 25.4%. This is mainly because the English and Chinese languages don't belong to the same genre and have large difference between the language pairs. But our method rated 129 (1:1) sentence pairs as alignment anchors which divide the bilingual text into aligned fragments. The length-based classic method was applied to these aligned fragments and got a high precision. Fig 6 shows 129 selected anchors distribution which is in the same trend with all the (1:1) sentence beads. Their only difference is the sparse extent of the aligned pairs.

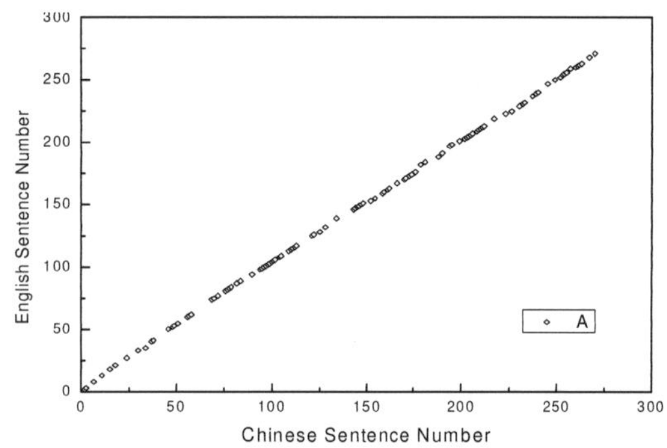

Figure 6 Distribution of alignment anchors

In order to evaluate the adaptability of our method, we select texts with different themes and styles as the test set. We merge two news bilingual texts and two novel texts. The data information is show in Table 3.

Our method is applied on the fixed data and receives the precision rating of 86.9%. The result shows that this alignment method is theme independent.

English text size	63.9K
Chinese text size	41.5K
English sentence number	510
Chinese sentence number	526

Table 3 Basic information of the fixed test data

(Haruno and Yamazaki, 1996) tried to align short texts in structurally different languages, such as English and Japanese. In this paper the aligned language pairs of English and Chinese belongs to structurally different languages as well. Our method gets the highest precision in aligning short texts. A bilingual news text is selected to be test data. The result is shown in table 4. There are two aligned sentence error pairs which are induced by the lack the corresponding translation.

English text size	5.6K
Chinese text size	3.4K
English sentence number	40
Chinese sentence number	38
Precision (%)	94.4

Table 4 Alignment results of short test data

It is difficult to attain large test set because doing so need more manual work. We construct the test set by merging the aligned sentence pairs in the existing sentence aligned bilingual corpus into two files. Then the two translated files can be as test set. Here we merge 2000 aligned sentence pairs. The file information is as follows:

English text size	200.3K
Chinese text size	144.2K
English sentence number	2069
Chinese sentence number	2033

Table 5 Basic information of the large test data

From the table 4, it is evident that there are many different styles of sentence beads. The method is developed on this large test set and gets the precision of 90.5%. The reason of the slight precision increase is that the last test set is relatively clean and the sentence length distribution relatively average. But overall, our method performs very well to align the real bilingual texts. It shows the high robustness and is not related to the languages, text themes, text length. This method can resolve the alignment problem of the real text.

7 Conclusion

This paper proposed a new method for fully aligning real bilingual texts using sentence location information, described concretely in section 3 and 4. The model was motivated by the observation that the location of a sentence pair with certain length is distributed in the whole text similarly. It uses the (1:1) sentence beads instead of the high frequency words as the candidate anchors. Local and global location characteristics of sentence pairs are involved to determine the probability which the sentence pair is an alignment anchors.

Every sentence pair corresponds to an alignment value which is calculated according to the formal alignment function. Then the process of BAM is performed to get the alignment anchors. This alignment method can restrain the errors extension effectively in comparison to the traditional alignment method. Furthermore, it has shown strong robustness, even if when it meets ill-quality texts that include incorrect sentences. To obtain further improvement in alignment accuracy sentence similarity based on an English-Chinese dictionary was performed. It need not segment the Chinese sentence. The whole procedure requires little cost to implement.

Additionally, we can adjust the alignment and similarity thresholds dynamically to get high precision alignment anchors, for example, applying the first test set, even if we get only 105 (1:1) sentence beads but the precision is 100%. We found that this method can perform the function of paragraph alignment very well and ensure simultaneous the alignment precision.

Of these pairs about half of total number of (1:1) sentence beads can be even extracted from the bilingual text directly to build a large scale bilingual corpus if the original bilingual text is abundant. And the rest bilingual text can be used as spare resource. Now, we have obtained about 500,000 English-Chinese aligned sentence pairs with high quality.

In the future, we hope to do further alignment on the basis of current work and extend the method to align other language pairs.

References

Wu, DeKai. 1994. *Aligning a parallel English-Chinese corpus statistically with lexical criteria.* In Proceedings of the 32nd Annual Conference of the Association for Computational Linguistics, 80--87, Las Cruces, New Mexico

Simard, M., Foster, G., and Isabelle, P. 1992. *Using Cognates to Align Sentences in Bilingual Corpora.*Fourth International Conference on Theoretical and Methodological Issues in Machine Translation (TMI-92), Montreal, Canada

Brown, P., Lai, J. and Mercer, R. 1991. *Aligning Sentences in Parallel Corpora.* ACL-91

Fung Pascale and Kathleen Mckeown. 1994. *Aligning noisy parallel corpora across language groups: Word pair feature matching by dynamic time warping.* In AMTA-94, Association for Machine Translation in the Americas, 81--88, Columbia, Maryland

Wang Bin, Liu Qin, Zhang Xiang. 2000. Automatic Chinese-English Paragraph Segmentation and Alignment. *Journal of Software,* 11(11):1547-1553 (Chinese)

Church, Kenneth W. 1993. *Char_align: A Program for Aligning Parallel Texts at the Character Level.* Proceedings of ACL-93, Columbus OH

Chen, Stanley. 1993. *Aligning Sentences in Bilingual Corpora Using Lexical Information.* In Proceedings of the 31st Annual Meeting of the Association for Computational Linguistics (ACL-1993)

Gale, W.A. Church, K.W. 1993. A Program for Aligning Sentences in Bilingual Corpora. *Computational Linguistics,* 19(2): 75-102

Haruno, Masahiko & Takefumi Yamazaki (1996), *High-performance bilingual text alignment using statistical and dictionary information,* In *Proceedings of ACL '96*, Santa Cruz, California, USA, pp. 131-138

M. Kay & M. Roscheisen. 1993. Text-Translation Alignment. *Computational Linguistics* 19:1

An Integrated Method for Chinese Unknown Word Extraction[1]

LUO Zhiyong
College of Computer Science
Beijing University of Technology
Beijing, PRC 100022
Center for Language Information Processing
Beijing Language and Culture University
Beijing, PRC 100083
luo_zy@blcu.edu.cn

SONG Rou
Center for Language Information Processing
Beijing Language and Culture University
Beijing, PRC 100083
songrou@blcu.edu.cn

Abstract

Unknown word recognition is an important problem in Chinese word segmentation systems. In this paper, we propose an integrated method for Chinese unknown word extraction for offline corpus processing, in which both context-entropy (on each side) and frequency ratio against background corpus are introduced to evaluate the candidate words. Both of the measures are computed efficiently on Suffix array with much less space overhead. Our method can also be reinforced when combined with a basic Segmentor by boundary-verification and arbitrary n-gram words can be extracted by our method. We test our method on Chinese novel *Xiao Ao Jiang Hu*, and obtain satisfactory achievements compared to traditional criteria such as Likelihood Ratio.

1 Introduction

The unique feature of Chinese writing system is that it is character-based, not word-based. The fact that there are no delimiters between words poses the well-known problem of word segmentation. Any Chinese Information Processing (CIP) systems beyond character level, such as information retrieval, automatic proofreading, text classification, text-to-speech conversion, syntactic parser, information extraction and machine translation, etc. should have a built-in word segmentation block. Currently, dictionary-based method is the basic and efficient one for word segmentation. A fixed Chinese electronic dictionary is required for most CIP systems. Yet there are many unknown words (out of the fixed dictionary) coming into being all the time. The unknown words are diverse, including proper nouns (person names, place names, organization names, etc.), domain-specific terminological nouns and abbreviations, even author-coined terms, etc. and they appear frequently in real text. This may cause ambiguity in Chinese word segmentation and lead to errors in the applications. Presently, many systems (Tan et al, 1999), (Liu, 2000), (Song, 1993), (Luo et al, 2001) focus on online recognition of proper nouns, and have achieved inspiring results in news-corpus but will be deteriorated in special text, such as spoken corpus, novels. As to the rests of unknown words types, it is still the obstacle of application systems, although they are really important for specific collections of texts.

For instance, according to our count on Chinese novel *Xiao Ao Jiang Hu* (《笑傲江湖》) (JIN Yong (金庸), 1967), there are almost 515 unknown word types (out of our 243,539-item general dictionary) of total 39,404 occurrences and total 112,654 characters, and there are 983,134 characters overall in this novel (that is, about 11.46% characters of the whole novel are occupied by unknown words.). And most of them, such as "东方不败"(person name), "辟邪剑谱"(normal noun), "日月神教"(organization name), etc. can't be recognized by most current CIP systems. It is important to note that without efficient unknown word extraction method, most CIP systems can't obtain satisfactory results.

2 Relative research works

Offline unknown word extraction can be treated as a special kind of Automatic Term Extraction (ATE). There are many research works on ATE. And most successful systems are based on statistics. Many statistical metrics have been proposed, including point-wise mutual information (MI) (Church et al, 1990), mean and variance, hypothesis testing (t-test, chi-square test, etc.), log-likelihood ratio (LR) (Dunning, 1993), statistic language model (Tomokiyo, et al, 2003), and so on. Point-wise MI is often used to find

[1] This paper is supported by NSFC (60272055) and 863 Project (2001AA114111)

interesting bigrams (collocations). However, MI is actually better to think of it as a measure of independence than of dependence (Manning et al, 1999). LR is one of the most stable methods for ATE so far, and more appropriate for sparse data than other metrics. However, LR is still biased to two frequent words that are rarely adjacent, such as the pair (the, the) (Pantel et al, 2001). On the other aspect, MI and LR metrics are difficult to extend to extract multi-word terms.

Relative frequency ratio (RFR) of terms between two different corpora can also be used to discover domain-oriented multi-word terms that are characteristic of a corpus when compared with another (Damerau, 1993). In this paper, RFR values between source corpus and background one will be used to rank the final candidate-list.

There are also many hybrid methods combined statistical metrics with linguistic knowledge, such as Part-of-Speech filters (Smadja, 1994). But POS filters are not appropriate for Chinese term extraction.

Since all the terms extraction approaches need to access all the possible patterns and find their frequency of occurrence, a highly efficient data structure based on PAT-tree (Chien, 1997), (Chien, 1998) and (Thian et al, 1999) has been used popularly for this purpose. However, PAT-tree still has much space overhead, and is very expensive for construction. Now, we introduce an alternative data structure as Suffix array, with much less space overhead, to commit this task.

In this paper, we propose a four-phase offline unknown word extraction method: (a) Construct the Suffix arrays of source text and background corpus. In this phase, Suffix arrays, sorted on both left and right sides context for each occurrence of Chinese character, are constructed. We call them Left-index and Right-index respectively; (b) Extract frequent n-gram candidate terms. In this phase, firstly we extract n-grams, appearing more than one time in different contexts according to Left-index and Right-index of source text, into Left-list and Right-list respectively. Then, we combine Left-list with Right-list, and extract n-grams which appear in both of them as candidates (C-list, for short). We also compute frequency, context-entropy and relative frequency ratio against background corpus for each candidate in this phase; (c) Filter candidates in C-list with context-entropy and boundary-verification coupled with General Purpose Word Segmentation System (GPWS) (Lou et al, 2001). In this phase, we segment each sentence, where each candidate appears, in the source text with GPWS and eliminate the candidates cross word boundary; (d) Output the final terms on relative frequency ratios.

The remainder of our paper is organized as follows: Section 2 describes the candidate terms extraction approach on Suffix array. Section 3 describes the candidates' filter approach on context-entropy and boundary-verification coupled with GPWS. Section 4 describes the relative frequency ratios and output of the final list. Section 5 gives our experimental result and Section 6 gives conclusion and future work.

3 Candidates extraction on Suffix array

Suffix array (also known as String PAT-array)(Manber et al, 1993) is a compact data structure to handle arbitrary-length strings and performs much powerful on-line string search operations such as the ones supported by PAT-tree, but has less space overhead.

Definition 1. Let $X = x_0x_1x_2..x_{n-1}x_n$ as a string of length n. For the sake of left and right context sorting, we have extended X by inserting two unique terminators ($, less than all of the characters) as sentinel symbols at both ends of it, i.e. $x_0 = x_n = \$$ in X. Let $LS_i = x_ix_{i-1}..x_0$ ($RS_i = x_ix_{i+1}..x_n$) as the left (right) suffix of X that starts at position i.

The Suffix array Left-index[0..n] (Right-index[0..n]) is an array of indexes of LS_i (RS_i), where $LS_{Left\text{-}index[i]} < LS_{Left\text{-}index[j]}$ ($RS_{Right\text{-}index[i]} < RS_{Right\text{-}index[j]}$), i<j, in lexicological order.

Let LLCP[i] (RLCP[i]), i=0..n-1, as the length of Longest Common Prefix (LCP) between two adjacent suffix strings, $LS_{Left\text{-}index[i]}$ and $LS_{Left\text{-}index[i+1]}$ ($RS_{Right\text{-}index[i]}$ and $RS_{Right\text{-}index[i+1]}$). These arrays on both sides are assistant data structures for speeding string search.

Figure 1 shows a simple Suffix array sorted on left and right context, coupled with the LCP arrays respectively.

We apply the sort-algorithm proposed by (Manber et al, 1993), which takes O(nlogn) in worst cases performance, to construct the Suffix arrays, and sort all the suffix strings in UNICODE order.

Figure 2 shows fragments of Suffix arrays of test corpus *Xiao Ao Jiang Hu* in readable style.

Sorted suffix arrays have clustered all similar n-grams (of arbitrary length) into continuous blocks and the frequent string patterns, as the longest common prefix (LCP) of adjacent strings, can be extracted by scanning through the suffix arrays sorted on left context and right respectively.

String "tobeornottobe"

#	0	1	2	3	4	5	6	7	8	9	10	11	12	13	14
String	$	t	o	b	e	o	r	n	o	t	t	o	b	e	$

Suffix array

#	0	1	2	3	4	5	6	7	8	9	10	11	12	13	14
Left-index	0	14	3	12	4	13	7	5	8	2	11	6	1	9	10
Right-index	0	14	12	3	13	4	7	11	2	5	8	6	10	1	9

LCP arrays on both sides

#	0	1	2	3	4	5	6	7	8	9	10	11	12	13	14
LLCP	0	0	3	0	4	0	0	1	1	2	0	0	1	1	/
RLCP	0	0	2	0	1	0	0	3	1	1	0	0	4	1	/

Figure 1: Suffix array example

…，只因巴结上东方不败，大权在手，作威作…	…？上官兄弟，听说东方不败下了令要捉拿童老…
…似乎正在走上东方不败的路子。他这次击败…	…抬着他，一来好叫东方不败不防，二来担架之…
…在黑木崖上与东方不败相斗，东方不败只握…	…杨莲亭头上砸去。东方不败不顾自己生死，反…
…武功路子便与东方不败一模一样，而岳不群…	…聊的玩意儿，只是东方不败与杨莲亭所想出来…
…闪跃进退固与东方不败相去甚远，亦不及岳…	…么会是威震天下的东方不败东方教主？众人回…
…。辟邪剑法与东方不败所学的《葵花宝典》…	…势道何等厉害，但东方不败两根手指拈着一枚…
…九剑之久，与东方不败之所学相比，那是更…	…也就没丝毫疑心。东方不败为了掩人耳目，对…
…只有隐忍，与东方不败敷衍。直到最近，才…	…了，升得好快哪。东方不败为甚么这样看重你…
…自知，终于为东方不败所困。他在西湖湖底…	…传言，天下武功以东方不败为第一，不知此言…
…了，心想他为东方不败所算，被囚多年，定…	…。 令狐冲心想："东方不败为练《葵花宝典》…
…之度外，才为东方不败所乘。任我行囚于西…	…般。冲哥，你记得东方不败么？他们都是疯子…
…去十余年来为东方不败尽力，言语之中，更…	…在眼里，但在见到东方不败之前先受如许屈辱…
…低垂，以防为东方不败的耳目知觉。当晚盈…	…，除了任教主和我东方不败之外，要算你是个…
…到"魔教教主东方不败"八字，脸色都为之…	…独孤九剑之久，与东方不败之所学相比，那是…
…兄和魔教教主东方不败暗中有甚么勾结？设…	…了再大的过失，连东方不败也决不会难为他任…
…那是魔教教主东方不败！'"众人听她提到…	…深，天下皆知，连东方不败也想到要擒拿了我…
…见过魔教教主东方不败一面，所谓勾结，所…	…长须老者，那自是东方不败了。殿中无窗，殿…
…知道魔教教主东方不败神功无敌，自称不败…	…亭在旁乱他心神，东方不败仍是不败。"想到这…
…敌，魔教教主东方不败更有"当世第一高手…	…祸便在眉睫吗？"东方不败仍是默不作声。童…
…是魔教的教主东方不败？此人号称当世第一…	…森森的妖氛鬼气。东方不败从身边摸出一块绿…

*Left part is fragment of Left Suffix array, starts at position of Chinese character "败"
*Right part is fragment of Right Suffix array, starts at position of Chinese character "东"

Figure 2: Fragments of Suffix array of *Xiao Ao Jiang Hu*

As show in Figure 2, on right sorted part which starts at the position of Chinese Character “东”, we can extract the repeated n-grams, such as “东方不败不”, “东方不败为”, “东方不败之”, “东方不败也”, “东方不败仍是”, “东方不败”, etc., in turn and skip many substrings, such as “东方”, “东方不”, etc., because they are not the LCP of adjacent suffix strings and only appear in the upper string “东方不败” for their all occurrences. We can apply the same skill on left sorted part which start at the position of Chinese character “败”, and extract “上东方不败”, “与东方不败”, “为东方不败”, “魔教教主东方不败”, “教主东方不败”, “东方不败”, etc., as repeated n-grams and skip many substrings, such as “不败”, “方不败”, etc., for the same reasons.

To extract candidate terms, we can scan through both left and right Suffix arrays and select all repeated n-grams into Left-list and Right-list respectively. The terms, which appear in both lists, can be treated as candidates (denoted by C-list). Extraction procedure can be done efficiently by coupled with the arrays of length of LCP on both sides via stack operations. The length and frequency of candidates can also be computed in this procedure.

For example in Figure 2, term “东方不败” should appear in both Left-list and Right-list, and it is a good candidate. Yet n-grams “东方不败也” is not a candidate because even though “东方不败也” does appear in Right-list, it does not exist in our final Left-list (It always appears as a substring of direct upper string “连东方不败也” according to right part of Figure 2).

Term	TC	Left Context-entropy	Right Context-entropy	RFR
令狐冲	5922	6.6804	4.9900	22743.7
了一	1267	4.7974	3.8534	0.9
岳不群	1184	5.9656	4.8688	10104.9
也不	1123	4.8512	4.1473	1.0
盈盈	1053	5.5446	4.7758	89.8
林平之	929	5.7310	4.7623	7928.6
岳灵珊	919	5.5887	4.5220	7843.2
我行	532	0.0930	4.4570	170.2
任我	528	5.5960	0.0412	1013.9
任我行	525	5.5891	4.4294	4480.6
东方不败	320	4.6805	4.8253	2731.0
五岳剑	284	4.0897	0.0585	2423.8
五岳剑派	281	4.0624	3.7344	2398.2
丹青生	176	4.3386	4.0105	1502.0
辟邪剑谱	156	1.7374	2.0613	1331.3
莫大先生	153	4.6941	4.4650	1305.7
蓝凤凰	103	4.3266	3.4258	879.0
计无施	97	4.2815	3.1410	827.8
黑木崖	80	3.0207	2.7821	682.7
不戒和尚	73	3.6620	3.9186	623.0

Table 1: Examples of candidates order by TC

Table 1 lists many examples of candidates extracted from *Xiao Ao Jiang Hu*, order by term count (TC).

4 Filter candidate terms

As what show in Table 1, not all the terms in C-list extracted in Section 3 can be treated as significant terms because of their incomplete lexical boundaries. There two kinds of incomplete-boundary terms: (1) terms as substring of significant terms; (2) terms overlapping the boundaries of adjacent significant terms. In this section, we will take measures, including Context-entropy test and boundary-verification with common Segmentor (GPWS) with general lexicon, to eliminate these invalid candidates respectively.

4.1 Measure on Context-entropy

According to our investigation, significant terms in specific collection of texts can be used frequently and in different contexts. On the other hand substring of significant term almost locates in its corresponding upper string (that is, in fixed context) even through it occur frequently. In this part, we propose a metric Context-entropy as a measure of this feature to filter out substrings of significant terms.

Definition 2. Assume ω as a candidate term which appears n times in corpus X, $\alpha = \{a_1,a_2,\ldots,a_s\}$($\beta = \{b_1,b_2,\ldots,b_t\}$) as a set of left (right) side contexts of ω in X.

Left and right Context-entropy of ω in X can be define as:

$$LCE(\omega) = \frac{1}{n}\sum_{a_i\in\alpha} C(a_i,\omega)\log\frac{C(a_i,\omega)}{n},$$

$$RCE(\omega) = \frac{1}{n}\sum_{b_i\in\beta} C(\omega,b_i)\log\frac{C(\omega,b_i)}{n}$$

$$\text{where} \quad n = \sum_{a_i\in\alpha} C(a_i,\omega) = \sum_{b_i\in\beta} C(\omega,b_i),$$

$C(a_i, \omega)$ ($C(\omega, b_i)$) is count of concurrence of a_i and ω (ω and b_i) in X.

Significant terms, which can be used in different context, will get high values of Context-entropy on both sides. And the substrings, which almost emerge because of their upper strings, will get comparative low values. The 3rd and 4th columns of Table 1 show the values of Context-entropy on both sides of a list of candidate terms. Many candidates, which almost emerge because of their direct upper strings, such as “我行”(in “任我行”(person name)), “任我”(in “任我行”(person name)) , “五岳剑”(in “五岳剑派”(organization name)), appear in relatively fixed contexts and should get much lower value(s) of one or both sides of Context-entropy.

4.2 Boundary-verification with GPWS

The candidate list of terms includes all of the n-grams, which appear in different context on both sides more than ones. The unique feature of Chinese writing system is that there are no delimiters between words poses a big problem: Many of candidate terms are invalid because of the overlapped factual words' boundary, i.e. these candidates include several fragments of adjacent words, such as “山派”(overlapping the boundary of common word “华山”(Hua Mountain)), “令狐公”(overlapping the boundary of common word “公子”(Sir)), etc. listed in Table 2. We eliminate these candidates by verifying boundaries of them with a common Segmentor (GPWS (Lou et al, 2001)) and a general lexicon (with 243,539 words).

GPWS was built as shared framework undertaking different CIP applications. It has achieved very good performance and great adaptability across different application domains in disambiguation, identification of proper nouns (including Chinese names, Chinese place names, translated names of foreigners, organization and company names, etc.), identification of high-frequency suffix phrases and numbers. In this part, we ONLY use the utilities of GPWS to perform the Maximum Match (MM) to find the boundaries of words in lexicon, and all of the unknown words (out of our lexicon) will be segmented into pieces. Coupled with GPWS, we propose a voting mechanism for boundary-verification as follows:

For each candidate term in C-list as *term*
Begin
  Declare *falseNum* as integer for the number of invalid boundary-check of *term*;
  Declare *trueNum* as integer for the number of valid boundary-check of *term*;
  falseNum = 0;
  trueNum = 0;
  For each sentence, in which *term* appears, in foreground corpus, as *sent*
    Begin
      Segment *sent* with GPWS;
      Compare the *term*'s position in *sent* with the segment result of GPWS;
      If *term* crosses the adjacent words boundary
        Set *falseNum* = *falseNum*+1;
      Else
        Set *trueNum* = *trueNum*+1;
    End
  If *falseNum* > *trueNum*
    Set boundary-verification flag of *term* to *FALSE*;
  Else
    Set boundary-verification flag of *term* to *TRUE*;
End

Assistant with the segmentor, we eliminate 38,697 items of total 117,807 in C-list in 96.85% of precision. Table 2 shows many examples of candidates eliminated by sides-verification with GPWS.

Candidate term	Segment result of GPWS for one sentence, in which term appears
山派	咱们/华山/派/却/也是/宁死不屈/。
令狐公	恭喜/令狐/公子/，/你/今日/大喜/啊/。
方证大	想起/那日/他/要/修书/荐/自己/去/见/少林寺/方/证/大师/，
那婆	那/婆婆/身子/也是/一/晃/，

Table 2: Examples of candidates eliminated by GPWS

5 Relative frequency ratio against background corpus

Relative frequency ratio (RFR) is a useful method to be used to discover characteristic linguistic phenomena of a corpus when compared with another (Damerau, 1993). RFR of term ω in corpus X compared with another corpus Y, RFR(ω;X,Y), simply compares the frequency of ω in X (denoted as f(ω,X)) to ω in Y (denoted as f(ω,Y)):

$$RFR(\omega;X,Y) = f(\omega,X)/f(\omega,Y)$$

RFR of term is based upon the fact that the significant terms will appear frequently in specific collection of text (treated as foreground corpus) but rarely or even not in other quite different corpus (treated as background corpus). The higher of RFR values of the terms, the more informative of the terms will be in foreground corpus than in background one.

However, selection of background corpus is an important problem. Degree of difference between foreground and background corpus is rather difficult to measure and it will affect the values of RFR of terms. Commonly, large and general corpora will be treated as background corpus for comparison. In this paper, for our foreground corpus (*Xiao Ao Jiang Hu*), we experientially select a group of novels of the same author excluding *Xiao Ao Jiang Hu* as compared background corpus for some reasons as follows:

(a) Same author wrote all of the novels, including foreground and background. The unique n-grams in writing style of the author will not emerge on RFR values.

(b) All of the novels are in the same category. The specific n-grams for this category will not emerge on RFR values.

So, most of the candidate terms with higher RFR values will be more informative and be more significant for the source novel.

On the final phase, we will sort all of the filtered candidate terms on RFR values in desc-order so that the forepart of the final list will get high precision for extraction.

The last column of Table 1 shows the RFR values of many candidates compared with our background corpus. Many candidates, such as "了一", "也不", which are frequent in both foreground and background corpus, will get much lower RFR values and will be eliminated from our final top list.

6 Experimental result

We use novel *Xiao Ao Jiang Hu* as foreground corpus compared with the rest of novels of Mr. JIN Yong as background corpus. The total characters of foreground and background corpus are 983,134 and 7,551,555 respectively. We read through the novel *Xiao Ao Jiang Hu* and 5 graduates manually selected 515 new terms (out of our lexicon) with exact meaning in the novel as follows for the final test:

(a) Proper nouns, such as person names: "令狐冲", "东方不败", "令狐大哥", place names: "黑木崖", "思过崖", "恒山别院", organization names: "日月神教", "五岳剑派" etc.

(b) Normal nouns, such as "辟邪剑谱", "吸星大法", etc.

(c) Others, such as "剧斗", "惊怖", etc.

By our method, we extract 117,807 candidates in this novel. Table 3 shows the result after filtering with Context-entropy on both sides and boundary-verification on different total extracted numbers; We also compared our integrated method to traditional measure LR. On lower total number levels, LR will overrun our method in unknown-word recall, and in turn overrun by us on higher levels. As to precision, our method always keeps ahead.

We also notice that both of the methods have much low precision in extraction. To retrieve terms with much certain, we rank the entire final list on RFR values in final phase. Most significant terms will comes in the front of ranked list.

Table 3 shows that our method Table 4 shows the top 12 of final list, and Figure 3 shows the performance of our method on different top levels when ranks the final list on RFR values.

7 Conclusion

Unknown word recognition is an important problem in CIP systems. Suffix array based method is an efficient method for exact arbitrary-length frequent terms. And most of substring of significant terms, which almost appear in fixed contexts, can be eliminated by Context-entropy values. Large lexicon can help to verify the unknown word doundaris and filter incomplete-boundary n-grams. Most significant informative candidates list on the top of final list according to RFR values for subsequent manual confirmation, and on the other aspect, RFR also reflects the internal character of the extracted terms.

Total Number Extracted		Word in Dict	Unknown Words	Precision	Unknown-words Recall
534	Our method	306	57	**0.68**	0.11
	LR	222	103	0.61	**0.20**
1325	Our method	668	126	**0.60**	0.24
	LR	421	171	0.49	**0.33**
2996	Our method	1411	225	**0.55**	0.44
	LR	888	287	0.39	**0.56**
6498	Our method	2877	346	**0.50**	0.67
	LR	1608	366	0.30	**0.71**
11684	Our method	4,643	512	**0.44**	**0.99**
	LR	2,428	427	0.24	0.83

Table 3: Result of our method compared to LR

Term	TF	RFR	Left Context-entropy	Right Context-entropy
令狐冲	5922	22743.7	6.6804	4.9900
岳不群	1184	10104.9	5.9656	4.8688
林平之	929	7928.6	5.7310	4.7623
岳灵珊	919	7843.2	5.5887	4.5220
令狐冲道	915	7809.1	5.5789	4.2271
仪琳	729	6221.6	5.5360	4.4128
田伯光	722	6161.9	5.5751	4.7080
恒山派	553	4719.6	4.7371	3.8601
任我行	525	4480.6	5.5891	4.4294
向问天	516	4403.8	5.4427	4.1689
左冷禅	482	4113.6	5.3223	4.7837
方证	414	3533.3	5.2607	2.6043

Table 4: Top 12 terms of final list order by RFR

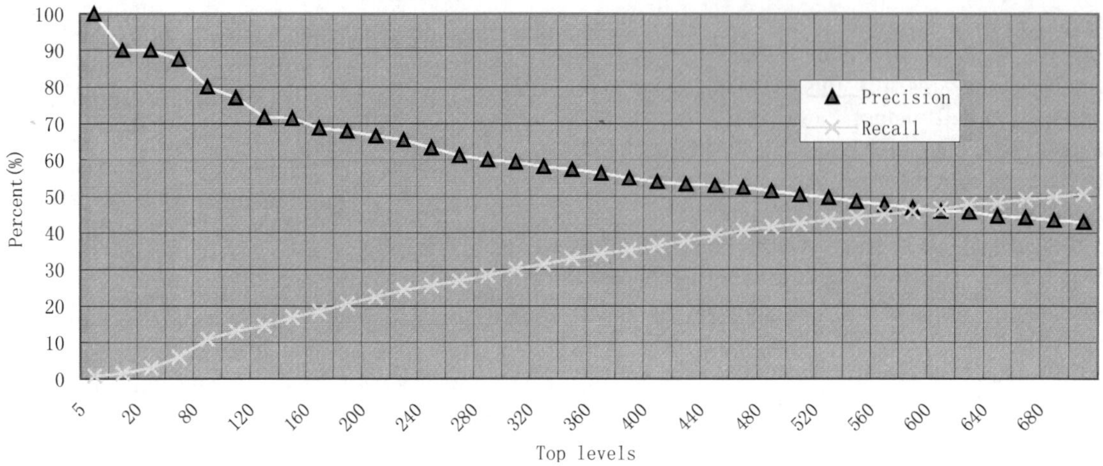

Figure 3: Test result on different top levels

References

Chien, L-F. 1997, *PAT-Tree-Based Keyword Extraction for Chinese Information Retrieval*. Proceedings of the 1997 ACM SIGIR, Philadelphia, PA, USA, pp. 50-58.

Chien, L-F. 1998, *PAT-Tree-Based Adaptive Key phrase Extraction for Intelligent Chinese Information Retrieval*. In special issue on Information Retrieval with Asian Languages, Information Processing and Management, Elsevier Press.

Christopher D. Manning, Hinrich Schutze. 1999. *Foundations of Statistical Natural Language Processing*, MIT Press.

Dekai Wu and Pascale Fung. 1994. *Improving Chinese tokenization with linguistic filters on statistical lexical acquisition*. In Proceedings of the Fourth ACL Conference on Applied Natural Language Processing (ANLP94), Stuttgart, Germany.

Frank Z. Smadja. 1994. *Retrieving collocations from text: Xtract*. Computational Linguistics, 19(1): 143-177.

Fred J. Damerau. 1993. *Generating and evaluating domain-oriented multi-word terms from texts*. Information Processing and Management, 29(4): 433–447.

H.Y. Tan, J.H. Zheng, K.Y. Liu. 1999. *A Study on the Automatic Recognition of Chinese Place Names*, Proceedings of the 5th Joint Conference on Computational Linguistics 99, Tsinghua University Press.

Kenneth W. Church and Patrick Hanks. 1990. *Word association norms, mutual information, and lexicography*. Computational Linguistics, volume 16.

Kunihiko Sadakane. 1998. *A fast algorithm for making suffix arrays and for Burrows-Wheeler transformation*, Proceedings of the ieee Data Compression Conference, pp. 129–138.

K.Y. Liu. 2000. *Automatic Segmentation and Tagging for Chinese Text,* Commercial Press.

Manber, U. and Myers, G. 1993. *Suffix Arrays: A New Method for On-Line String Searches*. SIAM Journal on Computing 22, 935-948.

R. Song. 1993. *Recognition of Personal Names Based on Corpus and Rules*, Journal of Computational Linguistics: Research and Applications, Beijing Language Institute Press.

R. Song. 1998. *The Geometric Structures of Chinese Words and Phrases*, International Conference on Chinese Grammers 98, Beijing.

Patrick Pantel and Dekang Lin. 2001. *A statistical corpus-based term extractor*. In E. Stroulia and S. Matwin, editors, Lecture Notes in Artificial Intelligence, pages 36–46. Springer-Verlag.

Ted E. Dunning. 1993. *Accurate methods for the statistics of surprise and coincidence*. Computational Linguistics, 19 (1): 61–74.

Thian-Huat Ong, Hsinchun Chen. 1999. *Updateable PAT-Tree Approach to Chinese Key Phrase Extraction using Mutual Information: A Linguistic Foundation for Knowledge Management*, Proceedings of the Second Asian Digital Library Conference, November 8-9, pp. 63-84.

T. Lou, R. Song, W.L. Li, and Z.Y. Luo. 2001. *The design and Implementation of a Modern General Purpose Segmentation System*, Journal of Chinese Information Processing, Issue No. 5.

T. Tomokiyo and M. Hurst. 2003. *A Language Model Approach to Keyphrase Extraction*. ACL-2003 Workshop on Multiword Expressions: Analysis, Acquisition and Treatment.

Z.Y. Luo, R. Song. 2001. *Integrated and Fast Recognition of Proper Noun in Modern Chinese Word Segmentation*, ICCC, Singapore.

Author Index